AN INTRODUCTION TO STUART DRAMA

AN
INTRODUCTION
TO
STUART DRAMA

BY

FREDERICK S. BOAS
M.A., Hon. LL.D., Hon. D.LITT.

OXFORD UNIVERSITY PRESS

Oxford University Press, Ely House, London W.1

GLASGOW NEW YORK TORONTO MELBOURNE WELLINGTON
CAPE TOWN SALISBURY IBADAN NAIROBI LUSAKA ADDIS ABABA
BOMBAY CALCUTTA MADRAS KARACHI LAHORE DACCA
KUALA LUMPUR SINGAPORE HONG KONG TOKYO

FIRST PUBLISHED JANUARY 1946
REPRINTED OCTOBER 1946
REPRINTED LITHOGRAPHICALLY IN GREAT BRITAIN
AT THE UNIVERSITY PRESS, OXFORD
FROM SHEETS OF THE SECOND IMPRESSION
1959, 1964, 1969

PREFACE

WITH this volume I complete a trilogy, which began with an *Introduction to the Reading of Shakespeare* in 1927, and was followed by an *Introduction to Tudor Drama* in 1933. It is owing to war conditions that this *Introduction to Stuart Drama* has not appeared till 1945.

I have here attempted to set forth what seem to me to be the most significant aspects of the plays of the chief dramatists whose work falls mainly or entirely between the accession of James I and the Restoration. The labours of scholars on both sides of the Atlantic have in recent years added considerably to our biographical knowledge of many of these dramatists. They have also led to some marked changes in our critical perspective. New light has thus been thrown on the dramatic range of Chapman and Heywood, Marston and Dekker, Webster and Ford, Shirley and Davenant. The stately progress of the Oxford *Ben Jonson* has brought into truer focus his classical tragedies, masques and last plays. In the so-called Beaumont and Fletcher *corpus* the respective shares of each of the pair and of Massinger can now be assigned with an approach to accuracy.

The fruits of such research are mostly to be found in collected editions and biographies or scattered through periodicals. I have aimed in this volume at bringing them together and making them accessible to those who are interested in Stuart drama without being professed scholars. With them in view too I have given special attention to the critical analysis both of plots and characterization without which an *Introduction* is apt to leave its readers at a loss. I hope that I may have been able to communicate something of what I have gained from the study of so many distinctive varieties of technique, and of dialogue in verse or prose, here quoted in modernized spelling. It will be evident that the period has been presented not as a decline from the Tudor dramatic apex but as having its own compelling attraction from first to last.

I have to thank the Oxford University Press for carrying through in the difficult conditions of to-day the publication of an *Introduction* which through its more comprehensive scope has markedly outgrown its two predecessors.

F. S. B.

August 1945

CONTENTS

CONTENTS

PRELIMINARY SKETCH

What cares these roarers for the name of King ?

THE Boatswain's exclamation in *The Tempest* concerning
the ungovernable ocean billows is equally apt in relation
to the waves raised by the creative breath of the dramatic
spirit. Elizabeth died on 24 March 1603 and was succeeded
by James I. In the eye of the historian that date is the
dividing line between the Tudor and Stuart periods. But
poets and playrights do not fall neatly within the limits of
regnal years. Marlowe had been cut off in his prime, but the
other leading dramatists of Elizabeth's latter days, Chapman,
Jonson, Dekker, Marston, Heywood, and Shakespeare himself did not reach their maturity till within the first Jacobean
decade. That decade too saw the flowering of the genius of
Beaumont and Fletcher in conjunction and of Webster.

It is true that the accession of a semi-foreign king with
a foreign consort could not but bring about some change of
atmosphere intensified by the crisis of the Gunpowder Plot
and by the growing friction between the sovereign and
parliament. But so far as the stage is concerned the great
Elizabethan period extends about half-way through the reign
of James. As 1616 saw the deaths of Shakespeare and
Beaumont and the publication of Jonson's first folio, it might
well seem to have the claim to be the terminal date. But
I should prefer to put this about three years earlier. The
dramatic activities of Shakespeare and of Beaumont ended
in or about 1613. Before that date Jonson had written all
the plays included in his first folio, though one of his masterpieces, *Bartholomew Fair*, followed in 1614. By that year
Chapman had completed his best work for the theatre and
Webster's tragic genius had reached the height of its achieve-

ment. The decade that produced Shakespeare's supreme tragedies and dramatic romances, Jonson's comic master-pieces and finest masques, the joint tragi-comedies of Beaumont and Fletcher, and the tragedies of Webster, Chapman, and Tourneur, stands unrivalled in England's theatrical annals and must be considered the culmination of that mighty dramatic movement which gathered head in the eighties of the sixteenth century. By a stretch of imagi-nation the radiant close of its full splendour might be seen in the brilliant theatrical festivities that celebrated the marriage of Princess Elizabeth and the Elector Palatine in February 1613, and its sunset glow in the fire that destroyed the Globe during a performance of *King Henry VIII* on the following 29th June.

From that time to the end of the reign in March 1625, which exceptionally forms something of a boundary line, there is a comparative relaxation in the stupendous dynamic energy of the preceding period. Even *Bartholomew Fair* in 1614, though it has its place in the front rank of Jonson's comedies, lacks the concentrated power of the other plays of his prime. Thenceforward till the end of the reign he deserted the professional stage. Chapman and Webster pro-duced little for it during these years, though the latter's *The Devil's Law Case* does not fall far below his two more famous tragedies. Fletcher, after losing Beaumont as a partner, found a powerful but more rhetorical and didactic ally in Philip Massinger, or with his single pen threw off a series of romantic comedies. Meanwhile comedy of middle-class London life was provided by Thomas Middleton, who also about 1623, in collaboration with William Rowley, struck a grimly tragic note in *The Changeling*, and in 1624 produced the first English Aristophanic comedy of political satire on the public stage.

The last half of James's reign had been darkened by a succession of calamitous events—the scandal of the Overbury murder, the outbreak of the Thirty Years' War, the execution of Sir Walter Raleigh, the fiasco of the Spanish marriage project. When Charles succeeded the future had still worse disasters in store. But for the time being the advent of an attractive young king with a gay French bride gave the promise of better things. Both Charles and Henrietta Maria were enthusiasts for the stage. The queen influenced the drama directly by spreading the cult of Platonic love which through Chapman and Middleton had found voice in the Jacobean theatre, but which received from her a fresh potent stimulus reflected in plays by John Ford, William Davenant, and others on the Caroline stage.

Another fashionable cult of somewhat earlier origin, that of melancholy, received a further impulse from the publication in 1621 of Richard Burton's *Anatomy*. It gives a distinctive tone and colour to the work of John Ford who carries on the tragic tradition while James Shirley takes the lead in sparkling social comedy. Nor were some of the older voices silent. Fletcher had died in 1625, but Ben Jonson in that year returned to the professional stage, and though none of the plays that he wrote during the next ten years compare with his masterpieces, they are far from deserving Dryden's condemnation as 'dotages'. It was the period during which Middleton and Massinger produced much of their most notable work. It has an obvious time-limit in 1642 with the outbreak of the Civil War and the closing of the theatres. But here, as with the substitution of 1613 for 1616, a somewhat earlier year, 1636, may be suggested as the effective terminus of the period. Scarcely any new play of importance appeared between that date and the beginning of hostilities. The visit of Charles and Henrietta Maria to Oxford in the August of that year, when three successful new plays were staged, culminating in the triumph of William Cartwright's *The Royal Slave*, forms a Caroline counterpart to the Jacobean dramatic festivities which had distinguished the royal wedding in February 1613.

By 1636 also Davenant had written the best of the

comedies which give him rank among the Caroline playwrights, though after an interval of two plague years he was
again theatrically active in 1638 and 1639. It was not till
the Commonwealth period in 1656 that with his *First Day's
Entertainment at Rutland House*, followed by the *Siege of
Rhodes*, he astutely evaded the Parliamentary inhibition of
plays by providing shows of an 'opera' type which blazed
the trail for the full renewal of dramatic activities, though
under changed conditions, after the Restoration.

The landmarks here briefly indicated may be of some help
in suggesting the perspective of what may be broadly termed
the half-century of Stuart drama as understood in the following pages. It is true, as has been seen, that the period of
its zenith closes about 1613. But the more deeply the record
is studied, the less ready shall we be to speak of any part of
it in terms of decline or of decadence. As the years pass, the
aspects change and the values vary. But we are conscious
throughout that not only the leading but the lesser figures
have their share of the authentic fire from the altar. However different their technique or their subject-matter, whatever comparative rank may be assigned to them in the
dramatic hierarchy, they have an instinct and faculty in
common. Their plays, taken as a whole, appealed alike to
popular audiences and to Court circles.

After three centuries of change in dramatic and literary
standards criticism inevitably detects flaws and imperfections even in the masterpieces. But not only in these but
in the rank and file of the plays of the period there is still
a compelling measure of attraction, whether it be in plot or
characterization, in interchange of dialogue or poetic flight.
The student of Stuart drama may miss the exhilarating
freshness of the dawn which greets him from the work of the
Tudor pioneers in the tragic and comic fields and of Kyd,
Marlowe, and the younger Shakespeare. But he will have
the compensating excitement and joy of exploring an ampler
and more richly varied domain, a 'country of escape', singu-

larly little touched by the deepening shadows of political and religious strife which at last was to end in a cataclysm that for a time almost, though not entirely, overwhelmed the English theatre.

THEATRICAL COMPANIES AND PLAYHOUSES

It does not come within the purpose of this volume to deal with the Stuart theatre for which readers must be referred to such stage-historians as Sir E. K. Chambers and Dr. G. E. Bentley. But it may be helpful to prefix a brief sketch of the leading companies and playhouses.

The dominant company and the only one that had a continuous existence throughout the period was the King's Men. Known during the later years of Elizabeth's reign from 17 March 1596/7 as the Lord Chamberlain's company, they received a new patent by which they became the servants of King James on 19 May 1603. Richard Burbage was their chief actor and among his fellows were Shakespeare, Kempe, Condell, and Heminges, who was the treasurer. The stability of the company was ensured by the fact that the leading actors were joint-owners of the theatres in which they played. From the winter of 1598–9 till the autumn of 1609 their house was the Globe on the Bankside. From the latter date they used the Globe only in summer, while the majority of their plays were presented during the winter at the Blackfriars theatre on the north side of the Thames. The Globe was burned down on 29 June 1613 during a performance of *King Henry VIII*, but it was rebuilt within a year. The death of Burbage on 13 March 1618/9, and the closing of the theatres for eight months after the accession of Charles on 27 March 1625 owing to the prevalence of the plague in London were severe blows. But the company was sustained by many evidences of royal and of popular favour, and it far surpassed its rivals in the number of Court performances. Nor could its primacy be challenged when it ranked among its playwrights Shakespeare, Beaumont, and

Fletcher and (though not exclusively) Ben Jonson, Chapman, Massinger, Middleton, Shirley, and Davenant.

The other leading company during Elizabeth's reign, the Lord Admiral's, moved in the autumn of 1600 into their new theatre, the Fortune, described as 'the fairest playhouse in this town', north-west of the City. Their star actor was Edward Alleyn, whose father-in-law, Philip Henslowe, was their financier. On the accession of James they became Prince Henry's men. In the following year Alleyn appears to have retired from the stage, though he remained the proprietor of the Fortune. None of his fellows, though they were actors of good standing, could replace him, but the attractions of the fine building and of the rich costumes and the music were a powerful magnet both to Londoners and foreign visitors. The death of the beloved Prince Henry in November 1612 was a grievous loss to the company which cannot have been compensated by the patronage of the foreign Palsgrave or Elector Palatine, the husband of Princess Elizabeth. In October 1618 by an agreement with Alleyn the actors gained a more independent position as lessees of the Fortune, but by an irony of fate this proved their undoing. On 9 December 1621 the playhouse was burnt down and all the apparel and play-books lost. As with the Globe a new Fortune took the place of the old, probably in the spring of 1623, but the fire in this case had been more disastrous, for it had destroyed the play-books, the company's repertory, which it tried with little success to replenish. The plague of 1625 seems to have given the Palsgrave's men their theatrical death-blow.

Another company, the Earl of Worcester's, which had acted chiefly in the provinces under Elizabeth, survived into the next reign, when it became known as Queen Anne's company. Its leading member and manager was Christopher Beeston. In 1604 it was performing at one of the oldest theatres, the Curtain in Shoreditch, but in 1605 it leased also the Red Bull playhouse in Clerkenwell. Early in 1617 the company made a further move to the Cockpit in Drury Lane, which became also known as the Phoenix theatre. On Shrove Tuesday, 4 March 1616/7 unruly apprentices and other rioters broke into the Cockpit, damaging the building, the costumes, and equipment, and burning the play-books. This disturbance seems to have been almost as disastrous to the Queen's men as the Fortune fire had been to the Palsgrave's, and Anne's death in March 1618/9 ended their activities as a London company, though some players continued to act in the provinces under her name. Part of the company, including Richard Perkins and Ellis Worth, appear to have been granted a patent as Players of the Revels and performed at the Red Bull till about the end of 1622. The others became dispersed among different existing companies.

Christopher Beeston, the manager, joined Prince Charles's men, of whom William Rowley was one of the leaders and the payee. This company is first heard of in London in a patent of 30 March 1610, when it was known as the Duke of York's. After the death of Prince Henry in November 1612 it took the title of Prince Charles's company, and in 1614 it became partly united with his sister's, the Lady Elizabeth's men, under the direction of Henslowe till his death in January 1615/6. When the Red Bull was vacated by Queen Anne's men in February 1616/7, Prince Charles's company moved there, and in 1619 they were transferred by Beeston to the Phoenix on the dispersal of the Queen's men. But by the middle of 1622 they moved once more to the Curtain and afterwards back to the Red Bull. When Charles succeeded to the throne and took over his father's players the company broke up.

The first Lady Elizabeth's company was established by a patent of 27 April 1611, and was under the control of Henslowe, with Nathan Field as the chief actor. From the autumn of 1614 their house was the Hope on Bankside, and, as already mentioned, they entered into co-operation with Prince Charles's men. This ceased with Henslowe's death, but four of their leading members, including Joseph Taylor, on 20 March 1615/6 joined the Prince's company while Field about the same time became one of the King's men. It was probably owing to these losses that the company was reduced to a provincial status.

But in May 1622 a new Lady Elizabeth's company is heard of as acting at the Phoenix, where it had probably been installed by Beeston, who had now allied himself with them. For nearly three years they prospered. Plays were written for them by many of the leading dramatists and they gave performances at Court during the Christmas season. But the long period of plague after the accession of Charles proved disastrous to them, and the company was broken up.

Some of the Lady Elizabeth's men were transferred to the company of the new queen Henrietta which the versatile Beeston organized from different elements, old and new, and which performed under his management at the Phoenix. It enjoyed a long period of prosperity, broken only by the closing of the theatre for seven months in 1630 owing to another plague epidemic. Their repertory included plays by a number of the chief dramatists of the day, especially the prolific output of James Shirley, who was a favourite at Court. But once again, in May 1636, the plague raged in London and theatres were closed. Anxious apparently for another change Beeston took this opportunity of breaking up the Queen's company. But with the goodwill of the Lord Chamberlain and the Master of the Revels it was reconstituted, with a new manager, Richard Heton, and began to act at the Salisbury Court playhouse in Whitefriars in October 1637, where it remained till the closing of the theatres.

About half a dozen of the original Queen Henrietta's men were retained by Beeston and included by him among the members of a new company for which he received a warrant on 21 February 1636/7 under title of the King's and Queen's Boys. They were also more familiarly known as Beeston's Boys, though the company certainly included a proportion of adult actors.[1] They opened at the Phoenix on 2 October 1637, but in a little more than a year they lost their manager, who was buried on 15 October 1638. He was succeeded by his son, William Beeston, who lacked something of his father's shrewdness. In April or early in May 1640 he, without obtaining a licence, produced a play of topical significance which displeased the king. An order was issued restraining the company for a few days from acting and Beeston was committed to the Marshalsea. He may still have been in prison when on 27 June William Davenant was appointed manager of the company in his stead. But some time in 1641 Beeston seems to have been reinstated, and held office till the closing of the theatres.

Another company containing, like Beeston's, an unusual number of boys, was that of the King's Revels, which was also known as the Children of the Revels. It was in existence in or before the autumn of 1629, when it was the first to occupy the new Salisbury Court theatre. Towards the end of 1631 the company migrated for a time to the Fortune, but it must have returned before July 1634, when it was described as the company of Salisbury Court by one of its members. From that date its manager was the Richard Heton already mentioned, and its chief playwright was Richard Brome. The long plague period of 1636–7 proved fatal to the company, but probably many of its members were absorbed in the second Queen Henrietta's company which, as has been seen, began acting at Salisbury Court in October 1637.

When the King's Revels men vacated Salisbury Court late in 1631 their place there was taken by a newly formed Prince Charles's (afterwards Charles II) company, licensed on 7 December of that year to their leader, Andrew Cane. Some time before July 1634 they had moved to the Red Bull, where they gained sufficient repute to be chosen to accompany the Court on a royal progress in the summer of 1634 and later to perform at Hampton Court and Whitehall. They

[1] See G. E. Bentley, *The Jacobean and Caroline Stage*, I. 324–5, note.

were even strong enough to survive the protracted inhibition due to the plague in 1636–7, though after they had resumed playing there were various disorders in the theatre, and they got into trouble in September 1639 by performing a piece satirizing various authorities. At Easter 1640 they migrated to the Fortune, where they remained till the closing of the theatres and where, according to contemporary evidence, their reputation declined.

In addition to the above and one or two less important organizations the Elizabethan children's companies continued to flourish and to be formidable rivals to their adult fellows during the earlier Jacobean period. The Children of Paul's, the boys of the choir school, had about 1600 a new master, Edward Pearce, who appears first as payee for a Court performance on 1 January 1601. Marston, Chapman, and Middleton were among those who wrote plays for this young company, and they presented the first work of Beaumont, and of Webster in collaboration with Dekker. Their last-known appearance was on 30 July 1606, when they acted before James and the King of Denmark. In the winter of 1608–9 Pearce accepted a 'dead rent' of £20 to cease playing in the house near St. Paul's Church.

The Children of the Chapel had a longer period of theatrical activity. With them also 1600 began a new departure. In September of that year Richard Burbage gave a lease of his Blackfriars playhouse for twenty-one years to Henry Evans, who co-operated with Nathaniel Giles, the Master of the Children. Giles had been granted a commission to impress boys for the service of the Chapel Royal, but he and Evans abused these powers for their own profit and were censured by the Star Chamber in 1602. Yet the company had striking stage successes. They acted Jonson's *Cynthia's Revels* and *Poetaster* and plays by Chapman and Marston. Their effective challenge at this time to the popularity of their adult rivals has been immortalized in Shakespeare's reference in *Hamlet* to the 'little eyases'. In February 1604 by a royal patent they were entitled the Children of the Queen's Revels. But in the following year they got into serious trouble over the production of several plays, especially *Eastward Ho* in 1605 and *The Isle of Gulls* in 1606, and their name was changed in 1606 to the Children of the Blackfriars. About the same time Robert Keysar, a London goldsmith, became associated with their management. Again trouble arose over Chapman's *Byron* in 1608, but this did not prevent their appearance at Court early in 1609 and a renewal early in 1610 of their patent as Children of the Queen's Revels. They had, however, lost their tenancy of the Blackfriars in August 1608, when Burbage obtained a surrender of the lease from Evans and henceforward used his playhouse for the King's Men in the winter months. The boys thereupon moved to White-friars, though some of them, now 'growing up to be men', were taken into the King's company. This second company of Children of the Queen's Revels, of which Philip Rosseter, a lutenist, became the chief manager, was mainly engaged in touring in the country, but it also appeared at Court in the Christmas seasons of 1612 and 1613 in important plays by Chapman, Beaumont and Fletcher. In the latter year it appears to have become amalgamated with the Lady Elizabeth's company under Henslowe, and after his death in 1616 its career was virtually ended.

Soon after the Children of the Queen's Chapel had temporarily lost her patronage in 1606 a short-lived boys' company was started in Whitefriars as Children of the King's Revels, with Martin Slater as manager. The first play bearing its name on the title-page was Sharpham's *Cupid's Whirligig* in 1607, and it performed in some popular pieces, though Middleton is the only dramatist of leading rank in their known repertory. Their activities probably closed before the end of 1608, though *Ram Alley* produced then was not printed till 1611.

In the Tudor period, in addition to the professional companies, the schools, the Inns of Court, and the Universities had been important theatrical centres. Under the Stuarts the stage activities of the schools continued, but on a reduced scale, and they produced no outstanding original play. The Inns of Court devoted their dramatic efforts almost entirely to the production of elaborate and lavishly mounted masques. The Universities on the other hand remained as fertile as before in the composition and performance of plays in Latin and English, the latter increasingly predominant, which drew royal visitors to Oxford and Cambridge till nearly the eve of the Civil War.

II

GEORGE CHAPMAN

COMEDIES OF INTRIGUE

FOREMOST among the Tudor-Stuart group of dramatists may be placed George Chapman. The circumstance that, though he was born at Hitchin in Hertfordshire, about the beginning of Elizabeth's reign, he did not attempt playwriting till near its close, helps to make him a link between the two periods. The man who had been the associate of Marlowe, Harriot, and Raleigh in the 'School of Night' and had completed Marlowe's unfinished *Hero and Leander*, survived long enough not only to celebrate the wedding of Princess Elizabeth in 1613 with his *Masque of the Middle Temple and Lincoln's Inn*, but to collaborate, shortly before his death in 1634, with one of the youngest of the Caroline dramatists, James Shirley, in comedy and tragedy.

Chapman's peculiar glory as translator of the *Iliad* and the *Odyssey*, and his distinctive achievement in his tragedies based on contemporary French history, have till recently overshadowed his work in the comic field. But both the extent and the importance of this are now receiving increased recognition. It is fortunate that we are able to date the *début* of Chapman as a comic playwright. Philip Henslowe enters in his *Diary* as a new play on 12 February 1595/6 *The Blind Beggar of Alexandria* acted at the Rose by the Lord Admiral's men. The piece was very favourably received, for twenty-two performances are recorded in the *Diary* up to 1 March 1596/7, and there was a later revival in May 1601. A quarto edition published by William Jones appeared in 1598, but the shortness of the text (about 1,600 lines) and the huddled close of the main plot, where two of the chief characters simply disappear, suggest that the printed version is imperfect. Yet it has several features of interest. The illicit passion of Queen Aegiale, wife of the aged King Ptolemy of Egypt, for the warrior Cleanthes, with its widespread fatal results, forms the main plot and combined with the humorous episodes foreshadows the type of tragicomedy developed to its height by Beaumont and Fletcher. These episodes revolve round the pretended 'blind beggar' with the Homeric name Irus, who with Protean versatility trebles also the roles of Count Hermes, Leon the usurer and Cleanthes the general. Playing in sublimated form the part of the *servus* of Latin comedy, and the Vice of the Morality he spins a web of mischievous intrigue and wins under different aliases two sisters as his brides. Finally as the conqueror Cleanthes he succeeds to the throne of Egypt, and in this elevation of one who avows that he is 'a shepherd's son at Memphis born' there seems to be an echo of the ascent of the Scythian shepherd Tamburlaine. There is still clearer proof of Marlovian influence in the blank verse in which the larger part of the play is written. It reproduces on occasion something of the music and colour of Kit's golden lines, but is pitched usually on a somewhat subdued note more suitable to its theme.

On 11 May 1597 Henslowe entered in his *Diary* the performance by the Admiral's men at the Rose, as a new play, of *The Comedy of Umers*. This is in all probability Chapman's *An Humourous Day's Mirth* which was printed in 1599 by Valentine Syms. The scene is laid in France during the reign of an unnamed king whose minion or favourite Lemot is the mainspring of the action, something after the fashion of the 'blind beggar' in the previous play. But here Chapman instead of echoing Marlowe and pointing the way to Beaumont and Fletcher is a pioneer in the comedy of humours of which Ben Jonson was soon to be the master. There are three couples whose relations are dominated by the humour of jealousy or suspicion in varied manifestations. The aged Count Labervele mistrusts his young and beautiful second wife Florilla in spite of her affectation of Puritan austerity. Old Countess Moren is similarly suspicious of her youthful husband. Another aged Count, Foyes, mews up his daughter Martia so as to force her into a marriage with the wealthy simpleton La Bestia.

With mischievous zest Lemot turns these humours to account and involves all the characters in an unduly complicated entanglement, culminating in a tavern scene which brings everyone, including the king and queen, on a variety of pretexts together. Florilla has listened to the persuasions of Lemot that she must expose herself to trial (Sc. iv, 230 ff):

If you will worthily prove your constancy to your husband, you must put on rich apparel, fare daintily, hear music, read sonnets, be continually courted, kiss, dance, feast, revel all night amongst gallants; then if you come to bed with your husband, with a clear mind and a clear body, then are your virtues *ipsissima*.

To which counsel the Puritan Countess lends the authority of a fictitious scriptural citation : 'it is written, we must pass to perfection through all temptation, Habbakuk the fourth.' Yet she does not stray beyond the limits of pardonable indiscretion with Lemot, and she can resume her Puritan pose free from any moral stain.

Martia runs into greater danger, for the king himself becomes enamoured of her, but she is safeguarded by her love at first sight of Dowsecer, son of Labervele by his first marriage. Dowsecer with his humour of contemplative melancholy stands apart from the more conventional types in the play. He enters with a philosophical quotation from Cicero on his lips and oblivious of all bystanders soliloquises on the crimes and follies of 'the shameless world'. His eloquence charms the king, who is thus prepared to surrender Martia to him. For by an unconvincing *volte-face* the confirmed 'isolationist' becomes the immediate victim of her charms, though he covers his surrender with a characteristic Platonic interpretation of it (vii. 213–7):

> thou hast not changed
> My soul to sense, but sense into my soul;
> And I desire thy pure society,
> But even as angels do to angels fly.

Most of Dowsecer's speeches illustrate Chapman's handling of blank verse in a more individual manner than in *The Blind Beggar*, and the prose dialogue in which the play is mainly written shows an advance in ease and flexibility.

Henslowe's *Diary* contains an entry on 2 July 1599 of a payment of thirty shillings to Chapman 'for his Boocke called the world Rones a whelles and now all foolles but the foolle'. This is the play which after one entire, and another partial, change of title was published by Thomas Thorpe in 1605 as *All Fools*. Henslowe's payment, it may be assumed, was made with a view to the performance of the comedy by the Admiral's men at the Rose, though there is no entry to this effect in the *Diary*, nor on the title-page of the quarto which records its presentation at the Blackfriars, and lately before his Majesty. About the turn of the century Chapman appears to have transferred his services from the Lord Admiral's men to the Children of the Chapel, known after 1603 as the Children of the Queen's Revels, acting at the Blackfriars theatre. The performance by them at Court as recorded in the Accounts of the Revels was on New Year's night 1604/5.

While no source has been traced for Chapman's earlier plays, *All Fools* is manifestly based on the *Heautontimoroumenos* of Terence, with some debt also to his *Adelphi* and *Eunuchus*. Thus the materials of the plot are borrowed but Chapman shows great dexterity in adapting typical Latin New Comedy characters and a highly complicated intrigue to the uses of the stage of his own day. The two heavy fathers, Gostanzo and Marc Antonio, in their contrasted relations to their sons Valerio and Fortunio, carry on the New Comedy tradition. But Valerio has been transformed from a prodigal involved in an amour with a courtesan into an Elizabethan gallant who has secretly married a beautiful but poor gentlewoman. His friend Fortunio has a closer tie with him than in the Latin play, for he is in apparently hopeless love with Valerio's sister, who is straitly guarded by her curmudgeonly father. And Chapman endows Fortunio with a younger brother, Rinaldo, who takes the place of the slave Syrus in the Terentian comedy. A scholar, disillusioned by an unhappy love affair, he is another of the dramatist's dominant figures who find delight in weaving a tangled web of mischief. By gulling Gostanzo into the belief that it is Fortunio, instead of his son Valerio, who has made an undisclosed marriage, and by persuading him to take the supposed wedded pair into his house, he starts a game of deceit and double-crossing that at the last, when all have been made fools, ends in disclosure of the truth and in fuller satisfaction for all than in the Latin original. And to add to the complications of an already involved plot, Chapman adds the sub-plot of the plebeian Cornelio's jealousy of his young wife. But with Terence as his tutor he keeps a firm hand on the complexities of the action, and it may be in emulation of his model that he casts the larger part of the dialogue in smoothly flowing verse that swells into rich melody in Valerio's outburst to Rinaldo :

> I tell thee, Love is nature's second sun,
> Causing a spring of virtues where he shines,
> And as without the sun, the world's great eye,
> All colours, beauties, both of art and nature,
> Are given in vain to man, so without love
> All beauties bred in women are in vain,
> All virtues born in men lie buried,
> For love informs them as the sun doth colour.
>
> *   *   *
>
> O 'tis the Paradise, the heaven of earth.

In contrast with *All Fools* the comedy *May-Day* is written almost throughout in prose, and here again Chapman was influenced by his source. For *May-Day* is an adaptation of *Alessandro*, a very popular piece by the sixteenth-century Italian humanist, A. Piccolomini. It is an example of the *commedia erudita* in which the classical New Comedy is given the background and atmosphere of the Italian Renaissance. *May-Day* was first published in 1611 by John Browne. It had been acted at the Blackfriars by the *chorus juvenum*, who introduce the play with a song and dance, the Children of the Chapel or the Queen's Revels who occupied the theatre till 1608. The date of production is uncertain, but several passages, including an imitation (III. iii. 277 ff.) of Sir Andrew Aguecheek's challenging letter in *Twelfth Night* and a garbled quotation (IV. i. 18–19) from Marston's *Antonio's Revenge*, suggest a year soon after 1600, in spite of an apparent quotation from Dekker's *Gull's Hornbook* (1609). In any case the source of *May-Day* must have been present to Chapman's mind when he was writing *All Fools*, where he adopted from *Alessandro* the names Gostanzo, Fortunio, and Cornelio, for which he substituted others in *May-Day*. Once again he showed his skill in adapting to the theatre of his own day a complicated plot involving not only the usual types of amorous cross-currents and intrigue but the further element of sex-disguise.

Under Chapman's vitalizing touch three figures stand out prominently. Though Alessandro gives his name to the Italian comedy, he is merely a confidant, a 'Charles, his friend'. His place is taken in *May-Day* by Lodovico, another of Chapman's irrepressible wire-pullers who has an equal zest in acting the go-between of two young lovers, whom he brings together by means of a rope-ladder, and in fooling to the top of his bent Lorenzo his uncle. Lorenzo is a typical figure of Renaissance comedy, the senile amourist, who counts on the favours of Franceschina, wife of Captain Quintiliano. But he is individualized by assuming the disguise of Snail, the chimney sweep, to gain access to his mistress, who thrusts him into her coal-house, whence he is dragged out by her husband. But Quintiliano is not seriously concerned about his wife's good name. 'Honour wooes me, preferment calls me, and I must lie pampered in a wench's lap, because she dotes on me.

Honour says no.' It is the voice of the *miles gloriosus*, but instead of its more strident and flashy tone, it has an ebullient ring, as in the scene (IV. iii) where the captain impresses on his 'lieutenant' Innocentio that 'the first model of a battle was taken from a banquet'. Quintiliano is one of the most diverting of Elizabethan swaggerers.

If *The Gentleman Usher*, printed by V. Syms for Thomas Thorpe in 1606, was, as seems probable, near in date to *May-Day*, it is surprisingly different in almost every aspect. And this is all the more notable because, though no performances have been recorded, the large proportion of music in the play and the introduction of masques indicate that like *May-Day* it was a Blackfriars production. But here Chapman, though he made use of a Plautine situation, the rivalry of a father and son for a maiden's love, and borrowed probably from the *Arcadia*, with modification, the idea of the disfigurement of a heroine's beauty, seems nevertheless to have been himself the chief originator of a plot which develops after a slow start into a romantic tragi-comedy. There is missing from it what had hitherto been the most distinctive figure in Chapman's comedies—a character who holds in his hands all the threads of the action. Instead in the gentleman-usher, Bassiolo, he is almost caricatured. In his affectations of speech and of dress, 'close stockings' and the 'most constant fashion of his hat', and in 'overweening thought of his own worth', Bassiolo is akin to his fellow major-domo, Malvolio, but to these he adds 'servile avarice'. Hence the heroine Margaret commends him to her lover Prince Vincentio as their go-between. When the prince bribes and flatters him with a show of hail-fellow familiarity he is ready to act as his letter-carrier. He offers himself too as Margaret's secretary, and indites a reply in high-flown, pedantic style (III. ii. 453–8) for which she substitutes her own more plain-spoken missive. But Bassiolo is too proud of his own composition not to hand it to Vincentio, and it serves as a hostage when, in fear of discovery and punishment by Margaret's father, he threatens to turn traitor to the lovers. Though the gentleman-usher gives the play its name there is better entertainment in the more lightly sketched humours of Poggio, whose habitual malaproprisms win for him the title of 'Cousin Hysteron Proteron', and whose delight in announcing evil tidings is pungently notified by Vincentio :

> The ass is great with child of some ill news,
> His mouth is never fill'd with other sound.

But the distinctive and abiding appeal of *The Gentleman Usher* lies in its romantic elements. Chapman soars into a transcendental, Platonic atmosphere in the scene (IV. ii. 132 ff.) where Margaret, to forestall forced nuptials between herself and her lover's father, the duke, offers herself to Vincentio by a far more sacred bond :

>   may not we now
> Our contract make, and marry before heaven?
> Are not the laws of God and Nature more
> Than formal laws of men? Are outward rites
> More virtuous than the very substance is
> Of holy nuptials solemnis'd within? . . .
> My princely love, 'tis not a priest shall let us,
> But since th' eternal acts of our pure souls
> Knit us with God, the soul of all the world,
> He shall be priest to us.

Vincentio, in token of their union, knits a scarf about her arm, declaring:

> As this is soft and pliant to your arm
> In a circumferent flexure, so will I
> Be tender of your welfare and your will
> As of mine own, as of my life and soul,
> In all things, and for ever.

Margaret with a similar gesture responds:

> In and for you shall be my joys and woes:
> If you be sick, I will be sick, though well:
> If you be well, I will be well, though sick:
> Yourself alone my complete world shall be,
> Even from this hour to all eternity.

Yet, as if to hold the balance between this supersensual union and the ideal pattern of customary wedlock, Chapman portrays the latter in its most gracious form in the relation between Strozza and his wife Cynanche. Strozza has been treacherously wounded while hunting, but he bears his pain with the help of his 'judicial patience', both Christian and Stoic, and his wife's ministering companionship (IV. iii. 2 ff.):

> Come near me, wife; I fare the better far
> For the sweet food of thy divine advice . . .
> Oh, what a treasure is a virtuous wife,
> Discreet and loving! Not one gift on earth
> Makes a man's life so highly bound to heaven;
> She gives him double forces, to endure,
> And to enjoy, by being one with him,
> Feeling his joys and griefs with equal sense.

But even with such allies as patience and his 'good angel', Cynanche, it is far from plausible that the arrow-head should, in accordance with Strozza's prophecy, fall, on the seventh day, out of his wounded side without medical aid. But the doctor is reserved for a more signal exercise of his art when Margaret, on Poggio's false report of Vincentio's murder, destroys her beauty with a blistering ointment and has it restored by a 'recureful mask'.

Even with the proofs already given of Chapman's dramatic versatility, it is astonishing to find that the panegyrist of Platonic and nuptial love in *The Gentleman Usher* should, probably a year or two later, have made a stage-play out of a contemporary sordid marriage lawsuit and scandal. The play itself is lost, but Chapman's authorship of it is attested out of his own mouth on the unimpeachable evidence of still extant legal records.[1] It was called *The Old Joiner of Aldgate* and was acted by the Children of Paul's on 28 February 1602/3 and probably later. Agnes Howe, the daughter of a barber-surgeon, had inherited a large estate from her aunt, and soon found a number of suitors, among them John

[1] See C. J. Sisson's *Lost Plays of Shakespeare's Age* (1936), Chap. II. 12–79.

Flaskett, favoured by her mother, and Thomas Field, her father's choice, both of whom had gone through some contract of marriage with her and who had invoked the law in support of their claims. The father turned for advice to Dr. John Milward, the preacher at Christ Church, who gave the problem an unexpected solution by himself marrying Agnes, without licence or asking of banns, at Barnet parish church soon after Easter 1601. Flaskett thereupon brought a suit against Milward, whose marriage was declared invalid, but this judgment was reversed on appeal on 20 February 1601/2. But Flaskett, a year later, obtained a re-trial of the case and it was at this point that he sought Chapman's aid. He thought that a play by a popular dramatist, ridiculing under transparent disguises the opponents of his claim to Agnes's hand and fortune, would help him as a litigant. And though Chapman denied that the piece had any personal applications, its list of *dramatis personae* made it evident that it was inspired by the Howe imbroglio. Snipper Snapper, a barber, was John Howe; Ursula, his daughter, was Agnes; Tresacres and Touchbox, her suitors, were Field and Flaskett; and a French doctor was Dr. Milward. Chapman sold the play to Thomas Woodford, manager of the Paul's boys, for the very handsome sum of twenty marks (£13. 6s. 8d.). And though it is not likely to have influenced the judgment of the Court, Flaskett in effect in February 1602/3 for a second time won his case. But Milward made a further appeal, which proved successful, to the Star Chamber, and it was here that he indicted Chapman, Woodford, and Edward Peers (Pearce), Master of the Children of Paul's, and thus preserved for posterity the record of a singular and unexpected phase of Chapman's dramatic activities.

But it was not long after this excursion into 'dramatic journalism' that Chapman returned to his most characteristic vein of combined romance and comic characterization in

Monsieur D'Olive, published in 1606 for William Holmes. The title-page describes it as having been acted at Black-friars by Her Majesty's Children, i.e. the Children of the Queen's Revels. The references in the first scene of the play to the calling in of monopolies on 7 May 1603 and to the lavish creation of knights, would be topical in the early years of James's reign, and the exceptional prominence given in the humorous scenes to the preparations for an embassy may well have been suggested by the public excitement over diplomatic missions to France, Spain, and the Low Countries in 1604–5. To that autumn or winter the play may be assigned.

The romantic main plot has two parts of separate origin which are held together by the figure of Vandome. He is another variant, in more serious guise, of Chapman's favourite character—the man who pulls all the strings of the action. He has returned from a three years' absence abroad and is confronted with a doubly strange situation. As a Platonic lover, in a different phase of idealist exaltation from that glorified in *The Gentleman Usher*, he had paid court to his 'matchless mistress', the Countess Marcellina. But her husband, Count Vaumont, had misjudged their relations and Marcellina in consequence had vowed never to show herself by day, and to leave her chamber only when night fell. As Vaumont repentantly laments to Vandome (I. i. 110 ff.):

> And thus my dear and most unmatched wife
> That was a comfort and a grace to me,
> In every judgment, every company,
> I, by false jealousy, have no less than lost
> Murther'd her living, and entomb'd her quick.

The last words give the key to Chapman's combination of two in themselves unrelated actions. In contrast with his mistress thus entombed alive Vandome learns that his sister, the wife of the Earl of St. Anne, has died but is unburied.

In a variant of a story associated with Herod and later with
Charlemagne, the Earl

> Retains his wife's dead corse amongst the living. . . .
> And in his chamber (as in life attir'd)
> She in a chair sits leaning on her arm,
> As if she only slept; and at her feet
> He, like a mortified hermit clad,
> Sits weeping out his life.

Vandome cures Marcellina of her perverse conduct in a
sufficiently conventional way. He draws her forth from her
entombment by persuading her that Vaumont has become
enamoured of a lady-in-waiting and that she will surprise
them in each other's arms. With St. Anne he goes more
subtly to work. Feigning that he is himself in love with
Eurione, the sister of Marcellina, he engages St. Anne to
plead his cause. But Eurione had been 'vow'd sister' to
St. Anne's wife and bore a strong resemblance to her. Thus
while the Earl is acting as proxy wooer he becomes enamoured of her, as Vandome had planned. He lays the body
of his wife below ground and welcomes Eurione as her living
counterpart (V. ii. 49 ff.):

> Matchless lady,
> Your beauties and your virtues have achiev'd
> An action that I thought impossible;
> For all the sweet attractions of your sex
> In your conditions, so to life resembling
> The grace and fashion of my other wife,
> You have reviv'd her to my loving thoughts,
> And all the honours I have done to her
> Shall be continu'd, with increase, to you.

St. Anne's strange obsession had however lasted long enough
to supply an excuse, however flimsy, for the introduction
into the play of its name part, Monsieur D'Olive. The King
of France had been uncle to the dead Countess and it was
thought that his intervention would procure her burial. For
the proposed embassy to the French Court D'Olive is put
forward in mockery by his associates, and from their de-

scription of his qualifications one is prepared to find him an egregious, affected blockhead and butt (I. i. 393):

'Tis the perfect model of an impudent upstart, the compound of a poet and a lawyer; he shall sure to th' Court . . . oh, 'tis a most accomplished ass, the mongrel of a gull and a villain, the very essence of his soul is pure villany; the substance of his brain, foolery; one that believes nothing from the stars upward . . . his wit is to admire and imitate, his grace is to censure and detract.

And in part at least D'Olive answers to this analysis when as a credential of his fitness for the embassy he repeats to the Duke his defence of tobacco against a Puritan assailant. But even here his verbal dexterity atones somewhat for his vanity, and it is displayed yet more fully in his dialogue with applicants for posts in his ambassadorial train, and in his final disquisition on these would-be followers (III. ii. 151 ff.):

I cannot look into the city, but one or other makes tender of his good parts to me, either his language, his travel, his intelligence, or something. Gentlemen send me their younger sons, furnished in complete, to learn fashions, forsooth; as if the riding of five hundred miles and spending a thousand crowns would make 'em wiser than God meant to make 'em.

And when he hears that 'the great ambassage', which he fondly hoped would become a date-mark rather than Agincourt battle or the loss of Calais, has come to naught, he takes the ruin of his dreams not without a touch of dignity. He scarcely deserves to be further befooled by a counterfeit letter from a Court lady making an assignation with him, if he comes disguised. But the lady is a cousin of Vandome, and thus another, though far-fetched, link is established between the romantic and the comic plots. And at the close the Duke instead of making mock of D'Olive, and allying himself with his tormentors, smilingly bids him reserve himself till fitter times and 'follow us to Court'.

In his dedicatory letter prefixed to *The Widow's Tears* Chapman states that it was 'of many desired to see printed', but it was not published by John Browne till 1612, six years after *The Gentleman Usher* and *Monsieur D'Olive*. It prob-

c

bably dates back to about 1606, and the title-page tells that
it was often presented at the Blackfriars and Whitefriars
theatres, doubtless by the Children of the Queen's Revels.
The main plot is based on the story of the Ephesian matron
as told by Petronius in his romance, the *Satyricon*, written
in the age of Nero. It has been matter for surprise that from
the idealist vein in the more serious parts of *The Gentleman
Usher* and *Monsieur D'Olive* Chapman passed so abruptly to
the cynical point of view of *The Widow's Tears*. But if *The
Joiner of Aldgate* had survived the transition would have
been less noticeable. Moreover, a curious link between
Monsieur D'Olive and *The Widow's Tears* has, I believe, been
overlooked. The two sections of the main plot in the former
play are concerned, as has been shown above, with problems
of 'entombment', literal and symbolic. This may well have
suggested to Chapman the idea of dramatizing a story where
a disconsolate wife does not, like St. Anne, keep her spouse's
body above ground, but accompanies it into the tomb.

But, after his usual fashion, Chapman largely transforms
and complicates his borrowed materials. He changes the
scene from Ephesus to Cyprus, a shrine of Venus, and adds
to the original story of the widow, now christened Cynthia,
whose ostensibly inconsolable mourning is so short-lived, a
parallel action introducing another widow of similarly
chameleon character, the Countess Eudora. And the link
between the two plots is furnished by Tharsalio, probably the
last and most vigorously drawn of Chapman's favourite
figure in his comedies, who sets in motion and keeps a hand
on all the springs of the action. As he steps upon the stage
he acknowledges as his guide the 'patroness of all good
spirits, Confidence', the Elizabethan equivalent of 'toujours
l'audace'. Formerly a page in the household of the Countess
who has vowed 'to preserve till death the unstained honour
of a widow's bed', he proclaims his resolve to woo and win
her out of hand. 'The castle's carried by a sudden assault,
that would perhaps sit out a twelve-months' siege.' Though

he has a rival in a Spartan lord of high degree, and though the Countess orders him to be thrown out by her servants, yet by sheer high-spirited effrontery, abetted (in a repellent scene) by the sensual promptings of a pandress to Eudora, he carries the day.

Tharsalio's challenging venture, though it is technically the underplot, fills the best part of the first three Acts. But the way is also being prepared for the rapid development of the main action. Tharsalio's brother Lysander has cherished an 'infallible belief' in the constancy of his wife Cynthia, which she oftentimes has vowed to him after his life 'till her own death had brought, forsooth, her widow-troth to bed'. But catching the infection of Tharsalio's cynical bravado he suddenly resolves to test his wife's vows of eternal fidelity by leaving her and spreading a report that he has been killed while on a journey. Here Chapman diverges from the *Satyricon* where the husband's death is real not feigned and follows or reverts to an older variant of the story. At first, after a mock funeral, Cynthia's constancy seems to stand the test. She hastens 'to follow her husband's body into the tomb, and there, for his company, to bury herself quick [alive]'. Here she and her handmaid drink nothing but their own tears and starve themselves to the point of death. But after five days Lysander, disguised as a soldier set to watch the bodies of certain criminals crucified near by, gains admission to the tomb. He urges upon Cynthia the futility of her conduct (IV. ii. 79 ff.):

> Say that with abstinence you should unloose
> The knot of life; suppose that in this tomb
> For your dear spouse you should entomb yourself
> A living corse . . . can your dear spouse
> Take notice of your faith and constancy?
> Shall your dear spouse revive to give you thanks?

When argument fails he resorts to the more concrete persuasions of food and drink to which first the handmaid and afterwards Cynthia herself yields. This paves the way for her complete surrender to the amorous advances of the supposed soldier.

In all this Chapman closely follows Petronius, but henceforward he introduces other complications of his own invention. Tharsalio spies Cynthia and her lover embracing and it is he who, to punish the 'soldado', takes down one of the crucified bodies which, by the law, has to be replaced by that of the negligent sentinel. To avert this, Cynthia, as in the *Satyricon*, proffers her husband's corpse instead, even though Lysander adds in the play a final acid test by proclaiming himself his murderer. But the preternaturally alert Tharsalio divines the identity of the soldier-wooer and reveals to Cynthia that it is her own husband. Thus what otherwise would have been a gruesome climax in Act V. iii, when Cynthia insists on taking the lead in the preparations for opening the coffin, is transformed into a brilliant piece of ironic comedy in which the 'widow' turns the tables upon the 'dear spouse' who has laid a trap for her.

Up to this point the play is, as an exhibition of plot-technique, a masterly achievement. But then comes a disconcerting collapse. Instead of the obviously needed scene of explanation and reconciliation between Lysander and Cynthia there is a tediously drawn-out trial scene before a blundering and fussy governor, a Dogberry *in excelsis*, where the action is brought to a muddled conclusion.

Three other extant comedies have an association with Chapman. He shares with Marston and Jonson the credit for the sparkling play, *Eastward Ho*, acted by the Children of the Queen's Revels and published in 1605. But as the design of the play was probably chiefly due to Marston, it will be discussed in relation to his work.[1] *Sir Giles Goosecap, Knight*, was published anonymously in 1606, as acted by the Children of the Chapel, and again in 1636 after a revival at Salisbury Court. There is no external evidence for Chapman's authorship of the play, but a strong and widely accepted claim for

[1] See below, pp. 138-41.

this has been made out on the ground of close correspondences in characterization, situations, and phraseology between *Sir Giles Goosecap* and works in the undoubted Chapman canon.[1] On this assumption the chief interest of the play would lie in the proof of Chaucer's influence on Chapman in the relation of its more serious plot to *Troilus and Criseyde*. On the other hand, *The Ball*, though it bears on its title-page, when published in 1639, the names of Chapman and Shirley, probably belongs to the latter alone.[2] The Master of the Revels, Sir Henry Herbert, in 1632, noted Shirley as its sole author and it bears throughout the evidence of his hand.

HISTORICAL AND PHILOSOPHIC TRAGEDIES

When Chapman's comic vein assumed the bitter quality of *The Widow's Tears*, it was evident that tragedy was henceforth to be his proper mode of expression. As early as 1598 Francis Meres had testified to his reputation in both kinds. But his earliest extant tragedy, *Bussy d'Ambois*, though its date is uncertain, seems by internal references, especially to 'the old queen', to have been written and acted after the accession of James I, perhaps in 1604, the leap-year, mentioned in Act I. ii. It was first published by William Aspley in 1607, 'as it hath often been presented' by the children of Paul's. An edition 'much corrected and amended by the Author before his death' [in 1634] appeared in 1641, with a prologue probably written for a revival of the play by the King's men at Court on 7 April 1634.

In contrast with Chapman's later tragedies no source of *Bussy d'Ambois* has been identified, though he may have been indebted to memoirs by Brantôme, Marguerite de Valois, and others and to recent floating tradition. Moreover, Marlowe's *The Massacre at Paris* pointed the way to another play dealing with the same period of French history and

---

[1] See T. M. Parrott's Introduction to the play in his edition of Chapman's *Comedies*, 889–97.

[2] See below, pp. 355–7.

introducing some of the same leading personages, King Henry III and the Duke and Duchess of Guise, though not in their relation to political and religious events but to the romantic figure of Louis de Clermont, Bussy d'Amboise. Born in 1549, Bussy was in Paris during the massacre of St. Bartholomew, when he killed a Huguenot cousin. Through his bravery and accomplishments he became a favourite of the Duke of Anjou, who appointed him in 1575 governor of Anjou. There he met and fell in love with Françoise de Maridort, wife of the Comte de Montsoreau, grand-huntsman to the Duke. A letter which he sent to the Duke concerning his intrigue with the Countess was shown by Anjou to the King, who passed it on to Montsoreau. The Count forced his wife to make a treacherous assignation with Bussy on the night of 15 August 1579 at their chateau, where he assassinated her lover and a companion.

In his choice of Bussy as a hero of tragedy Chapman was following in the track of Marlowe, though with a difference. In his ambition and arrogance, his headlong pursuit of his ends, whether as swordsman or paramour, he is akin to young Mortimer in *Edward II*. Indeed, as described by the King to the Guise, Bussy's own estimate of himself is more than justified (III. ii. 90 ff.):

> A man so good that only would uphold
> Man in his native noblesse . . . that in himself
> (Without the outward patches of our frailty,
> Riches and honour) knows he comprehends
> Worth with the greatest.

But this is too highly coloured a picture, and mingled with Bussy's grander qualities there is an element of coarseness in speech and action which robs him of the sympathy that goes out to Marlowe's protagonists, whatever their extravagances. Yet to the end his superb vitality makes him a dominant stage-figure and draws all eyes.

But if in characterization Chapman here is partly in debt to Marlowe, in his technique he mainly follows the semi-

Senecan model set by Kyd. He not only introduces the traditional Messenger in Act II and the Ghost in Act V, but his careful plot-construction shows the influence on him of classical examples. It is one of the virtues af *Bussy d'Ambois* that here as in his most distinctive comedies Chapman skilfully draws together threads of different origin. In the career of the historical Bussy his tragic end had no connexion with his earlier life at the French Court. But in the play the affray, with three combatants on either side, in which Bussy and Barrisor are the protagonists, so vividly described by the Messenger in Act II. i, springs from Barrisor's suspicion that Bussy is beginning to court Tamyra (as Chapman names the Countess) whom he has for long wooed. Thus Bussy's earlier gasconading exploits are related to the fatal climax of the tragedy which Chapman boldly transfers to Paris. And, as in his comedies, the dramatist gives a unity to the action by making one of the characters pull most of the strings. Here it is the Duke of Anjou who is represented as raising Bussy from a far humbler station than was the case, and afterwards, when he had grown jealous of his favour with the King, conspiring with the Duke of Guise for his overthrow. Anjou, moreover, has vainly sought the favours of Tamyra which she has granted to Bussy, and in revenge it is he (not the King) who shows the Count the paper that proves his wife's guilt, and who, with the Guise, suggests the stratagem by which she is forced to decoy her lover to his doom.

From first to last the play is pitched in a high key, with action and passion both at fever heat. And this reacted unfavourably on Chapman's style. In his comedies he had shown himself a master both of clear-cut, flexible prose and of lucid, flowing verse. But in developing the tragic theme of *Bussy d'Ambois* he aimed throughout at energy of expression at all costs. To this he was ready to sacrifice beauty of phrase and rhythm, and even a measure of lucidity. So far Dryden was justified in a famous criticism written in 1681 in complaining of those 'glaring colours which annoyed me in *Bussy d'Ambois* upon the theatre'. But he was wide of the mark when he accused Chapman of dressing up a dwarfish thought in gigantic words. He never spins out words to hide a poverty of ideas; the difficulties of his style in the play spring from excessive condensation, and from the plethora of illustrations by way of simile, metaphor, and other figures of speech. Even so there are not infrequent passages of crisp dialogue, of sustained and vital narrative, as in the Messenger's report of the Bussy-Barrisor encounter, or of stately soliloquy as when d'Ambois, fatally wounded, resolves to die standing:

> Prop me, true sword, as thou hast ever done!
> The equal thought I bear of life and death
> Shall make me faint on no side; I am up;
> Here like a Roman statue I will stand
> Till death hath made me marble.

And in words aptly borrowed from the lips of the dying Hercules, in Seneca's play, he bids farewell to a world in which he at last sees himself

> like a falling star
> Silently glanc'd, that like a thunderbolt
> Look'd to have stuck, and shook the firmament.

The success of *Bussy d'Ambois* upon the stage encouraged Chapman to seek another tragic hero in contemporary French annals. This two-part play, *The Conspiracy and Tragedy of Charles Duke of Byron*, was entered in the Stationers' Register on 5 June 1608, and published by Thomas Thorpe in that year. It had been 'acted lately' at the Blackfriars theatre by the Children of the Queen's Revels. It must have been first performed early in April 1608, for on the 8th of that month, the French ambassador, in a letter still extant, wrote: 'I caused certain players to be forbid from acting the history of the Duke of Byron; when, however, they saw that the whole Court had left the town, they persisted in acting it', and even represented the Queen of France boxing the ears of the king's mistress. But the Ambassador succeeded in getting three of the actors arrested and having the offensive scene cut out, for there is no trace of it in the play as published. Nor is this episode found in the work which otherwise by close verbal coincidences is shown to be Chapman's sole source, Edward Grimeston's *General Inventory of the History of France* (1607).

In Grimeston's volume based on contemporary French chronicles there was traced the career of a figure akin to Bussy, but who had historically been far more conspicuous. Charles de Gontaut, Baron de Biron, born in 1562, had won great military renown in the service of Henry IV and had been created Admiral and Marshal of France, Duke of Biron, and Governor of Burgundy. Intoxicated with success and aiming at an independent sovereignty, he entered into a conspiracy against Henry which was discovered and for which the King, after his confession of guilt, forgave him. Trading on this magnanimity Biron formed a second plot which was again betrayed. This time Henry refused pardon to the Marshal, who, confident to the last of a reprieve, was executed.

Here were the elements of a more poignant tragedy than that of Bussy. But for the first time Chapman, instead of being the master of his material, seems in part to be subdued by it. Though it is true that 'these poor dismembered poems' (as he calls the double play in his dedication) had suffered at the hand of the Master of the Revels, the cardinal defect of *The Conspiracy and Tragedy* cannot be ascribed to him. Like Browning at a later date in *Strafford* and Swinburne in his Mary Queen of Scots trilogy, Chapman overloads the action of his drama with a mass of historical detail outside the ken of the ordinary playgoer or reader, Jacobean or Victorian. This is specially true of *The Conspiracy*, where the figure of Byron, as the dramatic protagonist, does not stand out clearly enough from the background of diplomatic intrigue and rivalry between France, Savoy, and Austria.

Early in the play (Act I. ii. 31 ff.) he utters himself in words
that have a true Marlovian ring:

> 'Tis immortality to die aspiring,
> As if a man were taken quick to heaven;
> What will not hold perfection, let it burst . . .
> 　　　　　　　　　　　　　Happiness
> Denies comparison of less or more,
> And not at most, is nothing: like the shaft
> Shot at the sun by angry Hercules,
> And into shivers by the thunder broken,
> Will I be if I burst; and in my heart
> This shall be written: 'Yet 'twas high and right'.

But after this swelling exordium the movement is slow and
it is something of an anti-climax in Acts II and III that
Byron should be stirred to revolt mainly by reports of King
Henry's depreciation of his martial services. Act IV in what
appears to be its censored form consists entirely of a narrative of Byron's visit to the Court of Elizabeth and, though
flattering to an English theatrical audience, does not advance
the action of the play. The most significant part of this has
therefore to be compressed into Act V, where the final incite-
ment to Byron to conspire against the King is the refusal of
his request to be appointed governor of the citadel of Bourg.
The dialogue suddenly quickens and takes fire (V. i. 81 ff.):

Byr. But you will grant my suit?
Hen. 　　　　　　　　　　I swear I cannot,
　　Keeping the credit of my brain and place.
Byr. Will you deny me, then?
Hen. 　　　　　　　　　　I am enforc'd:
　　I have no power, more than yourself, in things
　　That are beyond my reason . . . Would you have a
　　　　king
　　That hath a white beard have so green a brain?
Byr. A plague of brain! What doth this touch your brain?
　　You must give me more reason, or I swear—
Hen. `Swear? What do you swear?
Byr. 　　　　　　　　I swear you wrong me,
　　And deal not like a king, to jest and slight
　　A man that you should curiously reward.

But Byron's thwarted assault on the King, Henry's reproaches, the Marshal's confession and pardon are ineffectively handled and make a lame conclusion.

Chapman may have been anxious to hurry on to the overwhelming catastrophe dealt with in *The Tragedy of Byron*. Yet here again the pace at first is slow while the Marshal once more turns traitor and plots with the perfidious La Fin. The heavily cut Act II, now merely a masque, but originally including the quarrel between Henry's queen and paramour, was doubtless 'good theatre', but it can have had nothing to do with the fortunes of Byron. These enter upon their downward slope in Act III, when in obedience to the King's summons and against the advice of his true friends, Byron self-confidently presents himself at Court. He cannot realize that he is marching to his doom, though Henry, Chapman's model of a righteous ruler, feels the awful responsibility of executing judgement (IV. ii. 63 ff.):

> O thou that govern'st the keen swords of kings,
> Direct my arm in this important stroke,
> Or hold it being advanc'd: the weight of blood,
> Even in the basest subject, doth exact
> Deep consultation in the highest king:
> For in one subject death's unjust affrights,
> Passions and pains, though he be ne'er so poor,
> Ask more remorse than the voluptuous spleens
> Of all kings in the world deserve respect.

The Marshal's arrest while he is playing cards with the queen and two courtiers is a very effective stage episode, though there is a reminder that *The Tragedy* is a Stuart, not an Elizabethan, play in Byron's punning encomium on Philip II of Spain as the 'worthy King of hearts'. In the last Act Chapman's too close adherence to the legal and formal details of Grimeston's narrative unduly protracts the dramatic action, but in the final scene beside the scaffold in the Bastille Byron rises to the majestic height of one who has nothing more to ask of life, and with whom in almost his first words it was 'immortality to die aspiring'. Thus to the

Bishop who bids him 'resign your sensual powers entirely to your soul', he proudly retorts (V. iv. 26 ff.):

> Let me alone in peace,
> And leave my soul to me, whom it concerns;
> You have no charge of it; I feel her free:
> But she doth rouse and like a falcon stretch
> Her silver wings, as threatening Death with death;
> At whom I joyfully will cast her off.

Yet at the very close in lines of exquisitely mournful cadence a note of hopeless frustration creeps in (V. iv. 245 ff.):

> And so farewell for ever! Never more
> Shall any hope of my revival see me;
> Such is the endless exile of dead men.
> Summer succeeds the Spring; Autumn the Summer;
> The frosts of Winter the fall'n leaves of Autumn:
> All these and all fruits in them yearly fade
> And every year return: but cursed man
> Shall never more renew his vanish'd face.

It was probably not long after 1611 that Chapman turned his attention to another French notable whose career under Francis I had in many aspects anticipated that of Byron under Henry IV. The 1611 edition of E. Pasquier's *Les Recherches de la France* gave an account, which the dramatist closely followed, of Philip de Chabot, born about 1580, who for his great services was created Admiral of France. The intrigues of enemies at Court lost him for a time the King's favour and he was tried and found guilty of treason. The later reversal of the sentence, on the production of fresh evidence, could not save Chabot from the annihilating effect of the trial which was followed by his death in 1543.

It was not till the year after Chapman's death that we first hear of the play, when it was licensed for performance by Sir H. Herbert on 29 April 1635. It was entered in the Stationers' Register on 24 October 1638, and published in 1639 as *The Tragedy of Chabot, Admiral of France*, as it was presented by Her Majesty's servants at Drury Lane. The title-page bore the names of Chapman and Shirley and internal evidence leaves little doubt that the play was written by the former and revised by the latter, who added or substituted some scenes of feminine interest. Chapman's own chief concern, as in the Byron plays, is with the conflict of character between the King and the greatest of his subjects. But here the subject is an innocent man, falsely condemned and sacrificed by an arbitrary sovereign. It is in Act II. iii that the clash between Francis and Chabot comes to a head. The King reminds him of the honours he has heaped on him and asks (ll. 75 ff.):

> And cannot all these powers weigh down your will?
> *Chab.* No, sir; they were not given me to that end,
> But to uphold my will, my will being just.
> *King.* And who shall judge that justice, you or I?
> *Chab.* I, sir, in this case . . .
> *King.*   What if I
> Grant out against you a commission,
> Join'd with an extraordinary process
> To arrest and put you in law's hands for trial?
> *Chab.* Not with law's uttermost!
> *King.*   I'll throw the dice.
> *Chab.* And I'll endure the chance, the dice being square,
> Repos'd in dreadless confidence and conscience
> That all your most extremes shall never reach,
> Or to my life, my goods, or honour's breath.

So uncompromising is Chabot that even when in Act IV. i. the King pardons all his faults and forfeits, he retorts:

> You cannot pardon me, sir . . .
> It is a word carries too much relation
> To an offence of which I am not guilty.

And at the close of the play, beside the Admiral's deathbed, Francis himself confesses that in Chabot was impersonated the justice which is the salvation of the state (V. iii, ll. 173 ff.):

> For justice being the prop of every kingdom,
> And mine broke, violating him that was
> The knot and contract of it all in him;
> It is already falling in my ear.

In drawing the picture of Chabot, too self-conscious an embodiment of righteousness to stir deeply the sympathy of a theatrical audience, Chapman was doubtless influenced by one of his own creations of slightly earlier date who had only a fictitious connexion with French historical events. In April 1612 there was entered in the Stationers' Register, and in 1613 there was published for John Helme, *The Revenge of Bussy d'Ambois*, 'as it hath been often presented at the private playhouse in the Whitefriars'. The Children of the Queen's Revels had begun to occupy the Whitefriars theatre in 1609 and the play falls between that year and 1612, probably close to the latter date. The success of *Bussy d'Ambois* stimulated Chapman to produce a sequel. But, as with Marlowe with Part II of *Tamburlaine*, the difficulty was to find material. There was a tradition that Bussy's sister and **her** husband, Baligny, had a design to take vengeance for his murder, but as it came to nothing, it could scarcely form the basis of a 'revenge' play. But Chapman was never happier than when he was partly inventing, partly piecing together, data from different sources, and thus producing a well-fashioned dramatic whole. He now brought upon the stage a brother of Bussy, Clermont D'Ambois, who had never existed, and who was charged by Bussy's ghost to avenge his murder. Here Chapman threw over the influence of Marlowe for that of Kyd and Shakespeare, and Clermont procrastinating his unwelcome task is akin to Hamlet. To fill up the necessary time before the execution of his mission Chapman hit upon the ingenious plan of borrowing from Grimeston an episode concerning Count d'Auvergne, who was treacherously arrested by agents of the king while attending a review of troops, and of substituting Clermont for d'Auvergne. This occupies a large part of the first four Acts. But in this play the action is of minor consequence. What became of absorbing interest to Chapman was the elaboration of the character of Clermont into a type of the Stoic way of life in its most exalted aspect. Here the dramatist drew upon the *Discourses* of Epictetus, from which he translated or adapted a number of passages. One of the most significant, declaring that the individual must act in harmony with the Universal will, is put into Clermont's lips in Act III. iv. 58 ff.:

> God hath the whole world perfect made and free,
> His parts to th' use of th' All; men then that be
> Parts of that All, must, as the general sway
> Of that importeth, willingly obey
> In everything without their power to change.
> He that, unpleas'd to hold his place, will range,
> Can in no other be contain'd that's fit,
> And so resisting th' All, is crush'd with it.

His character 'rightly to virtue fram'd', is delineated in full by the Duke of Guise in Act IV. iv. 14 ff., and is thus summed up:

> In short, this Senecal man is found in him,
> He may with heaven's immortal powers compare,
> To whom the day and fortune equal are;
> Come fair or foul, whatever chance can fall,
> Fix'd in himself, he still is one to all.

It is in this spirit, as of one fulfilling a divine decree, that Clermont at last executes justice upon Montsurry. But he does not long survive him. By another of the distortions of history which remind us that the Elizabethan age had passed Chapman represents the Duke of Guise, chief author of the St. Bartholomew Massacre, as a 'true tenth worthy', who listens eagerly to Clermont's doctrines and becomes his patron. When the news of the Duke's murder, another episode borrowed by the dramatist from Grimeston, reaches Clermont, he cannot live longer in a world where none is left favouring goodness, and in approved Stoic fashion he kills himself.

In his dedicatory epistle prefixed to the 1613 quarto Chapman complains that in its 'scenical presentation' the play had met with 'some maligners'. Nor can Jacobean gallants and groundlings be blamed if they failed to appreciate in the theatre a play which was a medley of perverted history and transcendental philosophic doctrine. But to those who turn over its pages to-day the figure of Clermont d'Ambois has a singularly appealing charm and in him English humanism in its later phase has bestowed one of its rarest gifts upon our drama.

Having presented a disciple of the Stoic doctrine in a Renaissance environment Chapman turned his gaze backward to its great Roman exemplar. For Cato of Utica is the real hero of *The Tragedy of Caesar and Pompey*. This play was entered in the Stationers' Register and published twice in quarto form in 1631, and again in 1653. In the dedicatory epistle Chapman speaks of it as 'written so long since', and it is probably to be dated not long after *The Revenge of Bussy*, about 1613. He also states that 'it never touched at the stage', yet the 1653 quarto describes it as acted at the Blackfriars and the detailed stage-directions suggest that the play was printed from a theatrical prompt-copy. In any case Chapman was justified in his belief that *Caesar and Pompey* was not primarily a piece for the stage. He drew his material from Plutarch, the *Lives* and the *Morals*, and the central part of the tragedy deals with the struggle between the two dictators for the mastery of the Roman world. As usual, Chapman allowed himself considerable licence with the historical facts, but unlike Shakespeare and Jonson in their different ways he could not give dramatic vitality to the personages and happenings of classical times.

But he achieved something different, not so much of theatrical as of biographical significance. At the head of the play he had put prominently the dictum 'only a just man is a free man'. Cato's career was shown to be framed upon this principle. But already in Chabot and in Clermont d'Ambois the spectacle of the 'just man' struggling with circumstance had been presented by Chapman. With a disregard of the limitations of the otherwise noble and spiritual Stoic creed he made Cato the mouthpiece of his own deepest meditations on the after-life. Thus not content with expounding to his

disciples in Utica the Stoic thesis that the good man is
justified in killing himself to escape falling into a tyrant's
hands, he speaks of death as the entrance to a second life.
When he is questioned (IV. v. 123 ff.):

> Hold you our bodies shall revive, resuming
> Our souls again to heaven?

he answers:

> Past doubt, though others
> Think heaven a world too high for our low reaches,
> Not knowing the sacred sense of him that sings:
> 'Jove can let down a golden chain from heaven
> Which tied to earth, shall fetch up earth and seas.'
> And what's that golden chain but our pure souls?

Here the translator of Homer gives his own spiritual
interpretation to lines from the *Iliad*. And when to forestall
the arrival of the victor, Caesar, Cato is about to fall on his
own sword, he affirms Chapman's conception of immortality (V. ii. 137):

> For we shall know each other, and past death
> Retain those forms of knowledge learn'd in life;
> Since, if what here we learn, we then shall lose,
> Our immortality were not life, but time.
> And that our souls in reason are immortal
> Their natural and proper objects prove,
> Which immortality and knowledge are.[1]

[1] Since this Chapter went to press, new light on Chapman's early years
has been thrown from Chanery Records by Miss Jean Robertson in *Mod.
Lang. Rev.*, July, 1945.

III

BEN JONSON

LIFE

WHEN Ben Jonson published.the quarto of his *Sejanus* in 1605 he stated that it differed in part from 'that which was acted on the public stage; wherein a second pen had good share'. It has been surmised that this second pen was Chapman, who alone among contemporary professional playwrights could rival Jonson in classical learning. In any case, the transition is natural in this survey from the chief Grecian of Elizabethan dramatists to the one who had in him most of the 'antique Roman'.

Benjamin Jonson (to give him once the full form of his familiarly shortened Christian name) was born almost certainly in or near London in 1572, probably on 11 June, a month after the death of his father, who had suffered persecution under Queen Mary, and later became a 'minister of the gospel'. About two years later the widow married a master-bricklayer who brought Ben up poorly. But a far-sighted friend sent him to Westminster School, where the second master, who taught the lower forms, was the antiquary William Camden. Under him, to whom long afterwards he acknowledged that he owed 'all that I am in arts, all that I know', he laid the foundations of his comprehensive learning.

But while Marlowe, the shoemaker's son, had proceeded from King's School, Canterbury, to Cambridge, Jonson, the bricklayer's stepson, was taken prematurely from Westminster and put into the 'craft' about 1589. Thus in later life he owed his degrees from both universities to 'their favour, not his study'. But he soon broke away from his uncongenial labour and at an uncertain date between 1591–2 and 1597 went for some time as a soldier to the war in

Flanders where, in characteristically classical fashion he killed a foeman in single combat. An adventure of a different kind was his early marriage, probably on 14 November 1594, to Anne Lewis whom he was later to describe as 'a shrew yet honest', and who bore him several children, of whom two died early.[1]

It was probably to support his young family that Ben began his connexion with the stage as an actor in a strolling company. Dekker, in *Satiromastix*, taunts him with having taken the part of Hieronimo in Kyd's *Spanish Tragedy* in 'a leather pilch by a play-wagon in the highway'. He also appeared as Zulziman in a lost play under Henslowe's management at Paris-garden—a bear-pit used at times for dramatic performances. He soon, however, found his real vocation. In the summer of 1597 he was employed to complete a satiric comedy *The Isle of Dogs* which Thomas Nashe, departing to Norfolk, had left unfinished. When it was produced the play was denounced to the Privy Council as 'containing very seditious and slanderous matter'. Jonson, with two other actors in the piece, was imprisoned in the Marshalsea, and though they were released in October, it was an ill-omened beginning of his career as a dramatist. But this did not prevent Henslowe from lending him twenty shillings on 3 December in earnest of a play, which Ben was to provide before Christmas, of which he showed the plot to the company. In the following year, 1598, he had attained sufficient reputation for Francis Meres in his *Wit's Treasury* to rank him 'among our best for tragedy'.

It was however in comedy that Jonson made his first popular success when *Every Man in His Humour* was produced at the Curtain theatre in September 1598. It did not appear under the auspices of Henslowe, but was acted by the Lord Chamberlain's company, with Shakespeare in one of the parts. A few days later he had a quarrel with Gabriel Spencer, one of the actors who had been imprisoned with him

[1] See Mark Eccles, "Jonson's Marriage", *R.E.S.* July, 1936.

during *The Isle of Dogs* scandal, and killed him in a duel. Again Jonson was arrested, and during his confinement he was put to the test by two Government spies, one of whom, according to a recent plausible interpretation of his epigram IX, was no other than the Robert Poley who had been present at the killing of Christopher Marlowe. Though they got nothing out of him, a priest who visited him in prison succeeded in converting him to Roman Catholicism. When he was put on trial in October he confessed that he had killed Spencer, but claimed benefit of clergy, and instead of hanging suffered confiscation of his goods and a brand on his thumb.

Once more he quickly surmounted what might have been disaster. Before the end of 1598 he began his connexion with the Children of the Chapel with *The Case is Altered*, soon to be followed by *Cynthia's Revels* (1600) and *Poetaster* (1601). For the Admiral's Company he collaborated in some lost plays and was paid by Henslowe in September 1601 for additions to *The Spanish Tragedy*, though if the evidence of style counts for anything, they cannot be those which appeared in the 1602 quarto of Kyd's play. He continued his connexion with the Lord Chamberlain's men with *Every Man Out of His Humour* (1599).

But while he kept the favour of these leading companies he was engaged in a violent stage-quarrel with two prominent dramatists, Dekker and Marston, of which further mention will be made below. There was a rift also in his domestic relations, for in February 1602 he is reported as living upon 'one Townesend', i.e. Sir Robert Townshend, a patron of himself and later of Fletcher. At a later date he moved to the house of Lord D'Aubigny, with whom he remained till the beginning of 1607. Another patron was Sir Robert Spencer, who engaged him to provide an entertainment on 25 June 1603 at Althorpe for King James, who had succeeded to the English throne on Elizabeth's death on 24 March, and who was on his way from Edinburgh to London. His accession boded well for Jonson, for the learned monarch was likely to be favourably disposed to the learned dramatist. And Ben's first play presented during the new reign, the tragedy of *Sejanus*, performed in the latter part of 1603 by the King's men, had a sufficient classical basis to satisfy the most exacting of scholarly tastes. But it met with popular disapproval, and in addition it involved Jonson in a charge of 'popery and treason' before the Privy Council, brought by the Earl of Northampton. This had no serious result, and when in 1605 Jonson voluntarily joined Chapman and Marston in prison as their collaborator in *Eastward Ho* the trio were soon released without further penalty. The Privy Council must have been fully satisfied of his loyalty and good-will, for on 7 November 1605, two days after the discovery of the Gunpowder Plot, they commissioned him to get into touch with a priest and others conversant with the plotters, though his attempts were unavailing.

The decade that followed was the golden period of Ben's career. Between 1605 and 1614 he produced his four master-pieces of comedy, as well as his second classical tragedy, *Catiline*, and also a series of masques at Court or in great houses. By 7 February 1607 he had again set up in a home of his own, for he then dated the dedication of *Volpone* 'from my house in the Blackfriars'. But in Jonson's complex nature there was too large a social, even convivial, element for him not to seek other than domestic enjoyments. At the Mermaid Tavern in Bread Street he met and was acclaimed by many of the finest spirits of the time. Beaumont and Herrick have paid first-hand tributes to his mastery at these 'lyric feasts', and Fuller has handed down the tradition of wit-combats between Jonson, the solid but slow Spanish galleon, and Shakespeare, the 'lesser in bulk but lighter in sailing' English man-of-war. Donne too he counted among his friends. And in higher social circles he was welcomed by members of either sex of the Sidney family—Sir Philip's nephew, the Earl of Pembroke, his daughter, the Countess of Rutland, and his niece, Lady Wroth. An even higher place in his affectionate loyalty was held by the Countess of Bedford. And by Sir Walter Raleigh, a prisoner in the Tower, he was chosen to be the tutor of his son during a foreign tour in 1612–13. He was back in London before 29 June 1613, when he saw the destruction of the Globe by fire during a performance of *Henry VIII*. In October 1614 the last of his greater plays, *Bartholomew Fair*, was acted very successfully at the Hope theatre and before the Court at Whitehall, but he did not include it in the folio edition of his works published in 1616. Nor did this contain the play performed in that year, *The Devil is an Ass*, which marks the beginning of his dramatic decline and ended his work for the professional stage for nine years. It was therefore all the more helpful to him that on 1 February 1616 King James had granted him a pension of 100 marks.

An epoch in Jonson's life was marked by his journey to Scotland, for which he set out on foot in the summer of 1618. He was welcomed in Edinburgh, where on 20 September he was admitted as a burgess of the city. About Christmas he paid a visit of two or three weeks to the landowner and poet, William Drummond, at Hawthornden, some miles from the capital. Here he talked freely, often caustically, about his contemporaries and himself, and the notes of these *Conversations* taken by his host are a prime source for Ben's life and opinions. At the end of the notes soon after the guest's departure Drummond on 19 January 1619 summed him up in realistic, if one-sided fashion, 'He is a great lover and praiser of himself, a contemner and scorner of others, given rather to lose a friend than a jest . . . he is passionately kind and angry, careless either to gain or keep, vindicative, but if he be well answered, at himself'.

On his return south he paid another visit to Oxford, where he stayed at Christ Church, and on 17 July 1619, on the recommendation of the Chancellor, Lord Pembroke, received the honorary degree of M.A. It was during the period after the publication of his first folio and his recognition by

Edinburgh and Oxford that Jonson's sovereignty in the London world of letters was fully acknowledged. It was symbolized by the 'throne' which he occupied in another famous Bohemian haunt, the Devil Tavern near Temple Bar. Here in the Apollo Room,[1] sitting under the Latin 'Rules' for club conviviality of his own composition, Ben held sway over his 'sons'.

From his *Execration upon Vulcan* when his library was destroyed by fire in November 1623 we learn that among the works which Jonson then had in hand and which perished in the flames were *The Discovery*, a poetical account of his Scottish journey; *Heroologia*, an epic in couplets on English worthies; a prose history of Henry V, and an English Grammar. His translation of Barclay's Latin romance, *Argenis*, which King James had commissioned, also was lost, though it had already been entered on 2 October in the Stationers' Register.

This disaster was the prelude to a darkening period in Jonson's career. The death of James in March 1625 brought to the throne a king with a French consort, both alien in their outlook and sympathies from Jonson. In 1628 he was stricken by paralysis which confined him to his room and cut him off from the tavern festivities where he had held sway over his 'sons'. His appointment in the September of this year as City Chronologer on the death of Middleton, brought an addition of 100 nobles (£33 6s. 8d.) to his slender income, but in November 1631 payment was stopped 'until he shall have presented unto this Court some fruits of his labours in that his place'.

Meanwhile he was attempting in vain to re-establish himself on the popular stage. *The Staple of News* (1626) failed to win favour and *The New Inn* in January 1629 was so completely damned that Jonson rounded upon the censurers of the play with the lofty, if too arrogant, invective

[1] Called after the fine terra-cotta bust of Apollo of which there is a photograph in Mrs. Esdaile's paper on 'Ben Jonson and the Devil Tavern' in the English Association's *Essays and Studies*, vol. XXIX (1944).

of *The Ode to Himself*. It was an added bitterness that for
five years he had not been invited to provide the libretto of
the Court masques. But now Charles, hearing of his mis-
fortunes, sent him a gift of £100, increased his pension from
100 marks to £100 and added an annual tierce of Canary
wine. The further compliment of being asked to collaborate
again with Inigo Jones in the masque performed at Whitehall on 9 January 1631, led to a violent quarrel when it was
soon afterwards published with Jonson's name first on the
title-page. Two further plays, *The Magnetic Lady* (1632) and
the probably revised *Tale of a Tub* (1634), in which Inigo
figured as Vitruvius Hoop, brought to a moderately satisfactory close Ben's labours for the public stage.

It is the most convincing proof of what has been well
called his magnetic quality that during these years of illness
and falling fortunes he continued to exercise his ascendency
over the choicest spirits of the age. His sick-room took the
place of the Mermaid or the Devil Tavern as their meeting-
ground.

> To him how daily flocked, what reverence gave,
> All that had wit, or would be thought to have.

So wrote Lord Falkland who, with the Earl of Newcastle and
Sir Kenelm Digby, was among the most notable of his
aristocratic associates who mingled with the younger poets
and dramatists in his chamber. The King himself signified
his pleasure to the City authorities that Jonson's salary, now
called pension, as Chronologer, should be renewed from
18 September 1634.

To the last he continued to exercise his versatile powers,
in the gleanings from his daily readings and his comments
embodied in his prose commonplace book, *The Discoveries*;
in the fragmentary sketch of an *English Grammar* intended
to replace the one destroyed in the fire; and probably in the
uncompleted pastoral drama *The Sad Shepherd*. Yet the
shadows darkened.   His only surviving son died in November 1635. With his straitened means he fell into debt, and

when death came at last on 6 August 1637, he seems to have left no will. Yet when he was borne to burial in Westminster Abbey the mourners included 'all the greatest part of the nobility and gentry then in the town'. Over the grave was set a slab with the terse epitaph that has captivated the imagination of posterity, 'O rare Ben Jonson'.

HUMOUR COMEDIES—COMICAL SATIRES

If one attempts to apply the epithet not to Ben's personality but strictly to his dramatic achievements, in what exact sense was it 'rare'? He was at once a rebel against the stage technique of the public theatre of his day and an exponent of it. His classical tastes and his austere artistic temper were in conflict with the prevailing loose structure of contemporary plays. He conformed in the main to the 'unities' in his plots and built them according to a strictly controlled design. But unlike the closet neo-classicists of his days he responded to the full exuberance of the llfe in Elizabethan England, especially the capital, and instead of being limited in range, his plays are as crowded with vital figures as those of the most 'romantic' dramatists of his time. It is true that these figures, though concrete and not abstract, are often typical rather than individually complex. As the Oxford editors of Jonson have said:

He seizes character under one aspect, because he sees it so; neglecting because he does not see them the cross-play of impulses, the inconsistencies and conflicts, the mingled strength and weakness of which they are normally composed. His observation was prodigiously active and acute; but its energy was spent in accumulating illustrations of a single dominant trait, not in distinguishing fine shades.

To Jonson with his analytical bias this ' single dominant trait' presented itself under the semi-physiological, semi-psychological aspect of a 'humour'. As in the body there were supposed to be four humours, 'choler, melancholy, phlegm, and blood' flowing continually, there were their counterparts in the general disposition. Hence (*Every Man out of his Humour*, Induction, 105-9):

> when some one peculiar quality
> Doth so possess a man that it doth draw
> All his affects, his spirits and his powers
> In their confluctions all to run one way,
> This may be truly said to be a humour.

It may, I think, be fairly said that the catchword 'humours' has been overworked in the interpretation of Jonson's dramatic art. A good many of the characters in his plays and much of their interest are not covered by its implications. But for this Jonson himself must bear the chief responsibility by entitling the two first plays that he thought worthy of print, *Every Man in his Humour* and *Every Man out of his Humour*. When he made his collection for the first folio of his works in 1616 he left out the early tragedies eulogized by Meres and his semi-romantic adaptation of two plays of Plautus, the *Captivi* and the *Aulularia*, called *The Case is Altered*, dating probably from 1597-8, which had been published without his authority in 1609. Even *Every Man in his Humour*, acted in 1598 and issued in quarto in 1601, was largely transformed before he admitted it to the folio. The scene had been originally laid in Florence and all except three of the characters had Italian names. In the folio London takes the place of Florence and all the names are anglicized. At many points the rhetorical diction which suited the original setting of the comedy is replaced by a more colloquial and homely idiom. Thus Jonson, while keeping true in the main to the 1598 structure and plot, brought the play into closer accord with his ideal of what comedy should be, as set forth in the prologue to the folio version of *Every Man in his Humour*. Here, after making much of the violations of the unities of time and place and the crude spectacular devices favoured by contemporary dramatists (though such gibes point back to stage conditions about 1598), he asserts that he will present

> deeds and language, such as men do use;
> And persons such as Comedy would choose,
> When she would show an image of the times,
> And sport with human follies, not with crimes.

It is follies that *Every Man in his Humour* exhibits though; in spite of the title, only some of these can be rightly termed humours even in a broad interpretation. Thus the relation between the elderly Knowell and his son Edward, the *jeune premier* of the comedy, is an Elizabethan variant of the attitude of Philistine fathers to their heirs traditional from the theatre of Plautus and Terence. Knowell is incensed against Edward, both on the customary ground of youthful extravagances and because he has been a devoted scholar,

> Dreaming on nought but idle poetry,
> That fruitless and unprofitable art,
> Good unto none but least to the professors.

The latter feature is more emphasized in the quarto version where in Act V. iii. 315 ff., young Lorenzo (Knowell) delivers the eloquent *apologia* on

> The state of poesy, such as it is,
> Blessed, eternal, and most true divine

which is omitted in the folio On the other hand, the letter from Edward's friend, Wellbred, which falls into his father's hands and leads him to set a watch upon his doings, is in a coarser vein than in the quarto and goes further to justify Knowell's indignant suspicions of his son's associates. Edward gets warning of this from Knowell's man, Brainworm in whom are combined features from the pliant *servus* of Roman comedy and the tricky Vice of the Moralities. But Jonson individualises him by giving him the 'humour' of a gusto for disguises. In the then too familiar figure of a needy discharged soldier he imposes upon Edward and (more surprisingly) upon his own employer, Knowell, who re-engages him as 'Fitzsword'. Afterwards he filches the clothes of a sleeping justice's clerk and thus attired serves a warrant and makes an arrest. But in court Justice Clement

repudiates a warrant without his signature and commits
Brainworm to jail. Then he reveals himself as Knowell's
servant, recounts his exploits during his 'day of metamorphosis', and is sentenced by the 'old merry magistrate'
merely to pledging him in a cup of wine, as he has done
nothing 'but deserves to be pardoned for the wit of the
offence'.

A still more striking variant of a traditional classical type,
the *miles gloriosus*, is Captain Bobadill. The braggart
soldier had become a familiar figure on the English stage
since Udall's Ralph Roister Doister. But Bobadill has
several markedly distinguishing characteristics. He is not a
voluble swaggerer. It is his humour to be 'mightily given to
melancholy'. As he says of himself, 'I am no general man
. . . I love few words.' These include his esoteric oaths, 'by
the foot of Pharaoh', 'by the body of Caesar'. Another sign
in Jonson's day, though not in ours, of his being 'no general
man' is his devotion to the newly found herb 'Trinidado' or
tobacco (III. v. 77 ff.):

I have been in the Indies, where this herb grows, where neither
myself nor a dozen gentlemen more, of my knowledge, have
received the taste of any other nutriment in the world for the
space of one and twenty weeks but the fume of this simple . . .
By Hercules, I do hold it, and will affirm it before any prince in
Europe, to be the most sovereign and precious weed that ever
the earth tendered to the use of man.

This provokes the Cockney water-carrier Cob, with whom
the Captain lodges, to an outburst against 'this roguish
tobacco; it's good for nothing but to choke a man and fill
him full of smoke and embers. . . . I'ld have it present whip-
ping, man or woman, that should but deal with a tobacco pipe.'
Whereupon Bobadill turns on him and beats him, and Cob
gets a warrant against him for striking 'his lawful host'. It
is characteristic of Bobadill's superior attitude that he
affects the pedantic love of the fencing-schools which was
anathema to the gay realist, Mercutio. If he were put at the

head of nineteen gentlemen of good spirit he would teach them 'the special rules, as your *punto*, your *reverso*, your *stoccata*, your *imbroccatta*, your *passada*, your *montanto*, till they could all play very near or altogether as well as myself. This done, say the enemy were forty thousand strong, we twenty would come into the field', and, according to Bobadill's fantastic method of computation, would without loss kill off all their foes in two hundred days. In the end Bobadill shows the white feather, protesting he has been served with a warrant of the peace, when Wellbred's half-brother, the plain country squire Downright, challenges him. He lets himself be beaten and disarmed.

Meanwhile he has been courted by Master Matthew, a town-gull, a fishmonger's son who apes gentility and seeks to 'wriggle into acquaintance with all the brave gallants about the town'. He has heard that Bobadill has 'absolute knowledge i' the mystery' of swordsmanship and takes lessons at his hands. He shares the Captain's preference for old-fashioned plays like *The Spanish Tragedy* and reads him crude love-verses, 'a toy of mine own, in my nonage'. He has a foil in the better-born country gull, Master Stephen, Knowell's nephew, whose literary aspirations are confined to manuals of field-sports:

'An a man have not skill in the hawking and hunting languages now-a-days, I'll not give a rush for him. They are more studied than the Greek or the Latin. He is for no gallant company without 'em.

He affects what he takes to be a fashionable melancholy and hauteur and is rallied by his sharp-witted cousin Edward: 'Come, wrong not the quality of your desert with looking downward, coz, but hold up your head, so! and let the idea of what you are be pourtrayed i' your face'. He is fascinated by the prospect of wearing the rapier which the disguised Brainworm offers for sale as a blade that 'may become the side or thigh of the best prince in Europe', and insists on buying it, despite Edward's remonstrances—only to learn later that it is not a Toledo but a weapon of the poorest quality.

The main link between the Knowell circle and the other character-group in the play is Edward's boon-companion, Wellbred, who lodges with his brother-in-law Kitely, a city merchant. Kitely's humour is jealousy in its Elizabethan sense of suspicion. It is significant that he is afraid of rebuking Wellbred and his familiars for their riotous behaviour in his house because (II. i. 114 ff.):

> They would give out, because my wife is fair,
> Myself but lately married, and my sister
> Here sojourning a virgin in my house,
> That I were jealous! nay, as sure as death,
> That they would say.

And they would be speaking truth. When he disobeys his wife's summons to breakfast because his head aches, and she is afraid that he has caught the 'new disease', he detects subtlety in her answers and interprets them in sinister fashion:

> A new disease? I know not, new or old,
> But it may well be call'd poor mortals' plague,
> For like a pestilence it doth infect
> The houses of the brain . . .
> Till not a thought or motion in the mind
> Be free from the black poison of suspect.

The working of this 'black poison' is shown in masterly fashion in Kitely's dialogue with Thomas, his cashier, in Act III. iii. He has a business appointment which will keep him away for two hours and will leave his wife's beauty unguarded. So he bids business 'go by, for once'. But when the cashier reminds him that his scrivener will be there with the bonds he declares that he must go. He then, with twists and turns, tells Thomas that he has a secret to impart on which his lips must be sealed. But when he bids him run after him with the news if Wellbred brings any gentleman to the house while he is away, he protests over and over that this is not the secret. When Cob, who has called at the house with water, tells him that there are five or six strangers there, he at once imagines that his wife has betrayed him. And when on his return he hears her describe Edward Knowell as 'a gentleman of an exceeding fair disposition and of very excellent good faith', he is convinced that he is her minion. His lunatic humour carries him to such extremes as to suspect his wife of trying to poison him and of having another lover in old Knowell, with Thomas as their go-between. He pursues her to their supposed place of assignation, Cob's house, whither she herself, catching his infection and incited by Wellbred, has gone in search of him. The scene (IV. x) in which they are all brought together at this rendezvous and which comes to a climax by Cob beating his innocent wife, Tib, for letting his doors lie open to all comers, is a capital example of Jonson's constructive skill. So too is the final scene in Justice Clement's court, where these and other entaglements are resolved by the genial sagacity of the old magistrate. Here too the news is broken to all that while they have been working themselves up to fury about imaginary amours, a real, though remarkably uneffusive, love-affair between Edward Knowell and Kitely's sister Bridget has come to a head in their secret wedding. Even in the less idiomatic quarto version *Every Man in his Humour* proved that Jonson was a master of sinewy and incisive prose. At the same time, with no less potent but more delicate touch, Shakespeare was achieving a similar result in the comic scenes of *King Henry IV*. Lyly's precedent of using prose as the chief medium of dialogue in comedy was now followed and confirmed by two master-dramatists, and henceforward it becomes the accredited instrument of the Comic Muse in England.

In the latter part of 1599 Jonson's next play, *Every Man out of his Humour*, was acted by the Lord Chamberlain's company at their new Globe theatre. It was published in quarto in 1600 for W. Holme and sold quickly. Holme issued a second quarto later in the year, and this was followed, also in 1600, by a third published for N. Ling. The title-page of the three quartos had the inscription, 'As it was first composed by the Author B.I.', but public opinion had obliged Jonson to substitute another ending for the one 'at the first playing' which included a long address of flattery to the queen impersonated on the stage. He added this original ending in an epilogue with a characteristically defiant preface. In the 1616 folio he omitted the quarto ending and restored the last twenty prose lines of the original text, though thirty-six of the forty verse lines of the address to the queen again appeared in an epilogue. Otherwise the chief changes in the folio were in textual minutiae, such as punctuation and lettering, on which Jonson laid much stress.

Where however Jonson was open to serious criticism was in his choice of a title, which suggested that the play would furnish a contrast and complement to *Every Man in his Humour*. This title in fact would be equally fitting to the second play, except in the closing scenes, where by one means or another the characters are forced 'out' of their humours. It is not in its portraiture but in its construction that *Every Man out of his Humour* differs fundamentally from its predecessor, and this Jonson indicated by calling it not a comedy but a comical satire. Instead of a loosely-knit plot he presents a series of episodes, almost or entirely unrelated to each other except by their satirical intention. In this he was a conscious innovator, for in the Induction Cordatus, speaking as 'the author's friend . . . inly acquainted with the scope and drift of his plot,' justified him by the precedent of the successive changes made in comedy by the Classical dramatists who 'augmented it with all liberty':

I see not then but we should enjoy the same licence or free power to illustrate and heighten our invention as they did; and not be tied to those strict and regular forms which the misuses of a few (who are nothing but form) would thrust upon us.

Thus while Jonson was ready to denounce the extravagances of romantic drama he was not prepared to be a neo-classicist of the rigid and pedantic type. But while right in general principle he was making an ill-judged new venture in *Every Man out of his Humour*. In what is virtually the opening speech in the Induction Asper, 'the presenter', declares:

> my language
> Was never ground into such oily colours,
> To flatter vice and daub iniquity;
> But with an armed and resolved hand
> I'll strip the ragged follies of the time
> Naked as at their birth.

And later he speaks of holding up a mirror,

> Where they shall see the time's deformity
> Anatomiz'd in every nerve and sinew
> With constant courage and contempt of fear.

This is the attitude of a satirist lashing out at a society completely diseased, not of a dramatist giving an objective presentation of a world mingled of good and ill. Thus the 'comical satire', as understood by Jonson, has not a sufficiently legitimate claim to a place on the stage.

Hence it is significant that nothing in the body of the play equals in precision and vigour of style either the dialogue in the Induction or the character-sketches of the *dramatis personae* which on this occasion Jonson prefixed, headed by Asper:

He is of an ingenious and free spirit, eager and constant in reproof, without fear controlling the world's abuses. One whom no servile hope of gain or frosty apprehension of danger can make to be a parasite either to time, place or opinion.

Indeed, a careful study of these penetrating analyses would go far to enlighten a reader about the purport of the play. As there is so little action, it will be sufficient here to indicate the groups within which the chief characters fall. There is the rich country farmer, Sordido, whose humour is to look in almanacks for prophecies of bad weather, and who when his own barns are bursting with corn grudges any of it

to his poor neighbours. Yet when some of them inadvertently
save him from hanging himself, and then curse him to his
face, he suddenly becomes a changed man. His brother,
Sogliardo, aspires to shake off all traces of the country
bumpkin and to buy the stamp of gentility. He puts himself
under the tuition of the cynical jester and *gourmet* Carlo
Buffone, who bids him live altogether in the city amongst
gallants, and pretend alliance with courtiers and great
persons. He introduces him to Fastidious Brisk, a gallant
who wears his clothes well and in fashion, but whose humour
is an affectation of speech and manner. As he describes
himself, 'I cannot frame me to your harsh, vulgar phrase, 'tis
against my *genius*'; or as viewed by Cordatus, who acts
throughout as 'grex' or chorus, 'labouring to avoid popularity [he] falls into a habit of affectation ten thousand times
hatefuller than the former'. The trio visit at his country-
house, Puntarvolo, a knight of an even more eccentric
humour, of whom the report goes that 'he has dialogues and
discourses between his horse, himself, and his dog; and that
he will court his own lady as she were a stranger ne'er
encountered before'. He is (surprisingly) godfather to
Sordido's son, Fungoso, who joins the company. He is a law
student, and his uncle Sogliardo wants to get the latest law
gossip from him. But he is entirely bent on observing the
fashionable gallant's clothes and finding means to copy
them. 'O (and I might have but my wish) I'd ask no more
of God now but such a suit, such a hat, such a band, such a
doublet, such a hose, such a boot.' But it is his ill fortune
always to be just in the rearward of the fashion.

A warmer feeling than envious admiration is entertained
for Fastidious Brisk by Fungoso's sister Fallace. She is
married to the honest and rich citizen Deliro, who is a
dotingly uxorious husband, anxious to forestall and gratify
her every whim. His reward is to have his favours insultingly
rejected, while Fallace falls in love with Brisk at first sight.
He in his turn seeks the good graces of the self-satisfied

beauty, Saviolina, but is discomfited when she is taken in by the gentlemanly veneer of Sogliardo and has to be convinced by the sight of his hand rough from ploughing that he is merely a country clown. Sogliardo suffers yet another humiliation when Cavalier Shift, whom he has taken to be a valiant soldier and dare-devil highwayman and who has become his sworn-brother, lets himself be beaten by Puntarvolo on a false charge of having poisoned his dog. Finally his mentor in the life of fashion, Brisk, is taken to the Counter prison, where he is visited by the infatuated Fallace, and where the pair are discovered by Deliro, whose eyes are at last opened. And the boastful man-about-town proves to be heavily in debt and cries that he is undone.

Thus each character in turn in a too protracted series of scenes is driven 'out of his humour', to the great satisfaction of Macilente, the man of scholarly parts, who envies in others the worldly success or wealth that has been denied to him. Played by the same actor as Asper 'the presenter', he is a critical observer, but doubles with this somewhat awkwardly the role of an agent in the cure of the other characters. His own conversion from his envious temper, as has been seen, was effected in the original performance by the sight of the queen, and the omission of this in the compulsorily revised version brings the piece to a lame ending.

It was characteristic of Ben to compensate for this by making Elizabeth, under the classical name in which Spenser and Raleigh had sounded her praise, the titular figure of his next play. *Cynthia's Revels* or *The Fountain of Self-love* was acted at the Blackfriars by the Children of the Chapel, probably in December 1600. It was published in quarto in 1601 by W. Burre. This text omitted, though they had almost certainly been already written, long passages in Acts III and IV and the first four scenes of Act V, chiefly satirizing Court amusements.

Cynthia's Revels, like its predecessor, is designated a

'comical satire' and departs even more widely from traditional types. Jonson proclaims this definitely in the prologue:

> In this alone his Muse her sweetness hath,
> She shuns the print of any beaten path;
> And proves new ways to come to learned ears.

But in describing the beaten path Jonson for once found himself in wandering mazes lost. *Cynthia's Revels* is a heterogeneous medley of mythological fancy, allegorical symbolism, and topical satire. As in *Every Man out of his Humour* the most effective dialogue is found in the Induction, where in a delightfully lively fashion three of the children quarrel as to which of them shall speak the prologue, and go on to make mock of the weaknesses alike of playwrights and their audiences. The scene is laid in Gargaphie (an Elizabethan Ruritania), where Cupid and Mercury descend. The former in the guise of a page is to join the train of the virgin huntress-queen Diana (Cynthia) who 'in regard of some black and envious slanders hourly breathed against her for her divine justice on Actaeon, as she pretends', has proclaimed solemn revels. Here the allusion to Elizabeth and Essex is unmistakable. Cynthia herself (V. xi. 14 ff.) elaborates it:

> For so Actaeon by presuming far
> Did (to our grief) incur a fatal doom. . .
> But are we therefore judged too extreme?
> Seems it no crime to enter sacred bowers,
> And hallowed places with impure aspect
> Most lewdly to pollute ?

But there is one difficulty. 'Fatal doom' seems to refer to the execution of Essex on 25 February 1601, but the play was acted before then. The Oxford editors of Jonson favour the view that the phrase is used only of the Actaeon of legend and the reference is to the offence of Essex in September 1599, when he entered 'sacred bowers' by bursting into the queen's chamber and found her with her hair about her neck. Mercury has been sent by Jove to summon the nymph Echo, still mourning for her beloved Narcissus, who had died while

gazing on the reflection of his own beauty in a fountain. Sh
appears beside it sighing out her grief in song, and names 'the
treacherous and murdering spring' the Fountain of Self-love,

> that who but taste
> A drop thereof may, with the instant touch,
> Grow dotingly enamour'd of themselves.

As the play takes therefrom its alternative title, one expects
the fountain to be a major influence, but it drops into the
background. Though Amorphus the traveller enters and
drinks from it, the interest shifts to the presentation of the
affected humours of him and his satellite, the prodigal young
heir Asotus. Amorphus, as his name implies, is 'one so made
out of the mixture and shreds of forms that himself is truly
deform'd'. Asotus 'is his zany . . . speaks as he speaks,
looks, walks, goes so in clothes and fashion: is in all as if he
were moulded of him.' This gallant wooes as his mistress 'a
nymph of a most wandering and giddy disposition, Argurion,
whose name betokens Money. Thus an allegorical element is
introduced, which attaches also to the other Court ladies,
Phantaste and Philautia, with their guardian, Moria, or
Folly, 'made all of voice and air, talks anything of anything.' Opposed to them is Cynthia's true attendant and
counsellor, Arete, or Virtue, who declares that

> This knot of spiders will be soon dissolv'd,
> And all their webs swept out of Cynthia's Court.

Yet Jonson thinks it worthwhile to linger interminably over
these 'webs', to depict in satiric detail the amusements and
follies of the pleasure-loving circle close to the throne. This
may have a semi-historical value, but far overleaps even the
most flexible of dramatic bounds.

At last, in Act V. v, the revels, which had been announced
in the opening scene, begin, and there is compensation for
the preceding *longueurs* in the exquisite hymn of invocation
to Cynthia, beginning, 'Queen and huntress, chaste and

fair'. The two masques presented before her are preludes to those which before long Jonson was to provide for the Court of King James. After thanking the performers Cynthia bids them unmask and is astounded to find that Cupid has posed as Anteros and Mercury as a page, while the light ladies and fops of the Court have been the counterfeits of sundry virtues antagonistic to their true selves. These mortals are condemned to penance and purgation before they are re-admitted to the service of Cynthia.

Their sentence is pronounced at her behest by the 'retired scholar' Crites, who, like Asper and Macilente, in the two *Humour* plays, has throughout been the satirical observer and denouncer of the follies before his eyes. Here he speaks for Jonson, and some of his characteristics, as described by Mercury (II. iii. 134 ff.), are those that Ben saw in himself:

He will think and speak his thought, both freely; but as distant from depraving another man's merit as proclaiming his own. For his valour, 'tis such that he dares as little to offer an injury as receive one. In sum he hath a most ingenuous and sweet spirit, a sharp and season'd wit, a straight judgement and a strong mind. Fortune could never break him nor make him less.

But even in his most arrogant mood Jonson could not have described himself as 'a creature of a most perfect and divine temper . . . it is clear, Nature went about some full work, she did more than make a man when she made him'; or, as in Arete's eulogy (V. viii. 18 ff.):

> Lo, here the man, celestial Delia,
> Who, like a circle bounded by itself,
> Contains as much as man in fulness may.
> Lo, here the man who not of usual earth,
> But of that nobler and more precious mould
> Which Phoebus self doth temper, is compos'd.

The question of how far Crites is to be identified with Jonson is complicated by the relation to him of Hedon and Anaides. Primarily they are a pair of empty-headed gallants whom Crites dismisses scornfully:

> The one, a light, voluptuous reveller,
> The other, a strange arrogating puff,
> Both impudent and ignorant enough.

So far they are ordinary 'humour' types. But they are distinguished by a common animosity to Crites and anger at his disdain of their insults (III. ii. 9ff.):

Hed. Look, here he comes. Laugh at him, laugh at him; laugh at him! Ha, ha, ha!

Ana. Foh! he smells all lamp-oil, with studying by candle-light.

Hed. How confidently he went by us and carelessly! . . . God's precious! this afflicts me more than all the rest that we should so particularly direct our hate and contempt against him, and he to carry it thus without wound or passion! 'tis insufferable.

It is natural to ask, had Jonson here any particular detractors of himself in mind? The quarrels of authors, whether in the days of Jonson or of Pope, are unedifying and of ephemeral interest, and in the so-called Elizabethan 'war of the theatres' there is much that is still obscure. But John Marston, though previously a collaborator with Ben, had apparently contrived to offend him in *Histriomastix* (1599). It is doubtful whether Clove, one of the minor affected fops in *Every Man out of his Humour*, was meant to be a retaliation, but as he borrowed a few items of Marston's rhodomontade, the latter took this for ridicule. In *Jack Drum's Entertainment* (*c.* August 1600) he caricatured Jonson in the person of Brabant senior. There can be little doubt that Ben gave a twist, so to speak, to the generalized characters of Hedon and Anaides to bring them into some affinity with Marston and with Dekker, who had also in some way fallen foul of him. At any rate, these two playwrights felt themselves attacked. Marston retorted immediately with *What You Will*, where Jonson is ridiculed as Lampatho. It was known that the couple were also preparing a more formidable joint counterblow. Determined to forestall this, Jonson, working at what for him may be called white-heat, produced within fifteen weeks *Poetaster*, wherein he delivered an unmistakably direct assault upon his two foes.

This comical satire, the last of the trio, was acted early in 1601 by the Children of the Chapel, and was published in quarto in 1602 by M. Lownes. It was reprinted in the 1616 folio with revision of details and some additions, including the last scene of Act III and the 'Apologetical Dialogue'. Jonson's primary aim was to castigate Marston and Dekker but, as was his wont in comical satires, he introduced many loosely related themes. His scene was now set not in an imaginary Gargaphie but in Augustan Rome, and his classical ardour could not resist the temptation to exploit various episodes familiar to him from the Latin poets. Horace, Crispinus, and Demetrius are the chief figures in the play, representing Jonson himself, Marston, and Dekker. But in the earlier scenes it is Ovid who fills the foreground, penning his verses when he should be studying his law-books. His Philistine father (a Roman forerunner of the elder Knowell) discovers him so engaged and hurls reproaches at him :

Is this the scope and aim of thy studies? Are these the hopeful courses wherewith I have so long flattered my expectation from thee? Verses? *Poetry*? Ovid, whom I thought to see the pleader, become Ovid, the playmaker?

But his railings cannot shake his son's allegiance to

sacred poesy, thou spirit of arts,
The soul of science and the queen of souls.

But for Ovid there is also a personal queen of souls in the emperor's daughter, Julia, who sends him an invitation by his fellow-poet, Tibullus, to meet her at the house of the jeweller, Albius. The scenes there are reminiscent of the two previous comical satires. Albius is a doting husband like Deliro in *Every Man out of his Humour*, made mock of by his better-born, termagant wife, Chloe. When Julia with the company of poets and their mistresses enters, the flow of repartee and the eagerness for entertainment, here not in the form of games but of song, carry us back to the Court scenes in *Cynthia's Revels*, though they are not, as there, tediously spun out. Crispinus is among the guests and is welcomed by Chloe as a gentleman born. Unlike Hedon in the *Revels* play he does not at once become a mouthpiece for scurrilous abuse. He pays flattering compliments to Chloe, assuring her that her love and beauties shall make him a poet. When he meets Horace out of doors instead of railing at him he plays the part of the bore whom the Roman satirist could not shake off in the *Via Sacra*. Horace at last escapes when Crispinus at the suit of his apothecary is arrested for debt, but is released when the swashbuckling Captain Tucca goes bail for him.

Tucca, though in a sense a supernumerary figure, is one of the most strongly featured in the play. He is a variant of the braggart soldier type, at the opposite pole from the melancholy and retiring Bobadill. His peculiarity (as it has been defined by A. W. Ward) 'is a buoyant blackguardism . . . and a picturesqueness of speech constituting him a walking dictionary of slang'. His lingo appears to have been partly based on that of a contemporary, Captain Hannam. He affects the military man's blustering contempt of civilians. He will not 'suffer knaves to be competitors with commanders and gentlemen. Are we parallels, rascal, are we parallels?' He pours scorn upon the arts. Playwrights are 'libertines, flat libertines'; Homer 'was a poor, blind, rhyming rascal that lived obscurely up and down in booths and tap-houses'. When a player passes him by without giving a salute, he bursts out (III. iv. 120 ff.):

A player! Call him, call the lousy slave hither! What, will be sail by and not once strike or vail to a man of war? ha! do you hear? you player, rogue, stalker, come back here! no respect to men of worship, you slave?

But when the actor returns a soft answer Tucca calls him 'honest vermin' and invites himself to supper with him And through Tucca's mouth Jonson makes his first direct attack on Marston's dramatic style when he bids the actor be acquainted with Crispinus.

Go! he pens high, lofty, in a new stalking strain; bigger than half the rhymers i' the town, again . . . he will teach thee to tear and rand, rascal; to him, cherish his muse, go: thou hast forty, forty shillings, I mean, stinkard; give him in earnest, do, he shall write for thee, slave.

As further proof of the captain's debased theatrical taste he orders his two young attandants to recite for the actor's benefit passages from old-fashioned plays, especially Jonson's favourite butt, *The Spanish Tragedy*. In the applause that follows a stander-by takes part and is described to Tucca by the actor (III. iv. 321 ff.):

A very simple, honest fellow, sir, one Demetrius, a dresser of plays about the town here; we have hired him to abuse Horace, and bring him in, in a play, with all his gallants.

Thus Dekker is introduced as a reviser of old plays, and as preparing a stage-attack upon Jonson, though the actor admits that nothing is known against him and that the author will have to devise what shall serve in some sort. We get a foretaste of what this is likely to be when at another gathering in the house of Albius Demetrius declares that Horace is 'a mere sponge; nothing but humours and observation; he goes up and down sucking from every society, and when he goes home squeezes himself dry again'. Tucca at any rate gets somewhat nearer the mark when he calls him 'a sharp-tooth'd satirical rascal, fly him . . . he will sooner lose his best friend than his least jest.'

But in Act IV the main interest shifts to Princess Julia and the Court, where at a banquet the poets and their mistresses impersonate the Roman deities, headed by Ovid as Jupiter and Julia as Juno, with Albius, Chloe, and Tucca added to the gay company as Vulcan, Venus, and Mars. But through the borrowing of a crown and sceptre from the players for this masquerade an over-zealous official warns the emperor that there is a conspiracy on foot, and when the

revel is at its height, he enters with Mecaenas and Horace
in his train, and in spite of their appeals for mercy for the
offenders, banishes Ovid for ever from the Court and commits
Julia to prison.

As Ovid at night steals beneath Julia's chamber window
and cries (IV. viii):

> Banished the Court! Let me be banished life,
> Since the chief end of life is there concluded:

we are irresistibly reminded of Romeo's lament, after his
sentence of exile:

> There is no world without Verona walls. . .
> Hence banished is banish'd from the world,
> And world's exile is death.

To us to-day the comparison of Jonson's and Shakespeare's
handling of the same romantic situation is of greater interest
than the sordid stage-quarrel. In my opinion Ben stands the
test unexpectedly well, and I cannot agree with the critics
who have more or less endorsed Gifford's view that he here
penned 'a truly ridiculous love-scene'. No one should expect
from 'Jonson's learned sock' the magical duet at dawn
between Romeo and Juliet, the very quintessence of love's
rapture and its pain. But the parting between Ovid and his
imperial mistress sundered by iron doors has a true emotional thrill and a subtle aptness to their fortunes. Julia
looking down upon her lover sees in this a symbol (IV.
ix. 5 ff.):

> I high, thou low! Oh, this our plight of place
> Doubly presents the two lets of our love,
> Local and ceremonial height and lowness:
> Both ways I am too high and thou too low;
> Our minds are even yet; oh, why should our bodies
> That are their slaves be so without their rule?

In the next world all this will be set right:

> The souls of parents rule not children's souls
> When death sets both in their dissolv'd estates;
> Then is no child nor father; then eternity
> Frees all from any temporal respect.

She is about to fling herself down to seek in death union with him when he bids her stay by declaring that love cannot endure without the bodily senses:

> Thou choosest death
> So thou might'st joy thy love in th' other life.
> But know, my princely love, when thou art dead,
> Thou only must survive in perfect soul,
> And in the soul are no affections:
> We pour out our affections with our blood,
> And with our blood's affections fade our loves.

It is a conception not unsuited to the poet of the *Amores* and it adds a poignancy to their final lingering farewell:

Julia.   Ovid, my love, alas, may we not stay
        A little longer (thinks't thou?) undiscerned?
Ovid.   For thine own good, fair goddess, do not stay.

*   *   *

Julia.   I will be gone then and not heaven itself
        Shall draw me back.
Ovid.   Yet, Julia, if thou wilt,
        A little longer stay.
Julia.   I am content.
Ovid.   O mighty Ovid! what the sway of heaven
        Could not retire, my breath hath turned back.

But he remembers that 'if both stay, both die', and he tears himself away with Julia's image in his heart. Here in this 'comical satire' Jonson has completely dropped the satiric role and shown, as nowhere else in his dramatic canon, an insight into the sacrificial ardour of frustrated love.

When Ovid thus quits the stage he makes way in Act V for an even greater Augustan poetic figure. Virgil appears at the Court and is greeted with reverence by the emperor, at whose bidding he reads aloud the passage (as translated by Jonson) from Book IV of his epic telling of the meeting of Aeneas and Dido in the cave. Such stress is laid on Virgil's pre-eminence not only by the welcome from Augustus but by the tributes from his brother poets, Horace, Tibullus, and Gallus, that the attempt has been made to identify him with one or other of the two master-spirits among Jonson's contemporaries, Shakespeare or Chapman. But the eulogies when analysed do not sufficiently fit either,[1] and if Virgil has any symbolic significance, it is as a standard of consummate art which, even more than the achievement of Horace, dwarfs the puny efforts of a Crispinus and a Demetrius.

At long last, after so many zig-zag windings of the plot, the pair suffer the penalties due to them. Tibullus indicts them on the statute of calumny and produces evidence under their own hands. Crispinus clothes his calumnies in fantastic phrases taken from Marston's plays, and Demetrius accuses Horace of being a plagiary, but has to admit imperfect knowledge of the classical authors from whom the thefts have been made. It is part of the punishment of Crispinus to take pills administered by Horace which cause him to vomit such fustian stuff as 'glibbery', 'lubrical', and 'spurious snotteries', after which nauseous restorative he is admonished by Virgil to complete his cure by reading Terence and the best Greeks, shunning 'wild outlandish terms', and letting his matter run before his words. Demetrius is more mildly treated by being condemned to wear a coat and cap that betoken him a slanderer. Finally, they have both to take an oath not to malign hereafter the person or writings of Horace 'or any other eminent man transcending you in merit'.

Jonson evidently felt confident that the verdict of his stage-court would be endorsed by public opinion outside. Instead, to his naïvely professed astonishment, the play bred tumult and stirred many hornets about him. These are the phrases in the 'Apologetical Dialogue,' which was Ben's counter-stroke. It was spoken only once on the stage and was suppressed by authority in the quarto, but appeared, after the storm had blown over, in the 1616 folio. Jonson had of course anticipated retaliation by Marston and Dekker, but he now found that other classes—lawyers, soldiers, and

---

[1] See the Oxford *Ben Jonson*, I. 431–7.

players—were in full cry against him. He protested that he
had not attacked individuals among them:

> I us'd no names. My books have still been taught
> To spare the persons and to speak the vices.

But when the identity of Horace, Crispinus, and Demetrius
was so unmistakable it was natural for spectators to seek for
living prototypes of other figures in the play. There is more
force in his plea that in representing Ovid's aversion to law-
studies he had the poet's own authority, and was in no way
concerned with English laws and their 'just ministers'. As
to soldiers, he could justly quote the epigram in which he
proclaimed his love for

> Your great profession, which I once did prove,
> And did not shame it with my actions then.

For the players he admits that he attacked some of them
sparingly, whereupon one and all they 'thought each man's
vice belong'd to their whole tribe'. In a different vein he
adds,
> Only amongst them I am sorry for
> Some better natures by the rest so drawn
> To run in that vile line.

It is tempting to find here a reference to Shakespeare, who,
according to the Cambridge author of the St. John's College
play, *The Return from Parnassus*, Part II (IV. iii), had taken
a part in the quarrel. Kempe, the comedian, declares, 'O,
that Ben Jonson is a pestilent fellow, he brought up Horace
giving the poets a pill, but our fellow Shakespeare hath given
him a purge that has made him bewray his credit.' The
allusion to *Poetaster* is evident, but Shakespeare's purge can
only be guessed at.

Even if Jonson's defence on these particular counts is
accepted, it is difficult to think that he himself can have
believed in his general claim (ll. 74–6):

> I can profess I never writ that piece
> More innocent or empty of offence:
> Some salt it had but neither tooth nor gall;

and that he merely wished to put to the blush those who had for three years been provoking him on every stage. In any case it was not with a blush but with derisive wrath that Dekker at once returned to the attack in *Satiromastix or The Untrussing of the Humourous Poet.* It was probably performed before 11 November 1601, when it was entered in the Stationers' Register. It was published in 1602 and acted publicly by the Lord Chamberlain's company and privately by the Children of Paul's.

Dekker would seem to have had in hand a romantic drama of the period of William Rufus[1] and to have grafted upon this, incongruously enough, his satirical rejoinder to Jonson's assault. Horace is discovered sitting in his study, with a candle by him burning, books lying confusedly, painfully hammering out an epithalamium for the wedding of Sir Walter Tyrell, which, he assures Asinius Bubo, are the best lines that ever he drew. He hears from Asinius that Crispinus and his 'journeyman poet', Demetrius, have sworn to bring his life and death on the stage 'like a bricklayer in a play' The taunt at his early plebeian vocation scarcely prepares us for the comparative mildness of the reproofs by his two victims when they enter. They assail him in his most obviously vulnerable point, his unctuous claim that his satire is merely general and not intended to wound individuals:

> Say you swear,
> And make damnation parcel of your oath,
> That when your lashing jests make all men bleed,
> Yet you whip none. Court, city, country, friends,
> Foes, all must smart alike; yet Court nor city,
> Nor foe, nor friend, dare wince at you: great pity!

But as the play proceeds the indictment becomes more bitter and in the end at a banquet graced by the presence of the King, Horace suffers a punishment in retaliation for, but different from, that inflicted on Crispinus at the court of Augustus in *Poetaster*:

[1] See below, pp. 152-3.

> Should we minister strong pills to thee,
> What lumps of hard and undigested stuff,
> Of bitter satirism, of arrogance,
> Of self-love, of detraction, of a black
> And stinking insolence should we fetch up!
> But none of these, we give thee what's more fit,
> With stinging nettles crown his stinging wit.

A wreath of nettles is placed on his head, and he is dressed up in a satyr's garb from which he is not 'untrussed', or stripped, till he has sworn to observe a number of conditions of which the most aptly trenchant is as follows:

> You must forswear to venture on the stage when your play is ended, and to exchange courtesies and compliments with gallants in the lords' rooms, to make all the house rise up in arms. and to cry, 'that's Horace, that's he, that's he, that's he that pens and purges humours and diseases'

Were the passages quoted entirely typical, it might fairly be said that honours were easy between the combatants or even that Dekker had on the whole the best of it. But he made what in modern eyes was the fatal mistake of purloining from *Poetaster* the figure of Captain Tucca, whom Jonson had narrowly saved from becoming unpalatable. By accentuating all his coarsest features, and making him take the vociferous lead in the denunciation of Horace, Dekker lowered the tone of *Satiromastix*. But to judge by the contemporary success of the play, Elizabethan audiences were ready enough to welcome the boisterous Captain again, even when 'translated' into more degraded form. Though Jonson put so bold a face upon the matter in his Apologetical Dialogue, and though *Poetaster* has in several ways more interest to-day than some of his better constructed plays, he realized that for the time being he had lost favour with the theatrical public, and ended by declaring:

> Since the Comic Muse
> Hath prov'd so ominous, I will try
> If Tragedy hath a more kind aspect.

ROMAN TRAGEDIES

The result was *Sejanus His Fall*, acted in 1603 by the
King's company, who under their former title of the Lord
Chamberlain's men had performed the two Humour plays.
E. Blunt entered the play in the Stationers' Register on
2 November 1604, but on 6 August 1605 transferred his right
to T. Thorpe, who published it in quarto later in the year.
This, as Jonson informed the readers, was not 'in all numbers . . . the same with that which was acted on the public
stage wherein a second pen had good share'. As has been
said above, Chapman has the likeliest claim to have been
the collaborator, and probably the passages for which Jonson
substituted 'numbers' of his own included those which had
given offence to the authorities. The 1616 folio makes a
considerable, number of minor emendations in spelling,
punctuation, and so forth, and has a few important changes
of reading.

Jonson found a convenient bridge from comedy to tragedy
by passing from the humours of the Court of Augustus in
Poetaster to the tragic happenings in the Court of his successor, Tiberius, in *Sejanus*. To his embittered mood the
caustic descriptions by Tacitus, and Dio Cassius, Suetonius,
and Juvenal, of early Imperial Rome offered congenial
material. To prove his historical accuracy, his 'integrity in
the story', he added in the quarto a profusion of marginal
references to, and quotations from, these and other sources.
Thereby unwittingly he did himself an injury, for he gave
the impression that the play was in the main a mosaic of
translated fragments. As a matter of fact the dialogue,
while based on the cited authorities, is for the greater part
of Jonson's own invention.

On the other hand he admitted that he had not observed
fully the laws of a 'true poem', according to classical precept.
He had violated the unity of time, he had dispensed with a
chorus, and could not reproduce 'the old state and splendour

F

of dramatic poems'. In default of these he had aimed at presenting 'truth of argument, dignity of persons, gravity and height of elocution, fulness and frequency of sentence'. These statements are of permanent interest for the light that they throw on Jonson's conception of tragedy. But they were beating the wind so far as Stuart playgoers were concerned. They cared nothing about 'integrity in the story', compliance with critical 'forms', or 'fulness and frequency of sentence'. They wanted, what they had got in Shakespeare's *Julius Caesar*, the presentation in melodious and lucid dialogue of contrasted characters—a Brutus, a Cassius, an Antony—Roman in origin but embodying eternal and universal types. Here Shakespeare gloriously followed the lead of Plutarch in North's translation. Jonson turning to a mass of classical sources became entangled in intricate historical issues unfamiliar to the Globe audiences. He made the same mistake as Chapman in his Byron plays of assuming in the ordinary theatre-goer or reader a detailed knowledge of events and persons in an unfamiliar past. Moreover, Jonson's most distinctive Elizabethan characteristic, his love of crowding his stage with characters, here proved itself a stumbling-block. How could an audience follow clearly the motives and actions of some forty *dramatis personae* headed by Tiberius and Sejanus and members of the imperial house with their satellites and agents? When on the top of all came Jonson's besetting theatrical vice of prolixity it is no wonder that the play was damned at the Globe.

Yet when all this has been said, *Sejanus* (as has not always been recognized) remains a remarkable achievement, with the stamp of its author's genius. Long and involved as is the 'argument', Jonson never loses his grasp of it, and all its parts fall fitly into his designed plan. And, as has been pointed out above, this implies more creative energy than appears on the surface. An example may be found in the central scene in the Senate in Act III, where Tiberius, after the death of Drusus, who had been their guardian, commends

the children of Germanicus, presumptive heirs to the imperial
throne, to the care of the conscript fathers; announces his
wish to be relieved of the burden of government, but asserts
his authority when Silius is indicted for sedition and takes
his own life upon the stage. If this dialogue of over three
hundred lines, punctuated with the satiric asides of Arruntius, be compared with the marginal references in the quarto,
it will be seen how much dramatic force Jonson has added
to what he found in his sources.

The creation of Arruntius from the slightest hints would
alone establish Jonson's originality. In the absence of a
classical chorus he, like Asper and Crites, speaks for the
author. He tries, as his opening words show, the degenerate
men of his own day by the standard of the heroes of the
last days of the republic (I. i. 89 ff.):

> Where is now the soul
> Of god-like Cato? he that durst be good
> When Caesar durst be evil, and had power,
> As not to live his slave, to die his master?
> Or where the constant Brutus that (being proof
> Against all charm of benefits) did strike
> So brave a blow into the monster's heart
> That sought unkindly to captive his country?

So in the background he follows with acid comments the joint
attacks of Tiberius and Sejanus on the few remaining parti-
sans of Roman liberties, and afterwards the breach between
emperor and favourite. Thus when after the suicide of
Silius, Tiberius affects grief, Arruntius exclaims in a grimly
pregnant simile:

> Excellent wolf!
> Now he is full he howls.

He is equally contemptuous of the mob when the favourite
falls and they wreak their vengeance on him (V. 800 ff.):

> Had Sejanus thriv'd
> In his design and prosperously oppressed
> The old Tiberius, then in that same minute
> Those very rascals that now rage like furies
> Would have proclaim'd Sejanus emperor.

Thus Arruntius sums up the struggle for ascendancy which is the leading motive of the play.

Sejanus with his limitless ambitions was no unfamiliar type to audiences to whom Marlowe had presented the Guise and Mortimer, and who were soon to see on the stage Chapman's Bussy d'Ambois and Chabot. His seduction of Livia and his fatal revenge on her imperial husband, Drusus, for striking him a blow would seem natural in the utterly unscrupulous wretch who could proclaim (II. 150 ff.):

> Adultery? It is the lightest ill,
> I will commit. A race of wicked acts
> Shall flow out of my anger, and o'er-spread
> The world's wide face.

But however grandiose his aspirations and his villainies, they lack the touch of redeeming glamour with which Marlowe or Chapman would have invested them. However highly he is advanced in the emperor's favour, Sejanus remains a man of the people. Thus for the first time he overleaps himself and starts his downfall when in III. 517 ff. he asks the emperor for the hand of the widowed Livia. On a stage where so much was made of the social gulf between the courtier and the citizen this point would have gone home. But what (as I think) must have puzzled the Globe audience, with its memories of the bluff Tudor sovereignty, and contributed to the failure of the play, was the spectacle of the imperial despot affecting humility (I. 391 ff.):

> Style not us
> Or lord, or mighty, who profess ourself
> The servant of the Senate, and are proud
> T' enjoy them our good, just and favouring lords.

And the tortuous hypocrisy of his speech (III. 530 ff.) to his 'most-loved Sejanus' (masterly in itself) on whom he is about to set a secret spy, must have sounded strange from the world-despot's lips.

From his lustful retreat in Capua he continues in Act IV to play a subtle game of cross-purposes that perplexes even

his satellites. But Sejanus, with Tiberius at a distance from
the centre of government, is sure that his fortunes have
reached their zenith (V. 3 ff.):

> I did not live till now; this my first hour
> Wherein I see my thoughts reach'd by my power.
> But this, and grip my wishes. Great and high,
> The world knows only two, that's Rome and I.

He treats with contempt omens of impending evil and his
confidence seems justified when news is brought that the
emperor has appointed a meeting of the Senate at which
Sejanus is to receive the tribunicial dignity. The audience
may now have been too fatigued to appreciate fully the
impressive climax that follows. The favourite, apparently
more secure than ever of his power, enters the assembly
amidst a chorus of abject acclamation. But when the
emperor's letter, with its characteristic windings, reservations,
and insinuations is read to the increasingly bewildered Senate
it culminates in the order to strip Sejanus of all his offices
and possessions. Here Jonson has worked up into a long
passage of his most effective prose a few sentences from Dio
Cassius and a memorable phrase from Juvenal's tenth satire.
He relied mainly on the same sources for his realistic picture,
after the Senate's condemnation, of the popular vengeance
on the body of the fallen favourite. The sudden descent
from so high a pinnacle to so vile an end should produce in
the theatre a measure of tragic terror, but it does not bring
with it pity, the nobler of Aristotle's two purgative emotions
aroused by tragedy. For Sejanus is wholly compact of evil,
and his fall is compassed by one equally evil, but more astute
and armed with more deadly striking power.

Sejanus was followed eight years later, in 1611, by Jonson's
second Roman tragedy, *Catiline His Conspiracy*, also acted
by the King's company. It was published in quarto in the
same year by W. Burre, and there were three later quartos
in 1635, 1669, and 1674. The 1616 and 1640 folio texts
differed from the 1611 quarto, mainly in extensive repunctu-

ation. It is surprising that *Catiline* should have gone through so many editions and been revived in 1668 at the Theatre Royal, with Hart in the name-part created by Burbage, and with a prologue spoken merrily by Nell Gwynn. For from Ben's own petulant address to 'the reader in ordinary', it is evident that after the first two acts the play had failed in the theatre, and it showed lack of judgement as well as arrogant obstinacy that in defiance of the popular verdict he dedicated it to the Earl of Pembroke as his best in its kind. For though in the period between *Sejanus* and *Catiline* he had reached his zenith in comedy, the second tragedy had a larger measure of the failings and less of the merits of the first. He reverted to two features of the antiquated Senecan technique by opening the play with a monologue by Sulla's ghost in Catiline's study and by introducing lyrical choruses between the acts. In his adaptation of Cicero's orations against the conspirators he even exceeded the prolixity of the speeches in the earlier play. Moreover, the subject of the tragedy was even more remote, as treated by Jonson, from the interests of a Stuart audience. A conspiracy, as *Julius Caesar* showed, might provide the material for a theatrical success. But the plot of the republican leaders against the dictator was a clear-cut issue, easily comprehensible. It was different with the conspiracy of Catiline and his satellites against the more abstract Roman old order, represented by the Senate and the consul Cicero. It is true that Cicero as the master of Latin prose was a name to conjure with in Renaissance humanist circles. But as a political figure he meant little to the average playgoers, as Shakespeare recognized in *Julius Caesar*, and Jonson had testily to rebuke their 'dislike' of his interminable oration in Act IV. Indeed, among the champions of the Senate, Cato, with his hatred of compromise and his blunt directness of speech, makes the strongest appeal to sympathy. So far as any character in the play may be said to speak for Jonson, it is he.

Yet the balance between the two Roman tragedies is not

all on one side. The revolutionary aristocrat has always a paradoxical attraction, and the patrician Catiline, in spite of his crimes, does not make the impression of playing, like Sejanus, a purely lone and selfish hand. He can at any rate conjure up a vision of a commonwealth not engrossed 'by a few, the giants of the state', while the rest (I. 354 ff.):

> However great we are, honest, and valiant,
> Are herded with the vulgar; and so kept . . .
> Ungrac'd, without authority or mark,
> Trembling beneath their rods; to whom (if all
> Were well in Rome) we should come forth bright axes.

He shows himself a leader of men not only by holding out to his followers a general prospect of a new order, but by his keen insight into the motives that sway them individually. And when the plot is betrayed by a woman's treachery he is ready to try the more desperate chance of the battle-field where (in Cato's elegiac words) he meets

> A brave bad death.
> Had this been honest now, and for his country
> As't was against it, who had e'er fallen greater?

Fulvia, the wanton who worms out of her lover Curius the secret of the conspiracy is one of the group of ignoble dames developed by Jonson, with a caustic brilliance unsurpassed in his comedies, from the sketches by Sallust and Cicero. In Act II Fulvia's waiting-woman, Galla, slyly irritates her mistress by dilating upon the accomplishments in the tongues and the arts of the rival, more elderly, courtesan, Sempronia, but adds, 'She's fain of late to seek more than she's sought to'. Catiline's paramour, Orestilla, she sums up as very rich, with good suits, but

> She cannot put 'em on. She knows not how
> To wear a garment.

When Sempronia is announced she at once poses as the power behind the scene who will get Catiline elected consul, and not Cicero, the 'new fellow':

                                    a mere upstart
            That has no pedigree, no house, no coat,
            No ensigns of a family.
Ful.   He has virtue.
Semp. Hang virtue! Where there is no blood; 'tis vice,
            And in him sauciness.

Then she suddenly shifts the talk to the comparison of grey
and white powders as dentifrices, and from this as abruptly
to the visits of Fulvia's lovers. The entry of one of them,
Curius, her 'special servant', cuts short this boudoir gossip.
The infatuated young patrician regains her capricious favours
at the price of revealing to her the plot in which he has
become involved.

In such scenes Jonson gives his blank verse the flexibility
and ease of the best conversational prose. In the more
serious passages it rises at time to an imaginative height
that he seldom elsewhere attained. Thus a conspirator
describes the sequel of the massacres under Sulla's pro-
scription (I. 247):   The rugged Charon fainted,
            And ask'd a navy rather than a boat
            To ferry over the sad world that came.

Catiline, urging on his soldiers to the final conflict, cries
(V. 412 ff.):

            Methinks, I see Death and the Furies waiting
            What we will do; and all the heaven at leisure
            For the great spectacle.

The victorious general thus reports his death in battle
(V. 677ff.):

            And, as in that rebellion 'gainst the gods,
            Minerva holding forth Medusa's head,
            One of the giant brethren felt himself
            Grow marble at the killing sight, and now
            Almost made stone began t'inquire what flint
            What rock it was that crept through all his limbs,
            And ere he could think more, was what he feared,
            So Cataline, at the sight of Rome in us,
            Became his tomb.

Such inspired flights help us to understand Ben's own partiality for this 'legitimate poem', as he called it in the dedication to Lord Pembroke. Nevertheless posterity as a whole has echoed the verdict of Pepys in December 1668 that it was 'the least diverting' piece that he had ever seen.

IV

BEN JONSON

MASQUES AND ENTERTAINMENTS

I T was not only on the two Roman tragedies that Jonson
lavished his wealth of classical learning during the first
decade of the Jacobean period. It was characteristic of him
to make use of it for lighter dramatic purposes. He was
called upon to help in providing the 'entertainments' with
which the advent of the new King and his family was
welcomed. The first of these was given by Lord Spencer at
Althorp to Queen Anne and Prince Henry on their progress
southwards. Here Jonson brings into rivalry a satyr of
mythological origin and the English folk-lore figures of
Queen Mab and her fairies, who have come to pay their
tribute to the royalties. The shaggy wood-god gives Queen
Anne a warning:

> Trust her not, you bonnibell,
> She will forty leasings tell,
> I do know her pranks right well.

And in tripping octosyllabics he recounts these pranks
much after the fashion of Mercutio in *Romeo and Juliet*. But
when he has skipped off, after being pinched black and blue,
Mab commands a song in honour of 'Oriana' (*quasi Oriens*
Anna), and presents her with a jewel. The fairies then hop
away 'in a fantastic dance', and the Satyr coming out again
offers Lord Spencer's heir garbed as a huntsman to the
prince's service, with his instruments, bow, horn, and dog as
gifts. Thereupon the wood sounded with hunting music, and
a brace of choice deer were 'fortunately killed' in the queen's
sight.

It was a charmingly appropriate show and it is no wonder

that Anne kept her eye on Ben for further service to herself.
But his next devices were primarily in honour of the King,
when on 15 March 1604 he passed through the City to his
coronation at Whitehall. Jonson provided the first part of
the entertainment, at Fenchurch, where an arch was erected,
on which were grouped a number of symbolical 'live figures',
two of which, Genius Urbis, and the river Tamesis, made
congratulatory speeches. Other devices were provided by
Dekker, but for the last part, at Temple Bar, Jonson was
again responsible. It took the form of the Temple of Janus,
wherein were assembled various classical personages, among
them again Genius Urbis and the Flamen of Mars. Genius
bids the Flamen remove his 'superstitious fumes' from the
altar to make room for

> My city's heat, which shall for ever burn . . .
> > here I fix it fast,
> Flame bright, flame high and may it ever last!

A stately *Panegyre* upon the opening of his first Parliament
on 19 May by James, where he is reminded that kings

> by Heaven are plac'd upon the throne
> To rule like Heaven;

and an Entertainment, in which the household gods in Roman
fashion welcomed the king and queen on May morning to
the home of Sir William Cornwallis in Highgate, gave further
proof of Jonson's versatile power of making happy use of
official and social occasions. It was natural therefore that
he should be called upon to furnish the Court masque for
Twelfth-Night 1605.

I have previously sketched the development of the Masque
under the Tudors,[1] with the opportunities that it gave to
highly-placed amateurs to display their talents in recitative,
song, and dance. But Elizabeth, even when on pleasure
bent, had a frugal mind, and Court entertainments were kept
within economic bounds. And her role was that of a spectator, not a performer. The Stuart fashion was one of lavish

[1] See *Introduction to Tudor Drama*, 58 ff.

expenditure in all directions, including amusements. And the continental consorts of both James and Charles were eager to take the lead in the Whitehall festivities. 'The most magnificent of queens, Anne' not only commissioned the 1605 Twelfth-Night masque, but gave directions that the performers, including herself and eleven of her ladies, should appear as black-a-moors at first. From this odd clue Jonson with the co-operation of 'master Inigo Jones' in 'the bodily part' ingeniously developed a *Masque of Blackness*. Oceanus in human form coloured blue and the river Niger as an Aethiop riding on two great sea-horses 'induced' the masquers, twelve nymphs, daughters of Niger, attended by twelve daughters of Oceanus as their torch-bearers, and placed in 'a great concave shell like mother-of-pearl'. When Oceanus asks Niger why he has wandered from the East into 'the extremest West', the river tells that his daughters, anxious to change their complexions, have been bidden in a vision to seek a land whose name ends in 'tania'. Thereupon the moon worshipped by the Aethiopians as their goddess under the name of Aethopia, 'was discovered in the upper part of the house, triumphant in a silver throne'. She announces to Niger that his daughters have reached their goal in this blest isle, Britania.

> For were the world, with all his wealth, a ring,
> Britania (whose new name makes all tongues sing)
> Might be a diamond worthy to inchase it,
> Ruled by a sun that to this height doth grace it.
> Whose beams shine day and night, and are of force
> To blanch an Aethiop, and revive a corse.

Thus an adroit reference is made to the 'new name' of the two kingdoms now united under a single crown and a flattering compliment turned to its wearer. The masquers then step forth from the shell and dance 'on shore', and as they thereafter are 'about to make choice of their men' (according to masquing fashion, from the audience), a song from the sea by a tenor voice, followed after several measures and corantos by another by two trebles, summons them back to their native element. But the moon comforts them with the assurance that if they perform certain rites on thirteen nights when she is full they will in a year 'for your pains perfecton have'.

This the first of Ben's masques had 'success in the nobility of its performance', but its intended sequel had to be postponed, as the Twelfth Nights of 1606 and 1607 were occupied by wedding masques, one of them from Jonson's pen. Then after an interval of three years, on 10 January (the Sunday after Twelfth Night) 1608, he was able to comply with the queen's command to 'think on some fit presentment, which should answer the former, still keeping them the same persons, the daughters of Niger, but their beauties varied, according to promise, and their time of absence excus'd, with four more added to their number'. This *Masque of Beauty* opens with the fierce wind Boreas blustering in to Januarius and telling him why the Ethiopian maidens have been delayed in their return. Four of their dark-hued sisters had set out to join them in order to share their transformation, but Night, angered at this insult to her colour, had storm-tossed them on to a floating island, where they were being sought by their twelve 'changed sisters'. Hereupon the gentle wind Vulturnus enters to announce that the island has been found and is floating close at hand. The drawing of a curtain discloses it, with a throne of beauty in the centre and divided by pillars into eight squares—in which the masquers were placed by couples. Flying Cupids and eight figures representing the elements of beauty completed the spectacle.

The river Thamesis receives the nymphs ashore. He was impersonated by Thomas Giles, the designer of the dances which now follow, of which Jonson gives a highly appreciative description and which won an encore from the king. Between the dances songs were sung on the themes of love and beauty, and before the last dance Januarius summons

the masquers back to 'beauty's perfect throne', hitherto
straying uncertain, but

> Now made peculiar to this place alone,
> And that, by impulsion of your destinies,
> And his attractive beams that lights these skies.

Jonson with his associates had reason to be satisfied with
their accomplishment of the somewhat exacting task set
them by Queen Anne, and when she received some months
afterwards in 1608 the presentation copy of the quarto,
published by Thomas Thorpe, of the two masques (now the
Garrick copy in the British Museum) she must have recognized from the marginal notes and references the wealth of
learning that had gone to their making. For the *Masque of
Blackness* there is also preserved in the Museum the MS. copy,
without the notes and with shorter descriptions of scenery
and dresses, prepared for the queen's use at the performance.[1]

The 1608 quarto contained also with continuous signatures
a masque in honour of the wedding of Viscount Haddington
and Lady Elizabeth Radcliff presented on Shrove Tuesday,
9 February. But Jonson had already published in 1606 his
Hymenaei, presented on 5 and 6 January of that year in
celebration of the marriage of the Earl of Essex and Lady
Frances Howard. In the framework of a classical wedding
ceremony Hymen announces the rites that are to unite 'two
noble maids of different sex'. But eight men issuing from a
globe 'figuring Man', representing the four humours and the
four affections, attempt to disturb the ceremony with drawn
swords, whereupon Hymen summons the aid of Reason,
'seated in the top of the globe, as in the brain or highest part
of Man', who quells the riot. Thereupon the upper part of
the scene opens to disclose Juno sitting in a throne attended
by eight ladies representing her powers as 'governess of
marriage'. They pair with the men and songs and dances
follow, concluding with an epithalamium adapted from

[1] This is printed as an appendix to the text of the two masques from
the 1616 folio in volume VII of the Oxford *Ben Jonson* (1941).

Catullus. But by this time the audience had had enough and would only listen to one of the fifteen stanzas, all of which Ben printed with a characteristic promise to 'forgive their ignorance whom it chanceth not to please'.

Jonson might have had further cause for annoyance had he foreseen that *Hymenaei* in the future would be of interest less for itself and its marginal apparatus of learning than for what may be called its prologue and (factually) its epilogue. The former is Jonson's lofty statement in his introduction to the quarto of his ideal in the composition of a masque.

'It is a noble and just advantage that the things subjected to understanding have of those which are objected to sense that the one sort are but momentary and merely taking; the other impressing and lasting. . . . So short-lived are the bodies of all things in comparison of their souls. . . . This it is hath made the most royal princes and greatest persons (who are commonly the personators of these actions) not only studious of riches and magnificence in the outward celebration or show (which rightly becomes them) but curious after the most high and hearty inventions to furnish the inward parts, and those grounded upon antiquity and solid learning.'

Jonson therefore turns his back on those who decry learning as wasted in these 'transitory devices', and offers his 'full tables' instead of their 'empty trenchers'. It was in this spirit that he was to provide Court entertainment for many a year, though gradually tempering his more solid fare with lighter elements. But Fate was to give a sharply ironical turn to the high-flown sentiments voiced in Jonson's first published masque. The union so auspiciously begun ended in a scandalous divorce in 1613. Thus when Jonson republished the masque in the 1616 folio, he omitted the names of the bridegroom and bride, the performers, and his collaborators, Inigo Jones, Giles, and the musician Ferrabosco, to whom he had made complimentary references.

Warned perhaps by the restiveness of the audience before the close of *Hymenaei* Jonson not only made the Haddington wedding masque considerably shorter but lighter in texture. Venus appears from the sky in her dove-and-swan drawn chariot and begs the three Graces to find her son Cupid who has disappeared. The first Grace begins the hue and cry:

> Beauties, have ye seen this toy,
> Called Love, a little boy,
> Almost naked, wanton, blind,
> Cruel now, and then as kind?
> If he be amongst ye, say;
> He is Venus' run-away.

Nine stanzas follow in this delightfully tripping style, and then Cupid appears armed, 'attended with twelve boys, most antickly attired that represented the sports and pretty lightnesses that accompany love'. At Cupid's behest they fall into a 'capricious dance, to as odd a music', nodding their 'antique' faces, and making other ridiculous gestures, which caused great merriment. Hereafter Venus seizes her 'little straggler', who bids her learn his latest feat from Hymen. This is the uniting in the presence of a sovereign

> That is so just to his great act and thought,
> To do, not what kings may, but what kings ought,

of a noble who saved him from the Gowrie conspiracy and a noble virgin as rich in 'virtue, blood and form' as in worldly wealth. Thereupon the husband of Venus, Vulcan, cleaves with his hammer a red cliff (in honour of the bride's surname) and discloses a silver globe containing the masquers representing the twelve signs of the Zodiac who preside at all nuptial hours. The masquers descend and dance while the Cyclops beat time with their hammers. And to ensure that the audience should this time wait till the close of the epithalamium Jonson astutely arranged a dance between every stanza, though in the quarto it appears as a continuous lyric. To-day we need no such interpolated lure to make us appreciate this splendid marriage ode linked together by the verbal and rhyming repetitions in the last half of each stanza and the concluding line, 'Shine, Hesperus, shine forth, thou wished star'.

It may have been the success of what Ben himself called the 'anti-masque of boys' in the Haddington masque that led the queen, when for the third time she gave a commission to Jonson, to direct him to precede the main masque by 'some dance or show that might . . . have the place of a foil or false-masque'. Thus when on Candlemas night, 2 February 1609, he presented before the Court *The Masque of Queens*, he for the first time included in his design an anti-masque in the full sense. The object of the main masque was to illustrate true Fame bred out of Virtue in the persons of twelve queens. By way of antithesis the scene opened as 'an ugly hell which flaming beneath smoked unto the top of the roof', whence came forth eleven witches to the accompaniment of 'hollow and infernal music'. As they begin to dance they call with charms thrice repeated upon their Dame, Ate, the mischief-maker, to appear. At last she enters, in her hand a torch made of a dead man's arm lighted, and girded with a snake. She bids her hags disturb this night dedicated to Fame and Glory:

> Mix hell with heaven and make nature fight
> Within herself; loose the whole hinge of things.

Each in turn tells of what she has prepared. Thus one declares:

> I have been gathering wolves' hairs,
> The mad dog's foam, and the adder's ears;
> The spurging of a dead man's eyes;
> And all since the evening star did rise.

Another brings the grisly recital to an end:

> I went to the toad breeds under the wall,
> I charmed him out, and he came at my call;
> I scratched out the eyes of the owl, before;
> I tore the bat's wing. What would you have more?

Thereupon the Dame invokes the fiends and furies to spread fog and darkness over all, but their incantations and foul

G

rites are of no avail, nor their magical dance in which they
'do all things contrary to the custom of men, dancing back
to back, hip to hip, their hands joined, and making their
circles backward to the left hand'. Then at a sudden loud
blast of music the witches and their hell into which they ran
vanished and instead there appeared a glorious building
figuring the House of Fame wherein was a throne, in the
form of a pyramid, on which were seated the twelve
queens.

It was some years since Shakespeare had done homage to
King James's belief in the malign power of witches by presenting them as unearthly, lurid figures in the tragic atmosphere of *Macbeth*. It was, if not so consummate, an even
more astonishing achievement of Jonson, in response to a
light-hearted command of Queen Anne, to bring within the
delicate framework of a holiday entertainment so eerie and
horror-striking a representation of these midnight hags. His
success in a sense defeats itself, for readers to-day if not for
the original spectators. Deprived of the living charms of the
Court beauties, the twelve queens, as described by Heroic
Virtue in the panoply of Perseus, ranging from the Amazon
Penthesilea to the reigning Bel-Anna herself, are somewhat
pallid figures. But from this point the masque depended for
its effect largely on the ingenious and splendid mechanism
devised by Inigo Jones. The throne whereon the twelve
queens were grouped was a *machina versatilis* which spun
round to reveal the figure of white-winged, trumpet-bearing
Fame. Her house, modelled on Chaucer's poem, gleamed
with golden statues of the poets, her 'substantial supporters',
and of the heroes of whom they had sung, and other rich
embellishments. Thence the masquers came forth in 'three
triumphant chariots', drawn respectively by eagles, gryphons,
and lions, with the hags as captives bound before their
wheels. After alighting they took part in elaborate dances
before again 'triumphing about the stage' in their chariots
and returning to the house of Fame to the accompaniment

of a song (set to Ferrabosco's music) which gives stately voice to Jonson's intended moral in the masque:

> Who, Virtue, can thy power forget,
> That sees these live, and triumph yet?
> Th' Assyrian pomp, the Persian pride,
> Greeks' glory and the Romans', died;
>   And who yet imitate
> Their noises tarry the same fate,
>   Force Greatness all the glorious ways
>   You can, it soon decays,
>   But so good Fame shall never;
> Her triumphs, as their causes, are for ever.

It was a theme that appealed to the high-souled young prince Henry of Wales, who commanded Jonson to print the masque with annotation citing his 'particular authorities'. On this account, as Ben explained to the queen in an autograph inscription in his presentation copy to her of the 1609 quarto, he dedicated it to the prince. In addition he wrote out for him in his own hand the masque in full. This MS., now in the British Museum, supplies the text of the masque in the Oxford *Ben Jonson*.

Prince Henry was soon to inspire Jonson further. In June 1610 he was invested with the title of Prince of Wales, and in celebration of the event a mock tourney or *Barriers* was held. The prince, under the name of Meliadus Lord of the Isles, had sent a challenge to the knights of Great Britain. As a framework for the tilt Jonson composed a semi-dramatic dialogue introducing the Lady of the Lake, King Arthur, and Merlin, who gives Meliadus a lecture on the patterns in British history that he is to follow before summoning Chivalry to wake from her deep sleep to bless the arms of the young knight who   here doth keep the field,

> According to his bold and princely word,
> And waits employment for his pike and sword.

Henry, as Prince of Wales, was now entitled to commission a masque himself, and at his behest Jonson presented on New Year's Day, 1611, *Oberon, the Fairy Prince*. Here, as in

the Althorp entertainment, he mingled figures from classical
and native folk-lore, but with finer artistry. The former, a
group of satyrs headed by Silenus, make their appearance
in what is virtually an anti-masque. Ben never wrote anything more charming than the octosyllabic dialogue in which
Silenus assures his 'wantons' as they eagerly question him,
that prince Oberon 'will do More than you can aim unto';
and afterwards bids them strike a charm into the ears of
the two 'sylvans' who have fallen asleep while on guard
outside Oberon's palace. Then at cockcrow the palace opens
and discloses 'the nation of fays', with Oberon in a chariot
drawn by two bears which to a loud triumphant music begin
to move forward. The speeches and songs of the main
masque follow, with courtly compliments to James and his
heir and with a succession of dances till the day-star
appeared 'and the whole machine closed'.

The Queen also during the same festive season called upon
Jonson for another masque. In *Love Freed from Ignorance
and Folly* he showed Love made captive by a Sphynx representing Ignorance with an attendant train of 'Follies which
were twelve she-fools'. But he is set free by the priests of
the Muses, ever ready to assist Love in any action of honour
and virtue, and 'inspire him with their own soul'. The
masque was short and simple in construction, but according
to contemporary testimony sixty-six musicians were employed in it, and this must have swollen its cost. The lavish
sums spent upon these Court entertainments were arousing
popular outcry, and Jonson met this challenge in characteristic and original fashion in his 1612 Twelfth Night masque,
Love Restored. Here he gave the anti-masque the novel form
of a prose dialogue in which Plutus the money-god inveighs
against the 'vizarded impudence' of those who are profaning
his deity. 'I will have no more masquing; I will not buy a
false and fleeting delight so dear. The merry madness of one
hour shall not cost me the repentance of an age.' Again,
Jonson mixes classic and native myth when he brings in

Robin Goodfellow bitterly complaining that he had 'run a thousand hazards to arrive at this place; never poor goblin was so put to his shifts to get in, to see nothing.' Plutus bids him go away and with him a masquer who has made excuses for the delay in beginning the show. 'I will endure thy prodigality nor riots no more; they are the ruin of states. . . . They are these make me hear so ill, both in town and country, as I do.'

Fate was later to prove that Jonson was here the *advocatus diaboli*, for of a truth the words put by him in irony into the mouth of Plutus were to be realized in fact when Stuart Court extravagance was to lead to the conflict with Parliament over taxation and to the Civil Wars with 'the ruin of states'. But the end was not yet, and in the masque Cupid enters in his chariot, heralded by a song:

> O how came Love, that is himself a fire,
>   To be so cold?
> Yes, tyrant Money quencheth all desire,
>   Or makes it old.
> But here are beauties will revive
> Love's youth and keep his heat alive.

Thereupon Cupid restored bids defiance to the money-god:

> Impostor Mammon, come, resign
> This bow and quiver; they are mine.
> Thou hast too long usurped my rites,
> I now am lord of mine own nights.

Though the predictions in *Hymenaei* of the happy issue of the Essex marriage had been falsified, Jonson was ready to celebrate the still more disastrous union (as it was to prove) of the divorced bride with the Earl of Somerset at the end of 1613. On this occasion he presented *The Irish Masque* on 29 December. Here he again used prose in the anti-masque, but he gave it a novel turn by making four Irish footmen talk to 'King Yamish' in their native dialect. They relate in circuitous fashion that 'a doshen of our besht Mayshters' had set out to attend a great wedding but they had lost their clothes on the voyage except for their Irish

mantles. The footmen dance 'to the bag-pipe and other rude
music', and are succeeded by their 'mayshters', wearing their
mantles, 'to a solemn music of harps'. Then an Irish gentleman brings in a bard whose prophecies concerning King
James and Ireland were to go singularly awry.

> This is that James of which long since thou sung'st
> Should end our country's most unnatural broils . . .
> This is the man thou promis'd should redeem,
> If she would love his counsels as his laws,
> Her head from servitude, her feet from fall,
> Her fame from barbarism, her state from want.

But for the moment, while the bard sings to two harps, the
royal presence has power to strip the oversea visitors of their
uncouth mantles and to reveal them in the full splendour of
their masquing attire.

On 31 December and on New Year's Day 1614 Jonson did
further honour to this ill-omened marriage. In *A Challenge
at Tilt*, two Cupids, in the guise of pages to the bridegroom
and the bride, dispute which of them is the true love-god,
and throw down their bows and quivers as gages for a tilt
which takes place on the following day, with honours equal.
Whereupon Hymen appears to reconcile them by telling that
they are both true Cupids and both the sons of Venus by
Mars, Eros and Anteros, the complement one of the other,
both necessary to the perfection of wedded love.

In 1615, after three years' interval, Jonson was again called
upon to supply the Court Twelfth Night masque. In *Mercury
Vindicated from the Alchemists at Court* he combined classical
myth not as often previously with folk-lore, but with the
pseudo-science with which he had already made play in one
of his comic masterpieces. Vulcan is disclosed in a laboratory
or alchemist's work-house and he spies Mercury thrusting
himself out of the tunnel of the middle furnace. He raises a
hue and cry. 'Help! He flies! He is 'scap'd. Precious golden
Mercury, be fixed! Be not so volatile!' Mercury after running once or twice about the room gives a lively recital of

his torments at the hands of 'Old Smug here of Lemnos and his smoky family.' The fire-god pursues him with a troop of thread-bare alchemists, who dance about Mercury, and form the first of what, in a novel development, are two anti-masques. He defies them and makes much of their pretensions.

In yonder vessels, which you see in their laboratory, they have inclos'd materials to produce men, beyond the deeds of Deucalion or Prometheus. . . . And what men are they, they are so busy about, think you? Not common or ordinary creatures, but of rarity and excellence such as the times wanted and the age had a special deal of need of; such as there was a necessity they should be artificial, for Nature could never have thought or dreamt o' their composition.

To refute him Vulcan calls forth 'creatures of the first class', who now appear in the second anti-masque as 'imperfect creatures with helms of limbecks on their heads'. Mercury bids these ridiculous monsters vanish, and the scene changes to a glorious bower, wherein Nature is placed with Prometheus at her feet, and standing about them the masquers, who in contrast to the deformed products of the alchemists' art are the noble offspring of Nature not as a stepdame but a mother.

The New Year and Twelfth Night masque of 1616, *The Golden Age Restored*, was a slighter composition, in verse of lyric charm, but for Christmas of this year Jonson again struck out on a new line, or rather turned an old one to his own use. For this show was not really a masque but a mummers' play in which 'Christmas, old Christmas, Christmas of London and Captain Christmas' presents his ten children led in by Cupid dressed as an apprentice, except for the wings at his shoulders, while his mother Venus as a deaf tire-woman from Pudding Lane pushes her way to the front to see him act before the king.

I could ha' had money enough for him, an I would ha' been tempted, and ha' let him out by the week to the King's players. Master Burbadge has been about and about with me; and so has old Mr. Hemings too; they ha' need of him.

In the year in which Shakespeare had died it is a curious reference in the Court festivities to two of his leading colleagues. After Christmas has sung a rollicking ballad describing his children, Misrule, Carol, Mince-Pie, and the rest, it is Cupid's cue. But his mother's interruptions put him out of his part and he is ordered off to make way for the dances. Jonson may here have broken away from the pattern of the masque, but he never wrote a piece of more genial comedy.

His remarkable versatility was once more in evidence in *Lovers Made Men*, presented at the country house of Lord Hay on 22 February 1617 in honour of Baron de Tour, Ambassador Extraordinary of the French king. In compliment to the foreign guest 'the whole masque was sung (after the Italian manner) *stylo recitativo* by Master Nicholas Lanier who ordered and made both the scene and the music'. It was thus, as pointed out in the Oxford *Ben Jonson*, 'in effect, the earliest operatic piece in the language'. It was a highly ingenious adaptation of a classical theme which might have seemed at first sight alien to the festival spirit. Charon is seen landing 'certain imagined ghosts' on the shore of Lethe, where they are received by Mercury. They are those who have passed through the fires and frantic seas of love and look on themselves as dead. To cure them of their illusion they are bidden drink of the waters of Lethe to which they stoop, 'and dance forth their anti-masque in several gestures, as they had liv'd in love'. After retiring for a space they reappear not as ghosts but men, to perform the dances of the main masque, and to learn from a dialogue between Cupid and Mercury that they may still love, but 'love with wit'. The heart must take the mind as its guide. It was scarcely the moral to be appreciated by a typical Frenchman.

The 1617 Christmas masque, *The Vision of Delight*, in which Phantasy calls forth an anti-masque of Phantasms, and Wonder in contrast exhibits the figures of the main masque

as the glories of the Spring, is chiefly notable for Jonson's
rare descriptions of the beauties of Nature. Its successor,
the Twelfth Night 1618 masque, *Pleasure Reconciled to Virtue*,
has more varied claims to attention. It was the first masque
in which Prince Charles, since his elder brother's death in
November 1612 heir-apparent to the throne, took a personal
part. In connexion with the performance a presentation
MS. was very carefully written which is still preserved at
Chatsworth, and has been taken as the basis of the text in
the Oxford *Ben Jonson*. The scene opens on Mount Atlas,
whence from an ivied grove 'to a wild music of cymbals,
flutes and tabors is brought forth Comus, the god of cheer,
or the belly, riding in triumph, his head crowned with roses
and other flowers'. He is accompanied by a noisily singing
rout and preceded by an attendant carrying the bowl of
Hercules, who commands the first anti-masque—a dance by
a Tun and Bottles. It is interrupted by the entrance of
Hercules, who is enraged to see   my cup

> Brought in to fill the drunken orgies up . . .
> Can this be pleasure, to extinguish man,
> Or so quite change him in his figure? Can
> The belly love his pain, and be content
> With no delight but what's a punishment?

He bids the grove vanish with its riotous crew. Thus
Comus disappears without having himself uttered a word,
but impersonating coarse and penalising debauchery. It is
generally assumed that he gave in part the cue for Milton's
enchanter. But when Jonson's masque was performed
Milton was aged nine. He was not in the Court circle and
how could he have known the masque before its publication
in the 1640 folio? However this may be, Milton's Comus
with his subtle spells and dazzling rhetoric belongs to another
order than Jonson's unvocal, bloated belly-god.

Pleasure and Virtue are then seen seated on the mountain,
and Hercules, the 'great friend and servant of the good',
is sung asleep, whereupon in a second anti-masque a number

of pigmies seek to steal his club and seize him. But when a song wakes him they run into holes, while Mercury descends to crown him, and to announce

> a cessation of all jars
> Twixt Virtue and her noted opposite,
> Pleasure.

To exemplify the reconciliation twelve masquers come forth from the lap of the mountain led by Daedalus the wise, who guides them through the mazes of symbolic dances, to whose significance Jonson pays a notable tribute.

> For dancing is an exercise
>   Not only shows the mover's wit,
> But maketh the beholder wise,
>   As he hath power to rise to it.

But though in these courtly revels Virtue lets Pleasure have her place and her soft sports, her own way of life is hard and exacting:

> She, she it is in darkness shines,
>   'Tis she that still herself refines,
>   By her own light, to every eye,
> More seen, more known when Vice stands by.
>   And though a stranger here on earth,
>   In heaven she hath her right of birth,
>   There, there is Virtue's seat.
>   Strive to keep her your own,
>   'Tis only she can mate you great,
>   Though place here make you known.

No more lofty note was touched by Milton than by Jonson here.

At the end of the folio text there is a disingenuous note, 'This pleas'd the King so well, as he would see it again when it was presented with these "additions".' There is evidence in contemporary letters that the masque did not find favour, and the 'additions', entitled *For the Honour of Wales*, performed on the following Shrovetide, were the substitution of a Welsh for a classical background and characters. As one of the Welshmen declares, it is 'a very vile and absurd as a

man would wisse . . . to pyt the Prince of Wales in an out-
landis mountain'. Thus Craig-Eriri takes the place of Atlas.
Music is supplied by 'the ancient Welsh harp', and there is a
dance of goats instead of tuns and bottles. As a climax there
is a paean on the Welsh nation as 'stout, valiant, courteous,
hospitable, temperate, ingenious, capable of all good arts'.
These 'additions' have lost most of their savour to-day, but
they served their purpose at the time. The revised version
of the masque was 'much better liked . . . by reason of the
new conceits and anti-masques, and pleasant merry
speeches'.

A break of three years followed before Jonson again
supplied the Twelfth-Night masque in 1621, and in *News
from the New World Discovered in the Moon* he broke away
even more decisively than in some previous instances, from
the accredited pattern of Court entertainment. For the
attraction of this show lies in the prose dialogue between a
printer, chronicler, and factor (or writer) of news—a pungent
comic sketch—and the fanciful description by two heralds
of life in the moon and its strange inhabitants, Epicenes and
their progeny Volatees, 'a race of creatures like men, but
are indeed a sort of fowl in part covered with feathers'. The
Volatees provide the anti-masque and are followed by the
main masquers, who have been rapt above the moon in
speculation of the virtues of King James and have now
returned to warm themselves in the sun of his presence. It
is a forced conceit and the songs and dances are on a
restricted scale.

A strong contrast was presented by a later 1621 composition by Jonson, *The Gypsies Metamorphosed*, commissioned
by the favourite, the Marquis (later Duke) of Buckingham,
and performed first at his residence, Burley-on-the-Hill, on
5 August, in the presence of King James. Its success was
so great that it was repeated two days later at Belvoir, where
the Earl of Rutland was the host, and again, in revised form,
about a month later at Windsor. It is much the longest of

Jonson's masques, and its contents are too diversified to fit neatly into the regular scheme. The text of the Windsor version is best preserved in a MS. (not autograph) now in the Huntington Library; that of the original version can be gathered in large part from an imperfect copy in the Cambridge University library of a duodecimo of 1640 in its first state.[1] The most important changes will be noted.

The gipsies enter with song and dance and proceed to tell fortunes. Their captain reads the king's hand, and from a MS. of this fortune-telling episode in the Public Record Office, we learn that Buckingham himself played the captain. The second gipsy, who reads the hand of Prince Charles, was Buckingham's brother-in-law, the Earl of Denbigh. His prophecy (to be mocked by the event) is of the prince's Spanish marriage, and even, in the Windsor version:

> Of a little James to play
>   Hereafter
> 'Twixt his gandsire's knees and move
> All the pretty ways of love,
>   And laughter.

Then at Burley and Belvoir the fortunes of the leading ladies were told. But at Windsor these were omitted, and those of the high Court officials present were substituted.

A number of rustic clowns and their wenches run in and perform a country dance, which is in effect the anti-masque, though it is not so called. During it the gipsies come prying about them, and afterwards while telling their fortunes pilfer their purses and other small treasures, which, however, are soon restored to them. They are then entertained by the singing of a ballad about the gipsies' first lord, Cocklorrel, and his feast to the Devil. It is in every sense very strong meat, but the clowns applaud 'an excellent song, and a sweet songster', and press to be admitted to the gipsies' company. But they are told in lines that catch the free and easy spirit of the vagabond life that

---

[1] For a detailed account see the Oxford *Ben Jonson*, VII. 541–64.

> There's much to be done
> Ere you can be a son
> Or a brother o' the moon.
> 'Tis not so soon
> Acquired, as desired.

This is set forth in vivacious detail, which is an awkward prelude to the reappearance of the gipsies 'changed' or 'metamorphosed' as Court gallants richly dressed who dance the main masque. There is nothing to explain their transformation, and Jonson himself in an epilogue to the Windsor performance had to confess that it was

> a thing not touched at by our poet;
> Good Ben slept there, or else forgot to show it.

At Windsor, too, Jonson added another feature in the stanzas blessing the sovereign and his senses, which in their coarser way are now as distasteful as the final flattering songs which hail the king as

> not lord alone of the estate,
> But of the love of men, and of the empire's fate;
> The muses' arts, the schools, commerce, our honours, laws,
> And virtues hang on him as on their working cause.

This, the most successful of Jonson's masques, is not among his most artistic achievements. It owed its vogue to the 'go' and colour of the gipsy scenes and to the attraction of its varied and illustrious personal associations.

The Masque of Augurs, first presented on Twelfth Night 1622, was on a much slighter scale, but it contained two curiously divergent elements. Its main interest lies in its first anti-masque, of which the scene is the Court buttery-hatch. Here appear a noisy group from St. Katherine's Docks, headed by Notch, a brewer's clerk, and Vangoose, 'a rare artist'. Notch tells the Groom of the Revels that having heard 'the Christmas invention was drawn dry at Court', he and his friends have presumed 'to fill up the vacuum with some pretty presentation'. This included a dance by bears, representing an ale-house sign. But Vangoose, a 'projector of masques', who, though a Briton born, has 'learned to misuse his own tongue in travel, and now speaks all languages in ill English', is anxious for something more grandiose, 'de Sofie van Persia, de Tartar Cham, met de groat King of Mogul'. When Notch objects that these 'are somewhat too big for the room' and suggests instead some Welsh pilgrims, Vangoose declares, 'Ick vill show yow all de whole brave pilgrims o' de vorld', and thus introduces the second anti-masque, 'a perplexed dance of straying and deformed pilgrims'.

All this is grotesquely irrelevant to the main masque wherein Apollo descends from above and summons a band of Augurs whose presages from the flight of birds are interpreted in terms most flattering to the King and his descendants:

> It is enough your people learn
> The reverence of your peace,
> As well as strangers do discern
> The glories by th' increase.

The text of the masque, as presented on Twelfth Night, was printed soon afterwards in quarto. It was performed again on 6 May, probably in the revised form in which it appears in the 1640 folio, where John Urson, the bearward, sings a rollicking ballad, and where Jonson also added a marginal Latin commentary on the symbolism of the main masque.

The 1624 Twelfth-Night masque *Time Vindicated* is another singular combination of a topical anti-masque and a classical main masque. But here Jonson made two new departures. For the first time in a masque he made a satirical attack on a poetic contemporary, George Wither, and probably in contrast with the rhyming couplets put into his mouth the other characters speak in blank verse. Wither figures as Chronomastix, the whipper of Time, and has among his admirers a quondam justice, who carries his poems in his pocket, his printer, and a schoolmaster who turns his works into Latin and makes his boys learn them.

They dance the first of the anti-masques, and are suceeded by another of tumblers and jugglers.

The scene abruptly changes and Saturn (as *Kronos* or Time) is seen sitting with Venus, at whose suit he promises to set free 'certain glories of the Time obscur'd'. These are the masquers who perform the main dance and then in graceful verse are challenged by Cupid and Sport respectively. Once again, in this elaborate masque, the scene changes to a wood, where Diana descends to the hunter Hippolytus, a model of what she would have Jacobean courtiers to be. She has called them,

> Out of the honour that I bore their parts
> To make them fitter so to serve the Time,
> By labour, riding, and those ancient arts,
> That first enabled men into the wars,
> And furnish'd Heaven with so many stars.

It is a summons, in the noble words of the final chorus, to be hunters in the highest sense:

> Man should not hunt Mankind to death,
> But strike the enemies of Man.

The marriage of Prince Charles to the Spanish Infanta which Jonson had foretold in *The Gypsies Metamorphosed* came to naught in the autumn of 1623, and the populace joyfully welcomed back the prince without a detested bride. In honour of his homecoming Jonson prepared for Twelfth Night 1624 *Neptune's Triumph for the Return of Albion*, where Neptune stands for the King and Albion for Charles. Owing to a dispute for precedence between the French and Spanish ambassadors the masque was not presented, and Jonson remodelled it into *The Fortunate Isles and their Union*, performed on 9 January 1625. In the two versions the anti-masque is completely different. *Neptune's Triumph* has a prolonged prose dialogue between the poet, 'a kind of Christmas engine', who has come to present a masque, and the king's master-cook who claims that nothing can be set forth in the banquetting-house without his approval. He maintains that it was in the kitchen that 'the art of poetry was learned and found out, or nowhere; and the same day with the art of cookery'. He argues with such eloquence that the poet hails him as a brother, and tells him the plot of his device, in which Neptune has sent out a floating island to bring back to safety his Albion from the Hesperian shores.

In the *Fortunate Isles* the poet and the cook are replaced by Johphiel, an airy spirit from the sphere of Jove, and Merefool, a melancholy, threadbare student, a disillusioned votary of the Rosicrucians. Johphiel, posing as their emissary, promises Merefool the gift of magic powers as various and unlimited as those of Faustus, and the sight of any past worthies whom he may name. The student proposes a number of Greek and other sages, but, according to Johphiel, they are all engaged at the moment, and he raises instead Scogan, who wrote in ballad-royal in Henry IV's time, and Skelton, poet-laureate to Henry VIII. Both rhyme after their own fashion, especially Skelton in his distinctive verse.

With the announcement of the approach of a floating island the main masque begins and is fundamentally, and in the main verbally, alike in both versions. But the island is now not the prince's ship, but one of the Fortunate Isles seeking union with the even more blessed Britannia:

> There is no hunger there, nor envy of State,
> Nor least ambition in the Magistrate;
> But all are even-hearted, open, free,
> And what one is, another strives to be.

And to crown the felicity there is the prospect near at hand of joining 'the bright lily and the rose', through the approaching marriage of Charles and Henrietta Maria of France.

Thus closed Jonson's long series of Jacobean masques. After six years' interval he presented two in the next reign, *Love's Triumph through Callipolis* on 9 January 1631 and *Chloridia* on the following 22 February. But these and two entertainments at Welbeck and Bolsover in May 1633 and July 1634 are of minor account. Taken as a whole it is an astonishing achievement. Not everything in it is to the credit side. With Ben's scrupulous insistence elsewhere on the observance of dramatic rules it is surprising that especially in the later masques he should have introduced so much that was alien to this special art-form. And even allowing for the demands of Court conventions, the incense offered at the shrine of one so unworthy of adoration as King James soon begins to cloy. Jonson was thus betrayed into panegyrics on the blessed state of Britain under Stuart rule which were to prove as wide of the mark as his predictions of a happy issue of the ill-starred Essex and Somerset weddings with Frances Howard and the abortive Spanish marriage of Prince Charles.

But when this has been said, the series of masques must be accounted the brilliant outcome of a genius which had its natural sphere elsewhere. Into this light, festive framework Jonson poured without stint the riches of his classical learning, the most graceful of his fancies, the most sustained of his lyric flights, and an abundant share of his humour and his realism. And to form a just estimate of the contemporary effect of these entertainments one must also give attention to the magnificent designs for the scenery and dresses by Inigo Jones, and recreate in imagination the music of Ferrabosco and the rhythmical intricacies of the dances which were the pivot of the show. It is a resplendent picture soon to be blacked out by parliamentary strife and civil war. But as yet these 'golden lads and lasses' went on their light-hearted way, heedless of the future when:

Some with lives that came to nothing, some with deeds best left undone,
Death came tacitly and took them where they never see the sun.

V

BEN JONSON

THE MASTERPIECES

THE first Jacobean decade was Jonson's crowning period, in which besides many of his most notable masques and his two Roman tragedies he produced his masterpieces of comedy. *Volpone, or The Fox*, was acted by the King's men at the Globe early in 1606, and later 'with love and acceptance', according to Jonson, before the two universities, though this may not mean more than in the cities of Oxford and Cambridge. It had been written in five weeks and was a consummate example of its author's constructive art, though in its lurid colouring it was more akin to tragedy than to comedy, and flouted his earlier dictum that the latter should 'sport with follies not with crimes'. Nor can the dominating passions of the characters be accounted as merely 'humours'.

Again Jonson drew upon a classical source. It was now not political history, as in the Roman tragedies, nor mythology as in the masques, but a peculiar feature of social life. In the satirists he found accounts of the *captator* or legacy-hunter who made presents to a wealthy acquaintance in the hope of reaping a profitable reward in his will. To bring so unfamiliar a figure and practice somewhat closer to a London audience Jonson transferred the scene from ancient to modern Italy, from Rome to Venice, which was to the Elizabethans the epitome of every luxury and vice. Volpone, a magnifico of the City of the Doges, salutes his gold with the poetic rapture of Marlowe's Jew of Malta:

> Open the shrine that I may see my saint;
> Hail the world's soul and mine! . . .
> > Let me kiss
> With adoration thee and every relic
> Of sacred treasure in this blessed room.

His joy in his wealth is all the greater because it flows in
without exertion on his own part.

> I gain
> No common way; I use no trade, no venture; . . .
> I turn no moneys in the public bank,
> Nor usure private.

He has neither wife nor child, so the prospect of being his
heir draws to his house

> Women and men, of every sex and age,
> That bring me presents, send me plate, coin, jewels,
> With hope that when I die (which they expect
> Each greedy minute) it shall then return
> Ten-fold upon them.

In his cynical designs Volpone has a skilful minister in his
wily attendant Mosca. He is suggested by the parasite of
classical comedy, but he is no vulgar specimen of the type.
As he says of himself, he is

> a fine elegant rascal, that can rise
> And stoop, almost together, like an arrow . . .
> This is the creature had the art born with him,
> Toils not to learn it, but doth practise it,
> Out of most excellent nature.

He helps his master to put himself into the pose of a sick
man almost *in extremis* wherein he receives his dupes,
significantly bearing the names of birds of prey. The first
is Voltore, the vulture, an advocate, bringing a piece of massy
plate. He is followed by Corbaccio, the raven, with a bag
of gold coins, who is persuaded by Mosca, as a crowning bait,
to make a will in Volpone's favour and disinherit his son.
Next enters Corvino, the crow, with a rich pearl, but who
has a richer one in his jealously guarded young wife, Celia,
with a luscious description of whose beauty Mosca inflames Volpone's desires. To win a sight of her the magnifico,
always keen to act a part, takes his stand under her window
in the disguise of a mountebank quack doctor, till he is
driven away by her furious husband. Yet this husband,
when told by Mosca that to restore Volpone he must have a

young woman to sleep with him, is ready to offer up his wife. Even in a world of unrelieved corruption Jonson here strains our credulity to breaking point.

Yet by a masterly stroke he saves the situation from becoming intolerable. Mosca, playing a subtle and risky game, warns Corbaccio's son, Bonario, that he is to be disinherited and bids him hide where he can overhear all. But before Corbaccio can return, Corvino hastens in with his wife and in spite of her tears and protests urges her to the shameful surrender. When they are left alone Volpone leaps from his sham sick-bed and wooes her in words that throw as dazzling colours round sensual joys as his opening speech had round his gold. We feel indeed that 'one word is too often profaned' when the exquisite song,

> Come, my Celia, let us prove,
> While we can, the sports of love.

is framed for so base a use.

When Celia's purity is proof against pleas and bribes, and Volpone seeks to force her, Bonario rushes from his hiding-place and saves her from dishonour. But by the craft of Mosca and the venal rhetoric of Voltore he is charged with attempted parricide and an assault on Volpone, in whose favour his father had disinherited him on account of his guilty relations with Celia. Never did Jonson display greater virtuosity than in Act IV, v and vi, where the four *avocatori* or magistrates are persuaded against their better instincts to condemn the innocent pair, though their sentence is deferred. The cut and thrust of the dialogue in court between all concerned in the trial is an outstanding proof of how flexible an instrument blank verse could be made. But the decisive argument with the magistrates is the apparently impotent silence of 'the old gentleman', Volpone, when he is brought in as a witness, and is 'returned with care'.

Mosca may well declare,

> Here we must rest; this is our masterpiece;
> We cannot think to go beyond this.

But intoxicated with his success Volpone hits on a new stratagem to trick his dupes by spreading a report that he has died. When they come flying 'to peck for carrion' they find, in another scene (V. iii) of consummate technique, Mosca deaf to all else while he makes an inventory of his master's treasures and finally shows to the discomfited rivals a will in which he is named sole heir. Not content with spying on this, Volpone with his passion for histrionics, invests Mosca with his own garb of a *clarissimo* and disguises himself as a *commandadore*, that they may follow the dupes into the streets and taunt them further. But the fox over-reaches himself. When the magistrates meet again to give sentence, Voltore recants his tale, and when Mosca, dressed as a magnifico, appears to solve the court's perplexities, he disclaims all knowledge of his master, 'I never saw his face.' Again the court lets itself be hoodwinked, and the order is given that Volpone is to be taken away and whipped. Driven to a corner, with the cry, 'the fox shall here uncase', he strips off his disguise and declares, 'I am Volpone and this is my knave.' Well may the chief magistrate exclaim, 'The knot is now undone by miracle.' Punishment suitably varied to the offence of each delinquent is decreed, though the Venetian caste system procures for Volpone himself, as 'by blood and rank a gentleman', a relative measure of leniency.

As something of relief to the sustained gloom of this darkest of comedies Jonson introduces, irrelevantly enough, three English visitors to Venice who provide a 'humours' element. Sir Politick Would-be says of himself to Peregrime, who has recently arrived from London:

> I do love
> To note and to observe . . . and know the ebbs
> And flows of state.

His passion is to be 'in the know'; to see beneath the surface of ordinary actions secret plots and plans, and out of his own brain to devise outlandish 'projects' for the benefit of

Venice and himself. Of all this he makes a confidant at first
sight of Peregrine, who takes revenge for his boredom by
setting on local merchants to burn Sir Politick's notes for
these projects and to guy him with an engine of his own
invention. Equally voluble is Lady Would-be, who makes
a victim of Volpone with her 'everlasting voice', prescribing
remedies for his feigned ills and discoursing upon the arts,
especially the Italian poets from Petrarch to Guarimi's
Il Pastor Fido.

How high a value Jonson set on this 'poem' is shown in
his lofty dedication of the 1607 quarto to 'the most noble
and most equal sisters, the two Universities', where after
indicting those who in 'stage-poetry' practise 'nothing but
ribaldry, profanity, blasphemy, all licence of offence to God
and man', he claims 'for their instruction and amendment'
to have laboured to restore 'not only the ancient forms but
manners of the scene', the easiness, the propriety, the innocence and last the doctrine, which is the principal end of
poesy, to inform men in the best reason of living.' No more
pregnant statement of the high moral purpose of dramatic
art has ever been penned, though it is questionable whether
it could be convincingly based on a stage exposure of villainy
so black that the only fitting solution would have been in
a tragic end.

But when three years later Ben provided a comedy not
for the King's men but for the Children of the Queen's Revels,
he abandoned this solemnly didactic vein for one that was
frankly sportive. In *Epicoene, or The Silent Woman* humours,
verging more closely on the farcical than in the earlier pieces,
form the staple of the plot, and they are exploited in prose
dialogue as finished and flexible as the blank verse of
Volpone. The central figure is the rich curmudgeon, Morose,
whose obsession is a hatred of noise. He lives in a street
so narrow at both ends that it will admit no creaking coaches
or carts. His room has double walls and treble ceilings; the
windows are close shut and caulked, so that he has to live

by candlelight. He talks with his servant through a 'trunk'
or tube, till he hits on 'a more compendious method' of
saving him the labour of speech by making him answer by
signs or bows. Morose's dread of female loquacity has kept
him hitherto a bachelor, but this conflicts with a spiteful
desire to disinherit his nephew Dauphine by marrying and
begetting a child. He thinks to cut the knot by taking as
his bride a young gentlewoman, Epicoene, who has a 'servant'
in the foolish knight, Sir John Daw, and whose voice has
a 'divine softness'. To his own spun-out speeches of courtship she makes answer in the fewest and most modest words,
'Judge you, forsooth', 'I should be sorry else', 'I'll leave it
to you, sir.'

But when they have been married by a parson who 'has
catch'd a cold and can scarce be heard six inches off', the
bride finds her voice and announces that she will not have
'unnatural dumbness in my house, in a family where I
govern.' Morose cries in dismay, 'She is my regent already.
I have married a Penthesilea, a Semiramis, sold my liberty
to a distaff.' A crowd of unbidden guests pours in to celebrate the wedding. Sir John Daw leads in a trio of 'collegiate'
ladies, 'an order between courtiers and country-madams that
live from their husbands . . . cry down or up what they like
or dislike in a brain or a fashion, with most masculine or
rather hermaphroditical authority'. Another addle-pated
knight, Sir Amorous La-Foole, is gulled into acting as a
server at the feast, and is followed by his cousin, the termagant Mistress Otter, whose hen-pecked husband calls her
'princess' and finds solace in his three carousing cups,
which he calls his bull, bear, and horse. A deafening medley
of music ordered by Dauphine and his friends, Clerimont and
Truewit, completes the uproar from which Morose seeks
refuge by climbing to the top of his house and sitting over a
cross-beam of the roof, till at last he comes down to oust the
intruders with his drawn sword.

All this works up to a mirthful climax in Jonson's happiest

lighter vein. But the scenes in which Morose is accused of
being mad, and in which Daw and La-Foole are egged on to
a duel and prove themselves poltroons, not only unduly
protract the action but must have seemed dangerously
reminiscent to theatre-goers who had seen *Twelfth Night*,
though Ben could never be a mere imitator. And no pen
but his could have made such an inimitable medley of learning and farce in the scene (V. iii) where Otter, disguised
as a parson and, Cutbeard, a barber, as a doctor of canon
law, argue whether Morose can get a lawful divorce from his
newly wedded bride. After he has been driven to humiliating
confessions and kept on the rack between hope and despair,
Dauphine offers to relieve him if he will make a financial
settlement on him. Thereupon he takes off Epicoene's
peruke with the electrifying announcement:

Then here is your release, sir; you have married a boy, a gentleman's son, that I have brought up this half year at my great
charges, and for this composition that I have now made with you.

The disclosure of a secret so jealously guarded till the last
possible moment not only from the other personages in the
play but from the audience in the theatre may have so dumb-
founded them as to account for the silence with which at
the end, as Drummond relates, *The Silent Woman* was received.
Here, in my opinion, is a technical flaw which in spite of its
otherwise brilliant technique robs the plot of the play of the
very highest rank. And on other grounds it appears to have
caused dissatisfaction in high quarters. A passage in Act V.
i. 24–5 was interpreted as a reference to Stephano, prince of
Moldavia, and the king's cousin, Lady Arabella Stuart,
whom he had courted. She made a complaint, and, according
to the Venetian Ambassador, the play was suppressed. In
the dedication of the 1616 folio version to Sir Francis Stuart
Jonson complains of 'how much a man's innocency may be
endangered by an uncertain accusation', and in a prologue
he protests against those who wrest what he doth write', and
'who make a libel which he made a play'. By 1616 Lady

Arabella was dead and Jonson printed the piece, including the impugned passage, without 'a line or syllable in it changed from the simplicity of the first copy'.

The cold reception of *The Silent Woman* may have prompted Jonson to return in the following year to a theme and treatment closer to that of *Volpone*. In *The Alchemist* he was again writing for the King's men, giving once more to his blank verse dialogue an extraordinarily supple and flexible quality, and handling another, more familiar, aspect of the *auri sacra fames*. As a by-product of the genuine scientific movements of the Renaissance period there was an intensified development of such medieval legacies as astrology, wizardry, and alchemy. Such practitioners as John Dee and Simon Forman gave alchemy in particular a repute in the highest quarters, and they had camp-followers who were more purely charlatans than themselves, and who were always ready to fish in troubled waters. Thus the actual prevalence of the plague in London in the autumn of 1610, and the evacuation of their houses by some of the richer citizens, gave Jonson the idea of using these very circumstances as the background of a play exposing the frauds perpetrated by alchemists and the follies and greed of their dupes.

Lovewit, a wealthy householder, has gone into the country to escape infection, leaving his premises in the care of his butler, Face, who feels sure that

> while there dies one, a week,
> O' the plague, he's safe from thinking towards London.

Face, posing as a captain, has thus opened Lovewit's doors to Subtle, an alchemist of the most completely quack type, with whom he is to share profits. And as a further lure to dupes they have taken into partnership a woman of the town, Dol Common, who, when the piece opens, is trying to end a furious quarrel between her two confederates. She just succeeds as the first of their victims arrives.

As in *Volpone*, Jonson brings on the stage a succession of credulous gold-hunters, but instead of the almost indistin-

guishably sombre Venetian trio he presents a number of
sharply individualized figures drawn from the London of his
own observation. They are headed by Dapper, a lawyer's
clerk, eager to get a 'fly', or familiar spirit, whose aid will
enable him to be a successful gambler and win cups at horse-
races. On parting with more than he bargained for of his
hard-earned cash, he gets a promise of this and also of the
favour of the fairy queen. He is followed by Abel Drugger,
a young tobacconist, about to set up shop and anxious to
be told

> Which way I should make my door, by necromancy,
> And where my shelves; and which should be for boxes.
> And which for pots. I would be glad to thrive, sir.

Drugger has his hand read by Subtle and is then given
instructions in a high-flown jargon for which he is mulcted in
a gold portagu, a coin he has treasured for half a year.

The next of Subtle's visitors, Sir Epicure Mammon, is a
dupe on a far more grandiose scale. He has already set the
alchemist to work with his art on materials that will produce
the philosopher's stone, the talisman to infinite wealth. He
dilates on this glorious prospect to his sceptical companion,
Surly, who seeks fortune by the more risky means (as
Mammon thinks) of dice and cards (II. i. 1ff.):

> Come on, sir! Now you set your foot on shore
> In *novo orbe*. Here's the rich Peru;
> And there within, sir, are the golden mines . . .
> This is the day wherein to all my friends
> I will pronounce the happy word, 'be rich'.

By virtue of this elixir its possessor can not only turn all
metals to gold, but

> Can confer honour, love, respect, long life,
> Give safety, valour; yea, and victory,
> To whom he will.

To crown all, there will be the unlimited sensual delights
on which he rhapsodises in a vein compounded at once of
grossness and of opulent fancy. But after a prolonged inter-

change of esoteric jargon between Subtle and Face the latter anounces that some materials are wanting to complete the 'projection', to procure which Sir Epicure has to hand out ten pounds. Hardly has he done so when he catches sight of Doll Common, and his thoughts switch off at once from all else to the eager desire to have 'conference' with her.

After the voluptuary there comes the saint, the deacon Ananias, on behalf of the holy brethren of Amsterdam, who, like Mammon, have been negotiating with Subtle for the philosopher's stone, and having already disbursed a large sum are anxious to see projection. After bombarding him with the pseudo-scientific lingo which is 'heathen Greek' to the deacon, Subtle bids him fetch his superior, the elder Tribulation Wholesome. Jonson in his broadside attack here on the Puritans skilfully discriminates between two types. Ananias is the out-and-out fanatic, convinced by his 'zeal' that 'the sanctified cause should have a sanctified course' Tribulation is an opportunist, ready to turn the profane to the advantage of the brethren (III. i. 11 ff.):

> We must bend into all means
> That may give furtherance to the holy cause.
>
> *   *   *
>
> The children of perdition are oft-times
> Made instruments even of the greatest works.

Thus he silences Ananias and parleys with Subtle, only to find that another call is needed on 'the holy purse'.

Well may Subtle call this his lucky day. But from this point things begin to go less smoothly for his gang. The dupes come back on one another's heels. Dapper, wanting his promised sight of the queen of the fairies, has to be further gulled and gagged with a piece of gingerbread. Sir Epicure suddenly returns for his 'conference' with Doll. Drugger, who is a suitor to a young widow, asks for her fortune to be told, and brings with him her brother, the 'angry boy' Kastril, anxious to be instructed in the whole technique of quarrelling. So impressed is he by Face's account of 'the Doctor's' powers that he fetches his 'suster', and thus starts rivalry for her favours between the two rogues. Lastly there is an apparent newcomer in a Spanish count, with whom 'Captain' Face has made acquaintance, but who is Surly returned in disguise to turn his suspicion of the impostors into certainty. Kastril is dazzled by the lure of an alliance between his sister and this hildalgo, though she protests:

> Truly, I shall never brook a Spaniard.
> Never sin' eighty-eight could I abide 'hem,
> And that was some three year afore I was born, in truth.

She is saved from worse than such a detested match by Surly's disclosure to her of his identity and the purpose of his return in disguise. Meanwhile Subtle brings off a last *coup* by means of an explosion which wrecks the works, and which he persuades Mammon is the retribution for his 'vice and lust'.

Another unforeseen explosive force now blows up the alchemist's 'works' in a different sense. Lovewit, the master of the house, unexpectedly returns, and hears from the clamouring neighbours that it has been visited day and night by a mixed company. Face, with his captain's beard shaved off, and in his true role of Jeremy, the butler, protests for a time that it is all a mistake. But at last he confesses the truth to Lovewit, and begs pardon for the abuse of his house, in return for which he will procure him a rich widow as a bride. Thus it is Lovewit, not Surly, who in the disguise of a Spanish count is wedded to Kastril's sister.

As a masterpiece of design, within the compass of the classical unities, *The Alchemist* takes its place at the head of Jonson's comedies. And its sparkling variety of interest and characterization stands out in relief against the sombre uniformity of *Volpone*. But it must be noted that Jonson has here deviated in disconcerting fashion from the lofty moral principles set forth in the dedication of the Venetian play. It is true that all the dupes pay the penalty of their greed, and that Subtle and Doll have to beat an ignominious retreat over the back wall of Lovewit's house. But their partner in knavery, Face, is let off scot-free by an indulgent master, who through no merit of his own carries off a matrimonial prize which by rights should have fallen to Surly, who had saved the widow's honour, and had alone seen through the trio's fraudulent schemes.

The Alchemist, published in quarto in 1612, was the last of the comedies to be included in the 1616 folio. Though *Bartholomew Fair* was acted by the Lady Elizabeth's servants at the Hope on 31 October 1614, and repeated on the following day at Court before the King, it was not published till 1631, in the same year as *The Devil is an Ass* and *The Staple of News*. These three plays opened the 1640 folio. The delay i n publication is surprising, for the piece at once gained the popularity at which it aimed. According to the Induction it claimed to be 'a new sufficient play . . . merry, and as full of noise as sport; made to delight all and to offend none'. In its unsparingly realistic portrayal of contemporary London life in some of its grossest and most uproarious phases it was designed to contrast with what in Ben's eyes were two forms of theatrical artificiality old and new. There was the out of date blood and thunder of *Jeronimo* (*The Spanish Tragedy*) or *Andronicus* still considered the best plays by those whose judgement has 'stood still these five and twenty or thirty years'. There was the recent Shakespearean fantastic romanticism of 'a servant-monster' and the like, tabooed by a dramatist who was 'loth to make nature afraid in his plays like those who beget *tales, tempests*, and such like drolleries'. It would have angered Jonson to foresee that the figures of Kyd's and Shakespeare's imagination were destined to more enduring vitality than any of the motley crowd whom he drew from the life at the great London carnival.

Yet to the theatre-goers of his day, many of them frequenters of the fair, the picture presented must have come home with outstanding force. Its counterpart is to be found less in other plays of the period than in the Dutch *genre*-paintings of low-life joviality at the *Kermesse*. It has been truly said that it is a play without a hero, and that it is the fair itself which 'provides a real unity of theme and tone'. Thus the figures that at once catch the eye are those who make a livelihood at the fair by more or less legitimate means. Foremost by reason of her gross bulk (depicted with a coarseness that recalls Skelton's Elinor Rumming) and by the fact that she dispenses at her booth the fair's choicest delicacy, roast pig, washed down by beer (besides more questionable commodities), is Ursula, 'the pig-woman', with her lean tapster and henchman, Mooncalf. Another favourite ware is the ginger-bread on the stall of Joan Trash, who protests that 'though I be a little crooked o' my body, I'll be found as upright in my dealing as any woman in Smith-field', and that she sells nothing but what is wholesome.

With no fixed pitch but going to and fro among the crowd are such hangers-on as the loud-voiced horse-courser, Knock'hum, the light-fingered cutpurse, Edgeworth, and his accomplice, the ballad-singer, Nightingale, who draws the ears of listeners while their pockets are being picked. A 'roarer', a bawd, and a harlot made up a still more disreputable trio. One figure among the stall-keepers stands out among the rest, for in his case Jonson appears to have blended realism with an element of personal satire. Lantern Leatherhead, the hobby-horse seller, deals in a variety of toys and musical instruments—rattles, drums, halberts, 'babies [dolls] o' the best, fiddles o' the finest'. He is also called by Joan Trash, when they are bandying words between their stalls, 'parcel-poet and an engineer'. This is a riddle, till Act V. iii., when Lantern (as he chooses to be called) appears as the manager and mouthpiece of a 'motion' or puppet-show of the 'ancient modern history of Hero and Leander'. To make this easier for an unlettered audience, the Hellespont is turned into the Thames, Leander into a dyer's son about Puddle-wharf, and Hero a wench o' the

Bank-side. One could wish that Jonson had chosen to desecrate some other tale of love than that which had been glorified by Marlowe in his last days. But it is yet another proof of his versatility that while turning classical legends to such graceful account in his masques he could produce a ribald burlesque version suited to the level of a Smithfield fair audience. And when John Selden spoke of 'Inigo Lanthorn', he seemed to imply that Jonson in the 'engineer' puppet-master was having a satirical hit at his collaborator, with whom his relations were already becoming strained.

Though Lantern is a 'parcel-poet', it is not he who supplies the verses for the puppet-show. Their author is surprisingly a proctor, who issues marriage-licences, John Littlewit, in whom Jonson may have glanced at his rival masque-maker, Daniel. The proctor wants to visit the fair to see his play, and he urges his wife, Win, to feign a longing to eat roast pig there. But there is an obstacle in her mother, Mistress Purecraft, who protests, 'O resist it, Win-the-fight, it is the Tempter, the wicked Tempter. You may know it by the fleshly motion of pig . . . pray against its carnal provocations, good child, sweet child, pray'. Ben here renews his attack on the Puritans but in a less subtle way. In *The Alchemist* Ananias was a true zealot and Tribulation a wily opportunist. But Purecraft, a rich widow, is a sanctimonious hypocrite, and so, in more redoubtable measure, is her suitor, formerly a Banbury baker, now an elder and prophet, Rabbi Zeal-of-the-land Busy. He has given up his trade because his cakes were served at such profane feasts as bridals, may-poles, and morrises. But his heart is still in the flesh-pots, and when the question of eating pig at the fair is put to him he is at no loss for a casuistical defence (I. vi. 70 ff.):

It may be eaten, and in the fair, I take it, in a booth, the tents of the wicked; the place is not much, not very much; we may be religious in the midst of the profane. So it be eaten with a reformed mouth, with sobriety and humbleness. . . . In the way of comfort to the weak, I will go and eat. I will eat exceedingly and prophesy.

There is a rival for the widow's hand in Winwife, with his 'gamester' companion, Quarlous, who also go to the fair. And there is another set of visitors of somewhat higher social quality. Bartholomew Cokes, a simple-minded young country gentleman from Harrow, has come to London to see the sights, especially the fair called by his name. His man, Waspe, who acts as a sort of 'bear-leader' to him, comes to Littlewit for a marriage licence between him and Grace Wellborn, ward of justice-of-the-peace Overdoo, whose wife is a sister of Cokes. While the others are seeing the sights, Overdoo, who has jurisdiction in the fair's powder-pie court, wanders amongst the booths in disguise to make his own discoveries of its 'yearly enormities'. But he blunders badly, and gets beaten and put in the stocks. A similar fate befalls Rabbi Busy, who has excepted roast-pig, but declaims against the other wares offered for sale: bottle-ale is a drink of Satan's; the hobby-horse is an idol; the ginger-bread stall is an idolatrous grove of images, which he overthrows. Cokes is gulled and loses his money and other valuables, and finally his bride-elect, who is gained by Winwife, while Quarlous secures widow Purecraft. It is a riot of complications in which mistress Overdoo and Win Littlewit find themselves in highly equivocal situations. There is a wealth of ingenuity in the weaving together of multiple threads, but the play makes its chief effect neither through plot nor characterization, but by its broad, ebullient presentation of a characteristic slice of London Jacobean life.

LAST PLAYS

It was unfortunate that Bartholomew Fair was not included in the 1616 folio, which would then have contained the full product of Jonson's dramatic genius at its zenith. By the date of its publication as noted above, it is linked with plays which exhibit the decline of his powers. That decline begins to show itself in *The Devil is an Ass*, a play acted at the Blackfriars by the King's company in the autumn of the year which saw the folio's publication. It was a sign of Jonson's loosening grip that he who had ridiculed the introduction of marvels and monsters on the stage should venture into what was for him the alien sphere of the supernatural. The opening scene, the prologue in hell, as it might be called, is indeed promising enough when Pug, 'the less devil' obtains from his chief Satan, leave to visit earth till midnight in the body of a cutpurse just hanged at Tyburn; and when Iniquity, the old Vice of the Moralities, with his doggerel couplets, is rejected as his companion as not of sufficient quality and fashion for these sophisticated times. But when Pug takes service with the wealthy squire, Fitz-dottrel, he is scarcely distinguishable from the general run of menials in the plays of the period. He proves himself an ass in comparison with some of the human scoundrels, but instead of being laughable in his stupidity, as comedy requires, he is merely dull. But he has one pregnant fling at earthly villainies (IV. iv. 170–1):

> You talk of a university! Why, Hell is
> A grammar-school to this!

A more ludicrously asinine figure is his employer. Fitz-dottrel is obsessed with a passion for self-expression. He thinks himself ruined,

> should he 'scape
> One public meeting, out of the belief
> He has of his own great and catholic strengths
> In arguing and discourse.

He has just contracted with the young gallant Wittipol for the gift of a rich cloak in which he will make a sensational appearance at the theatre (I. vi. 31 ff.):

> To-day I go to the Blackfriars playhouse,
> Sit i' the view, salute all my acquaintance,
> Rise up between the acts, let fall my cloak,
> Publish a handsome man and a rich suit . . .
> The ladies ask, 'Who's that?'

I

In return Wittipol is to have a quarter of an hour's talk at the measured distance of a yard or more, in Fitzdottrel's presence, with his beautiful young wife. The gallant addresses her in terms of fervid love, and when at her husband's behest she keeps silence, he changes places and speaks for her, making an assignation when Fitzdottrel is at the theatre. As his window faces that of Wittipol's friend, Manly, in Lincoln's Inn Chambers, they are able later to lean forth to each other and embrace while he courts her in those fancifully sensuous terms which form for Jonson the language of love. But Fitzdottrel, summoned by Pug, breaks in upon them, strikes his wife, and threatens vengeance on her gallant.

Meanwhile, however, Fitzdottrel's main interest (and with it that of the play) has been switched in other directions. It was a period when the Government was trying various economic schemes to meet its financial difficulties, and amongst them were plans for the drainage of the fens. Jonson was always quick to see the weaker side of what he considered fantastic designs, if not actual impostures. So here Fitzdottrel is made the gull of the 'projector' Meercraft, who has a plan for 'the recovery of drowned land'. The Norfolk squire is only to lend his countenance to the business as an 'undertaker', and his reward is to be made 'Duke of Drownland'. Another invention of Meercraft's fertile brain is a Court of Dependencies, to which impending duels are to be referred, and of which his cousin, Everill, is to be master. For this he needs to disburse a hundred pieces, and Fitzdottrel is so fascinated by the description of the court's procedure, that he is ready to provide double the amount.

This is ingeniously linked with a more commonplace deception practised on the squire. Wittipol disguised as a Spanish lady affects to train the future Duchess of Drownland in courtly speech and deportment. Fitzdottrel, fascinated by her charms, hands over his wife to her absolutely. 'She is your own. Do with her what you will.'

He also, in accordance with a rule of the Court of Depen-

dencies, as an intending duellist, makes a feoffment of his
estate and names the counterfeit Spanish lady as his heiress.
Wittipol, however, insists on the substitution of Manly, and
thereupon strips off his disguise and announces that the
feoffment will be for the benefit of Fitzdottrel's wife. For by
an edifying but dramatically most inconsistent development,
she and Wittipol, instead of turning the situation to amorous
account, adopt a highly virtuous attitude, the formerly
ardent wooer now declaring:

> Lady, I can love goodness in you more
> Than I did beauty.

The discovery of how he has been gulled brings tumbling
down the squire's edifice of make-believe:

> I will be what I am, Fabian Fitzdottrel,
> Though all the world say nay to't.

Here the play should by rights have ended, but to provide
a fifth act Fitzdottrel again lets himself be befooled, though
after a different fashion. At Meercraft's suggestion he affects
the hysterical symptoms and speech of a victim of witchcraft, and the allegation is put forward that he was not
compos mentis when he made the feoffment. The credulous
Justice Eitherside is taken in by the imposture, but Fitzdottrel suddenly declares that it is time he leave off counter-
feiting and confesses that he is not bewitched. It is an
inconsequent ending, though the squire's feigned ravings had
given Jonson the opportunity of ridiculing the widespread
belief in demoniacal possession.

It was not till after nearly ten years that he wrote his next
comedy, *The Staple of News*, acted by the King's company
in the spring of 1626, and published in 1631. But he was
still occupied with the congenial task of exposing impostures
and those who were duped by them. Here it was a recent
development, the manufacture of sensational, fictitious news,
at which he had already tilted five years before in the
masque, *News from the New World*. Cymbal, another of

Jonson's gang of 'projectors', has set up and equipped an
office, of which he is the master, to enter all the news of the
time and give it forth. It is to be gathered by four 'emis-
saries', bringing in their reports from the Court (fashion),
Paul's (the book trade), Exchange (commerce), and Westminster Hall (law and politics). In the 'great rooms' of the
office an examiner, registrar, and two clerks sort and file and
issue the news. One of the clerks, called Nathaniel and
described as 'a decayed stationer', who knows news well, is
evidently to be identified with Nathaniel Butter, a stationer,
who in 1622 had co-operated in producing a journal, *News
from most parts of Christendom*.

The Staple is seen in full working order in Act III. ii.
Fashionable visitors hear strange tidings from abroad—the
King of Spain is chosen Pope; Spinola is made General of the
Jesuits; a burning-glass has been found in Galileo's study
which will fire any fleet out at sea. Another item sounding
equally fantastic at the time now seems like an unconscious
prophecy of the submarine and its torpedo (ll. 79–82):

> It is an *automa*, runs under water,
> With a snug nose, and has a nimble tail
> Made like an auger, with which tail she wriggles
> Betwixt the coasts of a ship and sinks it straight.

Among humbler customers there is a she-anabaptist who
lays down sixpence for news of the saints at Amsterdam and
is told they expect the prophet Baal to be sent over to them.
Another customer learns that a colony of cooks is to be
landed on the coast of America to convert the cannibals into
'good, eating Christians'. And so the Staple proceeds merrily with its manufacture of news for the entertainment of
clients and the profit of the office, till suddenly it is blown
up and all its officers dissolved into vapour as unsubstantial
as the fictions they had spread.

In his treatment of this main theme Jonson shows much
of his distinctive quality, but he combines it somewhat
loosely with weaker elements. In the same house as the

office of the Staple there lodges a young prodigal, Peniboy, who has just come of age, and has succeeded (as he thinks) to his father's estate. For the father, by a clumsily unconvincing device, in the disguise of a 'canting' beggar, has announced his own death to Peniboy. The young heir is instructed by the lawyer, who is the Westminster-Hall 'emissary' of the Staple, that by his father's will he is to pay court to the lady Pecunia (Money). She is the ward of Peniboy's miserly uncle, who flatters her and seeks to keep her in his power while there is another rival for her favours in Cymbal, the Master of the Staple, who displays before her the attractions of his office. In the end her wooers suffer disappointment and learn their lesson. Peniboy's father throws off his disguise, bids his miserly brother

> To use her like a friend, not like a slave
> Or like an idol;

and puts his prodigal son through a penitential course before he is allowed to enjoy Pecunia with 'safe frugality'.

Here Jonson, who could be so scornful of the old-fashioned theatrical taste that revelled in *The Spanish Tragedy* and *Titus Andronicus*, harks back to the far more antiquated allegorical technique of the Moralities. It fits awkwardly into the topical main plot, but it has a delightful counterbalance in the naïve prattle about the Moralities between the four 'gossips' in the 'intermeans' between the Acts.

Tattle. My husband, Timothy Tattle (God rest his poor soul!) was wont to say, there was no play without a Fool and a Devil in't; he was for the Devil still (God bless him!). The Devil for his money, would he say. I would fain see the Devil.

*   *   *

Expectation. But was the Devil a proper man, gossip?
Mirth. As fine a gentleman of his inches as ever I saw trusted to the stage or anywhere else . . . he would carry away the Vice on his back quick to Hell in every play where he came, and reform abuses.

The later comments of this chorus on the news from the Staple were liable to be mistaken for Jonson's own, and in publishing the play he protested against such a sinister interpretation 'as if the souls of most of the spectators had lived in the eyes and ears of these ridiculous gossips that babble between the Acts'.

He was, however, to fare far worse with his next venture on the stage, *The New Inn*, 'never acted, but most negligently play'd' by the King's company, probably on 19 January 1629. It was a disastrous *première*, during which 'a hundred fastidious impertinents' rose from their seats and would not see the performance out. The quoted splenetic phrases are from the title-page and dedication of the octavo 1631 edition, which also contained Jonson's superbly indignant ode to himself:

> Come, leave the loathèd stage
>   And the more loathsome age:
> Where pride and impudence (in faction knit)
>   Usurp the chair of wit,
> Indicting and arraigning every day
>   Something they call a play.

Presumably readers were no more favourable than spectators, for *The New Inn* was not included in the 1640 folio and was not reprinted till the third folio in 1692.

If a play is written for performance in a theatre, it has to take its chance with the audiences, and from this point of view there is no appeal from their verdict. Nor can it be denied that Ben tried them unduly high. One cause of their resentment is a complete puzzle. They hissed because one of the characters, a chambermaid, was called Cis. They evidently detected, rightly or wrongly, a personal allusion, and Jonson changed the name to Prue. A much more serious handicap was the fantastically complicated series of disguises and impersonations in which so many of the leading characters were involved. This too had to be recognized by Jonson when he prefixed as a key to the printed text an 'argument' of the plot and a 'characterism of the chief actors'. Lord Frampul, who had been deserted by his wife, is keeping, under the disguise of Goodstock, the host, the inn of 'the light heart' at Barnet. His wife, who had left him because she had been able to bring him only daughters, not a male heir, is living at the inn, unrecognized by him, as an old Irish nurse and charwoman. Their younger daughter, Laetitia, is also resident there, and unrecognized, posing as a boy, Frank, and the son of the host. The elder daughter, Frances, after her mother's disappearance, has assumed the title and state of Lady Frampul, and wishing to make merry with the lords who are her 'servants' appoints a meeting with them as her guests at the inn of the light heart. Her maid, Prue, to provide her with feminine company for decorum's sake, dresses up the host's 'son' as a girl, Laetitia —which in truth she is. And to complete these transformations the maid richly arrayed, is appointed by her mistress to be queen of the sports at the inn.

As an offset to these complications there is an ineffective humorous by-plot. Sir Glorious Tipto, a somewhat shadowy type of the braggart soldier, is one of Lady Frampul's 'servants', but gives his whole attention to 'Fly', once a gipsy, now the host's chief retainer, and to the below-stairs 'militia' of the house, the drawer, tapster, and the rest.

If this were all, *The New Inn* would be of small account. But paradoxically this play of Jonson's declining years—and this helps to explain his indignation at its failure—contained his unique attempt to give dramatic expression to idealized love. There is lodging at the inn another 'servant' of Lady Frampul, of a different type from her merry-making guests. Lovel, 'a complete gentleman, a soldier, and a scholar', is in deep melancholy because Lady Frampul frowns on his suit. But he has an unsuspected ally in the quick-witted maid Prue, who as sovereign of the sports decrees that for two hours he shall have all the freedoms and favours of the lady's principal servant, and for each hour the right to take a kiss. So with Prue presiding over a court of love, with the lady and Lovel facing each other, he pleads his case in the

Platonic fashion to which Henrietta Maria had given vogue
(III. ii. 105 ff.):

> Love is a spiritual coupling of two souls,
> So much more excellent, as it least relates
> Unto the body; circular, eternal;
> Not feigned nor made, but born: and then so precious
> As nought can value it but itself; so free
> As nothing can command it but itself;
> And in itself so round and liberal
> As where it favours it bestows itself.

It is a strangely different note from any hitherto sounded in
Jonson's plays, and it instantly converts the defendant:

> Where have I liv'd in heresy so long
> Out o' the congregation of love,
> And stood irregular by all his canons? . . .
> What penance shall I do to be receiv'd
> And reconciled to the church of love?

In the second hour the question before the court is changed
to 'what true valour is which oft begets true love'. Again,
Lovel's oratory, defining its scope as 'always honour and the
public good', is found irresistible by Lady Frampul, though it
is a lengthy, philosophic disquisition more in place in the
academic lecture-room than on the stage. There is an inkling
of this even in the lady's admiring outburst (IV. iv. 138):

> Most manly utter'd all!
> As if Achilles had the chair in valour
> And Hercules were but a lecturer!

So sudden and complete is her surrender that Prue takes
it to be merely dissembling, that will end when the court is
dismissed. But Lady Frampul has in the two hours found
her true self—a more significant revelation than the discovery of the identities of her relatives with which the play
closes, while Prue's wit and loyalty are rewarded by the
hand of Lord Latimer, a 'servant' of her mistress.

Jonson's last play, *The Magnetic Lady*, or *Humours Reconciled*, acted by the King's company at the Blackfriars on or
soon after October 1632, fared no better than *The New Inn*.

Again the players let him down, not this time by indifferent
acting, but by the insertion of oaths which had incensed the
Master of the Revels and led, as he records in his office-book,
to a prolonged dispute. But the ill success of the comedy lay
deeper. Jonson wrote it with a premonition that it was to
be the end of his long labours for the stage. Through the
mouthpiece of a 'boy of the house', the chief of three characters in the Induction, he tells how from *Every Man in his
Humour* he had studied humours in manners of men till
'finding himself now near the close or shutting up of his
circle', he had conceived the idea of a magnetic lady who
would draw to her house a number of persons of different
humours 'to make up his perimeter'. These were to be finally
reconciled by the 'magisterial wit' of the lady's friend and
counseller, the mathematical scholar, Compass, and thus the
full circle of the comedy of humours was to be completed.

It was an ingenious conception and in its working out
Jonson shows that he retained to the last his skill in plot
construction. But the plot itself is of a conventional type
unusual with Jonson, and the humours, with one or two
exceptions, lack the vitality of his former creations. Lady
Loadstone herself is a shadowy figure whose magnetism has
to be taken for granted. The centre round whom the action
revolves is Placentia, her supposed niece, a rich heiress, for
whose hand there is sharp rivalry. Lady Loadstone favours
her lawyer, Practice, for whom she foresees high judicial
promotion. Sir Moth Interest, the girl's usurious uncle, who
has made a huge profit as guardian of her fortune, sponsors
his creature Bias, who would let Sir Moth retain a large part
of her dower. Lady Loadstone's 'gossip', Mistress Polish,
supports the suit of the affected courtier, Sir Diaphanous
Silkworm. Other professions under Lady Loadstone's roof
are represented by the quarrelsome soldier, Ironside, the
unscrupulous physician, Rut, and the pliable parson, Palate,
who all play their part in the imbroglio. It comes to a head
when Placentia, having given birth to an illegitimate child

is found not to be Lady Loadstone's niece but the daughter
of Polish, who substituted her in infancy for the true heiress,
Pleasance, who has been the lady's waiting-woman. But
both girls are so colourless that the revelation leaves the
audience cold, and Compass, though designated the recon-
ciler of the conflicting humours, is too much of an abstraction
to attract much sympathy when by a ruse he outwits Practice
and wins the heiress for himself. And it is little more than
the affinity of their names that helps to justify Lady Loadstone in offering herself and her estate to Captain Ironside
at the close.

But in two respects, apart from his constructive achievement, Jonson gives evidence of unflagging quality. Mistress
Polish may take rank with the creations of his prime. With
her irrepressible volubility, her sentimental reminiscences,
and her ingrained vulgarity, she is of kin, as has been truly
pointed out, to the Nurse in *Romeo and Juliet*, whom Jonson
may have had in mind. But he has added a sinister criminal
element which leads her to perpetrate the wrong to the
heiress, and, when cornered, to confess it boldly in the belief
(rudely disappointed) that Bias will still marry her daughter
and bring the part of the endowment settled on him by
Sir Moth.

And characteristic to the last of Ben's haughtily independent attitude are the rebukes which between the acts the
boy of the house administers to the two gentlemen for
misunderstanding the author's purpose. One of them takes
the lesson to heart:

> Our parts . . . are to wait the process and events of things
> as the poet presents them, not as we would corruptly fashion
> them. We come here to behold plays and censure [i.e. judge]
> them as they are made and fitted for us; not to beslaver our own
> thoughts with censorious spittle tempering the poet's clay, as we
> were to mould every scene anew.

It might be the voice of Jonson in the earliest days of his
stage career. And enough, I believe, has been said to show

that his last plays, whatever their imperfections, are far from deserving Dryden's condemnation of them as his 'dotages'. With the extraordinary calls that he had made on it for some thirty-five years his massive genius was still not without an apparently inexhaustible reserve. As securely as Shakespeare stands at the head of the Olympians of the English theatre, so does Jonson in the forefront of the Titans. Nature had endowed him lavishly with almost every gift that goes to the making of the supreme dramatist. He is pre-eminent among those who

> get so near—so very, very near!
> 'Tis an old tale: Jove strikes the Titans down,
> Not when they set about their mountain piling,
> But when another rock would crown the work.[1]

It is for lack of the crowning rock of transcendent poetic imagination that rare Ben Jonson just fails to win his way into the dramatic heaven of heavens.

[1] R. Browning, *Paracelsus*, Part V.

VI

JOHN MARSTON—THOMAS DEKKER

MELODRAMA AND CIVIC COMEDY

As with George Chapman so with John Marston, recent critical investigation has given a more generous estimate than has been traditional of his contribution to English drama. It has been increasingly realized that Ben Jonson's burlesque of the more vulnerable features of Marston's style in his serious plays has led to an undue depreciation of his distinctive qualities. There has been more appreciative recognition of his aims as a dramatist and of their effect on his technique and his dialogue.

Documentary research has also added to our biographical knowledge. The discovery of the entry of the christening of John Marston on 7 October 1576 in the register of the church of St. Mary Magdalene, Wardington, Oxfordshire, has established the year and place of his birth. At the age of sixteen, in 1591, he entered Brazenose College, Oxford, and took his B.A. in February 1593/4. From 1594 to 1606 he was a member of the Middle Temple, but like many other residents in the Inns of Court he devoted himself to literature instead of law. In May 1598 he published an erotic poem, *Pygmalion's Image*, and a series of *Satires*, followed in Spetember by another set of satires, *The Scourge of Villany*. In the epistle prefixed to this he attacked Jonson under the name of Torquatus and this was followed by 'the war of the theatres' between the playwrights.[1]

It has to be borne in mind therefore that Marston had graduated as a satirist before coming out as a dramatist and that he retained the satirist's temper in his new sphere. He also retained his daring and extravagant vocabulary which

[1] See above, pp. 63–6, 69–72.

might pass within the leaves of a book but which was a provocation to censorious ears when thundered from the stage. And it was unfortunate that Marston's first important venture as a playwright was not in the field of comedy but of tragedy, where his distinctive qualities were put to a severer test. The two-part play, published in 1602 as *The History of Antonio and Mellida* and *Antonio's Revenge*, was entered in the Stationers Register in October 1601. The mention in Part I, Act V. i. 8–10 of 'Anno Domini' 1599, and 'Aetatis suae 24' points to 1599 as the date of its composition, and Part II must have soon followed. Both were acted by the Children of Paul's.

No source of the play has been traced, but the introduction into the dialogue of *Antonio and Mellida* of a number of Italian verse lines suggests southern influence. In any case, the main plot and characterization are in conventional romantic vein. Antonio, son of Andrugio, Duke of Genoa, loves Mellida, daughter of Piero, Doge of Venice, who forbids their union, and favours the suit of Galeazto, son of the Duke of Florence. Venice has just overcome Genoa in a sea fight and Piero has set a price upon the heads of Antonio and his fugitive father. Antonio in the disguise of an Amazon comes to the Venetian Court and arranges with Mellida to fly with him. But the plan miscarries and Antonio has to seek out his father in exile. Thereupon Andrugio boldly determines to present himself at the Venetian Court with the words:

> Then here, Piero, is Andrugio's head,
> Royally casked in a helm of steel.
> Give me thy love, and take it.

Piero at once joyfully assents, but immediately afterwards to sad music a coffin is borne in supposedly containing Antonio's 'breathless trunk'. Piero in his transformed mood offers his life and his daughter's love if they 'would but redeem one minute of his death'. Whereupon Antonio leaps from the coffin, crying, 'I rise from death that never liv'd till now.' This finale, crudely motived though it is, exemplifies Marston's instinct for 'good theatre', which is illustrated also in his detailed stage-directions showing close familiarity with the conditions of the Elizabethan playhouse. He availed himself to the full of the musical accomplishments of the Paul's company. And he recognized the value of a comic underplot even if his satire of some of the courtly affectations of speech and deportment has little to do with the action of the play. It is curious that with his sense of the oddities of Euphuism he should not have realized the incongruous effect on an audience of a number of his chosen epithets and phrases. 'Glibbery', mocked by Jonson, is applied in *Antonio and Mellida* to love, ice, and an urchin; a wave has a 'sliftered paunch'; earth is bidden to 'chawn' her breast; a suitor asks Mellida to 'erect your gracious symmetry', and a friend urges Antonio to

> Buckle thy spirits up, put all thy wits
> In wimble action.

And there are passages in the dialogue where Marston flounders in his attempt to realize the aspiration of his prologue:

> O! that our Muse
> Had those abstruse and sinewy faculties,
> That with a strain of fresh invention
> She might press out the rarity of art.

Yet at times he succeeds in hitting the mark. There is true nobility in the cry of Antonio's father, conquered, exiled, and bereft (III. i. 59–62):

> There's nothing left
> Unto Andrugio but Andrugio:
> And that nor mischief, force, distress, nor hell-can take,
> Fortune my fortunes, not my mind, shall shake.

And there is felicitous imagery in Antonio's utterance in his despair (III. ii. 203–7):

> Each man takes hence life, but no man death:
> He's a good fellow and keeps open house:
> A thousand, thousand ways lead to his gate,
> To his wide-mouth'd porch: when niggard life
> Hath but one little, little wicket through.

Dramatic surprise was a favourite feature of Marston's technique, but he characteristically gave it undue licence when the gracious Piero at the close of *Antonio and Mellida* steps on the stage at the beginning of *Antonio's Revenge*, 'his arms bare, smear'd in blood, a poniard in one arm bloody'. In the interval between the two parts he has poisoned Andrugio and stabbed to death the courtier, Feliche, ostensibly caught in adultery with Mellida. With Marston's flair for piling up the agony the way is thus prepared for a double revenge action. Feliche's father, Pandulpho, is eager like Hieronimo in *The Spanish Tragedy* to avenge his son. Antonio, like Hamlet, to avenge his father. But the likeness to *Hamlet* goes much further and raises the problem of priority. The strong probability is that Marston knew either the pre-Shakespearean *Hamlet* or an early version (to which Gabriel Harvey seems to refer about 1598) of Shakespeare's play. He keeps the essential features of the Elsinore tragedy but varies the details. Piero reveals that he has poisoned Andrugio that he may marry his widow Maria. But instead of being like Gertrude his sister-in-law, she has been his early love who had preferred his rival to him. Mellida is prevented by her father (in spite of his consent at the end of Part I) from marrying Antonio, not, like Ophelia, because of difference in rank, but because Piero for political ends wishes her to be the bride of the heir to the duchy of Florence. Antonio assumes, like Hamlet, the pose of madness, but in addition he masquerades for a time in a professional fool's garb. His father's ghost appears to urge him to revenge, but it is in the church where he lies entombed not on the castle battlements. The ghost's opening words are in Marston's most incisive style and sum up the whole situation (III. i. 34–42)

> Antonio, revenge!
> I was impoison'd by Piero's hand:
> Revenge my blood; take spirit, gentle boy;
> Revenge my blood. Thy Mellida is chaste:
> Only to frustrate thy pursuit in love,

> Is blaz'd unchaste. Thy mother yields consent
> To be his wife, and give his blood a son
> That made her husbandless, and doth emplot
> To make her sonless.

But with Marston's curious uncertainty of touch he follows this up with lines of overstrained and tasteless imagery:

> Thou vigour of my youth, juice of my love,
> Seize on revenge, grasp the stern bended front
> Of frowning vengeance, with unpraized clutch,
> Alarum Nemesis, rouse up thy blood!

It is this incontinence of speech and a corresponding exaggeration in action that hinder much of Marston's intended tragic effect. He alienates the sympathy due to Antonio for his father's murder and Mellida's death, on a false report of his suicide, by making him kill Piero's innocent child, Julio. But there is true pathos in the dialogue between Pandulpho, bearing with him the body of his murdered son, and Antonio in his despair (IV. v. 53–8):

> *Pan.* I am the miserablest soul that breathes.
> *Ant.* S'lid, sir, ye lie; by the heart of grief, thou liest.
> I scorn't that any wretched should survive
> Outmounting me in that superlative,
> Most miserable, most unmatched in woe;
> Who dare assume that but Antonio?

The final scene in which the avengers take advantage of the masque in which they are appearing to bring Piero to his doom, while Andrugio's ghost 'placed betwixt the music houses' gloats over the spectacle, is partly reminiscent of the close of *The Spanish Tragedy*, and doubtless shared a good deal of its popular appeal on the stage. But once again Marston overshoots his mark by a superfluous accumulation of horrific details.

After this tragic surfeit he turned to comedy, though of a bitterly satiric type. *The Malcontent* was published in three different editions by William Apsley in 1604. The two earlier spoke of it as by John Marston; the third title-page had 'Augmented by Marston. With the Additions played by the

King's Majesty's servants. Written by John Webster'. The chief addition by Webster appears to have been the Induction introducing a number of the chief actors in the King's Company, including Burbage. Their frank talk makes it clear that the play had been written for the Children of the Queen's Revels acting at Blackfriars, but that as a retort to the Children's purloining of *Jeronimo* (probably the First Part) the King's men had adopted the play as their own. And as they could not like the boys lengthen out the performance with a great deal of music they had found it necessary to have the dialogue supplemented.

It is plain also from the Induction that *The Malcontent* had given offence to some of its hearers. Sly, the actor, twice calls it 'a bitter play', and Burbage answers, 'Such vices as stand not accountable to law should be cured as men heal tetters by casting ink upon them'. And in his own epistle to the reader Marston says of his 'supposed tartness' that 'unto every worthy mind it will be approved so general and honest as may modestly pass with the freedom of a satire.' But satire and drama have different aims and limits which Marston here confuses, so that the contemporary criticism of the play seems not without justification to-day. Malevole, the malcontent, is the disguised former Duke of Genoa, Altofronto, who has been dispossessed by his successor, Pietro, supported by the Duke of Florence, whose daughter, Aurelia, he has married after imprisoning Altofronto's wife, Maria. As Malevole reminds his sole confidant, Celso, he had played into his supplanter's hands by abjuring all the usual maxims of policy (I. iv. 9–14):

> I wanted those old instruments of state,
> Dissemblance and suspect: I could not time it, Celso,
> My throne stood like a point in midst of a circle,
> To all of equal nearness, bore with none;
> Rein'd all alike, so slept in fearless virtue,
> Suspectless, too suspectless.

In these lines Marston shows again that he is master at

K

times of clear and cogent expression. But when Malevole
in his disguise as an observer of Court affairs begins to rail
at all men and all things the unmeasured violence of his
invective becomes fatiguing and goes far to defeat its own
end. Pietro, not knowing who he is, says of him that

> his highest delight is to procure others vexation, and therein he
> thinks he truly serves heaven; for 'tis his position, whosoever in
> this earth can be contented is a slave and damn'd; therefore does
> he afflict all in that to which they are most affected.

There is much indeed to move his indignation. Aurelia
proves faithless to Pietro with two lovers, Ferneze and
Mendoza. The latter has been chosen as his heir by Pietro,
and to gain the throne quickly he suborns Malevole to kill
him while hunting. Malevole reveals the plot to Pietro, bids
him assume the disguise of a hermit, and announce his own
death. Thereupon Mendoza, saluted as Duke, banishes
Aurelia, plans to set free and marry Maria, and proposes to
Malevole and the 'Hermit' to make away with each other.
They join against this new usurper and seize him during a
masque which is to celebrate his enthronement. This recalls
the close of *Antonio's Revenge*, but here the villain's life is
spared, and Altofronto is restored to his wife and his crown.

In the working out of this complicated action Marston
shows his theatrical skill and his capacity for exploiting the
resources of his stage. These cannot make their full effect
in print, and Marston was fully conscious of this when he
lamented in this epistle to the reader: 'Only one thing
afflicts me, to think that scenes invented merely to be spoken
should be inforcively published to be read.'

By 1604 Marston had composed his quarrel with Jonson,
to whom he dedicated *The Malcontent* in the most cordial
terms. This reconciliation bore good fruit, for early in 1605
the two dramatists, together with Chapman, collaborated in
one of the most attractive plays of the period, *Eastward Ho*,
acted at the Blackfriars by the Children of the Queen's
Revels and published by William Aspley. The comedy in-

cluded satirical references in Act III. iii to the Scots, and in
Act IV. i to the new king's lavish creation of knights.
Marston and Chapman were arrested. Jonson, by his own
account, joined them voluntarily in prison, from which the
efforts of high-placed friends soon procured their release.
The other two playwrights ascribed the offending passages
to Marston, who had thus to suffer a sharper penalty than
the censure provoked in some quarters by *The Malcontent.*
Otherwise there is only internal evidence to suggest the conjectured distribution of the play between its three authors.
Seldom has there been such successful fusion of the work of
several hands. But it is the commonly accepted view that
credit should be given to Marston

for the general conception of the main plot and for the introduction and development of the chief comic characters . . .
Chapman was engaged mainly in the dramatization of the Italian
tale which furnished the underplot, while Jonson, in addition no
doubt to valuable advice as to the construction of the whole, did
little more than revise and finish the work of his collaborators.[1]

An allusion in the prologue makes it clear that the authors
of *Eastward Ho* had in mind Dekker and Webster's *Westward
Ho* recently performed[2], and in their main plot they were
in similar fashion presenting a picture of London city life.
But they dealt with it in a different spirit and developed their
theme on the lines of the prodigal-son story. Touchstone,
the Cheapside goldsmith, with his pride in his craft and his
rectitude and shrewdness, is a true civic worthy. He has
one apprentice, Golding, of similar character to himself,
while his fellow, Quicksilver, spends his time in idleness and
debauchery, and has frequently on his lips notorious tags
from popular plays that he has seen in the theatre. This pair
are matched by Touchstone's two daughters. As he puts
it (I. i. 79–83):

[1] T. M. Parrott, *The Comedies of George Chapman*, 847. See also Herford & Simpson's *Ben Jonson*, II. 37–46. Simpson, *P.M.L.A.* Sept. 1944,
see Jonson's hand especially in the last scenes.

[2] Nor out of our contention to do better
Than that which is opposed to ours in title.

As I have two prentices, the one of a boundless prodigality, the other of a most hopeful industry, so have I only two daughters; the eldest of a proud ambition and nice wantonness, the other of a modest humility and comely soberness. The one must be ladyfied, forsooth, and be attired just to the court-cut and long tail.

This daughter, Gertrude, is about to marry a needy knight, Sir Petronel Flash, who is to fulfil her dream of rising into a new social level. As she tells her sister, Mildred, 'though my father be a low-capped tradesman, yet I must be a lady, my mother must call me madam'. Nor does her vulgar-minded mother make any demur to her declaration, 'I must be a lady to-morrow, and by your leave, mother (I speak it not without my duty, but only in the right of my husband), I must take place of you, mother.'

But Sir Petronel's only motive in marrying into the city is to get hold of Gertrude's inheritance to finance a voyage that he has planned to Virginia with a sea-captain, Seagull, and two other adventurers. And there blows for a few moments through this London play a breath from the New World when Seagull gives a fanciful account of the treasures waiting for them in the country of their quest. Sir Petronel intends to leave his bride behind, but to take with him the young wife of the old usurer Security. Here there is skilfully inter-woven with the main action an underplot apparently based upon a story in the *Novellino* of the Italian Masuccio. Security is made an accomplice in his own dishonour, in the belief that the disguised woman who is brought by Quick-silver on board Petronel's ship is not his wife, Winifred, but the wife of his lawyer, Bramble. But the voyagers never get farther than the Thames, for in a fierce storm and with a drunken company their ship is wrecked off Cuckold's Haven. This episode, with the successive landing of all who have been aboard, is vividly portrayed with a masterly employment of the resources of the Blackfriars stage.

Sir Petronel and Quicksilver, after their rescue from the 'rude Thames', are arrested and charged by Touchstone, the one 'on suspicion of felony' and the other as 'being accessory in the receipt of my goods'. And the bitterest drop in their cup is that they have to appear before Golding, now married to Mildred, who has been elected to the civic office of alderman's deputy, and who after a stern examination sends them to the 'Counter' prison. The disillusioned Gertrude bewails that she has been made a lady by a knight 'which is now as good as no knight . . . and instead of land i' the country all my knight's living lies i' the Counter; there's his castle now'. She has to throw herself upon the charity of her despised sister, whose husband meanwhile comes to the relief of those whom he has sent to jail. By a stratagem he gets Touchstone to visit the Counter, where the hitherto inexorable goldsmith is so affected by the demonstrations of repentance by Quicksilver and Petronel that he forgives them their offences, and a general reconciliation takes place. When penning the realistic prison scenes in the last act the authors of *Eastward Ho* did not anticipate that they would so soon themselves, in Jonson's words, be 'committed to a vile prison' and have to be delivered by higher authorities than an alderman's deputy.

The Dutch Courtesan was entered in the Stationers' Register on 26 June 1605, and a quarto was published in the same year 'as it was played in the Blackfriars by the Children of her Majesty's Revels. Written by John Marston'. If it followed closely on *Eastward Ho*, the more genial tone derived from Marston's collaboration with his fellow playwrights was of short duration. For *The Dutch Courtesan* suffers from the intemperate and fatiguing violence of expression which is his besetting weakness. He claims that 'the difference betwixt the love of a courtesan and a wife is the full scope of the play', but to achieve this he wades through so much mud that we are inclined to apply to him words used by a character in the play: 'In very good truthness, you are the foulest-mouth'd, profane, railing brother, call a woman the most ungodly names'. The courtesan

Franceschina is furious because young Freevill is breaking
his connexion with her to marry 'a lawful love, my modest
Beatrice'. But his place as the courtesan's lover is taken by
his friend Malheureux who, hitherto an austere moralist, is
inflamed by the sight of her beauty into delirious passion.
Franceschina as the price of her favours insists that Malheureux shall kill Freevill. All this is on conventional lines, but
with his customary ingenuity and command of stage resources Marston so develops the plot that Malheureux,
though he only pretends to murder his friend, is arrested,
imprisoned, and condemned to execution, from which he is
saved at the last moment when Freevill, who has been in
hiding and disguised, reveals himself. These complications
excite more interest than Freevill's courtship of the somewhat colourless Beatrice, who is eclipsed by her spritely
sister, Crispinella, who has something in her akin to the other
Beatrice of *Much Ado about Nothing*, but with a far freer
tongue. When her sister cries, 'Fie! you speak too broad',
she retorts in words which might serve as a justification for
Marston's own extreme frankness: 'I consider nature without
apparel, without disguising of custom or compliment; I give
thoughts words, and words truth, and truth boldness.' How
aptly here and elsewhere maxims of Montaigne are made to
flow from Crispinella's lively lips!

But there is still a livelier figure in Cocledemoy, the
'knavishly witty companion' who is the centre of the underplot. Here we meet again with city tradesmen, though they
make a poorer showing than in *Eastward Ho*. Cocledemoy,
in a series of disguises, outwits and robs a vintner, Mulligrub,
and his wife, and finally gets him arrested on a false charge
of stealing his cloak by constables as muddle-headed as
Dogberry and Verges. Mulligrub, like Malheureux, is led to
execution and saved at the last moment, after he has for-
given Cocledemoy, by that worthy's disclosure of himself
and confession that all that he has done has been 'for wit's
sake'. The parallel entanglements and solutions of the

serious and the comic plots are a striking piece of stage craft.

Parasitaster, or The Fawn, entered in the Stationers' Register 12 March 1606, was published in two editions in that year, the second being 'corrected of many faults'. Acted first by the Children of the Queen's Revels and afterwards by those of Paul's, it reverted to the Italian background of *The Malcontent* and to the situation of a duke in disguise watching over the development of the action. But here the widowed Hercules, Duke of Ferrara, has a specific aim—to see how his son Tiberio progresses in the courtship of the Duke of Urbin's daughter, Dulcimel, on behalf of his father, who really wishes his cold-blooded son himself to become enamoured of her. And this is brought about by Dulcimel herself, who artfully makes her purblind father, in his own despite, the agent of her amorous advances to Tiberio and of a midnight marriage in her chamber.

Hercules, in his role of 'fawn' or parasite, makes less impression than Altofronto as the malcontent, and the group of foolish and dissolute courtiers do not arouse strong interest. But once again Marston shows his remarkable faculty of using the resources of a children's company to secure an effective ending to a play. Hercules devises in honour of the Duke of Urbin the sport of 'Cupid's Parliament', produced with dancing, music, and allegorical figures, in which offenders against the love-god's statutes are summoned to the bar, and each courtier in turn has to confess his guilt, and even the Duke himself is convicted.

On 17 March 1606, five days later than *The Fawn*, another play by Marston, *Sophonisba, or The Wonder of Women*, was entered in the Stationers' Register and published in the same year. With *Sophonisba* the dramatist breaks, in various ways, new ground. For the first time he draws his plot from classical history, probably using Appian's *Roman History* as his chief source. But, as he tells 'the general reader', he had not laboured

> to tie myself to relate anything as an historian but to enlarge everything as a poet. To transcribe authors, quote authorities, and translate Latin prose orations into English blank verse, hath in this subject been the least aim of my studies.

Here, in spite of their recent collaboration, he seems to be hitting at Jonson, whose *Sejanus* had been published in the previous year. In any case, Marston's treatment of his classical theme is essentially different from Ben's neo-Senecan method. And it is equally remote from Shakespeare's transfiguring art which gives universal significance to the figures in his Roman plays. It has been truly said by the dramatist's latest editor that 'it looks forward to the heroic drama of the age of Dryden, and has more in common with *All for Love* than with any work of its own period'.[1]

The tragic fortunes of Sophonisba, beautiful daughter of the Carthaginian general, Hasdrubal, provided Marston with a subject suitable to his spectacular stage-technique. Wedded to a Libyan king, Massinissa, she surrenders him on their wedding night to the call of Carthage (I. ii):

> *Soph.*   Go, best man,
> And make me proud to be a soldier's wife
> That values his renown above faint pleasures . . .
> *Mass.* Wondrous creature, even fit for gods not men,
> Nature made all the rest of thy fair sex
> As weak essays, to make thee a pattern
> Of what can be in woman.

There is a rival for her love in Syphax, another Libyan king, who has joined the Roman general, Scipio, in his campaign against Carthage. To detach him from this allegiance the Carthaginian Senate arranges to have Massinissa treacherously poisoned and his bride and kingdom bestowed upon Syphax. An honest patriot, Gelosso, reveals the plot to Massinissa, who now leagues himself with Scipio. Meanwhile Sophonisba has been sent to the palace of Syphax at Cirta,

[1] H. Harvey Wood, *Plays of John Marston*, III. xiv.

but she is deaf to his pleading and his threats, and in an ingeniously contrived scene escapes from his chamber through a cave to a forest, where she is followed and again seized by Syphax.

At this point (Act IV. i. 91 ff.) Marston had the unfortunate inspiration of introducing an episode suggested by the invocation to the witch Erictho in Lucan's *De Bello Civili*, Book VI. Syphax summons her to his aid, and she promises to bring Sophonisba to his bed, but herself assumes the loved one's shape to cheat Syphax. But even this unpleasant superfluous scene had its compensation for the Blackfriars audience and the reader of to-day. The stage-directions show how the musical resources of the boys' company were used to build up the scene. 'Infernal music plays softly whilst Erictho enters, and when she speaks, ceaseth'. A song, 'Hark, hark, now rise, infernal tones', is followed by a treble viol, a bass lute, &c., which 'play softly within the canopy', and after this there is another short song, when 'nuptial hymns enforcèd spirits sing'.

Massinissa defeats Syphax in single combat, but spares his life and hastens to Sophonisba. But Scipio orders him to give her up as 'a Roman prisoner to the Senate's doom The Libyan king is torn between his love and his oath of allegiance to Rome. Again Sophonisba, as on their marriage night, proves herself to be the wonder of women (V. iii. 83 ff):

> *Soph.* List to her in whose sole heart it rests
>   To keep thy faith upright.
> *Mass.*   Wilt thou be slaved?
> *Soph.* No, free,
> *Mass.*   How then keep I my faith?
> *Soph.*   My death
>   Gives help to all. From Rome so rest we free;
>   So brought to Scipio, faith is kept in thee.

She drinks poisoned wine, and the play ends with the mournful solemnity of Massinissa presenting Sophonisba's body to the Roman general:

> Look, Scipio, see what hard shift we make
> To keep our vows. Here, take, I yield her thee.
> And Sophonisba, I keep vow, thou'rt still free.

In the face of such a moving and finely wrought climax it
is a perverse criticism that dismisses the whole play as
'second-rate in both design and execution'. A poetic dramatist of to-day is at any rate nearer the mark when he
singles out *Sophonisba* as the best of Marston's plays. In
dealing with his classical theme he has achieved a broad
simplicity of plan and, except in the Erictho episode, he has
restrained his impetuous torrent of speech within the bounds
of pregnant and effective dialogue.

Sophonisba was probably Marston's last extant completed
play. In June 1608 he was again in trouble with the government and was committed to Newgate. It has been conjectured that he was the author of a piece acted at the
Blackfriars satirising the king's interest in Scottish mines,
and known only through contemporary allusions.[1] His imprisonment may have prevented his finishing *The Insatiate
Countess*, published with his name in 1613, anonymously in
1616, and in 1631 in two issues, one of which assigned it to
him and the other to William Barksteed. It was not included
in the collected edition of his plays in 1633. If Marston had
the chief hand in the play it was an astonishing recoil from
the picture of the 'wonder of women' to that of the deliriously
lustful Countess Isabella, whom he found in Painter's *Palace
of Pleasure*. There is nothing in the treatment, except
occasional poetic flashes, to make the theme more plausible
or less unpleasant. And an equivocal underplot, also derived
from Painter, though it has ingenious complications, is
almost swamped in a deluge of gutter-snipe vocabulary.

No work could have been a less fitting prelude to Marston's
ordination in 1609, and his presentation in 1616 to the living
of Christchurch in Hampshire, which he resigned in 1631,
three years before his death in London on 25 June 1634 and

[1] E. K. Chambers, *Elizabethan Stage*, II. 53–4.

his burial in the Temple Church on the following day. There are few stranger contrasts in stage-history than between Marston's feverishly active decade of play-making and the obscurity of his quarter of a century as a parish priest.

THOMAS DEKKER

Though to a less extent than with Marston recent research has added some important particulars to the biographical record of Thomas Dekker. Neither the date nor the exact place of his birth has however yet been identified. But in the dedicatory epistle to his prose tract, *English Villanies* (1632) he speaks of his 'three-score years', indicating that he was born in or about 1572. And in another tract, *The Seven Deadly Sins of London* (1606), he apostrophises the capital, 'from whose womb received I my being', but does not specify further the locality. Nothing more is known about him till January 1597/8, when Henslowe records payment to him as a playwright, followed on 4 February 1598/9 by another payment of forty shillings to discharge him from the Counter prison. Henceforward plays, often written in collaboration, and prose pamphlets came in quick succession from his pen. A brief notice of some of the pamphlets, which show Dekker's exceptional knowledge of varied phases of London life, and which serve as biographical landmarks, may here precede the discussion of his plays. In *This Wonderful Year* (1603) and *A Rod for Runaways* (1625) he anticipates Defoe in his realistic descriptions of the visitations of the plague in those two years. There is further reference to the plague in *Work for Armourers* (1609), but the pamphlet deals with many of the darker aspects of London life which give Dekker an opportunity for the display of his humanitarian spirit. In lighter satirical vein, published in the same year, is *The Gull's Hornbook*. Here he sketches a day in the life of a young Jacobean gallant, with instructions for his behaviour in the ordinary, the tavern, and theatre and other places of fashionable resort. It still remains a social document of first-rate importance for the period. To the same year, 1609, belongs a work of a very different type, *The Four Birds of Noah's Ark*, a collection of prayers breathing a true spirit of devotion.

Dekker had provided part of the entertainment for King James on 15 March 1604, when he progressed through the City to his coronation at Whitehall.[1] On 29 October 1612, he furnished in *Troja-Nova Triumphans* the mayoral pageant in honour of Sir John Swinerton. Yet his many-sided activities did not save him from again falling on evil days. In 1613 he was once more in prison, and a letter to Edward Alleyn is dated from 'King's Bench, 12 September 1616'. His confinement may even have lasted till 1620, for in *Dekker his Dream*, mainly in verse, published in that year, he speaks of 'the bed in which seven years I lay dreaming', with apparent reference to the period of his imprisonment.

He was again in trouble with the law in February 1625 when, in connexion with proceedings arising out of the performance of the play, *Keep the Widow Waking*, he had to answer Star Chamber interrogations, and on 24 March 1626 undergo examination.[2] In October 1628 and 1629 he was again chosen to furnish the mayoral pageant. The date of his death was till recently in doubt, but the record of his burial on 25 August 1632 has now been found in the registers of St. James's Church, Clerkenwell.

Dekker's two earliest extant plays, *The Shoemaker's Holiday* and *The Comedy of Old Fortunatus*, both published in 1600, were acted before Queen Elizabeth by the Lord Admiral's servants and are therefore, strictly speaking, of Tudor rather than Stuart origin. But they are among the first-fruits of a dramatic activity that extended into the Caroline period, and *The Shoemaker's Holiday*, performed on New Year's Day 1600, gives a picture of citizen-life in London which can have been little affected by the change of dynasty. Here, as in *Eastward Ho*, the tradesfolk of the city are shown in relation to their social superiors, but they fill more of the

[1] See above, p. 83.   [2] See below, pp. 164–5.

centre of the stage and are drawn with even greater sympathy and understanding. Simon Eyre, the 'true shoemaker and a gentleman of the gentle craft', is one of the most vital figures in the range of Elizabethan comedy. With exuberant pride in his vocation he cries, 'Prince am I none, yet am I nobly born, as being the sole son of a shoemaker'. This pride includes also his workmen, Hodge the foreman and Firk the journeyman, 'my fine knaves, you arms of my trade, you pillars of my profession'. When by a stroke of fortune he suddenly becomes rich and is elected sheriff of the city his first thought, after his wife who will be made a lady, is for them. 'Where be my fine men? Roger, I'll make over my shop and tools to thee; Firk, thou shalt be the foreman.' When he reaches the peak of civic dignity as Lord Mayor, he is still his jovial, warm-hearted self. 'By the Lord of Ludgate, it's a mad life to be a Lord Mayor; it's a stirring life, a fine life, a velvet life, a careful life.' On the same day that the king comes to dine with him he entertains also his fellow prentices of London; 'they shall have fine cheer, gentleman-like cheer.' And as a perpetual memorial of his mayoralty he procures that every Shrove Tuesday shall be a shoe-makers' holiday.

Deftly intertwined with the realistic scenes are two love-stories of followers of the gentle craft. Ralph, Eyre's junior journeyman, is pressed for a soldier and torn from his newly married wife, Jane, who during his absence works in a shop as a sempstress. Here she is courted by Hammon, a rich citizen, who deludes her into a promise of marriage by a false report that Ralph has been killed in the wars. But he has only lost a leg and comes back to his old trade, just in time, with the help of his fellow-shoemakers, to rescue her from Hammon outside the church where she is to be made his bride.

Hammon is ingeniously made a link with the other, major, love-plot, for he has previously wooed in vain Rose, the daughter of Sir Roger Oately, Eyre's predecessor as Lord Mayor. She has given her love to the scapegrace but nobly born Lacy, nephew of the Earl of Lincoln. It throws a vivid light on the Elizabethan caste system that not only does the Earl violently oppose the match, but that the Lord Mayor himself declares:

> Too mean is my poor girl for his high birth,
> Poor citizens must not with courtiers wed.

Lincoln believes that all will go well, for he has procured Lacy's appointment as chief colonel of some companies ready to serve in France. But Lacy, who during his travels had served as a shoemaker at Wittenberg, seeks employment with Eyre in the disguise of Hans, a Fleming, and when carrying a pair of shoes to Rose, arranges for them to be married secretly. Lincoln, hearing that she has taken flight with a shoemaker, guesses the truth and tries to stop the wedding, but is duped by Firk into laying hands on Ralph and Jane after she has been rescued from Hammon. Lacy's desertion of his military post is pardoned by the indulgent king on the ground that it was not due to cowardice but love, and as a truly democratic ruler he bids Lincoln remember

> that love respects no blood;
> Cares not for difference of birth or state.
> The maid is young, well born, fair, virtuous,
> A worthy bride for any gentleman.

And to make up for the honour that he lost in France the King redeems it by knighting Lacy—a gratuitous mark of royal favour but in keeping with the sunny atmosphere of the play.

In astonishing contrast to the realistic characterization and the skilful plot-construction of *The Shoemaker's Holiday* are the nebulous romantic elements and the loose texture of Dekker's other 1600 publication, *Old Fortunatus*. Henslowe records in his *Diary* that the Admiral's men had revived between 3 February and 24 May 1596 '1 parte of *Fortunatus*'. In November 1599 he paid Dekker £6 for 'the hole history of *Fortunatus*', followed by two other payments. The comedy was acted at Court on 27 December 1599. It was entered in the Stationers' Register on 20 February 1600 as 'old Fortunatus in his newe lyverie' and published in the same year. Dekker had thus revised and enlarged an older play, by himself or another. It was based on a German folk-tale which had some affinities with the story of Dr. Faustus. To Fortunatus there is offered by Fortune the choice of one of her gifts, 'wisdom, strength, health, beauty, long life, and riches'. He chooses the last and receives a purse whose wealth will be inexhaustible by him and his two sons. Later at the Court of the Sultan of Babylon he flies away with another talisman, a hat which has the power of transporting its wearer wheresoever he will. With the purse and the hat he boasts himself to be a monarch who grips all the world. But at this moment Fortune strikes him down because he has

> played the ruffian, wasted that in riots
> Which as a blessing I bestowed on thee,

though in the play little has been seen of such excesses. In dying he bestows the purse and hat upon his sons. The prodigal Andelocia seizes on the purse and betakes him to the court of King Athelstan of England, whose daughter, of whom he becomes enamoured, robs him of the purse. In retaliation he claps horns on the heads of the princess and two courtiers, who revenge themselves by strangling him and also doing to death his virtuous brother Ampedo.

A 'pleasant comedy', is a singular title for a piece in which the three chief characters meet with a tragic doom. But it is difficult to classify a play which combines the allegorical figures of a morality, the music and pageantry of a masque, and the naïf supernaturalism of a fairy-tale, transporting the spectators from Cyprus to Babylon and thence to Anglo-Saxon England. It doubtless provided Elizabeth with an enjoyable Christmas entertainment closing with the obeisance of Fortune and Virtue to her as 'sacred deity'. The piece abounds in passages of graceful verse, and Shadow, Andelocia's servant, is an engagingly nimble-witted clown. But

I do not rank *Old Fortunatus* as high among Dekker's plays
as many critics have done.

On the other hand, I think that the attention concentrated
on the relation of *Satiromastix*, published in 1602, to the
poetomachia, discussed in Chapter III, pp. 63–72, has ob-
scured the interest of the main plot of this play on which
the controversial features appear to have been grafted. The
scene is laid in the England of William Rufus, who plays as
unhistorical a part as Athelstan in *Old Fortunatus*. Sir
Quintilian Shorthose is holding a wedding feast on the day
of the marriage of his daughter Celestine to Sir Walter
Terrill. King Rufus attends the feast, becomes inflamed by
the bride's beauty, and dares 'Wat' to send her to the Court
before they spend their first night together. He swears by
'a double-guarded oath' as husband and subject that

> This night untainted by the touch of man
> She shall a virgin come.

Though women are earthly moons that 'change their orbs
(their husbands)' and 'steal to their sweet Endymions', he
knows that his bride is not one of these. And so it proves.
Celestine pleads urgently against being sent to Court, but
Terrill insists on the sanctity of an oath:

> 'Tis law within a man, the seal of faith,
> The bond of every conscience; unto whom
> We set our thoughts like hands; yea such a one
> I swore, and to the King: a King contains
> A thousand thousand; when I swore to him,
> I swore to them.

It is difficult to realize that these words were written
before the accession of the first Stuart king with his doctrine
of divine right. Terrill's situation curiously anticipates that
of Marston's Massinissa when his oath to Scipio compels him
to deliver his Sophonisba to the Romans. And it looks as if
there was to be a similar solution. For Celestine drinks what
she believes is poisoned wine and is borne seemingly lifeless
into the presence of the King; Terrill has kept his oath.

> Here take her, she was mine
> When she was living, but now dead she's thine.

But the drink was only a 'somniferous potion' and Celestine awakens from her trance to be greeted by her wondering husband as 'too constant far to be a woman', and saluted by the repentant King as 'mirror of maidens, wonder of thy name'. This plot gives scope for Dekker's qualities of grace and tenderness which are set against the boisterous comedy of the wooing of the widow Minever by the three rival knights, Sir Quintilian Shorthose himself and two of his guests, Sir Adam Prickshaft and the Welsh Sir Vaughan ap Rees, who all have to own defeat by the military swaggerer, Captain Tucca.

Dekker must have had Terrill and Celestine still in mind when he began *The Honest Whore*,[1] for again a gallant follows the apparently lifeless body of his beloved. Count Hippolito has won the heart of Infelice, daughter of the Duke of Milan, who forbids the match because the Count belongs to a family that has been hostile to his own. The Duke has ordered a doctor to give her a soporiferous draught which brings about the appearance of sudden death, and she is given a stately funeral which her frantic and incredulous lover seeks in vain to stop. When Infelice wakens from her stupor she is told that she was overcome by news of Hippolitos's death, though she protests that she has no such memory, and she is sent to recover at Bergamo. The Duke then seeks to turn the pretence into reality by bribing the doctor to poison Hippolito, which he merely affects to do.

Meanwhile Hippolito's gay friend Matheo believes that he can divert him from his grief by bringing him into the company of his mistress, the harlot Bellafront. But the unforeseen happens. Bellafront falls in love at first sight with Hippolito and swears to him that she would be as loyal 'as a poor gentlewoman could be':

> Therein I'll prove an honest whore
> In being true to one, and to no more.

[1] His name alone appears on the title-page of the 1604 and later editions, but according to Henslowe, Thomas Middleton collaborated in the play.

But he brushes her oath aside as a trick of her trade and in the most burning words that yet had flowed from Dekker's pen unfolds to her the loathesomeness of a harlot's life. In her repentant despair she attempts suicide, rejects all lustful offers and in vain begs Matheo, her first betrayer, to make due recompense by marrying her. Then in page's disguise she forces her way into Hippolito's chamber and entreats his pity. Tenderness and pathos meet in their dialogue, as he points to a picture of Infelice (IV. i):

Hip.   I cannot love thee, nor I must not: see
         The copy of that obligation
         Where my soul's bound in heavy penalties
Bell.   She's dead, you told me, she'll let fall her suit.
Hip.   My vow's to her, fled after her to Heaven.
         Were thine eyes clear as mine, thou might'st behold her
         Watching upon yon battlements of stars,
         How I observe them. Should I break my bond,
         The board would rive in twain, these wooden lips
         Call me most perjured villain. Let it suffice
         I ha' set thee in the path; is't not a sign
         I love thee, when with one so most, most dear,
         I'll have thee fellow? All are fellows there.

This is but cold comfort for Bellafront, who feigns madness and betakes herself to the Bethlem monastery, where Dekker has London rather than Milan in mind and where, with little plausibility, he collects his *dramatis personae* at the close of the play. It is here, of all places, that the doctor arranges for Hippolito and Infelice to meet to be joined in wedlock by friar Anselmo, and here they are pursued by the Duke, who comes too late to prevent their union, and who since 'Fate hath conquered' gives them his blessing. In this moral mood he orders Matheo to make amends to Bellafront by marrying her.

Apart from this strange medley of free-will visitors to Bethlem monastery and from the pitiful group of resident madmen, there is one figure who has been brought there under duress. It is the climax of the humiliations suffered

by the linen-draper Candido, centre of the farcical underplot.
His shop with its display of 'fine hollands, fine cambrics, fine
lawns' is as vividly pictured as that of Simon Eyre, but what
poles apart from the jovial, masterful shoemaker is his meek,
all-enduring fellow tradesman. To humour some mischievous
gallants he will ruin a piece of his costliest lawn by cutting
out a pennyworth from its centre, and even when they run
off with a silver and gilt beaker, instead of prosecuting them,
he invites them to dinner.

When he has to attend a meeting of the Senate in a cere-
monial gown (where Dekker again has London civic custom
in mind), and his wife hides the key of the chest where it is
kept, he makes shift by arraying himself in a 'carpet' or
table-cloth, with holes cut for his head and arms. Finding
on his return his prentice wearing the gown he dons the dress
of a prentice, and speaks as such till his wife has him arrested,
as a madman, and carried to Bethlem. When repenting she
follows him there to beg his release he is still unmoved,
declaring, 'Is patience madness? I'll be a madman still.' The
Duke, after bidding them 'join hearts, join hands', asks
Candido, 'What comfort do you find in being so calm?' His
answer lifts the underplot at its close to an unexpectedly lofty
level:

> Patience, my lord; why, 'tis the soul of peace;
> Of all the virtues 'tis nearest kin to Heaven,
> It makes men look like gods. The best of men
> That e'er wore earth about him was a sufferer,
> A soft, meek, patient, humble, tranquil spirit,
> The first true gentleman that ever breathed!

Though a good many plays of the period have a second
part, *The Honest Whore* is singular in having waited for a
quarter of a century for this addition. And it is equally
curious that its outstanding figure should be one who had
received only a casual mention in the first part—Bellafront's
father, Orlando Friscobaldo, who plays a part more characteristic of Chapman's than of Dekker's technique, holding in
his hands all the main threads of the action and in particular

watching in disguise over the daughter whom he had discarded when she turned to sin. In order to show that Bellafront's conversion is real and that she remains 'honest' with every temptation to relapse, Dekker has to darken other of the figures in the play. Matheo, now her husband, had in the first part been a dissolute scapegrace, but he is now degraded into the vilest of scoundrels who that he may 'fly high' is ready to sell his wife's honour and to pawn the very clothes off her back. And what is still more difficult to accept, her saviour Hippolito now reverses his role and tempts her again to sin. Stuart drama can show no more paradoxical passage than the dialogue in Act IV. i, where Hippolito delivers a defence of the harlot's vocation and Bellafront rebuts it with a counter-plea.

It is the disguised Friscobaldo who furnishes Infelice with the letter, ring, and purse that are the proofs of her husband's purposed infidelity. And one of the most effective situations in the play is where Infelice by a false confession of guilt traps Hippolito into an indictment of the frailty of women and then turns the tables on him with a mocking echo of his own words (III. i):

> O men,
> You were created angels pure and fair,
> But since the first fell, worse than devils you are.
> You should our shields be, but you prove our rods.
> Were there no men, women might live like gods.

Friscobaldo puts Bellafront to the hardest test of all when in Act IV. i he appears for a while undisguised and rejects her starving petition to save her from renewed shame:

> That cunning bawd, necessity, night and day
> Plots to undo me; drive that hag away,
> Lest being at lowest ebb, as now I am,
> I sink for ever.

Frisc.   Lowest ebb, what ebb?

Bell.   So poor, that though to tell it be my shame,
> I am not worth a dish to hold my meat:
> I am yet poorer, I want bread to eat.

Frisc.   It's not seen by your cheeks.

But her plight tears at his heart-strings and to save her from further outrage by Matheo, he gets a warrant from the Duke for his arrest on the charge of robbing two pedlars, who are in reality Friscobaldo's servants. But the Duke is more gravely concerned with his son's infatuation with Bellafront, and he orders a wholesale arrest of the city harlots, including her. Thus the second part closes in Bridewell (transported from London to Milan) after a fashion closely parallel to the Bethlem scenes in the first part. There is even the repellent succession of three harlots on the stage to balance that of the three madmen. It is Friscobaldo, once more throwing off his disguise, who cuts all the knots by declaring that his daughter is honest, her husband a knave (though with a chance still to mend), and the supposed pedlars his own servants. He thus releases too the linen-draper, Candido, now matched with a second wife as patient as himself, who has been the innocent receiver of the goods stolen from the counterfeit pedlars, and thus as undeservedly lodged in Bridewell as formerly in Bethlem.

In such parallel adjustment of the two parts of *The Honest Whore* Dekker shows much technical skill, and his command over dialogue in verse, and even more in prose, shows to full advantage. Friscobaldo is one of his most original creations and has received eloquent acclaim. Bellafront in her sufferings and constancy gains something of sacrificial lustre. But I wish that this could have been won at some other price than Hippolito's fall from grace and the attempted violation of his vows to the so hardly won Infelice.

The Whore of Babylon, entered in the Stationers' Register in April 1607, and published in the same year, was acted by Prince Henry's servants, formerly the Lord Admiral's men. It may have been a revision of their play, *Truth's Supplication to Candlelight*, for which Henslowe records a payment to Dekker in January 1600 and the purchase of a robe for Time in the following April. Truth and Time, but not Candlelight, appear in *The Whore of Babylon*, which in any case belongs in its present form to the reign of James I, to whom there is a flattering reference as 'a second Phoenix'. The play has little of either Dekker's realistic or romantic vein, but is a crudely serious and allegorical dramatization of recent history. Elizabeth appears as Titania, the fairy queen, contrasted with the Empress of Babylon (more coarsely designated in the title) representing the Papacy.

A number of the leading events of the Queen's reign are represented under the thinnest disguise. She is wooed in vain by Spain, France, and Rome, but grants her favours to the Low Countries. Paridel (Parry), Campeius (Campion), and Lopeus (Lopez) conspire against her. Dekker shows something of his true dramatic quality when he represents Campeius as tempted into the service of Babylon by the prospect of rewards which his own country had denied to his learned attainments:

> In disputation
> I dare for Latin, Hebrew, and the Greek
> Challenge an University; yet (O evil hap!)
> Three learned languages cannot set a nap
> Upon this threadbare gown: how is Art curs'd!
> She has the sweetest limbs and goes the worst.

The most effective moment in the play is when Titania hesitates to seal the doom of a former favourite, evidently Essex, though the allusion to him is only metaphorical, 'the moon that from your beams did borrow light'.

> Must we then
> Strike those whom we have lov'd? Albeit the children
> Whom we have nourished at our princely breast
> Set daggers to it, we could be content
> To chide, not beat them (might we use our will);
> Our hand was made to save, but not to kill.

When she is exhorted not to spare him because of his noble birth, she signs the death-warrant with a grim flourish:

> Give me his axe . . . how soon the blow is given!
> Witness, so little we in blood delight
> That doing this work, we wish we could not write.

There is the true voice of Dekker and we hear it again in different tone in the answer to Titania's query concerning the Armada, 'Why swells this fleet?'

> Thus they give out that you sent forth a Drake
> Which from their rivers beat their water-fowl,
> Tore silver feathers from their fairest swans,
> And plucked the halcyons' wings that rove at sea,
> And made their wild-ducks under water dive
> So long that some never came up alive.

In his account of the great sea-fight Dekker embodies too much statistical material to make it dramatically effective, but it is proof of the theatrical appeal of the victory twenty years afterwards. But there is one event whose omission is eloquent. With James upon the throne there could be no allusion to the execution of his mother, Mary Queen of Scots.

In 1612 was published *If this be not a Good Play, the Devil is in It*, 'a new play, as it hath been lately acted, with great applause, by the Queen's Majesty's servants: at the Red Bull'. As reference is made to the murder of Henry IV of France on 14 May 1610, the play must be later than that date. Its technique bears a general likeness to that of *The Whore of Babylon* in that it combines in a series of dissolving views supernatural and historical characters. But the latter fill a much smaller space, and instead of Titania and her fairies there are Pluto and his infernal agents, whence the play gets the latter half of its title. As to the other half, opinions will differ as to whether the piece is a 'good' one, according as it is judged as a whole or from individual scenes. In any case Dekker must have the credit of adapting and expanding in dramatic form the English prose version of the continental story of *Friar Rush* and of having 'stumbled upon the very idea afterwards carried out in Goethe's *Faust*, —the recasting of an old devil-story in terms of modern society'.[1]

[1] C. H. Herford, *Studies in the Literary Relations of England and Germany in the Sixteenth Century*, 317. Herford first pointed out the relation between the English *Friar Rush* and Dekker's play.

This story told how a devil, in the disguise of a friar, corrupted a monastery. He is an agent of the arch-fiend who in the English *Friar Rush* holds an infernal council before sending him to earth. The idea there given is effectively worked up by Dekker. Pluto appears in a violent quarrel with Charon, who refuses to be any longer 'Hell's drudge, her galley-slave', unless his fare for each soul ferried over is raised to twopence. Then follow three devils, Roughman, Shacklesoul, and Lurchall, each of whom is despatched on a special mission. To Shacklesoul is allotted the original role of Friar Rush, who serving in the kitchen of a strict Neapolitan monastery incites the inmates to gluttony and to the further vices that flow from it. But even to this basic part of the legend Dekker adds a pathetically attractive figure, the virtuous Sub-Prior, who when all his brethren are falling away from grace resists every temptation—even the bait of gold to which Friar Rush feels sure that he will succumb.

Lurchall's sphere of operations is the city where he becomes clerk to Baskervile, a close-fisted, usurious trader. Dekker thus has the opportunity of presenting another picture of the city life which he knew so well. The opening stage-direction in this scene carries with it an office atmosphere.

A table is set out by young fellows like merchants' men, books of accounts upon it, small desks to write upon. They sit down to write tickets, Lurchall with them.

Prompted by his clerk, Baskervile plunges into even lower depths of fraud and villainy, till he meets his fit doom in being carried by Lurchall down to hell.

A more singular addition by Dekker to the story is the mission assigned to Roughman, who becomes the tempter of the newly crowned King of Naples. This youthful monarch, in the spirit of the modern slogan, one good deed a day, dedicates to each week-day a specific beneficent act. But while he is considering Saturday, Roughman, a 'Helvetian', is announced and counsels him to devote the day to pleasure.

Henceforth, in spite of the warnings of his two uncles, his course is one of dissipation and lawlessness. He even refuses to receive Erminhild, daughter of the Duke of Calabria, his affianced bride. She is one of Dekker's affectionately constant women, and when her father wages war on her behalf against Naples she entreats him not to injure the king. She thus doubly becomes his saviour, for overcome by her loyalty the king begs her forgiveness and escapes not only the dangers of battle but the damnation to which Roughman had consigned him. This scene of reconciliation takes place in the monastery where by an ingenious technique parallel to that at the close of the two parts of *The Honest Whore* Dekker assembles all the chief characters. There follows a lurid *finale*, which doubtless earned part of the 'great applause' for the play, where the devils are shown 'leaping in great joy, discovering behind a curtain' Ravaillac, Guy Faux, and others standing in their torments. However much the presentation of these may have appealed to the Red Bull audience, we feel to-day that Marlowe showed finer dramatic insight when we did not attempt to follow Faustus into Hell.

One other play, *Match me in London*, apparently belongs to Dekker's later years. It was entered in the Stationers' Register late in November 1630, and published in the following year. It must have been written before 21 August 1623, when Herbert licensed it for the Lady Elizabeth's servants acting at the Cockpit as an old play formerly allowed by Sir George Buck. But Dekker, in his dedication of it to Lodowick Carlell, speaks of himself as 'a priest in Apollo's temple many years' and laments that his voice is 'decaying with my age'. Though the play has found its modern admirers, I think that Dekker's apologetic tone is justified. The scenes in the shop of the linen-draper, Cordolente, lack the buoyancy of those in which his fellow tradesman, Candido, had displayed his wares. And the pursuit of his wife, Tormiella, by a former suitor, favoured by her father, and by a violently enamoured king, is on well-worn lines. But Tormiella can claim to close the procession of devotedly constant women in Dekker's single-handed plays.

To the plays from his own pen there has to be added a mass of collaborative work too large and varied to be enumerated in full here. *The Virgin Martyr*, with Philip Massinger, is discussed below.[1] He took part with the youthful John Webster in the historical piece, *The Famous History of Sir Thomas Wyat* and in the two merry comedies of intrigue, *Westward Ho* and *Northward Ho*, printed in 1607, of which the former seems to have preceded and the latter to have followed *Eastward Ho*. His was probably the major hand in *The Roaring Girl*, written by him and Middleton, acted by Prince Henry's men at the Fortune, and published in 1611. It was characteristic of Dekker in this lively comedy to represent the contemporary virago Moll Cutpurse in an unduly favourable light. She touches pitch without herself being defiled, passing among rogues and thieves, in whose canting slang she shows herself an adept, and giving kind-hearted help to those in trouble. He shared with John Ford in *The Sun's Darling: A Moral Masque* (March 1623/4) and with Ford and William Rowley in *The Witch of Edmonton*, acted by Prince Charles's men at the Cockpit in 1621 and at Court on 29 December of that year, but not published till 1658. The play was topical and probably written rapidly. It was intended to exploit the popular interest in the execution of Elizabeth Sawyer on a charge of witchcraft, as set forth in a pamphlet, now non-extant, by Henry Goodcole. But it needs the genius of a Marlowe or a Shakespeare to transfigure such supernatural themes. The Mother Sawyer of the play, though she doubtless drew plaudits from the Cockpit and Court audiences, just fails to be either sufficiently impressive or pathetic. So long as she is an old bent crone, falsely accused of being a witch, beaten and ill-used, she excites pity. But when, like Faustus, she sells herself, body and soul, to the devil, in the shape of a black dog 'familiar',

[1] See 304-6.

and uses him to wreak spiteful vengeance on her enemies, she forfeits sympathy without exciting terror.

In the loosely connected secondary plot the balance of interest is again somewhat similarly disturbed. Frank Thorney seems the gallant lover when he braves his father's anger by marrying secretly Winnifred, Sir Arthur Clarington's maid, who is with child. But to avert the threatened sale of the estate that he would inherit he consents to make a second match with Susan, daughter of the rich yeoman, Carter, who brings him a large wedding dowry. Stuart drama is fertile in marriage complications, but Frank's bigamy is almost unique and his situation is highly equivocal. But it leads to a finely-wrought scene (III. ii) between the two 'wives', when Susan welcomes Winnifred in boy's disguise as attendant on Frank:

> Thou may'st be servant, friend, and wife to him:
> A good wife is them all. A friend can play
> The wife and servant's part, and shift enough:
> No less the servant can the friend and wife.

With a deeper meaning than Susan realizes, Winnifred assures her:

> I'll be all your charge,
> Servant, friend, wife to him.

Frank seeks deliverance from his dire entanglement by stabbing Susan to death with his knife and accusing two suitors of her and her sister as the murderers. But this results from contact with the devil-dog, and it is this strange fiend that later impels Susan's sister, Kate, to the discovery under Frank's vest of the bloody knife with which he has done the fatal deed. This supernatural soliciting is all the more irrelevant because Mother Sawyer has no cause of ill-will against Frank or Susan. Nor are we prepared for the witch's edifying end as she is led to execution:

> Bear witness, I repent all former evil;
> There is no damnèd conjurer like the devil.

Frank, too, goes to his doom with prayers for forgiveness

from all whom he has wronged and in the hope that his example

> Might teach the world hereafter what a curse
> Hangs on their heads who rather choose to marry
> A goodly portion than a dower of virtues.

It is not, however, in its moral lessons or its plot that the attraction of the *Witch of Edmonton* now lies. This is to be found in the tender loyalty of Winnifred and Susan to Frank, in the racy picture of the yeoman and his household; and in the simplicity, at once laughable and affecting, of Cuddy Banks, with his fellow morris-dancers, who sees in the witch 'a motherly woman', and to whom the devil-dog is 'a fine gentle cur, and well brought up, I warrant him'.

It is tempting to see in Winnifred and Susan, and in Cuddy, typical Dekker figures, but with a trio of collaborators such identification, however plausible, is necessarily speculative. It is a paradox that the only composite play in which Dekker's part is beyond doubt is not extant. In *The Late Murder in Whitechapel, or Keep the Widow Waking*, performed at the Red Bull in September 1624, probably by Prince Charles's men, he again had Rowley and Ford and also Webster as his associates in a rapidly written topical piece, about which remarkable details have recently been discovered in legal records.[1] At the Old Bailey on 3 September 1624 Nathaniel Tindall was found guilty of the murder of his mother in Whitechapel on the previous 4 April and was afterwards executed. On the same day at the Old Bailey Tobias Audley, a young tobacconist, was put on trial for felony against Anne Elsdon, a rich old widow, whom he had married on 23 July, when she was in a drunken coma, and whom he had afterwards ill-treated and plundered. He was remanded to Newgate. The case was later transferred to the Star Chamber, and dragged on till the summer of 1626, but before then both Audley and the widow had died.

In the Bill of Information laid before the Star Chamber on

[1] See C. J. Sisson, *Lost Plays of Shakespeare's Age* (1936), 80–124.

26 November 1624 Dekker, Rowley, and others were accused of conspiring with Audley and his confederates, and of devising 'one scandalous interlude or play' to the great disgrace of Anne Elsdon, called *Keep the Widow Waking*. It is from the deposition of Dekker himself that we learn that with this low comedy plot of which a contemporary ballad gives the details, there had been incongruously combined the sensational Whitechapel matricide. Dekker told the court that he had written the first act of the play and 'a speech in the last scene of the last act of the boy who had killed his mother'. He thus both introduced and concluded a catch-penny theatrical venture which did little credit to any of the quartet who had hands in it. It is an irony that Dekker to whom we owe some of the pleasantest stage-pictures of contemporary London life should thus, on his own confession, be found making dramatic capital near the close of his career out of some of the seamiest episodes in the capital's underworld.

VII

THOMAS HEYWOOD

ROMANTIC AND CHRONICLE-HISTORY PLAYS—
DOMESTIC DRAMAS

THOMAS HEYWOOD, to an even greater degree than Dekker and for a longer period, was a versatile writer in many fields in addition to that of drama. Heywood, according to his own testimony, was a native of Lincolnshire, and his latest biographer makes it probable that he was a son of Robert Heywood, rector of Rothwell and of Ashby-cum-Fenby, and that he was born after July 1573 and before 1575.[1] He was probably the Thomas Heywood who entered Emmanuel College, Cambridge, as a pensioner, about 1591; the statement in 1658, twenty-seven years after his death, that he had been a Fellow of Peterhouse, is of doubtful value.

From Cambridge he seems to have proceeded direct to London and to have taken a part at once in dramatic work. It has been plausibly suggested that his peculiarly difficult writing is that of hand B in the play of *Sir Thomas More*. On 14 October 1596 Henslowe notes a loan of 30 shillings 'for hawodes bocke', evidently a play that had been commissioned for the Admiral's men. Heywood must have been an actor as well as a dramatist, for on 25 March 1598 he entered into a contract with Henslowe as his 'covenant servant' not to play anywhere publicly about London for two years except in his house, which was then the Rose. Other plays from his pen are noted by Henslowe, and in *Palladis Tamia* Meres already includes him among 'the best for comedy'. After the close of his engagement with Henslowe he became associated as actor, sharer, and dramatist with the Earl of Worcester's company, and when their title was changed to Queen Anne's men he appears third in the list of them in a draft patent.

[1] See A. M. Clark, *Thomas Heywood* (1931), 1–6.

Between 1600 and 1608 some of Heywood's earlier plays had appeared in print. In the latter year he turned his pen to account in a different field by publishing a translation, at second hand through a French version, of Sallust's two historical memoirs, *Catiline* and *Jugurtha*. This was followed in 1609 by an excursion into more legendary classical antiquity in *Troia Britannica*, a poem of seventeen cantos, almost throughout in *ottava rima*. Here Heywood skilfully versifies a succession of episodes from Greek mythology, followed by the story of the rise and fall of Troy. In the last cantos, accepting the medieval fanciful genealogy, he traces the descent of the British monarchy from Brutus, the grandson of Aeneas, and the sequence of kings and queens till his own day.

Various points of internal evidence suggest that Heywood's most important prose work, *An Apology for Actors*, was written or revised about the same period as the above translation, though it was not published till 1612. Here Heywood, with a wealth of professional experience to which none of his predecessors could lay claim, plunged vigorously into the long-standing controversy concerning the stage and players in which Gosson and Lodge, Rainolds and Gager had been prominent. It was common to the disputants on either side to base their condemnation or their defence of the theatre and all its works on moral grounds. In this respect Heywood is a man of his age, for he puts in the forefront of his 'apology' for the stage its ethical influence. There is a lofty sense in which this argument holds good, but it is not one that would approve itself to Puritan critics. Heywood was on safer ground when he claimed that the variety of theatrical entertainment in London was 'an ornament to the city', which excited the admiration of foreign visitors. And he struck a more unusual note when he asserted that dramatists and actors had helped to refine English from a rude and unpolished tongue into 'a most perfect and composed language.' But to-day we would gladly exchange some of his general arguments for further enlightening details about the Elizabethan theatre, as when he quotes Thomas Kyd as the author of the anonymous *Spanish Tragedy*.

Of Heywood's domestic life in London little is known. But he appears to have been resident in the Clerkenwell district from about 1603, and he has been conjecturally identified with the 'Thomas Hayward' who on 13 June 1603 married at St.Antholin's Church Anne Butler, a servant to Mr. Venn,[1] though one would have expected his wife to be of higher social status. To this couple at least six children were born by 1615. With a family to provide for, and the fortunes of Queen Anne's company declining, Heywood again fell into financial difficulties. In the dedication of his Γυναικεῖον or *Nine Books of Various History Concerning Women* to the Earl of Worcester in 1624 he spoke of one woman, Care, who never forsakes him day or night. This folio is a huge compilation based chiefly on Heywood's extensive reading of classical and later miscellanies. It has been aptly termed his 'Legend of Good, Bad, and Indifferent Women', from goddesses downwards, though in general it is a defence of the sex against its detractors.

He appears to less advantage in dedicating a reprint in 1631 of Sir Richard Barckley's *The Exemplary Lives* to the disgraced favourite Somerset, who, in spite of his nefarious record, had a singular fascination for the *literati* of the period. In the same year in succession to Dekker he began to provide a series of mayoral pageants, continued in 1632, 1633, 1635, and 1637. In the autumn of 1634 he was flying at still higher game in the composition, with Inigo Jones, of a masque in honour of the king's birthday.[2] About the same time he was producing another of his bulky miscellanies, chiefly in decasyllabic couplets, *The Hierarchy of Blessed Angels*. Drawing mainly upon the pseudo-Dionysius he describes the different ranks of the beings intermediate between God and man, and from other sources gives a

[1] A. M. Clark, *op. cit.*, 57–8.   [2] See below, pp. 397–9.

similar catalogue of devils and of the witches who are their allies and agents.

A further miscellany, *Pleasant Dialogues and Dramas*, was ready for licensing in August 1635, but did not appear till 1637. It included a few short dramatic pieces by Heywood, and some of his prologues and epilogues spoken at public or private performances, together with dialogues from Erasmus, Textor, and Lucian oddly adapted from prose into verse. With untiring industry Heywood continued to pour out pamphlets of very varied types, under his own name or anonymously. Some of the latter have been identified from internal evidence by his biographer, Mr. Clark, who has traced a growing Puritan tendency in these publications of his later years. The final record of him is the entry in the register of St. James's, Clerkenwell, of the burial in the church on 16 August 1641 of 'Tho. Heywood, Poet'.

The Four Prentises of London: With the Conquest of Jerusalem is probably the earliest of Heywood's extant plays. In his prefatory epistle to the quarto of 1615 he speaks of it as 'written many years since, in my infancy of judgement in this kind of poetry and my first practice', and asserts that 'as plays were then some fifteen or sixteen years ago it was in the fashion'. Heywood here ignores the achievements before the close of the sixteenth century of Kyd, Marlowe, and Shakespeare, yet no doubt among the groundlings and even those of higher station there was also at that period a welcome for such more artless productions as *The Four Prentises* in which dumb shows and a presenter are employed to eke out the dramatic action. And in spite of its immaturity *The Four Prentises* combines elements which were often to reappear in Heywood's plays—pictures of London civic life, romantic adventure by sea and land, and pseudo-history. The Earl of Boulogne, who has supported William of Normandy in his conquest of England, has been dispossessed by the French king and is living in London as a citizen, where he has apprenticed his four sons to different trades, Godfrey

M

a mercer, Guy a goldsmith, Charles a haberdasher, and
Eustace a grocer. They are content with their humble lot
except the youngest brother, Eustace, who has a severer
master than Dekker's Eyre or Candido.

> Methinks I could endure it for seven years
> Did not my master keep me in too much.
> I cannot go to breakfast in a morning
> With my kind mates and fellow prentises,
> But he cries, 'Eustace, one bid Eustace come'
> And my name 'Eustace' is in every room. . .
> He will allow me not one hour for sport:
> I must not strike a football in the street
> But he will frown; nor view the dancing-school
> But he will miss me straight; not suffer me
> So much as take up cudgels in the street
> But he will chide; I must not go to buffets,
> No, though I be provoked; that's the hell;
> Were't not for this, I could endure it well.

In such intimate touches, different from Dekker's realism,
Heywood already shows something of his distinctive quality.

When the old Earl announces that he is going on pilgrimage
to the Holy Land, and when the drums beat to summon all
who will follow the Conqueror's eldest son, Robert, on a
crusade, they are at once on fire to answer the call, though
they will carry the arms of their several trades in their
ensigns. There follows a succession of wildly romantic
episodes—shipwrecks, fights with banditti, duels between
brothers who fail to recognize each other, with a sentimental
undercurrent supplied by Bella Franca, who has followed her
brothers and finds a mate in the Italian Prince Tancred, and
by the French king's daughter who becomes the bride of
Guy. The crusading brothers speak throughout in the
'Ercles vein:

> *Eust.* Survey me well! brave Hector I resemble,
> Whose very brow did make the Greeks to tremble.
> *Guy.* But I, Achilles, proud ambitious boy,
> Will drag thy corse about the walls of Troy.

Yet amidst all the extravagance, as has been insufficiently

recognized, there are traces of Heywood's dramatic insight. In the pagan host the contrast is skilfully drawn between the old Soldan of Babylon who seeks at first to make terms with the Christians, if they come merely as pilgrims, and the young fire-eating Sophy of Persia, who is for instant war:

> Before the Christians shall attain these walls
> With dead men's faces we will pave the earth.

When the Crusaders have their first sight of Jerusalem their reverent emotion finds touching expression. And when the conquest of the holy city is achieved the investment of the old Earl, reunited to his family, as patriarch, and the refusal of the elder son, Godfrey, to wear any crown but one of thorns, lend an unexpected element to an otherwise too symmetrical close.

The combination of domestic scenes, romantic adventure, and a historical background reappears at a considerably later date in Heywood's dramatic activity and in a much maturer form in the two-part play, *The Fair Maid of the West*, published in 1631, 'as it was lately acted before the King and Queen with approved liking' by Queen Henrietta's company. As the prologue and epilogue were 'spoken to their two Majesties at Hampton Court', this performance took place there. It has been conjectured that Part I was originally acted at a much earlier date.

The Crusaders are now replaced by the Elizabethan gallants setting out from Plymouth in a somewhat similar spirit with the Earl of Essex in 1597 on the island voyage to the Azores to do battle with the Spaniards:

> How the streets
> Glister with gold! You cannot meet a man
> But tricked in scarf and feather that it seems
> As if the pride of England's gallantry
> Were harboured here.

Among this 'brave society' is a gentleman of fortune, Captain Spencer, enamoured of Bess Bridges, a tavern wench, the fair maid of the west, to defend whom from insult he kills a man. Before setting sail he bestows on Bess his trunks and picture and his Windmill Tavern at Foy in Cornwall, whither he bids her depart. When he reaches Fayal in the Azores misfortune still dogs him. Intervening in a duel he is wounded, as he thinks, to death, and commissions his friend Goodlack to carry to Bess at Foy his legacy of five hundred pounds a year, which she is, to forfeit to Goodlack if he finds that there is any scandal on her name. It is, however, spotless, and Goodlack's own attempts, for the annuity's sake, to defame her break down before her devotion, where Heywood sounds one of his most tender notes, to Spencer's picture (III. v):

> O thou, the perfect semblance of my love,
> And all that's left of him, take one sweet kiss
> As my last farewell! Thou resemblest him
> For whose sweet safety I was every morning
> Down on my knees, and with the lark's sweet tunes
> I did begin my prayers; and when sad sleep
> Had charmed all eyes, when none save the bright stars
> Were up and waking, I remembered thee;
> But all, all to no purpose.

From this point the action develops on wildly romantic lines. Bess uses her legacy to fit out a ship to bring back the body of Spencer from Fayal, but he had recovered from his wound and it was another Englishman of the same name whose death had been reported to Goodlack. By a series of hairbreadth adventures, including sea-fights with the Spaniards, Bess and Spencer are brought in separate ships to Morocco. Here the King of Fez is captivated by the charms of the English maid and under her influence plays the part of the noble savage, tempering justice with mercy and finally uniting her to her long-lost lover. But again amidst so much that is extravagant fantasy Heywood keeps in sure touch with some realities. The constancy of Bess shines throughout with a radiant glow, while the brave spirit of Elizabethan gallants and sea-dogs, and the salt-breezes of the Spanish Main, give a refreshing verve and tang to the play.

Part II opens with another of the surprises which are not uncommon, as has been seen, in Elizabethan stage sequels. The hitherto chivalrous king and his queen, Tota, have lustful designs on Bess and Spencer on their very marriage night, but are tricked into each other's arms. Meanwhile, Bess and Goodlack escape to her ship in the harbour, but Spencer has perforce to remain behind. An incredibly altruistic Bashaw is so touched by his woes that he gives him leave to follow Bess to the ship and is prepared to answer for this with his life. Once more Heywood amidst preposterous happenings touches a chord of true humanity. For Spencer, in spite of the pleadings of his bride, returns at the appointed hour and saves the Bashaw's head. But not to save his own life will he obey the command to surrender his bride:

> Wert thou the king of all the kings on earth,
> Could'st thou lay all their sceptres, robes and crowns
> Here at my feet, and had'st power to instal me
> Emperor of th' universal Empery,
> Rather than yield my basest ship-boy up
> To become thy slave, much less betray my bride
> To thee and to thy brutish lust, know, King
> Of Fez, I'ld die a hundred thousand deaths first.

But he is spared his self-sacrifice by the return of Bess with Goodlack and Roughman, who offer themselves for execution, 'three for one', and so move the king by their noble action that he grants life and liberty to all and bestows on Bess an ample dowry. With this anticipation of some of the sentimental flights of Restoration heroic drama Part II of *The Fair Maid of the West* should have closed. But there were still two acts to be filled in, and here Heywood reverts very nearly to his more primitive technique in *The Four Prentises*. With the aid of a chorus and a dumb-show Bess and Spencer are again parted during a fight with pirates on their homeward voyage. Three Italian dukes become enamoured of the lovely Englishwoman, and through a strange mischance she has to suffer an apparently cruel repulse by her

husband before they are finally restored to each other's
arms.

In Act V of *The Fair Maid of the West*, Part I, Heywood
eulogized Queen Elizabeth as

> The only phoenix of her age,
> The pride and glory of the Western Isles.

In the first part of the singularly titled play, *If You Know
Not Me, You Know Nobody*, published by Nathaniel Butter
in two parts in 1605 and 1606 respectively, he had already
made her the centre of a chronicle-history play. Many years
afterwards Heywood in a prologue written for a revival at
the Cockpit protested against the 'most corrupted copy'
issued by Butter without his consent. The play, he asserts,

> Did throng the seats, the boxes and the stage
> So much that some by stenography drew
> The plot: put it in print (scarce one word true).

Yet in its mangled form it gained remarkable popularity, for
by 1632 eight editions had appeared of Part I without any
material textual alteration, and by the same date four of
Part II, the last of which has an extended version of the
closing episode.

Whatever the crimes of the stenographer may have been
it is difficult to suppose that the piece was ever anything else
than a loosely jointed affair in the kaleidoscopic style of *The
Four Prentises*. But though dramatically of little value
Part I is of interest as one of the few plays dealing with
Elizabeth before she became queen and as indicating that a
presentation of her early 'troubles' appealed to popular
sentiment after her death. Throughout she bears herself
with dignity and proves herself an adept in verbal fence.
When the Bishop of Winchester and the Constable of the
Tower try to prove her guilty of treason she scornfully rejects
the charge:

Const.   Madam,
> The Queen must hear you sing another song
> Before you part with us.

Eliz.   My God doth know
    I can no note but truth; that with heaven's King
    One day in choirs of angels I shall sing.
Winch. Then, madam, you will not submit?
Eliz.   My life I will, but not as guilty.
    My lords, let pale offenders pardon crave:
    If we offend, law's rigour let us have.

When Sir Henry Beningfield refuses to let her have ink and paper because it is not in his commission, she cries,

    Good jailer, be not so severe.
Bening. Good madam, I entreat you, lose that name
    Of jailer; 'twill be a by-word to me and my posterity.
Eliz.   As often as you name your commission,
    So often will I call you jailer.

Contrasted with her persecutors are those who seek to lighten her sufferings, Gage, Sussex, Gresham, and, above all, King Philip. The favourable light in which the foreign and Roman Catholic king is shown is one of the most striking features of the play. This is all the more remarkable because it closes with a ringing Protestant panegyric on the open Bible from the lips of Elizabeth, who on her accession is presented with a copy by the Lord Mayor:

    This book that hath so long concealed itself,
    So long shut up, so long hid, now, lords, see
    We here unclasp: for ever it is free.
    Who looks for joy let him this book adore;
    This is true food for rich men and for poor.

Part II is only in the loosest sense a sequel to Part I. During more than two-thirds of the play the queen disappears and the central figure is the wealthy and benevolent London merchant, Thomas Gresham, whose one failing is his quarrel with another notable citizen, Sir Thomas Ramsey, which is composed by the Dean of St. Paul's. The dean further improves the occasion by showing the pictures of a number of former charitable citizens, and Gresham is thus fired to his great enterprise of building a 'Burse', 'a place for merchants to assemble in'. The pictures of all British sovereigns 'from Brute unto our Queen Elizabeth', with which he planned to embellish it, are lost in the wreck of one of his ships; a new king of Barbary repudiates a contract in which Gresham had invested £60,000. But in the true spirit of a royal merchant he proceeds with his design till the building, 'stately, fair and strong', is completed, and is opened by Elizabeth herself, who christens it the Royal Exchange and knights its founder. A somewhat laborious comic element is supplied by Gresham's scapegrace nephew, John, and his employer, the worthy haberdasher, Old Hobson, who in his humbler grade rivals Gresham's civic patriotism, and when the queen sends to borrow from him a hundred pounds forces double the sum upon her messenger. Heywood proves himself a genuine interpreter of the spirit of London, but he lacks Dekker's power of realistic portraiture of city life, and he encumbers his dialogue with too much prosaic detail. This is also true of the account of the defeat of the Armada related by three 'posts' in the last act which is quite unconnected with the fortunes of Gresham and his 'Burse'.

The chronicle-history method of *If You Know Not Me, You Know Nobody* was applied by Heywood to the legendary annals of Rome in *The Rape of Lucrece*, first published in 1608 as acted by the Queen's servants at the Red Bull, and reprinted with some revision and additional songs four times by 1638. If, as has been conjectured, Heywood was influenced by the appearance of an edition of Shakespeare's *Lucrece* in 1607, and drew Tarquin and Tullia after the model of Macbeth and his wife, the play must have been published soon after its performance. In any case it has nothing of higher dramatic quality than the opening scenes where Tullia urges her husband to kill her father, the aged King Servius:

> I am no wife of Tarquin's, if not king . . .
> Thou art a man: oh, bear my royal mind,
> Mount heaven and see if Tullia lag behind.
> There is no earth in me, I am all fire;
> Were Tarquin so, then should we both aspire;

and the murder itself in the Capitol with its swift verbal thrust and parry followed by the clash of steel in which Servius is slain and is trodden under foot by Tullia. Thenceforward Heywood keeps in touch with Livy's narrative, though he foreshortens the historical perspective by introducing prematurely the Etruscan king Porsena's assault on Rome and the exploits of Horatius and Mutius Scevola.

Of the scenes concerning the heroine of the play Heywood succeeds best with the lively banquet in the camp when the Roman lords decide to visit their wives without warning at night; and the domestic interior where Lucrece sits up late waiting with her maids, and offers her husband and her other unexpected visitors 'such welcome as a poor unprovided house can yield'. The scenes in which Tarquin's son, Sextus, violates the chastity of Lucrece and in which she denounces him to her husband, father, and friends before taking her own life go somewhat heavily, but in the closing episodes where vengeance overtakes the house of Tarquin, above all the ravisher Sextus, there are renewed fire and movement. But the popularity of the play evidently was largely due to a curiously incongruous feature—'the several songs in their apt places by Valerius, the merry lord among the Roman peers'. How little 'apt' some of these very frolicsome songs are to the central theme of the tragedy may be seen from the addition in an epilogue to the 1638 quarto of one on 'the cries of Rome'; including references to the prisoners of Newgate and to white Worcestershire salt.

In Roman history Heywood found a less abundant mine than in classical mythology. In a fourfold series, *The Golden Age* (1611), *The Silver Age* (1612), *The Bronze Age* (1613), and *The Iron Age* (published in two parts, 1632) he dramatized a succession of episodes from the beginning of Saturn's reign to the fall of Troy. It is the nearest parallel in the Elizabethan theatre to the Miracle Cycles ranging from the Creation to the Last Judgement. The fortunes of the Hellenic gods and heroes might have been deemed caviare to the general in the Stuart age. But *The Golden Age* was 'sundry times acted at the Red Bull' by Queen Anne's servants and won 'the approbation of auditors', and *The Silver Age* was performed at Court. And so fertile a pen as Heywood's could not fail to provide varied entertainment out of such episodes as Jupiter posing as Amphitryon, the triangle of Mars, Venus, and Vulcan, the labours of Hercules, and the tragic fate of Meleager. *The Iron Age*, though not published till 1632, was probably produced soon after the others. The two parts, as Heywood states, were 'often (and not with the least applause) publicly acted by two companies upon one stage at once, and have at sundry times thronged three several theatres with numerous and mighty auditories'. This, too, is somewhat surprising, though the great figures of the Trojan war, of both sexes, were already familiar on the Elizabethan stage. Heywood could not rival Marlowe's raptures over Helen or Shakespeare's philosophic brooding in *Troilus and Cressida*, but he could make his own appeal by the ingenious fancies with which he embroidered his mighty theme. Thus in Act III of Part I he introduces a banquet scene, during a truce in the hostilities, with Trojan and Greek leaders seated side by side, waited on by royal and other Trojan ladies, and then taking part in a 'lofty dance'. Thereafter Helen is brought in and placed between Paris and Menelaus, who each wooes her anew with antithetical pleas till she decides in favour of Paris, whereupon the strife begins afresh.

Even the four *Ages* did not exhaust Heywood's interest in Greek mythology and legend. His *Pleasant Dialogues and Dramas* (1637) include a number of short pieces on these subjects wherein he acknowledges his debt to Lucian and Ovid and to Renaissance humanists.

Another debt of Heywood to a classical source has been comparatively recently discovered. *The Captives, or The Lost Recovered*, one of the plays in the British Museum MS. volume, Egerton, 1994, was identified by A. H. Bullen as being in

Heywood's peculiarly difficult script and was printed by him in volume IV of *Old English Plays* (1885). It was entered by Sir Henry Herbert in his office-book on 3 September 1624 as a new play for the Cockpit company, 'written by Hayward'. The main plot is closely based on the *Rudens* (the *Rope*) of Plautus. But the scene is shifted from Cyrene in Africa to Marseilles, a modern atmosphere is introduced, and except the heroine Palaestra all the characters are given different names. A girl of unknown parentage, she has fallen into the hands of a brothel-keeper, Mildewe, but she keeps her innocence and is beloved by a young merchant, Raphael, who pays 300 crowns to Mildewe to secure her liberty. But Mildewe proves false, and instead of delivering her to Raphael sets sail with her and her friend, Scribonia, for England. The vessel is, however, immediately wrecked in a storm and the two girls are thrown up on the sea-shore, where they find refuge in a monastery which Heywood substitutes for the Temple of Venus in the *Rudens*. But Mildewe and a rascally associate have also escaped drowning and he claims the girls as his chattels and goods, his slaves bought with his private coin. But they find a champion in an English merchant, Ashburne, who has found an asylum in Marseilles from pursuing creditors, and who, on hearing that they are his countrywomen, declares (III. ii):

> England's no brood for slaves . . .
> None is lord with us
> But such as are freeborn . . . Our Christian laws
> Do not allow such to be bought or sold.

Meanwhile a fisherman in Ashburne's service has caught in his net a box lost in the wreck, which in an amusing exercise of 'sea-sophistry', where Heywood skilfully expands and anglicizes the Plautine legal phrases, he claims as his own (IV. i):

What I catch is mine own, my lands, my goods, my copy-hold, my fee-simple, mine to sell, mine to give, mine to lend and mine to cast away; no man claims part, no man share, since fishing is free and the sea common.

Upon examination the box proves to contain valuables belonging to Mildewe, which eventually come in part to the finder, and also a casket with property of Palaestra and evidence that she is the long-lost daughter of her rescuer, Ashburne, who gladly gives her hand to her lover, Raphael. To amplify further the simpler Plautine happy ending Scribonia proves to be the cousin of Palaestra, and her father opportunely arrives to bless her union with a friend of Raphael and to inform Ashburne that he has inherited a fortune from an uncle.

Heywood's modernization of the *Rudens* in *The Captives* is a successful piece of work and he was scarcely well advised in adding a quite unrelated underplot concerning the intrigue of an amorous friar and the trick by which one of his monastic brethren is deluded into the belief that he has murdered him. This story from a *novella* by Masuccio di Salerno had already been used by Marlowe, with variations, in *The Jew of Malta*.[1]

Plautus again served Heywood's turn in *The English Traveller*, published in 1633, as acted in the Cockpit by the Queen's company, but probably dating from about the same time as *The Captives*. It was now, however, the sub-plot that was borrowed from the Roman source, the *Mostellaria* (the *Ghost-Story*). The father of the dissipated young Lionel, returning suddenly from a sea-voyage, is kept away from his own house, occupied by a crowd of revellers, by his servant, Reignald, who persuades him that it is haunted by the ghost of a man murdered there by the former owner of the house.

Reignald further hoaxes the old man into the belief that his son, to escape from the haunted house, has bought on very favourable terms a neighbour's premises with money for whose return a usurer is now pressing the young scapegrace. All this with the ensuing complications and their solution is effectively anglicized by Heywood, though the

---

[1] A. M. Clark in his *Thomas Heywood* (1931), Appendix III, argues that Heywood interpolated this plot into Marlowe's play. See, on the other hand, F. S. Boas, *Christopher Marlowe* (1940), 148–50.

crafty servant, the Tranio of Plautus, is essentially a type belonging to Roman comedy.

This sub-plot, as in *The Captives*, is very loosely related to the main action, from which the *English Traveller* takes its title. Geraldine has returned from a prolonged journey which has taken him as far as the Holy Land and is effusively welcomed by his neighbour Wincott, the elderly husband of a young beauty (I. i):

> I would have you
> Think this your home, free as your father's house,
> And to command it, as the master on't;
> Call boldly here and entertain your friends,
> As in your own possessions: when I see't,
> I'll say you love me truly, not till then.

Though Geraldine and Wincott's wife had been sweethearts before her marriage, he does not abuse the husband's confidence, but they solemnly vow to wed after his death. Delavil, however, a false friend, so works upon Geraldine's father by Iago-like innuendoes that he is convinced of his son's guilt and forbids him to enter Wincott's house. At last, however, a message from Wincott brings him there at night, and he discovers the wife in her bedchamber with Delavil. Love and friendship are together blotted out for him for ever, but he does not take vengeance with his sword or even with his lips (IV. iii):

> Heaven will find time to punish: I'll not stretch
> My just revenge so far as once by blabbing
> To make your brazen impudence to blush.

He determines instead to leave again the country that has bred two such monsters. But Mistress Wincott's hypocritical entreaties to him not to travel:

> O sir, should you miscarry I were lost,
> Lost and forsaken,

force him to break silence and to denounce her treachery to his 'unspotted and unbounded love'. Overwhelmed by his reproaches, she dies repentant and confessing her guilt. It is a strange situation, for Geraldine's fury has been roused not by the wrong to the husband but to himself, and this accounts for the curiously varied estimates of his character and of the moral bearing of the play as a whole.

But the paradox arises from the fact that Heywood had many years before reached his highest dramatic level in portraying a husband's treatment of a guilty wife and he had needed a variation from the theme of *A Woman Killed with Kindness*. This play dates from 1602/3, for on 12 February of that year Henslowe recorded in his *Diary* a payment of £3 to Heywood for it on behalf of Worcester's men, and on 6 March another sum of £3 in full payment for it. On 4 and 5 February he had already paid £7 15s. for a woman's gown of black velvet for the play, and on 7 March he added ten shillings to the tailor who made a black satin suit for it. It is a classic instance of the author being ranked below the properties in the financial scale. Quarto editions appeared in 1607.

In *A Woman Killed with Kindness* Heywood drew neither from romantic imaginings nor from classical sources. He concentrated his powers upon a highly emotional domestic situation set in the background of a Yorkshire country house of which the daily routine is attractively presented. Its owner, Frankford, has just married, and congratulates himself in being the happiest of men (II. i):

> I am possessed of many fair revenues,
> Sufficient to maintain a gentleman.
> Touching my mind, I am studied in all arts . . .
> I have a fair, a chaste and loving wife,
> Perfection all, all truth, all ornament.

But after she had borne him two children this paragon of women betrays him with Wendoll, whom Frankford, in compassion of his small means, has made an inmate of his house. The chief weakness in the play is that Heywood makes no attempt to depict a conflict of emotions in Mistress Frankford. She surrenders with merely a sigh to the enchantment of the seducer's tongue (II. iii):

> What shall I say?
> My soul is wandering, and hath lost her way.
> Oh, Master Wendoll! Oh!

The revelation of their guilt by a faithful servant still leaves Frankford unconvinced, though in the highly effective scene of the game of cards (III. ii) his equivocal words are evidence of his suspicions. But even when he has caught the pair sleeping in each other's arms, he does not execute the swift justice on them sanctioned by the tradition of the revenge tragedies. His excuse is the converse of Hamlet's, who would not kill Claudius at prayer (IV. vi):

> I would not damn two precious souls,
> Bought with my Saviour's blood, and send them laden,
> With all their scarlet sins upon their backs,
> Unto a fearful judgment.

And in lines as poignant as Heywood ever penned Frankford prays that it might be feasible to reverse the past and retrieve lost innocence:

> O God! O God! that it were possible
> To undo things done; to call back yesterday;
> That Time could turn up his swift sandy glass,
> To untell the days, and to redeem these hours,
> Or that the sun
> Could, rising from the west, draw his coach backwards . . .
>   that I might take her
> As spotless as an angel in my arms.

On one who has been so idolized he cannot inflict the stern doom for which in her repentant agony she craves, and on an Elizabethan audience surfeited with outcries of revenge his 'sentence' must have fallen with surprising effect:

> I'll not martyr thee
> Nor mark thee for a strumpet; but with usage
> Of more humility torment thy soul,
> And kill thee even with kindesss.

She is to retire properly furnished and attended to his manor seven miles off and never to see or have communication with him or their children. But this kindness has almost as swift a result as an avenging sword, for Nan Frankford will not have food or drink or sleep and sinks to her death-bed, where her husband comes to take his last farewell. And in revealing contrast with the lurid close of neo-Senecan revenge tragedies is the sanctified light that glows over the scene where Frankford answers his wife's cry for pardon:

> As freely, from the low depth of my soul,
> As my Redeemer hath forgiven his death,
> I pardon thee. I will shed tears for thee, pray with thee;
> And in mere pity of thy weak estate,
> I'll wish to die with thee . . .
> Even as I hope for pardon at that day
> When the great Judge of Heaven in scarlet sits,
> So be thou pardoned. Though thy rash offence
> Divorced our bodies, thy repentant tears
> Unite our souls . . .
> My wife, the mother to my pretty babes!
> Both those lost names I do restore thee back,
> And with this kiss I wed thee once again.

Among the episodes of reconciliation in Elizabethan drama this stands out unique.

As has been seen, Heywood's sub-plots have little relation to the main action. So here Sir Francis Acton, Mistress Frankford's brother, forms the slender link between them. A match between his and Sir Charles Mountford's dogs and hawks, where Heywood shows his technical knowledge of falconry, ends in an affray where Mountford's party kill two of Acton's men. This leads to his imprisonment, from which he has to buy his release with all his fortune except a small house and estate, and he accepts the offer of a loan from a false friend and neighbour, Shafton, who wishes to add this property to his own. But when Mountford refuses to sell his only remaining inheritance to redeem the debt Shafton has him consigned to closer confinement than before. The plead-ings of his devoted sister, Susan, for help from his relatives are in vain, but Acton, who has been enchanted by her beauty, pays the money that secures Mountford's release. Thus arises a situation at once curiously akin to, and different from, that between Claudio and Isabella in *Measure for Measure*. Mountford cannot endure the thought that he is indebted to his hated enemy, and he suggests to his sister that she should discharge the obligation with interest by sacrificing her honour to Sir Francis (V. i):

> What moved my foe
> To enfranchise me? 'Twas, sister, for your love,
> With full five hundred pounds he bought your love,
> And shall he not enjoy it? Shall the weight
> Of all this heavy burthen lean on me,
> And will you not bear part?

He assures her that he himself will not survive her shame, and she gives a verbal assent to the bargain, though declaring that she will kill herself before fulfilling it. This gives an artificial twist to the situation and we feel that in a sense Acton has been tricked when he is so overcome by the offer of Susan's honour in redemption of Mountford's debt that he bestows on her his hand and fortunes. But Heywood probably wished to emphasize the contrast between the reward of her loyal chastity and Nan Frankford's penalty for her deceitful sin.

The Wise Woman of Hogsdon, printed in 1638, probably was written and acted not long after *A Woman Killed with Kindness*, to which it contains a reference in Act III. ii, 'We shall else have thee claim kindred of the woman killed with kindness.' The phrase was proverbial, but the use of 'the', instead of 'a', implies that the allusion is specifically to Nan Frankford. But whatever its date may be, I do not rate the play as highly among Heywood's domestic dramas as several critics have done. It is true that it has a vigorous movement, that it contains some capital scenes, such as the opening game of dice and those in which mockery is made of the pedantic schoolmaster's Latin; and that the scattered threads are skilfully drawn together at the close. But the characters are either shadowy or lacking in attractive qualities. Young Chartley is a fickle scapegrace who is tricked into marriage with the Luce whom he had courted and then deserted to pay court to her namesake (an awkward duplication) who consoles herself with his 'blunt' friend Boyster, while Grace, a third object of his roving affections, finds a mate in his 'conceited' friend Sencer. And it would be difficult to imagine a less pleasing *dea ex machina* than the wise-woman of Hogsdon (Hoxton), witch, beldam, hag, and worse, who pulls most of the strings and gives the play its name.

There are several other plays bearing only Heywood's name on the title-page which further illustrate the width of his range, but which do not add much to his dramatic significance. *A Maidenhead Well Lost*, printed 1634, claims on the title-page to have been acted with much applause by the Queen's company at the Cockpit. But it appealed to a less healthy taste than most of Heywood's plays. The Prince of Florence is warned on the eve of his marriage, for reasons of state, to Julia, daughter of the Duke of Milan, that she is unchaste, and he declares that if he finds her so, he will repudiate her. The charge is true, for she has borne a son to the Prince of Parma. But to deceive the Prince of Florence Julia's place on the marriage night is taken by Lauretta, the exiled daughter of a Milanese general, with whom he had secretly fallen in love. In this the villain of the piece, Stroza, had meant to make her a tool, but she outwits him, wins the hand of the prince and restores Julia to Parma's arms.

A Challenge for Beauty, printed 1636, was acted by the King's company at Blackfriars and the Globe. There is no claim that it was received with applause and probably its incredibly fantastic plot was not redeemed for theatre-goers by the patriotic features introduced into it. Isabella, Queen of Portugal, exacts from all around her idolatry of her beauty, virtue, and birth, and banishes the noble Spaniard Bonavida because his praise is not extravagant enough. Unless he can return with a woman to match her he is to suffer death. In England he finds such a paragon in Helena, sister of the sea-captain Ferrers, who is a chief figure in the loosely con-

nected (after Heywood's fashion) underplot. But Bonavida's
return with merely the report of Helena's perfections incenses
the queen to renewed fury. She has him thrown into prison
and sends two sychophant courtiers to England to obtain by
a trick the ring which Helena had vowed to keep as the
pledge of her loyalty to him. When the Queen shows this
to him as a proof of her infidelity he is so prostrated that he
begs for the death sentence to be carried out, in default of
which he will take his own life. But at the last moment
before his public execution Helena appears and by an
ingenious stratagem forces her two traducers into a declaration of her innocence. Thereupon the Queen makes an
unexpectedly whole-hearted surrender to the English beauty
and her lover:

> Be ever mine: next·her, you that have travell'd
> To fetch me o'er this mirror which I'll casket
> As my best jewel.

The Royal King and the Loyal Subject, acted by the Queen's
company, was not printed till 1637, but the epilogue speaks
of it as an 'old' play, written when rhymed lines were in
favour, and when 'doublets with stuffed bellies and big
sleeves' and trunk-hose were the fashionable wear. This has
suggested a date very early in the seventeenth century. But
the highly artificial plot is more characteristic of a period
when the divine right of kings was being emphasized by the
Stuart monarchy. It is based on William Painter's translation in his *Palace of Pleasure* of a novel by Bandello, but
the scene is transferred from the Orient to England under a
legendary king who, incited by jealous courtiers to exalt his
own 'royalty', heaps upon his loyal subject, the Marshal who
has saved his life in battle, a series of gross humiliations. To
these, even when they involve risk to the honour of his two
daughters, he submits with a meekness that passes belief.
And when at last he has found an ingenious means of
reconciling the king, he is brought, in a superfluous fifth act,
within an ace of the final outrage of a public execution. The

similarity here of his situation to that of Bonavida in *The Challenge for Beauty* points a contrast (whether or not present to Heywood) between the truly loyal subject and the mouthpiece of passive obedience.

All the above plays, with the addition of the autograph *The Captives* and some half dozen Court and city masques, are, on the evidence of the title-pages, from Heywood's pen. Two other plays bear his name with that of a collaborator. *Fortune by Land and Sea* was published in 1655 in a badly-printed quarto, as written by Heywood and William Rowley and acted by the Queen's servants. As we now know that Rowley died early in 1626, the queen was probably Anne, not Henrietta, if the reference is to its first production. But in any case Heywood had the main hand in the play. The domestic drama, exemplifying 'fortune by land', belongs to his familiar choice of themes. The 'fortune by sea' of the pirate Clinton and his purser has thus tended to be claimed for Rowley, though the author of *The Fair Maid of the West* had no lack of interest in maritime adventure. But Mr. Clark has found that scenes in the pirate plot are verbally parallel with passages in a pamphlet, *A True Relation of the Lives and Deaths of the two most famous English Pirates, Purser and Clinton* (1639), which on internal evidence can be assigned to Heywood, who appears thus to have made double use of his own work.[1]

About the other play, *The Late Lancashire Witches*, by Heywood and Richard Brome, our information is much more precise. It was acted by the King's company at the Globe in the summer of 1634 and published in the same year. Like *The Witch of Edmonton* in 1621 it was hastily written to make capital out of a sensational witchcraft trial. But now the fate of not one unhappy woman but a group of beldames was involved, and it was discreditable to the two dramatists that they should for their own profit have worked up popular feeling against the victims of a widespread savage

[1] See *op. cit.*, 180–2.

credulity. As Heywood was much the senior partner, and as in Γυναικεῖον and *The Hierarchy of Angels* he had already shown his belief in witchcraft, he must be accounted the chief offender.

The Pendle district of Lancashire had a bad reputation as a haunt of witches. A boy belonging to it, Edward Robinson, in February 1634, brought accusations of satanic practices against a number of his neighbours, seventeen of whom were found guilty and imprisoned in Lancaster Castle. The case was remitted in turn to the Privy Council, the Bishop of Chester, the Secretary of State, and finally to the King, who on 30 June issued a pardon to the accused. Meanwhile several of them had died in prison and even after the pardon the others, though not executed, remained in confinement in the castle. Some lines in the epilogue have been taken to show that it was performed while the king's 'great mercy' was still under consideration, but a petition of the players, dated 20 July in the Lord Chamberlain's book concerning their 'designed comedy of the Lancashire witches', indicates that it was not finished then.[1]

The witches when they first appear in Act II are merely called Meg, Maud, and Gilian, but later they are known by the names of three of the four women who had been brought up to London for a medical examination, mistresses Diccinson, Spenser, and Hargreaves, to whom a Granny Johnson is added. Young Robinson, their original accuser, is designated only 'Boy'. With their attendant spirits they have something more of authentic diablerie about them than the witch of Edmonton, and they exercise their black arts in the most varied fashion. They transform human beings into animals; they give a topsy-turvy turn to normal family relations; they render a newly-wedded bridegroom impotent; they foil the hunters' sport by taking the form of a hare and hounds. In league with these village cronies is a woman of higher station, Mrs. Generous, wife of a landowner whose noble character

---

[1] See G. E. Bentley, *The Jacobean and Caroline Stage*, I. 40–1 (1941).

is indicated by his name. Though she had a possible prototype during an earlier Pendle witch scare in 1612, her role
here is a creation of the dramatists and the situation that
results between her and her husband is one after Heywood's
heart. When Generous finds that his adored wife is ready to
confess that she is a witch and that she has promised her
soul to the devil, so far as she can claim interest in it, he
is thunderstruck.

> O cunning Devil! Foolish woman, know
> Where he can claim but the least little part,
> He will usurp the whole; th'art a lost woman.

She pleads to make atonement by penitent tears, and as
he folds her in his arms our thoughts are carried back for
the moment to the sacred scene of reconciliation between
Frankford and Anne:

> Well I do remember, wife,
> When I first took thee 'twas for good and bad.
> O change thy bad to good, that I may keep thee,
> As then we passed our faiths, till death us sever. . .
> Only thus much remember, thou had'st extermin'd
> Thyself out of the blest felicity
> Of saints and angels, but on thy repentance
> I take thee to my bosom once again,
> My wife, sister and daughter.

It strikes us as a desecration that after this Mrs. Generous
should return at once to her black magic and that her husband, after visual proof of her infamy, should himself feel
bound to deliver her to justice, which she meets without any
further affectation of remorse. The play was intended to
drive home the lesson that there could be no limited lia-
bility in a contract with the devil.

In the prefatory address to the 1633 quarto of *The English
Traveller* Heywood claimed that by then there were two
hundred plays in which he had 'either an entire hand or at
the least a main finger'. In the same year he wrote prologues
and epilogues for the revival of Marlowe's *Jew of Malta* at
the Cockpit and at Court and a preface to the only extant

edition. Whether he had also a 'finger' in the text of that edition cannot be determined with certainty,[1] but his sponsoring of the forty years' old melodrama is one of the most interesting links between the Tudor and the Stuart stage. The astronomical figure furnished by Heywood himself of his dramatic productions has inevitably stimulated editors and critics to attribute to him a number of anonymously published plays on the internal evidence of their resemblance to one or other of his acknowledged works, though this must always be a doubtful criterion. Thus the two parts of *King Edward the Fourth* (1600) have a likeness in their chronicle-history style to the two parts of *If You Know not Me, You Know Nobody*, and the treatment of the sinning wife, Jane Shore, and her forgiving husband anticipates in its more sentimental degree the situation in *A Woman Killed with Kindness*. In another anonymous play which has been claimed for Heywood, *How a Man may Choose a Good Wife from a Bad* (1602), the situation is reversed, and it is the wife who forgives and reclaims an erring husband. A similar theme in grimmer fashion and carried to a fatal close is treated in *A Yorkshire Tragedy* (1608), played at the Globe and attributed on the title-page of the quarto to Shakespeare, but claimed by the latest biographer of Heywood as his work.[2] The same critic supports strongly the tentative suggestion of A. H. Bullen that *Dick of Devonshire*, printed in 1883 from the same MS. volume as *The Captives*, is by Heywood.[3] It combines with a romantic sub-plot the account of the exploits of Richard Pike, of Tavistock, who was left behind by the expedition of 1625 at Cadiz and performed remarkable feats of prowess. The breezy atmosphere of these scenes and the attitude towards the relations of England and Spain are akin to features in plays of the Heywood canon On the other hand, Charles Lamb has found little support recently in assigning to Heywood *The Fair Maid of the*

[1] See above, p. 180n.
[2] See A. M. Clark, *Thomas Heywood* (1531), Appendix V.
[3] *Ibid.*, Appendix II and Bullen's *Collection of Old English Plays*, vol. ii.

Exchange (1607) in which a cripple plays a leading part and helps the youngest of three brothers to defeat his elders in the rivalry for the hand of the fair maid, Phillis Flower.

VIII

JOHN WEBSTER—CYRIL TOURNEUR

POETIC REVENGE TRAGEDIES

THE dramatists who have followed one another through the preceding pages had brought to the theatre a prodigal store of gifts, but these had not included poetic imagination in its quintessential quality. It was this which distinguished Marlowe alone among Shakespeare's predecessors and also, though in strongly contrasted manifestation, John Webster alone among his successors. On Webster's life even the most recent research has been able to cast little light. He states that he was born free of the Merchant Taylors' Company, which implies his father's connexion in some way with that company and suggests that he was born in London. The date is uncertain, and there is no documentary evidence concerning him before an entry in Henslowe's *Diary* in May 1602 of a payment to Webster with other dramatists of £5 in earnest of a play *Caesar's Fall*. Similar payments for his share in other plays follow in October and November. In 1604 he added the Induction to Marston's *Malcontent.* Thereafter the only landmarks are the dates of the publication of his own plays and those in which he had a share, and some other writings, including verses prefixed to other men's works. He must have been alive in October 1624, when he composed the Lord Mayor's pageant, *Monuments of Honour.* Ten years later he is one of the dramatists to whom Heywood alludes in the past tense in his list of their familiar names in his *Hierarchy of the Blessed Angels.*

The fame of no other Elizabethan dramatist is so securely based upon so comparatively narrow a foundation. Webster has his place in the first rank by virtue of the three plays of which he is sole author, and of which the earliest, *The White Devil*, was published in 1612, a decade after Henslowe's first mention of him. Webster in his preface to the quarto confesses that he was a long time in finishing this tragedy, which was acted by the Queen's men at the Red Bull in the winter season, probably of 1611–12. The plot of *The White Devil* is based upon events in the tempestuous life of Vittoria Accorombona, a North Italian beauty, born in 1557 and murdered in 1585. Whether Webster obtained his knowledge of her career from written or oral sources is doubtful, but while he retained many of the historical features he largely altered others to fit in with his dramatic design.[1] He introduced also into his dialogue echoes of his varied reading— from Montaigne, Sidney's *Arcadia*, Guazzo's *La Civil Conversatione* (as has been recently shown), and even in Act V from Shakespeare to whose 'right happy and copious industry' he had paid tribute in his preface to the play. But upon all his materials Webster's genius wrought so effectively that few plays in the Elizabethan canon have so authentic a stamp of individual inspiration: yet it is not surprising that, as he declares, he was led to publish it because in the theatre 'it wanted a full and understanding auditory'. It needed a more subtle-brained audience than the gallants and groundlings in a Jacobean public theatre to take in rapidly the pregnant and often obscurely allusive dialogue which even for the reader of to-day needs the help of scholarly interpretation. Something of a parallel may be found in Victorian drama in Browning's *Strafford*.

Nevertheless from the beginning Webster presents vividly his chief personages—Vittoria and her mild, cold-blooded husband Camillo; her brother Flamineo, the unscrupulous and cynically humorous secretary of the Duke of Brachiano and go-between in his amorous intrigue with Vittoria; and Brachiano's gentle wife, Isabella, sister of Francisco, Duke

[1] For a detailed account of the historical events and of their relation to Webster's play see F. L. Lucas, *The Works of John Webster*, I. 70–90.

of Florence. Francisco and Cardinal Monticelso, uncle of
Camillo, warn Brachiano against his evil courses which
involve the dishonour of their kindred. But they speak to
deaf ears. In Act II. ii, Webster makes use of the traditional
device of the dumb show to indicate not what is about to
happen, but what is actually taking place off the stage. A
conjurer presents to Brachiano his wife kissing his picture
which has been infected with poison, and instantly expiring.
Whereupon he laconically comments, 'Excellent, then she's
dead'. In a second show Flamineo knocks down and strangles
Camillo, during a competition with a vaulting horse, whereupon Brachiano again tersely observes, ''Twas quaintly
done'.

It is in the same spirit of cynical nonchalance, and with
the same pungent economy of words that Vittoria confronts
her judges, Francisco and Monticelso, when she is put on her
trial in Act III. ii. When the prosecuting lawyer begins his
indictment of her in Latin she interrupts:

> Pray, my lord, let him speak his usual tongue,
> I'll make no answer else.
> *Fran.*   Why, you understand Latin.
> *Vit.*   I do, sir, but amongst this auditory
> Which come to hear my cause, the half or more
> May be ignorant in't.

When the lawyer then substitutes a high-flown English jargon
she is no less scornful, 'Why this is Welsh to Latin'. Even
when the Cardinal himself bursts forth:

> Were there a second Paradise to lose,
> This devil would betray it,

she retorts instantly,

>   O poor charity!
> Thou art seldom found in scarlet.

When he calls her whore, and in answer to her query, 'What's
that?', expounds 'their perfect character', she nonchalantly
replies, 'This character 'scapes me'. Unfortified like Portia
at Venice with a good case and legal weapons, Vittoria by

sheer force of will and intellect dominates the court at Rome.
To the Cardinal's reproof:

> She comes not like a widow: she comes armed
> With scorn and impudence: is this a mourning habit?

she makes the withering reply:

> Had I foreknown his death, as you suggest,
> I would have bespoke my mourning.

When the accusation against her shifts from murder to
adultery with Brachiano she pleads for herself in an image
that transports us for a moment out of the stifling atmosphere of the law-court:

> Condemn you me for that the Duke did love me?
> So may you blame some fair and crystal river
> For that some melancholy distracted man
> Hath drown'd himself in't.

And has not Vittoria sufficient cause for scorn of the blear-
eyed judges who condemn her to a house of convertites while
they acquit Flaminco together with his innocent brother,
Marullo, and do not even put the arch-criminal Brachiano
on trial? By the superb, relentless consistency of his deline-
ation Webster has made of this scene in *The White Devil* one
of the peak points of Elizabethan drama.

The ascendency of Vittoria in the law-court is maintained
by her in the house of convertites when Brachiano opens
Francisco's feigned love-letter to her and turns upon her
with angry reproaches (IV. ii. 88 ff.):

> Your beauty! Oh, ten thousand curses on't.
> How long have I beheld the devil in crystal!
> Thou hast led me, like an heathen sacrifice,
> With music and with fatal yokes of flowers
> To my eternal ruin.

By her towering personality and her stinging retorts she
forces her haughty paramour into the confession:

> Once to be jealous of thee is t'express
> That I will love thee everlastingly,
> And never more be jealous.

With Flamineo urging appeasement, though cynically protesting, 'no oaths for God's sake', they agree to flee together to the Duke's palace at Padua.

The hitherto rapid sweep of the play is now for a time arrested. Webster does not, like many of his contemporaries, complicate his action with a sub-plot. But such episodes as the election of Monticelso to the Papacy, the assuming by Francisco of the disguise of a Moor and the declaration of love to him by Zanche, Vittoria's Moorish waiting-woman, and the murder of Marcello by Flamineo, divert the attention that is expectant of the catastrophe. This is set in motion in Act V. iii, when Lodovico, who had cherished a silent love for the murdered Isabella, takes revenge on Brachiano by poisoning the helmet, which he wears when fighting at barriers. The prolonged dying agony of the Duke, with its succession of 'strange distractions', and the appearance of his ghost to Flamineo, throwing earth upon him and showing him a skull, are more in the tradition of revenge tragedy than distinctive of Webster's dramatic genius. But this asserts itself again in the final scene when Lodovico, with an accomplice, completes his mission of vengeance by trapping Flamineo and Vittoria. When the former is bound and questioned, 'What dost think on?' his lips are sealed:

> Nothing; of nothing; leave thy idle questions,
> I am i'th way to study a long silence.
> To prate were idle. I remember nothing.
> There's nothing of so infinite vexation
> As man's own thought.

When Lodovico threatens Vittoria she turns upon him in scorn: You, my deathsman!
> Methinks thou dost not look horrid enough:
> Thou hast too good a face to be a hang-man.

The order to kill Zanche draws from her the imperious protest:

> You shall not kill her first; behold my breast,
> I will be waited on in death; my servant
> Shall never go before me.

Even the cold-hearted Flamineo cannot withhold his tribute
to her:

> Th'art a noble sister,
> I love thee now.

In the sombre image,

> My soul like to a ship in a black storm,
> Is driven I know not whither

she pronounces her own epitaph, and the moralising tag
which is thrust into her dying lips:

> O happy they that never saw the Court,
> Nor ever knew great men but by report,

are the only words that fall from her which she could never
have uttered. Flamineo lets us hear his own accents to the
last in his declaration:

> I have caught
> An everlasting cold. I have lost my voice
> Most irrecoverably.

Their executioners are handed over to justice, but their
poison and their daggers cannot rob these magnificent
Renaissance figures of a triumphant immortality.

It was from a similar quarry that Webster again drew in
The Duchess of Malfi, published in 1623, 'as presented privately at the Blackfriars, and publicly at the Globe', by the
King's men. As William Ostler, of this company, who acted
the chief male part, died on 16 December 1614, the play
must have been produced before that date. The parallels
in phrase between the play and Webster's *A Monumental
Column* (December 1612) and the debt of both to the
Arcadia, of which a new edition appeared in 1613, suggest
1613–4 as the probable date of composition. As in *The White
Devil* Webster was dramatizing (as is now known) historical
facts, but here they had reached him in the disguise of
fiction. The story of the Duchess of Amalfi was told by
Bandello in one of his *novelle*, of which a French version
appeared in Belleforest's *Histoires Tragiques*, englished by

William Painter in his *Palace of Pleasure*, which was Webster's immediate source, though he handles it freely and
gives it his own distinctive stamp.

Once more we breathe the hot-house atmosphere of the
north Italian ducal courts and of Papal Rome with their family
entanglements and intrigues. Murder and lust again confront
us. But they are viewed from a different angle, and though
Webster's imaginative genius links *The Duchess of Malfi* with
The White Devil as twin creations, the spirit of the later play
is in striking contrast with that of its predecessor. The
central figure is not a Vittoria trampling on every obstacle
to her desires and standing contemptuously erect before her
accusers, but a woman nobly born stooping to conquer by
making the tender of her love to one far below her in station,
Antonio, the Master of her Household. This difficult situation
is treated with delicate art, culminating in the exquisitely
coy avowal (I. i. 519 ff.):

> This is flesh and blood, sir,
> 'Tis not the figure cut in alabaster
> Kneels at my husband's tomb. Awake, awake, man!
> I do here put off all vain ceremony,
> And only do appear to you a young widow
> That claims you for her husband, and, like a widow,
> I use but half a blush in't.

But even at this moment there falls the shadow of impending
doom in the cry of the waiting woman, 'it shows A fearful
madness. I owe her much of pity'. Between the Duchess
and her vision of wedded bliss with Antonio stand the forbidding figures of her brothers, a Cardinal, and Duke Ferdinand of Calabria. They wish to keep her patrimony in their
own hands, they deplore a stain upon the escutcheon of their
proud House of Arragon, and they even have, or affect, that
horror of a widow's second marriage of which there is the
impress in *Hamlet*. They find an agent in Bosola, released
from seven years' punishment in the galleys, for whom they
procure a place in the service of the Duchess. He is as

unscrupulous as Flamineo, but instead of his cynical humour he is of a melancholy and sourly jealous temper. When Ferdinand learns from him that the Duchess has borne a supposedly illegitimate child he goes post-haste to Amalfi to reproach her and to leave her a dagger wherewith to kill herself. Even her announcement that she is married cannot assuage his fury. But if his ears are deaf to the tender pathos of her plea it is not so with us (III. ii. 127 ff.):

Duch.   Why might not I marry?
I have not gone about in this to create
Any new world or custom.
Ferd.   Thou art undone;
And thou hast ta'en that massy sheet of lead
That hid thy husband's bones and folded it
About my heart. . .
Duch.   Why should only I,
Of all the other princes of the world,
Be cased up like a holy relic? I have youth
And a little beauty.
Ferd.   So you have some virgins
That are witches. I will never see thee more.

He keeps this vow literally, for when he again visits the Duchess as a prisoner in her own castle he comes to her in the dark. The gruesome devices with which he seeks to terrorize her—the dead man's hand, 'the artificial figures of Antonio and his children, appearing as if they were dead', the dance of madmen howling their dismal music—doubtless appealed to the cruder elements in the theatrical taste of Webster's day, but they are merely excrescences on his genius. That reveals its true quality in the inspired dialogue between the Duchess and her waiting-woman, Cariola (IV. ii. 12 ff.):

Duch. This is a prison.
Car.   Yes, but you shall live
To shake this durance off.
Duch.   Thou art a fool;
The robin-redbreast, and the nightingale
Never live long in cages.

Car.   Pray, dry your eyes.
       What think you of, madam?
Duch.   Of nothing,
       When I muse thus I sleep.
   Car. Like a madman, with your eyes open!
Duch. Dost thou think we shall know one another
       In th' other world?
   Car.   Yes, out of question.
Duch. O that it were possible we might
       But hold some two days' conference with the dead!
       From them I should learn somewhat, I am sure
       I never shall know here.

It is the same thought that fortifies her when Bosola and
the executioners appear with bell, coffin, and strangling
cords. Amazed at her serene facing of these terrors, he cries,

                       Doth not death fright you?
Duch. Who would be afraid on't?
       Knowing to meet such excellent company
       In th'other world.

She can even give a playful turn to the executioners' grim
task (IV. ii. 237 ff.):

       Pull and pull strongly, for your able strength
       Must pull down heaven upon me.
       Yet stay! heaven's gates are not so highly arched
       As princes' palaces—they that enter there
       Must go upon their knees.

Her children share her fate, and even Bosola is moved to
ask Ferdinand when he shows him their bodies, 'Alas, how
have these offended?' In the Duke's answer there is already
a sign of his oncoming lycanthropic frenzy:

                       The death
       Of young wolves is never to be pitied.

But he cannot endure to look upon the Duchess:

       Cover her face: mine eyes dazzle: she died young.

Again it is Bosola who sees deeper:

       I think not so: her infelicity
       Seemed to have years too many.

o

And when he finds that he is to be cheated of his promised reward for his villainy he flatters himself for the moment with the belief that the Duchess may yet be called back to life (IV. ii. 369 ff.):

> She's warm, she breathes . . . her eye opes,
> And heaven in it seems to ope, that late was dead,
> To take me up to mercy.

But her lips merely move to breathe two words, 'Antonio' and 'Mercy'

Throughout these scenes of Act IV Webster's genius burns with a constant glow, all the more impressive because their wistful, tender charm wrung out of the very heart of tragedy is in such contrast with the power and passion of the corresponding scenes in *The White Devil*. The final act could not but be anti-climax. Yet it is notable in two ways. The threads of the plot are ingeniously interwoven so that the criminals become unwillingly the agents of retribution on one another. Bosola kills in the dark Antonio, whom he meant to save, and then wounds the Cardinal, who by warning the household to disregard cries in the night from the frenzied Duke or from himself has cut himself from rescue. Ferdinand, roused by the struggle, gives death-wounds to his brother and Bosola, but the latter kills him before dying himself. It is not however in the tragic loading of the stage that the main significance of the finale lies. It is in the chill spirit of hopeless melancholy of which each actor in turn is spokesman. Antonio's dying cry is:

> Pleasure of life what is't? Only the good hours
> Of an ague.

Ferdinand in his distraction accounts the world but a dog-kennel. The Cardinal's last prayer is 'to be laid by and never thought of'. Bosola, in an echo from Sidney's *Arcadia*, laments:

> We are merely the stars' tennis-balls, struck and bandied
> Which way please them;

and sighs his farewell:

> Oh, this gloomy world!
> In what a shadow, or deep pit of darkness,
> Doth, womanish and fearful, mankind live!

If allowance is made for the difference between a tragedy and a tragi-comedy, we are in a similarly gloomy world in *The Devil's Law-Case*, published in 1623, 'as it was approvedly well acted by her Majesty's servants'. Queen Anne died on 2 March 1619, and though a company in the provinces continued to bear her name for some years, a compliment to her nation, the Danes, in Act IV. ii, suggests that it was written while she was still alive. In any case five or six years had passed since the two great tragedies, and in the interval an eclipse, though by no means a total one, had shadowed Webster's splendidly imaginative vision. There are flashes of it in *The Devil's Law-Case*, but they are intermittent and subdued as compared with the earlier irradiating glow. Hence many critics have overlooked in the play the evidences of other elements in Webster's genius and technique. His frequent economy of phrase, his masterful power of devising dramatic situations, his skill (till it fails just as the close) in interlacing varied threads are all displayed. And these are the more remarkable because no source for the play has been traced, though precedents and parallels for some of its leading incidents have been cited.

But the crucial feature linking it with *The White Devil* and *The Duchess of Malfi* is that in the three plays a woman, to compass what she has set her heart on, defies the code of her own world and takes all the risks. Here it is the Neapolitan rich citizen's widow, Leonora, mother of the merchant Romelio and his sister, Jolenta. The girl loves and is loved by the nobleman Contarino, who in asking her mother for her hand gallantly begs for the widow's 'picture' which Leonora misinterprets to be her own portrait and is thus led to become enamoured of Contarino herself. Thus abetted by the cynical and immoral Romelio, akin to Flamineo and

Bosola, she seeks to force Jolenta into a loveless marriage
with Ercole, a knight of Malta and Contarino's friend from
youth. The two men are thus driven into a quarrel (II. i.
240 ff.), which Lamb described as 'the model of a gentleman-
like and well-managed difference' followed by a duel in which
each wounds the other. Contarino sends news that in his will
he has left everything to Jolenta; and Romelio, disturbed by
tidings of the loss of some of his ships and determined to
prevent Contarino from altering his will, visits him in the
disguise of a Jewish doctor and stabs him, as he thinks,
mortally. But instead he repeats an extraordinary cure
recorded by Grimeston in his translation of Goulart's
Histoires Admirables and relieves the patient by lancing the
wound. Ignorant of this, Romelio bluntly announces to his
mother, 'I have killed him'. Leonora can no longer conceal
her passion (III. iii. 242):

> I am twenty years elder
> Since you last oped your lips.
> *Rom.* Ha?
> *Leon.* You have given him the wound you speak of
> Quite through your mother's heart.

In burning words she gives voice to the frustrated longing
of an elderly heart:

> Why did I not
> Make my love known directly? 'T had not been
> Beyond example for a matron to affect
> I' th' honourable way of marriage
> So youthful a person. Oh, I shall run mad.

To justify her senile passion she cites the precedent, which
must even after some twenty years, have been fresh in the
minds of some of the theatrical audience in the Red Bull,
of Elizabeth and Essex (III. iii. 304 ff.):

> that worthy princess
> Who loathed food and sleep and ceremony
> For thought of losing that brave gentleman
> She would fain have saved, had not a false conveyance
> Expressed him stubborn-hearted.

To take vengeance on her son for the supposed murder of Contarino she has him dragged into a court of justice, where through the mouth of a rascally lawyer—whose long-winded oratory is a triumph of Webster's verbal mastery—she declares that Romelio is the bastard issue of her adultery with a friend of her husband and that her daughter is her husband's only legitimate heir. But when the name of the friend is given as Crispiano, and he proves to be no other than the presiding judge in the court who had gone to the East Indies four years before the alleged intimacy and has just returned after forty years' absence, Leonora's case collapses and Crispiano cries:

> But this is a mere practice 'gainst her son!
> And I beseech the Court it may be sifted
> And most severely punished.

The turning of the tables upon the accuser is as startling as in *The Merchant of Venice* and Webster's consummate handling of this astounding law-case entitles it to rank beside the most famous of Shakespeare's trial-scenes. But from this point the action becomes unduly entangled. Romelio has no sooner been relieved from the slur of bastardy than Ercole, who had recovered from his wound, rises in the court to denounce him as the murderer of Contarino. But as his accusation is unsupported, it has to be decided by a duel—the second one in the play, and 'continued to a good length', till it is interrupted by Leonora and a Friar with the news that Contarino is alive and is in fact acting in disguise as Ercole's second. Then as a climax to the surprises Contarino declares to Leonora that he has vowed his life entirely to her. Ercole seems to claim Jolenta, and Romelio is ordered to marry a nun whom he has seduced. It is a lame ending and has contributed to the undervaluation of a play which otherwise in its superb virtuosity and its dialectrical mastery is not unworthy to keep company with Webster's two tragedies.

On these three great plays of his middle period Webster's

fame rests secure. But in earlier and later years he took part in much collaborated work for the stage. His youthful association with Dekker in three dramas has been mentioned above,[1] and also their partnership with Rowley and Ford in 1624 in *The Late Murder in Whitechapel*.[2] *A Cure for a Cuckold*, written and acted probably in 1625, was not published till 1661, when it was ascribed to Webster and Rowley, to whom recent criticism has added Heywood. Its main plot deals with and elaborates a theme treated by Marston in *The Dutch Courtesan* (1605)[3] and by Heywood in *The Parliament of Love* (1624). A woman promises to give herself to a lover only on condition that he kills his best friend. In both *The Parliament of Love* and *A Cure for a Cuckold* the lover asks the friend to be his second in a duel, and only when they reach the ground reveals that he is not to be his second but his enemy. This scene (Act III. i) on Calais sands is by unanimous verdict from Webster's pen and gives a solution to the agonizing situation characteristic of his subtle brain. Lessingham, the lover, when they reach the ground, expresses to the newly-wed Bonvile the ideal conception of friendship between two men which is one of the loftiest features in Stuart drama:

> You left your bridal-bed to find your death-bed;
> And herein you most nobly expressed
> That the affection between two loyal friends
> Is far beyond the love of man or woman,
> And is more near allied to eternity.

This adds to the shattering effect of the disclosure that it is Bonvile who is to be killed. But after refusing to fight he finds another way of satisfying Lessingham:

> Thou camest to kill thy friend,
> And thou mayst brag thou hast done't; for here for ever
> All friendship dies between us.

Webster too is credited by all with the scene (Act IV. ii) in

---

[1] See above, p. 162.   [2] See above, pp. 164–5.
[3] See above, pp. 141–2.

which Lessingham assures his mistress, Clare, that he has fulfilled her bidding and is answered by another equivocation, that she had meant him to kill herself as his best friend. She had loved Bonvile and rather than see him wedded to another woman she had courted death at Lessingham's hand. But now that he is dead,

> Never did wine or music stir in woman
> A sweeter touch of mirth; I will marry you,
> Instantly marry you.

From such an offer Lessingham recoils with horror, but when Bonvile, to Clare's amazement, reappears without a scratch and tells her that Lessingham 'has kill'd me for a friend', he urges the marriage between them which, after further complications, forms the unsatisfactory end of an unequal play.

Another posthumously published drama in 1654, *Appius and Virginia*, bore only Webster's name on the title-page. This claim has found few supporters and the attempt has even been made to substitute Heywood for Webster. Critical opinion now mainly favours a division of the play between them, though there is considerable diversity concerning their separate shares. The earliest mention of *Appius and Virginia* is in a playhouse list of 10 August 1639, and the conjectures about its date have differed widely. The argument for 1625–7, resting in part on the apparently topical references in the complaints of the Roman soldiers to the hardships of English expeditionary forces in the Low Countries and elsewhere, seems to me to have most weight.[1]

The plot is based on the familiar story, as related by Dionysius of Halicarnassus, with some additional details from Livy, of the lustful pursuit of Virginia by the Roman decemvir Appius, and her death at her father's hand to save her honour. As compared with the kindred early Roman story of Tarquin and Lucrece it offers fewer dramatic possibilities, for Virginia is almost a passive figure—at the opposite

[1] See F. L. Lucas, *John Webster*, III. 125 ff.

pole from the women of predominant will who had been Webster's creative masterpieces. But alone or in conjunction with Heywood he worked up effective elements in the action. The crafty plotting of Appius together with his tool Clodius is vividly portrayed and elaborated. Virginius stands forth in bold relief not only as a father in his own house but as the central figure in the camp among the turbulent soldiery whose grievances derive their sting not from republican Rome but Caroline England. And in the trial scene before Appius (Act III. i), as might be expected, Webster (for here his hand is evident) found his chief opportunity. Again, as in *The Devil's Law-Case*, he introduces a lawyer to make the worse the better reason by seeking to prove that Virginia is, as Clodius claims, the daughter of his bondwoman. And the apparently judicial attitude of Appius, asking the advocate pithy questions and rebuking interrupters, till the time comes to throw off his mask and to give sentence in favour of Clodius, is a masterly achievement. And even Webster's greatest plays contain nothing more exquisite than the farewell of Virginius to his child before he kills her:

> Let me forget the thought
> Of thy most pretty infancy, when first
> Returning from the wars, I took delight
> To rock thee in my target; when my girl
> Would kiss her father, in his burgonet
> Of glittering steel, hang about his armed neck,
> And viewing the bright metal smile to see
> Another fair Virginia smile on thee.

When Appius is overthrown by a popular revolt, he, like other of Webster's well-born villains, in contrast with the plebeian Clodius, can meet his doom, self-inflicted, with an unexpectedly lofty spirit:

> As I offended, will I pay the mulct,
> And this black stain laid on my family,
> Than which a nobler hath not place in Rome,
> Wash with my blood away.

His warning to corrupt judges to learn from the lesson of

his fall is only one of the moralizing tags which close so inappropriately many Stuart plays.

CYRIL TOURNEUR

The fame of another poetic dramatist, Cyril Tourneur, rests upon even a narrower basis than that of Webster, for only one extant play bears his name on the title-page, and the post-Restoration attribution to him of another, greater, play, though generally accepted, has been challenged on internal grounds. Till recently little was known of his life and the facts now ascertained have little bearing on his literary career. The date of his birth is uncertain, but may be placed in the decade 1570–80. There is no record of his school or university, and the first fixed date concerning him is the publication of the poem, the *Transformed Metamorphosis* in 1600. In 1609 appeared his *A Funeral Poem upon the Death of Sir Francis Vere*, who among other services in the Low Countries had been Governor of Brill, where in 1598 he had dismissed from the office of Lieutenant-Governor Richard Turnor, probably a relation of Cyril. In 1612 he wrote a prose *Character* of Robert Cecil, first Lord Salisbury, which remained in MS. till 1930. Later in 1612 he joined with Webster and Heywood in a collection of poetic elegies on Prince Henry.

Henceforward he seems to have turned from a literary to an active career. In December 1613 he was paid for carrying letters from London to Brussels. In August 1614 a letter from Nimuegen speaks of his military service in that neighbourhood. In 1617 he was back in England and suffered a period of imprisonment on an unknown charge, but was released on a guarantee by Sir Edward Cecil. Under Cecil's command he took part in the ill-fated expedition to Cadiz in October 1625. Among those attacked by disease during it was Tourneur, who died soon after his return, on 28 February 1625/6.

The Atheist's Tragedy: or the Honest Man's Revenge, 'as in divers places it hath often been acted, written by Cyril Tourneur', was published in 1611. No source of the plot has been found, but it belongs to the group of revenge tragedies, and also shows Shakespearean influence. Portia's speech on mercy and Hamlet's meditations in the graveyard are echoed in III. iv and IV. iii, and the declaration of Edmund in *King Lear*, 'thou, Nature, art my goddess', might have been the inspiration of the play. For the distinctive quality of *The Atheist's Tragedy* lies neither in the vengeance that overtakes the central figure, D'Amville, nor in the macabre horrors calculated to raise the hair of a Stuart audience, but in the mainspring of the atheist's actions throughout the play. To Tourneur's contemporaries atheism meant more than religious disbelief; it implied revolt against the accepted moral and social standards. Thus in the opening scene D'Amville and his 'instrument' Borachio agree that man and beast are equal creatures of Nature, that Death ends all and that wealth is the sole source of happiness. D'Amville applies this not only to himself but to his children,

> For from my substance they receive the sap
> Whereby they live and flourish. . .
> There's my eternity. My life in them
> And their succession shall for ever live.

His brother, Lord Montferrers, is old and sickly, with an only son, Charlemont, to whom D'Amville lends money that he may go to the Dutch wars, and thus be separated from his beloved Castabella, heiress of the rich Lord Belforest, whom D'Amville has marked out to be the bride of his elder son, the weakling Rousard. Charlemont consigns her to the charge of Belforest's chaplain, Languebeau Snuffe, a hypocritical Puritan, who lets himself be bribed to further D'Amville's schemes. The contradiction between this presician's professions and his life serves, as D'Amville declares, to confirm him in his atheism. He finds another ally in Castabella's step-mother, Levidulcia, who plies the girl with sensual arguments against her preference of

> the' affection of an absent love
> Before the sweet possession of a man.

It is the Nurse's plea to Juliet to take Paris instead of Romeo, in less vulgar form, and when Belforest also cries (I. iv. 132 ff.):

> Passion o' me, thou peevish girl! I charge
> Thee by my blessing and th' authority
> I have to claim th' obedience: marry him

we seem to hear again the voice of old Capulet. But we are not prepared for the electrifying outburst of D'Amville's younger son, Sebastian,

> A rape! a rape! a rape! . . . Why, what is't but a rape to force a wench to marry, since it forces her to lie with him she would not?

But his protest is in vain. Disguised as a soldier Borachio in a spirited piece of narrative verse tells a false tale of how Charlemont was killed at the siege of Ostend, where Tourneur draws upon his own military experiences. Montferrers overcome by the news and fearing the approach of his own death is induced by Snuffe to make his will, leaving everything to his brother, D'Amville. Thereupon with Borachio's help he murders him by pushing him into a gravel pit as he is returning home by night, and in a passage of almost lyrical ecstasy (II. iv. 120-56) the pair exult over the perfect execution of their plot, the most judicious murder that
The brain of man was e'er deliver'd of.

The outbreak of a thunderstorm causes D'Amville characteristically to greet it as a brave noise that speaks encouragement (II. iv. 169 ff.):

> Now Nature shows thee how it favour'd our
> Performance: to forbear this noise when we
> Set forth, because it should not terrify
> My brother's going home, which would have dash'd
> Our purpose: to forbear this lightning
> In our passage, lest it should have warn'd him
> O' the pitfall. Then propitious Nature wink'd
> At our proceedings; now it doth express
> How that forbearance favour'd our success.

It is in the tradition of the Senecan revenge play that the ghost of Montferrers should appear to Charlemont when he falls asleep on outpost duty and warn him to return to France. But the ghost breaks with the tradition in the exhortation:

> Attend with patience the success of things,
> And leave revenge unto the King of Kings.

Charlemont in a different way strikes a new note, when he seeks at first to dismiss the apparition as a dream and proceeds to analyse the nature of dreams. But convinced of its reality he returns to find monuments erected to his father and himself and Castabella married to Ronsard. Thrown into prison by D'Amville till he can repay his loan, he is set free by the generosity of Sebastian, though in his confinement he shows the Stoic temper of a Clermont D'Ambois (III. iv.):

> I've lost a signiory
> That was confined within a piece of earth,
> A wart upon the body of the world.
> But now I am an emperor of a world
> This little world of Man. My passions are
> My subjects.

Still obsessed by the idea of enriching his issue, and fearful that neither of his sons is a 'good life', D'Amville makes to his daughter-in-law the monstrous proposal of a union with her to continue the succession of her blood. When she shrinks back in horror from incest, he cries:

> Incest? Tush!
> These distances affinity observes
> Are articles of bondage cast upon
> Our freedoms by our own objections.
> Nature allows a general liberty
> Of generation to all creatures else.
> Shall man
> To whose command and use all creatures were
> Made subject be less free than they?

There is the true atheist voice, in the Elizabethan sense, and in Castabella's answer we hear Tourneur's loftiest note:

O God!
Is Thy unlimited and infinite
Omnipotence less free because thou doest
No ill?
Or if you argue merely out of Nature
Do you not degenerate from that, and are
You not unworthy the prerogative
Of Nature's masterpiece, when basely you
Prescribe yourself authority and law
From their example whom you should command?

This dialogue takes place in a churchyard where D'Amville has also planned the murder of Charlemont by Borachio. But it is the assailant who is killed, and Charlemont now rushes in disguised as his father's ghost, to save Castabella from D'Amville's lust. Then he surrenders himself to the watch as the slayer of Borachio, and Castabella proclaims that she will share his fate. But this gives short satisfaction to D'Amville, who has to look upon the bodies of his two sons, the elder dead from disease and the younger killed by Belforest, who has caught him in an intrigue with his wife. This annihilation of his posterity, for whom he has contrived his plots and crimes, destroys D'Amville's confidence in Nature as supreme arbiter:

Sure there is some power above
Her that controls her force. . .
Nature, thou art a traitor to my soul,
Thou hast abus'd my trust. I will complain
To a superior court to right my wrong.
I'll prove thee a forger of false assurances.
In your Star-chamber thou shalt answer it.

In this superb imaginative sweep, this agonized appeal to a supernatural power, lies the true 'atheist's tragedy'. Meanwhile in the earthly court where Charlemont and Castabella are put on trial and face death with serene composure D'Amville finds himself forced to ask 'from whence the peace of conscience should proceed' and gets the answer, 'the peace of conscience rises in itself'. As a distraught tribute to their constancy he offers himself to act as executioner, and in lifting the axe accidentally strikes out his own brains. He sees in this however no accident but the final proof that (V. ii):

> Nature is a fool. There is a power
> Above her that hath overthrown the pride
> Of all my projects and posterity. . .
>   Yon power
> That struck me knew the judgment I deserved
> And gave it.

It is the atheist's dying recantation that lingers in our ears at the close of the play rather than the liberated Charlemont's acknowledgment that here is the hand of Heaven, and that, as the Ghost had enjoined, 'Patience is the honest man's revenge'.

It is doubly unfortunate that another play by Tourneur, *The Nobleman*, entered in the Stationers' Register 15 February 1611/2, and re-entered by Humphrey Moseley, 9 September 1653, was one of those burnt by Warburton's cook, if the story is to be believed. Not only would it have been of value on its own account, but it would have been of help in the attempt to solve the riddle of the authorship of *The Revenger's Tragedy*. This play was entered by George Eld in the Stationers' Register on 7 October 1607 and was published by him in the same year as acted by the King's company but without the name of the author. In 1656 the bookseller Archer, in a list of plays assigned it to Tourneur, as did Kirkman in similar lists in 1661 and 1671. Such an attribution half a century after the date of publication cannot be considered decisive and has to find support, if any, in internal evidence. What then is the impression made by *The Revenger's Tragedy*? It opens with abrupt explosive force as the central figure Vindice clasping the skull of his dead love, victim of the aged Duke's lust, indicts not only him but his heir, Lussurioso, his bastard son, Spurio, and the Duchess, his second wife. Vindice's very name stamps him from the beginning as the revenger, and he invokes vengeance, 'murder's quit-rent', to keep her 'day, hour, minute'. But for a time attention is fastened not on him but on the Duchess and her offspring. Her youngest (nameless) son has been guilty of a rape on the wife of the lord Antonio, and is put on trial. His mother and eldest brother, Ambitioso, plead for him, but the court gives sentence of death on the following morning, which the Duke overrules till the next sitting. But this does not appease the Duchess (I. ii. 102 ff.):

> Indeed, 'tis true an old man's twice a child;
> Mine cannot speak: one of his single words
> Would quite have freed my youngest, dearest son
> From death or durance:

and she vows vengeance by breaking her marriage troth with the Duke's bastard son.

Meanwhile Vindice has in disguise taken service with Lussurioso, who employs him as an agent to tempt to sin his sister Castiza. On her refusal he bribes their mother to plead with her till she cries with bitter irony:

> I cry your mercy, lady, I mistook you—
> Pray did you see my mother? Which way went you?
> Pray God I have not lost her.

Vindice renews his pleas and the verse catches the swift rhythm of his eager argument (II. i. 196 ff.):

> O think upon the pleasure of the palace,
> Secured ease and state: the stirring meats
> Ready to move out of the dishes, that e'en now
> Quicken when they are eaten;
> Banquets adorned by torch-light, musics, sports. . .
> Nine coaches waiting—hurry, hurry, hurry.
> *Cast.* Aye, to the Devil.

When again Gratiana comes to Vindice's support once more Castiza turns on her with icy irony:

> Mother, come from that poisonous woman there.
> *Gra.* Where?
> *Cast.* Do you not see her? She's too inward, then.

Vindice feigning to bring Lussurioso to his sister diverts him

from his purpose by crying out that Spurio is sleeping with
the Duchess, whereupon Lussurioso bursts into the ducal
bedchamber, shouting, 'villain, strumpet', only to find that
he has aroused his father, who to punish this outrage dooms
him to death, but revokes the sentence. Snatching at the
chance of getting rid of the heir to the dukedom the two
elder step-brothers show the death-warrant to the prison
officers, who mistakenly carry it out upon their youngest
brother still in confinement for rape. These are ingenious
complications and the dialogue moves with terse and pregnant force. But it is not till Act III. iv that there is a return
to the central theme when Vindice, still feigning a pander's
part but now for the Duke, appears with the skull of his
betrothed which he apostrophises:

> Madam, his Grace will not be absent long.
> Secret? Ne'er doubt us, madam; 'twill be worth
> Three velvet gowns to your ladyship.

Thereupon he launches into a vitriolic indictment of the
fleeting charms of sex, mounting to the macabre climax:

> See, ladies, with false forms
> You deceive men, but cannot deceive worms.

This skull is not to be only a useless property but to bear a
part in its own revenge, for Vindice has poisoned its lips, and
when the Duke kisses them his fate is sealed. Then the
revenger throws off his disguise (III. iv. 167 ff.):

> Look, monster, what a lady hast thou made me,
> My once betrothèd wife.
> *Duke.* Is it thou, villain? Nay, then—
> *Vin.* 'Tis I, 'tis Vindice, 'tis I.

To complete the Duke's torture he is bidden behold the
embraces of his bastard and his wife. Well may he ask,
'Is there a hell besides this?'

Thus the revenger's first aim is achieved, but Lussurioso
determines to be rid of the agent who had brought him
within an ace of execution. But stripped of his disguise
Vindice is reintroduced into Lussurioso's service. His pose

is now one of melancholy discontent, which offers easy scope for bribery (IV. ii. 112 ff.):

Lus.   I think thou art ill-moneyed.
Vin.   Money! ho, ho!
          'T has been my want so long, 'tis now my scoff:
          I e'en, forget what colour silver's of.
Lus.   Somewhat to set thee up withal.
Vin.   O mine eyes!
Lus.   How now, man?
Vin.   Almost struck blind;
          This bright unusual shine to me seems proud;
          I dare not look till the sun be in a cloud.

He is now given the task of murdering himself on the charge of seeking to corrupt his sister and mother, and enraged by the memory of his mother's pliancy he and his brother, Hippolito, threaten her with their daggers and assail her with reproaches that made Charles Lamb's ears tingle and a hot flush spread over his cheeks. She breaks down in repentant tears (IV. iv. 53 ff.):

          To weep is to our sex naturally given:
          But to weep truly, that's a gift from Heaven.
Vin.   Nay, I'll kiss you now. Kiss her, brother:
          Let's marry her to our souls, wherein's no lust,
          And honourably love her.
                 *   *   *
          The duke's son's great concubine!
          A drab of state, a cloth-o'-silver slut,
          To have her train borne up, and her soul trail i' the dirt!

Vindice's cynical humour, while he prepares for revenge for the insult of his sister's honour, finds scope in dressing up the Duke's unburied body in his own discarded disguise and thus persuading Lussurioso that his father was killed by his cashiered agent—as, of a truth, he had been.

And now the revels with which Lussurosio's installation is celebrated bring all to a head. In their rivalry for the succession to the throne the bastard and the two step-brothers plan to murder Lussurioso and one another in a masque, but are forestalled by Vindice and Hippolito, who in similar fashion kill the new Duke and his attendant nobles. The 'intended murderers' disappointed of their victims turn their weapons on one another, while the dying Lussurioso groans, 'my tongue is out of office'. Thereupon the revenger whispers in his ear:

> Now thou'lt not prate on't—'twas I Vindice murdered
> thee.

Lus. Oh!
Vin. Murdered thy father.

And trusting that Antonio who now becomes the head of the state will recognize that the rape of his wife has been 'quited well with death on death', Vindice reveals the secret of the old Duke's murder:

> We may be bold to speak it now.
> 'Twas somewhat wittily carried, though we say it.
> 'Twas we two murdered him.

Ant. You two?
Vin. None else i' faith, my lord. Nay, 'twas well managed.

To his consternation Antonio orders his and Hippolito's arrest and instant execution. The latter gives proof of wavering when he tries to shift the responsibility from himself, ''s foot, brother, you begun'. But Vindice goes glorying to his doom (V. iii. 121 ff.):

> Thou hast no conscience; are we not reveng'd?
> Is there one enemy left alive among those?
> 'Tis time to die when we're ourselves our foes. . .
> Y' faith we're well—our mother turn'd: our sister true.
> We die after a nest of dukes—adieu!

It is the climax of the revenge tragedy, initiated by Kyd and developed by Marston and others. Vindice takes his farewell in the same spirit as Hieronimo. Could anything be more alien from the last pronouncements of the two chief figures in *The Atheist's Tragedy*? D'Amville, unwilling executioner of himself, has to confess the break-down of his 'nature' creed. Charlemont acknowledges that he did right to forbear from being his own revenger. The discussion of Tourneur's claim to *The Revenger's Tragedy* has, in my opinion, taken too little account of this radical contrast between it and *The Atheist's Tragedy*. This outweighs the resemblances in their *macabre* features and their sensual, sombre atmosphere. Against the likeness that has been traced between the imagery in both plays may be set the parallels with Middleton's phraseology and with Marston's technique. And the versification of *The Revenger's Tragedy* is marked by such maturer power than *The Atheist's Tragedy* that some of Tourneur's supporters have been driven, on mere conjecture, to reverse the chronological order of the two plays. The authorship of *The Revenger's Tragedy* therefore remains, as I think, an open question. But with (in Swinburne's phrase) the 'fiery jet' of its 'molten verse', its revealing flashes of dialogue, its mastery of stage situations, and its unflinching presentation of an intellect and will consecrated solely to revenge, it stands in the front rank of Stuart drama.

IX

THOMAS MIDDLETON—WILLIAM ROWLEY

DRAMAS OF SEX COMPLICATIONS

FROM playwrights whose fame rests upon lofty achievement within the restricted domain of poetic tragedy attention may turn again to some of their contemporaries who with versatile gifts experimented, alone or in collaboration, in various dramatic spheres.

Recent research has set the biography of Thomas Middleton in a new light. Dyce in his introduction to the first collected edition of his works (1840) had conjectured that he was born not earlier than 1570 and he had been followed by later editors and stage-historians. But the record of his baptism on 18 April 1580 has been discovered in the register of the church of St. Lawrence in the Old Jewry.[1] He was the only son of William Middleton, gentleman, and his wife, Anne Snow. His school is unknown, but it has now been proved that he entered The Queen's College, Oxford, in April 1598. In spite of the legal knowledge which he turned to account in dialogue and plot-construction it appears that he cannot be identified with any of the three Thomas Middletons admitted to Gray's Inn in 1593–6.

With the discovery of the date of his birth his earliest publications, in verse, *The Wisdom of Solomon Paraphrased* (1597), *Micro-Cynicon* (1600), *Six Snarling Satires* (1599), and *The Ghost of Lucrece* (1600) are seen to be youthful efforts. They were followed in 1604 by the more mature prose pamphlets, *Father Hubbard's Tale* and *The Black Book*, both showing an intimate acquaintance with the London life of his day.

[1] Mark Eccles, 'Middleton's Birth and Education' in *R.E.S.*, October 1931.

Meanwhile Middleton had started as a dramatist. There are entries in Henslowe's *Diary* in May 1602 of payments to him as part-author of two non-extant plays, *Caesar's Fall* and *Two Harpies*. In October and November of the same year he received six pounds from Henslowe for *The Chester Tragedy*, which has also disappeared. Henceforward his dramatic output was prolific, and besides plays he composed in 1613 two city pageants, and in 1614 *The Masque of Cupid* to celebrate the marriage of the Earl of Somerset and Lady Frances Howard. In 1620 he was appointed City Chronologer and Inventor of its 'honourable entertainments', the last of which from his pen is dated 1626. It has recently been shown from the *Repertory* of the City of London that his work in 1625 and 1626 was not considered satisfactory and that payment was deferred or refused.[1] He lived in his later years at Newington Butts, and was buried in its parish church on 4 July 1627.

Considering Middleton's varied literary activities and his social and civic connexions the references to him by his contemporaries are surprisingly few, and both the canon and chronology of his plays are still under debate.[2] His authorship of a group of comedies acted by one or other of the children's companies, and published between 1602 and 1608 has been accepted by his editors on the doubtful evidence of some of the early play-lists. *Blurt, Master Constable* (1602), *Michaelmas Term* (1607), *The Phoenix* (1607) acted by the Children of Paul's, and *The Family of Love* (1608) by the Children of the King's Revels, were issued without an author's name on the title-page, as were later editions of *Michaelmas Term* and *The Phoenix* in 1630. The attribution to Middleton of *Blurt, Master Constable* has been strongly challenged, and though internal evidence of style has been held to support his claim to the other three plays, it cannot

[1] R. C. Bald, 'Middleton's Civic Employments' in *Modern Philology*, August, 1933.
[2] See R. C. Bald, 'The Chronology of Middleton's Plays' in *R.E.S.*, January, 1937.

be considered completely decisive. On the other hand *Your Five Gallants* (no date, but entered Stationers' Register 22 March 1607/8), acted at Blackfriars, has his name; *A Mad World, My Masters* (1608), acted by the Children of Paul's, has his initials; and *A Trick to Catch the Old One* (1608), 'as it hath been often in action both at Paul's and the Black-friars; presented before His Majesty on New-Year's Night last', has his initials, while a later 1616 edition has his name.

A Trick to Catch the Old One deserved the popularity with both the public and the Court indicated by the title-page, and it may be taken as representative of Middleton's early group of comedies. They introduce us into the world of middle-class London life, portrayed with a light-hearted cynicism, where youth is chiefly given over to dissipation and age makes a god of money. The characters are, for the most part, types rather than individuals, and their fortunes do not move us deeply. But agreeable entertainment is provided by well-contrived, swiftly moving plots and by easy and vivacious, though not highly polished, dialogue. In *A Trick to Catch the Old One* Theophilus Witgood, a young spendthrift country gentleman, has been forced to mortgage his estate to his uncle Pecunius Lucre, a usurious city mer-chant. Witgood loves Joyce, niece of Walkadine Hoard (Middleton specializes in out-of-the-way Christian names) whom Lucre has antagonized by over-reaching him in a bargain. But he is living with a courtesan whom he gets to pose as a rich country widow about to marry him, with four hundred a year 'in woods, in bullocks, in barns, and in tye-stacks'. This will 'conjure up a kind of usurer's love' in Lucre towards him. 'I know the state of an old man's affection so well; if his nephew be poor indeed, why, he lets God alone with him; but if he be once rich, then he'll be the first man that helps him'. And so it proves. When Lucre hears the news his nephew is transformed into 'lusty Witgood, thrice-noble Witgood', to whom he is ready to advance fifty pounds and whom he declares in the 'widow's' hearing to be heir to his house and all.

But complications follow thick and fast. Lucre has a step-son, Sam Freedom, hitherto another suitor to Hoard's niece, whom his mother now urges, with 'two hundred a year of thyself, beside thy good parts—a proper person and a lovely', to cut out Witgood in the widow's affections. A third, least expected, rival appears in Hoard, who grasps at this oppor-tunity not only 'extremely to cross my adversary and con-found the last hopes of his nephew, but thereby to enrich my state, augment my revenues'. To defeat Witgood on the very day that the match with the widow is to be concluded he arranges to carry her off beforehand by boat and marry her instantly. Lucre pursues them and, not knowing that the widow has now become Hoard's wife, offers, in the hope of cheating his adversary of the coveted prize, to free Wit-good from his mortgage. While Hoard is chuckling over the full measure of his happiness, a bolt falls from the blue. Witgood claims the widow by virtue of a pre-contract with her and in order to buy him off Hoard enters into a formal bond to satisfy his creditors.

The whole of this *imbroglio* in Acts III and IV is very skilfully managed by Middleton, who carries along the action at break-neck pace and turns his knowledge of legal detail to deft use. But the disclosure of the widow's real identity in the short final act is too forced and abrupt as it comes from Hoard's brother Onesiphorus, and his friends Limber and Kix (another trio of extraordinary names) who have merely caught sight of the courtesan for a moment in the opening scene of the play. Hoard has to accept the fate he has brought on himself:

> I must embrace shame, to be rid of shame!
> Conceal'd disgrace prevents a public name.

The courtesan and Witgood, now married to Joyce, kneel down and as 'reclaimed' they renounce their evil ways. But this belated moralizing sits awkwardly on a play which wins most appreciation if its standards of conduct are not taken too seriously.

It is more difficult, even if one is not a precisian, to be similarly indulgent to *A Chaste Maid in Cheapside*, which is one of a later group of Middleton's comedies. It was published, after his death, in 1630, with his name, as often acted at the Swan by the Lady Elizabeth's servants. This company's appearances at the Swan theatre appear to have been between 1611 and 1614, and references in the play suggest that it was performed soon after the enforcement of orders for the strict keeping of Lent in 1613.

Except under the genial eye of Dekker the citizens and their womenfolk fare ill, as a rule, with Elizabethan dramatists. But in Yellowhammer, the goldsmith of Cheapside, and his wife, Maudlin, they sink to their lowest level. They have set their hearts on forcing their daughter, Moll, the chaste maid, into a marriage with the profligate Welsh knight, Sir Walter Whorehound, though she loves a young gentleman Touchwood. She flies to him and (Act III. i) is being wedded with a ring, which Touchwood has tricked Yellowhammer into making, when her father and the knight rush in and carry her off. A second time (Act IV. iii) she tries to reach her lover by a boat on the Thames, but is overtaken by her mother, who drags her back by the hair after she has attempted to drown herself. All this part of the action is carried through with Middleton's unflagging vivacity, but again the *dénouement* is more forced. Touchwood attacks and wounds Whorehound and spreads a report of his own death from the encounter, while Moll also feigns death from grief. There is an elaborate double funeral, which must have been an effective stage-spectacle (V. iv), with 'recorders dolefully playing' and 'a sad song in the music room', till the two supposed corpses suddenly rise from their coffins and are united by the parson who had come to perform the burial rites.

Moll's fate is thus in the end happier than that of her

brother Timotheus, or Tim, who provides the only whole-some element of light comedy in the play. When he comes home with his tutor in Act III. ii he has just 'answered under bachelor' at Cambridge and is mightily offended when his mother offers him plums to eat, and still more when she threatens to make his tutor 'whip him':

> 'Life, whip a bachelor! You'd be laughed at soundly.
> Let not my tutor hear you, 'twould be a jest
> Through the whole university.

The tutor has brought Tim 'in league with logic', and the pair carry the Cambridge Latin disputations into Chelsea. But Latin means nothing to the Welshwoman, supposed niece of Whorehound and heir to some nineteen mountains, whom the shy scholar is set on to court, and who answers him in equally incomprehensible Welsh. She is really the knight's mistress, and it is a cynical dispensation that leaves him at the close married to her, with his mother's reminder that he can prove her by logic an honest woman.

Whorehound's amour with the Welshwoman is a pecca-dillo compared with his relation with Mistress Allwit, by whom he has had half-a-dozen children and is expecting another. For grossly cynical audacity there is nothing in Stuart drama that can outdo the speech in I. ii in which Allwit glories in the advantages of being a cuckold. And when the child is born 'a fine plump black-eyed slut', he congratulates himself on merely having to bid the 'gossips' for the christening, while the expense of the feast, of nurses, and charwomen falls upon Whorehound. The scene (III. ii) after the christening in Mistress Allwit's bedroom, where the gossips and Puritan neighbours gather to chatter and to partake of comfits and wine not wisely but too well, is painted with coarse Skeltonic realism. As they depart Allwit hears that Whorehound is about to marry Moll and makes a frantic attempt to stop the match by describing to Yellow-hammer, under an assumed name, the knight's relations with himself and his wife. But these relations are brought to an abrupt close by Touchwood's sword, for Whorehound fearing that his end may be near repents (in Middleton's unconvincing fashion) of his sins and denounces the Allwits, who retaliate by thrusting him out of their house whence he finds himself taken to prison.

To complete the sorry picture there are Sir Oliver and Lady Kix abusing each other because after seven years' marriage they are without an heir, till with the equivocal aid of Touchwood's elder brother one is on the way. This Touchwood senior, in contrast, is perpetually finding himself a father both within the bands of matrimony and in less legitimate ways. From these plays which may be taken as representative of Middleton's comic vein in his earlier and middle periods the transition may be made to the important miscellaneous group of his dramas dealing with darker or deeper themes.

The Witch is preserved in a manuscript, now in the Bodleian library, transcribed by Ralph Crane between 1620 and 1627. In a dedicatory letter Middleton speaks of it as 'this ignorantly ill-fated labour of mine' that has lain 'long in an imprisoned obscurity'. It was evidently not a success on the Blackfriars stage and was not published till 1778. Written almost throughout in fluent blank-verse, with a large proportion of feminine ending, it has the marks of Middleton's later style, and may be dated about 1616. Some of its features may have been intended to recall the marriage of the Earl of Somerset and the divorced Countess of Essex with its sequel in the murder of Sir Thomas Overbury and the execution of their agents.

It is not surprising that audiences who had been accustomed to enjoy Middleton's briskly moving comedies of London life were slow to respond when he presented to them a play of which the main plot was based on a gruesome medieval story which he had found in Machiavelli's *Florentine History* or Belleforest's *Histoires Tragiques*. A Duke, whose capital is Ravenna, has married the daughter of his conquered enemy and forces her on festive occasions to drink from a cup which he has made out of her father's skull. To revenge herself the Duchess apparently plays him false with a young courtier, Almachildes, though a courtesan takes her place, while he is blindfolded. She then discloses herself and gives him the choice of death or of killing the Duke. The Duchess believes that he carries out the murder, but becomes alarmed at the threat of a popular rising and plans to do away with Almachildes and marry the governor of Ravenna. Thereupon the Duke, who has lain apparently lifeless, starts up, embraces the Duchess fervently and declares that he will bury her father's skull.

This is a far from convincing solution and the handling of the whole story is somewhat confused. There is more of Middleton's geniune quality in the sub-plot, in which the soldier, Sebastian, and Isabella, the governor's niece, are the chief figures. Sebastian, returning from three years' warfare, finds that his beloved Isabella has just been given in marriage by her uncle to Antonio. Yet he still claims her as his own:

> She is my wife by contract before Heaven
> And all the angels.

He enters her household in the disguise of a servant and finds that Antonio is still keeping as his mistress the courtesan Florida. He discloses this to Isabella and tells her that she will find them together in the house of his friend Fernando. Meanwhile Isabella discovers that Antonio's wanton sister Francisca has given birth to an illegitimate child, and 'to be quit with her in the same fashion', Francisca accuses her to Antonio of unchastity. He is tricked into attacking her supposed lover while she is seeking him at Fernando's house. After further complications, Antonio conveninetly clears the way by falling to his death through a trap-door.

But the main feature of interest in this over-elaborated sub-plot is Sebastian's reiterated proclamation of a more sanctified union between himself and Isabella than earthly

marriage can confer. It finds its highest utterance in
Act IV. ii:

> We're registered
> Husband and wife in Heaven; though there wants that
> Which often keeps licentious men in awe
> From starting from their wedlocks, the knot public ;
> 'Tis in our souls knit fast; and how more precious
> The soul is than the body, so much judge
> The sacred and celestial tie within us
> More than the outward form, which calls but witness
> Here upon earth to what is due in Heaven.

It is one of the earliest expressions of the Platonic love
doctrine which was increasingly to influence Stuart drama.

This and other aspects of the play have been unduly, though
inevitably, overshadowed for readers of to-day by the three
scenes (I. ii, III. iii, V. ii) from which *The Witch* gets its title.
Sebastian, Almachildes and the Duchess in turn invoke the
supernatural aid of Hecate, with her attendant hags, Stadlin
and Hoppo and her son, Firestone. Their spells have surprisingly little effect on the action, and Hecate's speeches are
largely verbal echoes of Reginald Scot's *Discoverie of Witchcraft*. Middleton's additions to them are for the most part
disagreeably sensual or trivial, though in one striking speech
Hecate confesses to Sebastian that she cannot unloose the
marriage tie (I. ii):

> We cannot disjoin wedlock;
> 'Tis of Heaven's fastening. Well may we raise jars,
> Jealousies, strifes and heart-burning disagreements
> Like a thick scurf o'er life . . . but the work itself
> Our power cannot disjoint.

But the opening words of two songs in these scenes, 'Come
away, come away' (III. iii) and 'Black spirits and white'
(V. ii) are found, with the stage-direction, 'Music and a
song' in *Macbeth*, III. v. 33 and IV. i. 43.

Though *The Witch* is the later play there can be no reason-
able doubt that these songs and the figure of Hecate found
their way from it into the first folio, partly corrupt, text of
Shakespeare's tragedy. Hecate is a commonplace sorceress

intruding among the mysterious and terrible weird sisters whose exhortations are far apart from the songs in their rhythm and fanciful prettiness. On the other hand, with Scot's *Discoverie* at his elbow, and with the widespread interest in witches fostered by King James himself, it need not be assumed that Middleton was indebted for his general conception of witch scenes to Shakespeare.

Medieval history, though now relating to his homeland, furnished Middleton with the main theme of another play, *Hengist, King of Kent or The Mayor of Quinborough*. It was not printed till 1661, when it was published by Henry Herringman under its second title, 'as it hath been often acted with much applause at Blackfriars by His Majesty's Servants'. Two manuscripts in the same hand are extant, one in the Duke of Portland's library, the other long in the possession of the Kentish Lambarde family, now in the Folger Library in Washington. These contain 175 lines not in the quarto, which has however 25 lines not in them. In particular the MSS. have an entirely different ending, doubtless the original one, with 43 lines, including an epilogue, for which the quarto substitutes 11 lines. The MSS. give also the text of two songs, and their much more frequent stage-directions, especially concerning music, suggest that they are transcripts from a prompt-copy. The Portland MS. gives both titles; the Folger MS. has no title-page, but has *Hengist, King of Kent* at the end of the play.[1]

The inclusion of a presenter and of dumb shows led several critics to place *Hengist, King of Kent* (to use the primary title) among Middleton's earlier works. But these features had a longer dramatic life than was often supposed. The editor of the play from the MS. text has, in my opinion, shown conclusively that on metrical grounds it must be assigned to a period beginning with *The Chaste Maid in Cheapside*. It is first mentioned on a Revels office slip, con-

[1] The text has been edited from the Folger MS., with a collation of the Portland MS. and the 1661 quarto by R. C. Bald (1938).

taining a cancelled play-list which must date between 1615 and 1620, and the presumption on various grounds is that it belongs to about 1619.

Middleton's chief source was Holinshed's *Chronicle*, supplemented by Fabyan's *Chronicle*. Here he found in early British history an impressive groundwork. On the death of King Constantine the ambitious noble, Vortiger, drags his eldest son, Constantius, from a monastery to the throne, so that under his reluctant rule power may be vested in his own hands. He then has Constantius treacherously murdered and seizes the crown himself, though hated by the people. Worsted in battle by the Picts and Scots, he summons to his aid Saxons from Germany headed by Hengist and Horsus, who are afterwards joined by Hengist's wife and daughter, Roxena. Vortiger rewards Hengist with a gift of land in Kent and Thong-castle, and afterwards, forsaking his lawful wife, marries Roxena, 'to the high offence of God and great displeasure of his subjects'. They depose him in favour of his son, Vortimer, who is poisoned by his step-mother, whereupon Vortiger is restored, but meets his fate at the hands of Constantine's younger sons, Aurelius Ambrose and Uther, who burn him in his castle.

Here was ample material for tragedy, and in Vortiger Middleton drew a figure who is a Stuart counterpart to Marlowe's Guise and Shakespeare's Gloucester. Either of them might have spoken his opening words after Constantine's death:

> How near was I to a sceptre and a crown! . . .
> Well, though I rise not king, I'll seek the means
> To grow as near to one as policy can.

His treatment of Constantius is effectively portrayed. When the pious king groans beneath the killing weight of his office, Vortiger assures him (I. i. 147 ff.):

> To be oppressed is not required of you, my lord,
> But only to be king; the broken sleeps
> Let me take from you, sir; the toils and troubles,

> All that is burthensome in authority
> Please you to lay it on me, and what is glorious
> Receive it to your own brightness.

His insistence that Constantius must marry and that he must feast on fast days adds ingenious touches of the playwright's own invention. And after the murder of the king and Vortiger's seizure of power Middleton at first handles the situation with a notable sense of dramatic economy. Vortiger uses the Saxons not, as in the *Chronicle*, against Picts and Scots but his own rebellious subjects, and the battles which fill so much space in Holinshed are reduced to the stage-direction, 'noise of skirmish within'. The entrance of Simon, the tanner, with a hide in his hand in Act II. iii, makes more plausible Hengist's request for just so much land as 'yon poor hide will compass', which by a trick becomes a large part of Kent.

But thenceforward Middleton gives way to the obsession which leads him so often to overload his plots with abnormal sexual complications. It was not enough for him to expand Holinshed's statement that Vortiger forsook his wife and married Roxena. He attributes to him a repellently tortuous plot against Castiza, as his wife is significantly called in the play. Forced from the religious life to marry him, Vortiger knows that her purity is unassailable and that she will give him no pretext to put her away. Yet he is determined to replace her by Roxena (III. i):

> Why should not the mind,
> The nobler part that's of us, be allowed
> Change of affections, as our bodies are
> Change of food and raiment? I'll have it so.

In concert with Horsus he devises a plan by which Castiza is seized and blindfolded, and forced to have intercourse with himself, while she imagines herself the victim of a rape. When therefore Vertigor during a banquet in Hengist's castle (IV. ii) puts each lady to the test of swearing that she has never known the will of any man besides her husband's

Castiza cannot take the oath and is denounced by Vortiger. He then puts the test to Roxena, who is ready to swear that she is 'as free from man as truth from falsehood'. But she is forsworn, for she has been the mistress of Horsus, who in the play is not of kin to her father Hengist, and who in all his actions is moved by his passion for her.

To give scope for these amorous complications Middleton confines to a dumb show the crowning of Vortimer, his murder by Roxena and the restoration of Vortiger. But in Act IV. iii he returns to another main theme of the play, the treacherous ambition of Hengist, who seizes Vortiger during a peace parley, wrings from him the title of King of Kent, and obliges him to fly with Roxena to Wales. Here they are besieged by Constantine's younger sons, and seeing his doom so near, Vortiger proclaims from the castle walls to his foes that it was the 'Stygian soul' of Horsus that was the 'sole plotter' against his religious queen, Castiza. Whereupon Horsus reveals that he has followed him merely to make him a cuckold with Roxena. As they stab each other mortally, the castle goes up in flames and Roxena meets death by fire. Vengeance has overtaken the guilty except Hengist, who now is led in a prisoner and confesses boldly that he has been foiled in his hope of acquiring the whole kingdom. The defiant dignity of his farewell and the ironic retorts of Aurelius, to whom the vacant throne now falls, bring the play to a notable close (V. ii):

Heng.   I have a thirst
           Could never have been full quenched under all:
           The whole must do't or nothing.
Aur.   A strange drought!
           And what a little ground shall death now teach you
           To be content withal!
Heng.   Why let it then,
           For none else can; you've named the only way
           To limit my ambition . . .
                            Life to me,
           'Less it be glorious, is a misery.
Aur.   That pleasure we will do you. Lead him out.

It is strange that *Hengist, King of Kent* should ever have
been taken to be one of Middleton's early works. Not only
have the versification and the dialogue the marks of his
mature hand, but in dealing with his material he shows his
grasp of the essential difference between a chronicle-history
play and a historic tragedy. Largely through the skilful use
of dumb-shows he subordinates events to character-deline-
ation. But, as has been seen, this takes a somewhat abnormal
form. Moreover, the main interest shifts disconcertingly
from Constantius to Vortiger and from him to Hengist and
Horsus. Thus it came about that it was the underplot of
Simon the Tanner that made the greatest contemporary
appeal, as Herringman recognized when he published the
play as a 'comedy' and with the title of *The Mayor of
Quinborough*. Except that he appropriately brings in the
hide for the measurement of the land granted to Hengist,
Simon has no connexion with the main action. But he
provides delightful entertainment in the two scenes where
he is chosen Mayor (III. iii) over his rival Oliver, the Puritan
fustian-weaver, and where (V. i) he welcomes officially a
professed company of actors who have taken 'the name of
country comedians to abuse simple people with a printed
play or two, which they bought at Canterbury for sixpence'.
This is an ingenious variation of 'the play within the play'
device, and Simon is a figure of the richest fun in his droll
comments in the interlude of *The Cheater and the Clown*, and
in his interruption of the action to take the clown's part
himself till by one of the new additions he is blinded by meal
thrown in his eyes and his purse is picked.

The subject of abnormal sexual passion was still keeping
its fascination for Middleton when he wrote *Women Beware
Women*. The play was not printed till 1657, when it was
issued by H. Moseley, together with *More Dissemblers besides
Women*. Its date must therefore be conjectural, but on
grounds of style and versification it may be placed about
1620. Middleton is not likely to have been indebted (as

Q

Langbaine stated) to the English version by A. Hart of
The Tragicke Loves of Hipolito and Isabella, as this was not
published till 1628, the year after his death. He must have
used the French original *Les Amours Tragiques d'Hypolite et
Isabelle* (1610), though he transferred the scene from Naples
to Florence. Isabella's domineering father, Fabricio, insists
not only that she shall marry the rich doltish ward of Guardiano, but that she shall love him. Her aunt, Livia, who
has 'buried two husbands in good fashion' intervenes on the
girl's behalf (I. ii):

> O, soft there, brother! . . .
> You may compel, out of the power of father,
> Things merely harsh to a maid's flesh and blood;
> But when you come to love, there the soil alters,
> You're in another country.

This is only the prelude to a more active part by Livia.
Her other, favourite, brother Hippolito confesses to her that
he loves his niece, Isabella, and to further his incestuous
passion she tells the girl falsely that her father is not really
Fabricio but a Spanish marquis who had beguiled her
mother. Isabella, overjoyed at the news delights her father
by now pressing him to hurry on her marriage with the
foolish ward, that she may have a screen for an intrigue with
the lover who, as she thinks, is now outside the forbidden
affinities.

Meanwhile Livia becomes also the instrument in another
amorous complication where Middleton links with the uncle
and niece plot another based, with variations, on the
historic story of Bianca Capello, who after a lowly marriage
became the mistress of Francisco de Medici. Bianca appears
in the opening scene of the play as the bride who has just
eloped from her wealthy parents in Venice to the home of
her Florentine husband, the poor 'factor', or merchant's
agent, Leantio. He is displaying her exultingly to his old
mother:

> And here's my masterpiece; do you now behold her!
> Look on her well, she's mine; look on her better;
> Now say if 't be not the best piece of theft
> That ever was committed?

It is a charming picture of domestic bliss—a rare thing in Middleton's plays. But Leantio has soon to start on his commercial travels, and Bianca left behind is spied at a window, as he takes part in a festival procession, by the Duke, who becomes enamoured of her, and employs Guardiano to arrange for a meeting with her at Livia's house. The scene (Act II. ii) is Middleton's masterpiece of high comedy. With the subtle arts of a 'witty' society woman Livia sends an invitation to Leantio's mother, reproaches her for making herself so strange when she is a near neighbour, and insists on her staying to supper. The mother has at last to confess that she has left at home alone a young gentlewoman—her son's wife:

Liv.   Now I beshrew you;
    Could you be so unkind to her and me,
    To come and not bring her? Faith, 'tis not friendly.
Moth. I feared to be too bold.
Liv.   Too bold! O, what's become
    Of the true hearty love was wont to be
    'Mongst neighbours in old time? . . .
    Leave her behind! poor gentlewoman! alone too!
    Make some amends, and send for her betimes, go.

Bianca is brought and is escorted by Guardiano round the house to see the pictures and the monument, while Livia and the mother play at chess. The game, with its references to the black and white kings and other pieces, is, as it were, a pointer to the later remarkable play in which Middleton was to exploit his familiarity with chess in unique fashion; and Livia's double-edged comments show her preoccupation with the more serious game that is taking place in the upper part of her house. For Guardiano, drawing a curtain in the balcony, reveals the Duke, who by material allurements draws Bianca into his arms:

> Can you be so much your beauty's enemy,
> To kiss away a month or two in wedlock,
> And weep whole years in wants for ever after?
> Come, play the wise wench, and provide for ever.

Admirable, too, is the next scene (III. i), where Leantio
returns after his few days' absence with radiant anticipations
of joy, only to find his bride grown cold and querulous and
his matrimonial dream shattered. He is soon to find the
cause in Bianca's attraction for the Duke, who seeks to
placate him with an appointment as captain of a fort.
Bitterly he exclaims (III. ii):

> Is she my wife till death, yet no more mine?
> That's a hard measure: then what's marriage good for?
> Methinks, by right I should not now be living
> And then 't were all well.

But the unexpected, and the unconvincing happens. Livia
falls in love with him at first sight and offers him herself and
her wealth. From this point the plays takes a melodramatic
turn unequal to the brilliant workmanship of the earlier
acts. Leantio, to taunt Bianca, now lodged at Court, shows
her Livia's love-letters to him; Bianca tells the Duke, who
incites Hippolito against his sister's low-born abuser.
Regardless of the fact that he himself is sinning with his
niece, Hippolito fights with Leantio for his sister's honour
and kills him. Livia enraged by the loss of her lover reveals
how she had tricked Bianca with a false tale of her birth
and plans revenge. The opportunity comes with the wedding
of the Duke, who by Leantio's death is set free to marry
Bianca and thus, as he claims, to clear himself from his
brother the Cardinal's rebuke for living with her in sin. In
honour of the nuptials Livia and Guardiano present a
masque in which Hippolito and Isabella are to meet death
by concealed poison, but in which through mistakes and
counter-plotting the two presenters and the Duke and
Bianca also share their fate. It is indeed a 'tragic loading'
of the stage from which the Cardinal draws the moral of the

ruin wrought by lust. But it is for its lighter and more genial
scenes rather than its catastrophic close that *Women Beware
Women* takes so high a place in Middleton's canon.

WILLIAM ROWLEY

It was probably at a somewhat earlier date that he had
found an inspiring collaborator in William Rowley, of whose
career, except as an actor, little is known. By 1612 he was
a leading member of Prince Charles's company, as he received the payment for its performances at Court. In 1615
he was a representative of the company before the Privy
Council. His distinctive role was that of a fat clown. In 1621
he was still one of Prince Charles's men, for he wrote an
elegy on his fellow, Hugh Attewell. In 1623 he joined the
King's company, and appears four times in lists of its
members. Together with Dekker he was cited in the Bill
of Information laid before the Star Chamber on 26 November
1624 to appear as one of the authors of *Keep the Widow
Waking.* But the words 'now dead' were later interlined, and
no deposition by him has been found. He is most probably to
be identified with the 'William Rowley house-keeper', whose
burial is recorded in the registers of St. James's Church,
Camberwell, on 11 February 1626. On the following February
16 'Grace relict of William Rowley' appeared before a notary
public and renounced the administration of his goods.

A Fair Quarrel was published in 1617 'as it was acted
before the King and divers times publicly' by the Prince's
servants. It has Middleton's and Rowley's names on the
title-page, and it is therefore curious that the latter in a
dedicatory epistle makes no reference to his collaborator.
Their respective shares cannot be fully determined, but that
the main plot, for which no source has been traced, is from
Middleton's hand is, as I think, proved not only by the
versification but by its origin in the sexual mystifications
which continually attracted him. In a heated dispute
Captain Ager is called by his superior officer, described only

as the Colonel, 'the son of a whore'. As Ager declares
(II. i. 2 ff.):

> There is not such another murdering piece
> In all the stock of calumny: it kills
> At one report two reputations,
> A mother's and a son's. If it were possible
> That souls could fight, after the bodies fell,
> This was a quarrel for 'em.

Before taking vengeance on the traducer he gets from his
mother the assurance of her chastity, but as soon as she
realizes that he is about to imperil his life on behalf of her
honour she forswears herself and confesses, 'I was betrayed
to a most sinful hour.' He is shattered by this bolt from
the blue:

> I should be dead, for all my life's work's ended.
> I dare not fight a stroke now, nor engage
> The noble resolution of my friends.

Thus when his would-be seconds lead him to the duelling-
ground he confounds them by declaring 'I will not lift a
finger to this quarrel.' He has to bear their reproaches
(III. i):

> How? Not in this? Be not so rash a sinner. . .
> If you fail virtue here, she needs you not
> All your time after; let her take this wrong,
> And never presume then to serve her more!
> Bid farewell to th' integrity of arms.
> And let that honourable name of soldier
> Fall from you like a shiver'd wreath of laurel
> By thunder struck from a desertless forehead.

When the Colonel comes on the field Ager greets him with
soft words and with a plea against the use of weapons to
decide quarrels, which has a curiously modern sound:

> Why should man
> For a poor hasty syllable or two,
> And vented only in forgetful fury,
> Chain all the hopes and riches of his soul
> To the revenge of that, die lost for ever?
> For he that makes his last peace with his Maker
> In anger, anger is his peace eternally.

The Colonel's answer is to proclaim the Captain 'a base submissive coward', whereupon Ager crying, 'Now I have a cause; A coward was I never', fights with the Colonel and leaves him wounded and repentant on the field.

The psychology of these scenes may be debatable, but the action and the dialogue, including the comments by the 'friends' of the duellists, flow with the rapid and spontaneous movement in which Middleton shows his finest art. Then, as often with him, there is a falling-off in the later acts. Ager's mother confesses that she has belied her reputation to prevent him from endangering himself, whereupon he agonizes her by declaring that if the Colonel recover he will still call him to account. But he is forestalled. The Colonel has been stricken with remorse and from his sick bed cries to his friends (IV. ii):

> O kind lieutenants,
> This is the only war we should provide for,
> Where he that forgives largest, and sighs strongest,
> Is a tried soldier, a true man indeed
> And wins the best field.

It is a lofty sentiment from the lips of a Stuart man-at-arms. But the Colonel's repentance takes a fantastic form when he makes his sister his sole inheritrix—on condition that she offers herself, with her whole estate, to Ager as his wife. And though no word has hitherto passed between them the Captain clasps her to his heart, acknowledging the Colonel's 'conquering way'.

With the main plot of *A Fair Quarrel* there is very loosely connected another of more conventional type. Lady Ager's brother, Russell, is determined that his daughter, Jane, shall marry the rich Cornish clodhopper, Chough. But she has already secretly united herself by a 'jugal knot', of which Heaven is the only witness, to Fitzallen, a poor kinsman of the Colonel. Russell has him arrested on a false charge, and Jane, who is about to bear a child by him, discloses her state to a physician, who takes advantage of this to attempt to make her a victim of his own lust. When she defies him, he denounces her as 'naught' to Chough on the morning when at her father's command, she is to become his bride. Confronted by a new-born child, the proof of her guilt, Russell now presses on her wedding, with a greatly-increased dowry, to the released Fitzallen, who thereupon proclaims (V. i):

> Sir, this is mine own child;
> You could not have found out a fitter father;
> Nor is it basely bred, as you imagine,
> For we were wedded by the bond of Heaven
> Ere this work was begun.

This half-hearted assertion of the doctrine of Platonic love, and the complication of the sub-plot have their counterpart in Middleton's other work. But it is probable that Rowley's hand is to be chiefly found in the coarser and far-fetched humour of the scenes where Chough and his servant Trimtram take lessons in the 'roaring-school' for bullies, and turn to use its outlandish vocabulary of 'hippocrene', 'tweak', and the rest. Like the Simon scenes in *The Mayor of Quinborough* this seems to have made more of a contemporary hit than the subtleties of the main plot, for when *A Fair Quarrel* was republished later in 1617 it had (in IV. iv) 'new additions of Mr. Chough's and Trimtram's Roaring'.

Another joint-composition of Middleton and Rowley, *The Spanish Gipsy*, was acted by the Lady Elizabeth's company at the private house in Drury Lane (the Phoenix) and Salisbury Court, and before Prince Charles at Whitehall on 5 November 1623. It was printed in 1653 and again in 1661. The play, based on two novels of Cervantes has found favour with editors, but it belongs to a conventional type of romantic comedy and, in my opinion, exhibits little of Middleton's most distinctive qualities. Roderigo, son of the Fernando, the corregidor of Madrid, ravishes the beautiful Clara de Cortes, not knowing that she is the beloved of his friend, Louis de Castro. Her noble bearing after the outrage arouses in him a purer passion for her, and the scene between them, when he protests his penitence (I. iii) reaches a higher level than any that follows. We feel at the close that his sin has sat too lightly on him to justify his winning Clara as his bride. Though Louis threatens to ask 'satisfaction' for his loss, his role in the play is not mainly that of a lover. He is dominated by the resolve to seek vengeance on Count Alvarez, who twelve years since killed his father in a duel and whose whereabouts as an exile is unknown. The Count with his wife, Fernando's sister, and Constanza, a young daughter of the widowed corregidor, has in disguise sought refuge with a band of gipsies. The gipsy scenes have chiefly the mark of Rowley's work, and they are enlivened by songs and merry-making. But the lyrical quality of the songs is not high and the *soi-disant* gipsies are of the operatic type. They stir our interest most when they present before Fernando a play in the composition of which their host takes a hand to catch out his son after the fashion of Hamlet with the 'mousetrap' and King Claudius. Here, too, there is a sudden interruption of the performance, which is followed by the revelation of the identity of the 'gipsies', and by a reconciliation between Alvarez and Louis and the reunion of Fernando and his daughter, now betrothed to a high-born lover who for her sake had also adopted the gipsy disguise.

The association of Middleton and Rowley reached its peak in *The Changeling*, acted, as Sir Henry Herbert records, on 4 January 1623/4, by the Queen of Bohemia's company, at the Court at Whitehall in the presence of King Charles. It was not published till 1653 and it is highly paradoxical that one of the most grimly powerful of Stuart tragedies should take its title from a character in a farcical underplot which has the loosest relation to the main action. In this underplot Alibius, a doctor who keeps a home for the cure of fools and madmen, is wildly jealous of his young wife, Isabella. In the hope of winning her favours Antonio, 'the changeling', and Franciscus become his counterfeit patients and are thus the centre of some Bedlam scenes which here are grotesque instead of painfully realistic. These bear the mark of Rowley

whose hand has also been conjecturally found in the opening
and closing scenes of the main plot founded upon a story
in John Reynolds's *God's Revenge against Murther* (1621).
Its stupendous development is however due to Middleton
working at the highest pitch of his mastery over characterization and dialogue.

Beatrice-Joanna, daughter of Vermandero, governor of
the castle of Alicant, is about to be married to the man of
her father's choice, Alonzo de Piracquo. But she is seen in
church by a visitor from Valencia, Alsemero, and the pair
fall violently in love at first sight. Shrinking, like Lady
Macbeth, from nothing, not even murdei, to compass her
ends, Beatrice finds an instrument to get rid of Piracquo in
one of her father's attendants, the broken-down gentleman,
De Flores, whose sight she has hitherto loathed and dreaded:

> I never see this fellow but I think
> Of some harm towards me, dangers in my mind still;
> I scarce leave trembling of an hour after.

De Flores (to use another irresistible Shakespearean parallel)
has not only Iago's complete lack of scruple but his deceptively bluff demeanour, for he is greeted by such epithets as
'kind' and 'honest', and has given Beatrice no inkling of his
infatuation with her physical charms. The dialogue in which
without loss of dignity she enlists for her fell purpose the
man whom she has hitherto spurned like a cur is a masterpiece of economical dramatic construction which cannot be
more than illustrated by partial quotation (II. ii):

Beat.   De Flores!
De F. (*aside*)   Ha, I shall run mad with joy.
          She called me fairly by name De Flores,
          And neither rogue nor rascal. . .
Beat.   When we're used
          To a hard fall, it is not so unpleasing;
          It mends still in opinion, hourly mends;
          I see it by experience
De F. (*aside*)   I was blessed
          To light upon this minute; I'll make use on it.

Beat.   Hardness becomes the visage of a man well;
        It argues service, resolution, manhood,
        If cause were of employment.
De F.   'Twould be soon seen
        If e'er your ladyship had cause to use it;
        I would but wish the honour of a service
        So happy as that mounts to.
Beat.   We shall try you,
        O my De Flores!
De F.   How's that? She calls me hers!
        Already, *my* De Flores!

After warning him that 'there's horror in my service, blood
and danger' she gives him money to 'encourage' him and
promises further precious reward. She fails to catch the
sinister implication in his retort:

> I have assured myself of that beforehand,
> And know it will be precious;

and when he has assured her that Piracquo shall be seen no
more, she flatters herself that she will be rid of 'two in-
veterate loathings at one time', Piracquo and the 'dog-face'
of De Flores. Her eyes begin to be opened when, after the
treacherous murder of Piracquo in the castle-vault, De Flores
with a grimly humorous gesture presents to her a 'token',
the dead man's finger and ring (III. iv):

Beat.   Bless me, what hast thou done?
De F.   What is that more
        Than killing the whole man? I cut his heart-strings. . .
Beat.   'Tis the first token my father made me send him.
De F.   And I have made him send it back again
        For his last token. I was loth to leave it;
        And I'm sure dead men have no use of jewels.

This incident, of the dramatist's invention, is made by
Middleton, with consummate art, the opening for the gradual
revelation of De Flores' design upon the person of Beatrice.
She bids him keep the ring for its value in ducats, and adds
3,000 florins or, when he contemptuously ejaculates 'salary!',
whatever sum will content him, if only he will take flight.
Then he shows his hand:

De F.   You must fly too, then.
Beat.   I?
De F.   I'll not stir a foot else.
Beat.   What's your meaning?
De F.   Why are not you as guilty? E'en, I'm sure,
           As deep as I; and we should stick together . . .
           Nor is it fit we two, engaged so jointly,
           Should part and live asunder.

Beatrice at last realizes what De Flores means in putting
pleasure before wealth, but with subtle psychological insight
Middleton makes the girl, who has not shrunk from plotting
murder, incredulous of the outrage of which lust will not
stop short:

           Why 'tis impossible thou canst be so wicked,
           Or shelter such a cunning cruelty,
           To make his death the murderer of my honour!
           Thy language is so bold and vicious
           I cannot see which way I can forgive it
           With any modesty.
De F.   Pish! you forget yourself;
           A woman dipped in blood, and talk of modesty!

In De Flores' searing phrase, she has become 'the deed's
creature', and she has to pay the full price.

Through her waiting-woman Alsemero learns of her trans-
gression with De Flores and charges her with it. But in the
deepest sense there is truth in her disclaimer while at the
same time she reveals to him the crime which she had
perpetrated for his sake (V. iii):

           To your bed's scandal I stand up innocence,
           Which even the guilt of one black other deed
           Will stand for proof of; your love has made me
           A cruel murderess.

When De Flores enters Alsemero turns upon him:

           My wife's behind with you, she tells me,
           For a brave bloody blow you gave for her sake
           Upon Piracquo.

Even now De Flores can retort with his usual cool effrontery:

> Upon? 'Twas quite through him, sure.
> Has she confessed it?

Als.   As sure as death to both of you;
> And much more than that.

De F.   It could not be much more;
> 'Twas but one thing, and that she is a whore.

Again Beatrice protests her innocence, but when De Flores
gives her a mortal wound she confesses, 'Mine honour fell
with him and now my life' and she dies begging her husband's
forgiveness. But, as has been seen, Middleton had a peculiar
flair for handling sexual complications, and he achieves the
paradoxical feat of leaving us with the sense that Beatrice,
in spite of her sins, is at heart a chaste woman. De Flores, too,
wins at the close, as he takes his own life, the reluctant
admiration that must go to even a villain who has set his
heart on one object and is satisfied when that is attained:

> her honour's prize
> Was my reward; I thank life for nothing
> But that pleasure; it was so sweet to me,
> That I have drunk up all, left none behind
> For any man to pledge me.

It is the unfaltering ruthlessly logical sequence of every
word and act of Beatrice and De Flores that places them in
the very forefront of Stuart dramatic creations.

It is the crowning evidence of Middleton's theatrical versatility that within a half year of the Court performance of
The Changeling he had completed a satiric political comedy,
A Game at Chess, licensed by Sir H. Herbert on 12 June 1624.
Middleton had already made effective use of chess in *Women
Beware Women*, where the talk about the game had throughout a double meaning.[1] He was now to make the audacious
venture of using his knowledge of chess as the basis of a
topical dramatic allegory, on Aristophanic lines. Gondomar,
the powerful Spanish ambassador, favoured by King James
but hated by the populace, had achieved the chief triumph

[1] See above, p. 235.

of his diplomacy in arranging for the visit of Prince Charles and the Duke of Buckingham to Madrid in February 1623 to bring about a match between the Prince and the Spanish Infanta. But the plan went awry, and Charles returned in October without a bride amidst demonstrations of general rejoicing. The popular feeling found expression in a number of pamphlets of which Middleton made extensive use.[1]

The central figure of the play is the Black Knight, Gondomar, who boasts that he has achieved his purposes under a jesting guise (I. i. 278 ff.):

> What I have done, I have done facetiously,
> With pleasant subtlety and bewitching courtship,
> Abused all my believers with delight.
> They took a comfort to be cosened by me;
> To many a soul I have let in mortal poison,
> Whose cheeks have cracked with laughter to receive it.

Later, in a speech closely based on one of the contemporary pamphlets, he is more explicit about his methods (IV. ii. 61 ff.):

> To inform my knowledge in the state
> And strength of the White Kingdom, no fortification,
> Haven, creek, landing-place 'bout the white coast,
> But I got draught and platform, learned the depth
> Of all their channels, knowledge of all sands,
> Shelves, rocks, and rivers for invasion proper'st,
> A catalogue of all the navy royal.

Next in importance to the Black Knight is the singular figure of the Fat Bishop, Marco Antonio de Dominis, who had been Archbishop of Spalatro, had come to England in 1616, had joined the Anglican Church and been appointed Dean of Windsor and Master of the Savoy. Though de Dominis had his redeeming qualities he appears in the play purely as a self-seeking and hypocritical turn-coat. He feels that he has not received any advancement suitable to the greatness of his person and his parts (III. i. 9 ff.):

[1] This has been most fully shown, with detailed extracts, by R. C. Bald in his edition of *A Game at Chess* (1929).

I am persuaded that this flesh would fill
The biggest chair ecclesiastical
If it were put to trial.
To be made Master of an hospital
Is but a kind of diseased bed-rid honour;
Or Dean of the poor Alms Knights that wear badges.
There's but two lazy beggarly preferments
In the White Kingdom, and I've got 'em both:
My merit does begin to be crop-sick
For want of other titles.

To push his claims he eagerly circulates his books, 'his fat and fulsome volumes', as the Black Knight calls them, among Protestant dignitaries. To stop this mischief the Black Knight contrives that he shall be bribed to a reconciliation with Rome, so that he shall be made

the balloon ball of the Churches,
And both the sides shall toss him; he looks like one.

The Black King is Philip IV of Spain and the Black Duke his minister, Olivares. In the other house the White King is James; the White Knight is Prince Charles and the White Duke is Buckingham. In some of the later scenes there is pointed reference to their visit to Madrid, and the play ends with the White Knight's checkmate to the Black King:

White Knight. The game's ours—we give thee checkmate by
Discovery, King, the noblest mate of all.
Black King. I'm lost; I'm taken!

The play put on at the Globe by the King's men on 6 August 1624 had an immediate 'success of scandal'. According to a letter-writer of the day it was 'followed with extraordinary concourse and frequented by all sorts of people, old and young, rich and poor, masters and servants, papists and puritans, wise men &c., churchmen and statesmen'. It was performed continuously for nine days—not the first 'run' in the history of the English theatre, but longer than any previously recorded. The actors, according to one contemporary account, took £100 a day, and another report puts the receipts considerably higher. But the Spanish ambassador lodged a protest, and on 17 August the theatre was closed by order of the Council, before whom the players appeared on the following day. They could plead, however, that they had Herbert's licence, and no extreme steps were taken against them. They were soon allowed to act again after giving surety that they would never appear in *A Game at Chess*. Against Middleton himself a warrant was issued, but he could not be found, and after his son had been brought before the Council and questioned the proceedings seem to have been dropped. But the Council's action probably accounts for the fact that none of the printed editions of the play (one dated 1625 and the others probably belonging to the same year) bears the name of either the author or the printers. But there are several extant MSS. which have either Middleton's full name or his initials. Of all his varied dramatic output it was the greatest 'draw' in his own day. But the Black Knight, the Fat Bishop and the rest are period figures, not types of permanent significance, and thus *A Game at Chess* has now merely the interest of a museum piece.

X

FRANCIS BEAUMONT AND JOHN FLETCHER

BURLESQUES AND TRAGI-COMEDIES

THE dramatic collaboration of Middleton and William Rowley had fruitful results. But such collaboration on a wider scale, attained its cardinal achievement in the collection of plays published in the two folios of 1647 and 1679 under the names of Francis Beaumont and John Fletcher. This comprehensive claim was challenged on the appearance of the 1647 volume by Sir Aston Cokayne, who pointed out that many of the plays included were written after Beaumont's death and that Massinger had a considerable hand in them. Metrical and stylistic investigation has confirmed Cokayne's testimony, and one important MS. play has also been added to the Fletcher-Massinger canon. A minor share has with more or less certainty been assigned to other dramatists. Thus Beaumont's part has been reduced to the authorship in whole or part of about ten of the more than fifty 'Beaumont and Fletcher' plays. But these include the masterpieces of the collection and the names of the 'two full, congenial souls' may still be linked together as the classic example of Stuart dramatic partnership.

John Fletcher was the elder of the pair, born in December 1579 at Rye, where his father was the vicar, afterwards becoming bishop successively of Bristol, Worcester, and London. The bishop's death in 1596 may account for the fact that there appears to be no record of his son having attended a university or one of the Inns of Court. Nothing is known of his career previous to his commendatory verses prefixed to Jonson's *Volpone* in 1607. His own activity as a dramatist began about a year afterwards with *The Faithful Shepherdess*, followed by intimate personal and professional association

R

with Beaumont. According to Aubrey, they 'lived together in the Bank side, not far from the play-house, both bachelors . . . the same clothes and cloak between them'. If the dramatist was the John Fletcher married at St. Saviour's, Southwark, on 3 November 1612, this must have entailed their separation. Thereafter Fletcher's record is again a blank except for his continuous dramatic productivity till his death in August 1625.

Of the shorter life of Francis Beaumont somewhat more is known. Hs was born in 1584 or 1585 at the family seat of Grace-Dieu in Leicestershire, and was a son of a judge of the Common Pleas. He was educated at Broadgates Hall (now Pembroke College), Oxford, and at the Inner Temple, where he took part in a set of Christmas revels. An erotic poem, *Salmacis and Hermaphroditus*, issued anonymously in 1602, preceded by five years the publication of his first play, *The Woman-Hater* in 1607. His commendatory verses on *Volpone* in the same year and his verse epistles to Jonson indicate that he had become one of the company of the sons of Ben. If the domestic alliance between him and Fletcher did not end in 1612, it must have come to a close not long after, when Beaumont married about 1613 Ursula Isley. He contributed a masque to the festivities in honour of Princess Elizabeth's wedding in February 1613. His career came to almost as premature a close as that of Marlowe, through his death on 6 March 1616.

It is curious that not one of the few plays which can be assigned to either of the pair with probability before the beginning of their partnership gives a foretaste of the results of their collaboration. The internal evidence for discriminating between the work of the two playwrights, sometimes conflicting with the doubtful bibliographical ascriptions, though it is to be generally trusted, cannot be taken as conclusive in points of detail. Fletcher's verse is distinguished by several peculiar characteristics. He is fond to excess of double (or feminine), sometimes triple or quadruple, endings, and often stresses this extra syllable by the use of a weighty word. He varies his rhythm by the frequent introduction of trisyllabic feet. On the other hand he does not as a rule avail himself of the freedom of the run-on line, but keeps to the earlier tradition of the end pause. He scarcely ever uses rhyme and seldom finds prose necessary for his purposes.

Beaumont differs from Fletcher in all these characteristics. He avoids as a rule double endings, especially with stressed syllables. His lines are usually run-on and he intermingles rhyme with his blank verse. He makes considerable use of prose. But it has to be borne in mind that the general practice of the two playwrights was apt to be modified by some peculiarity in the piece on which jointly or singly they were at work.

The difficulties of attribution begin with the first play which can be dated with approximate certainty. *The Woman-Hater* was licensed for printing on 20 May 1607, 'as it hath lately been acted by the Children of Paul's', and was published in the same year. It seems to have been performed before July 1606, after which the Paul's boys disappear from view. The quarto of 1607 does not give the author's name. A later quarto in 1648 assigns it to Fletcher, and a third in 1649 to Beaumont and Fletcher, while Davenant, in a prologue to this edition, speaks of it as from Fletcher's pen. Yet on internal evidence the general consensus of criticism is that Beaumont was either the sole author or that Fletcher's share was slight. *The Woman-Hater* was a comedy of humours of the Jonsonian type, though pushed to a more fantastic extreme. Gondarino, from whom the play takes its name, prides himself on hating his wife after death and for her sake all women. The beautiful Oriana, sister of Count Valore, and beloved (though she knows it not) by the Duke of Milan, sets herself to overcome the aversion of this 'cold, frosty' lord to her sex. In revenge he denounces her to the Duke as 'naught', and in confirmation of this traps her into a house of ill-fame, where however she proves herself ready to lose her life before her virtue and finds a reward in the Duke's hand.

But the more original part of the play is in the under-plot, which Beaumont elaborated from an anecdote in the treatise by Paulus Jovius *De Romanis Piscibus*. The courtier Lazarillo has dedicated himself entirely to the joys of glut-tony. He is ravished by the news that the head of an umbrana, the choicest of all piscatorial delicacies, has been sent to the Duke for his table. Lazarillo, who hunts 'more after novelty than plenty,' determines to taste of 'this most sacred dish'. But his chase proves to be a long one, for the Duke sends the fish's head to Sandarino, who passes it on as a stop-mouth to a mercer to whom he owes money. The mercer hands it over to a pandar, and thus Lazarillo has to seek it in the ill-famed house where Oriana has been trapped and to offer marriage to a courtesan that he may at last enjoy it.

Meanwhile further complications have arisen. Count Valore has in his employ an intelligencer who brings 'informations, picked out of broken words, in men's common talk which, with his malicious mis-application, he hopes will seem dangerous'. With a fellow of the same kidney he sets watch on Lazarillo and overhears him declare that the fish's head will make him 'greater than the Duke'. The inference seems plain. 'There, there's a notable piece of treason; greater than the Duke, mark that!' So Lazarillo finds himself arrested for treason, but is liberated by the Count, who makes it plain that he is nothing worse than a 'hungry courtier'. The ingenious interweaving of the different threads and the vivacious handling of the dialogue save the piece from being merely a display of extravagant 'humours'.

The burlesque element in *The Woman-Hater* was to find richer expression soon afterwards in *The Knight of the Burn-ing Pestle*, first published in 1613. The Induction shows that the play had been acted by boys. As the MS. had been sent for publication by Robert Keysar, the company was the

Children of Blackfriars.[1] The date of performance was probably 1607, for the Induction states that 'this seven years there hath been plays in this house'.

It is possible, however, that the date was 1610, when the theatre would have been the Whitefriars. The quarto of 1613 was anonymous. A later edition in 1635 ascribed the play as acted by the Queen's men at the Cockpit to both Beaumont and Fletcher; so did another edition also dated 1635, but probably issued later. Internal evidence suggests that Beaumont's was the sole or, at least the predominant hand. The burlesque spirit of the play is characteristic of him, and though no English translation of *Don Quixote* appeared before 1612 he seems to have been sufficiently acquainted with Cervantes' mockery of Spanish chivalry to turn it to account against the military ardour of the London citizens which had been glorified upon the stage by Thomas Heywood and others. It was a brilliant inspiration to let Ralph, a grocer's apprentice, with some practice as an amateur actor, able to quote from Shakespeare and Kyd, and with a taste for romances like *Palmerin of England*, enact the part of a bougeois Quizote with a burning pestle portrayed upon his shield, and with two fellow apprentices as his *obligato* squire and dwarf. His adventures, especially with Tapstero, the host of the Waltham inn, and with the giant Babarossa, the barber-surgeon, are set forth with an admirable sense of fun which, as successful twentieth-century revivals prove, has not yet lost its savour. And when after these exploits Ralph is chosen Lord of the May and Captain of the London train-bands, we recognize even through the satire the spirit of the 'valiant men and freemen' of the capital—the spirt of which there has been splendid proof in our own day.

In contrast with the mock-heroic figure of Ralph stands the irrepressibly cheerful, bibulous Merrythought, with his inexhaustible store of care-free songs, while his elder son's

[1] See above, p. 11.

flight with his faithful Luce, and his younger's with his doting mother bring an element of sentiment into the piece. But more outstanding than these are the two characters who form a running chorus throughout the play—Ralph's master, the grocer, and his wife, voluble, good-natured Cockneys, beyond themselves with pride in the role to which their prentice has been called..

If Beaumont began by an exaggeration of Jonsonian humours there is some reason to believe that Fletcher began by an exaggeration of the nearest element to farce in Shakespeare. *The Woman's Prize or The Tamer Tamed* was first published in the folio of 1647. But when Herbert licensed it for performance at Court in 1633, he noted it as 'an old play, by Fletcher', whose hand is apparent in it throughout. References in it to the siege of Ostend, which ended on 8 September 1604, and the assumption that the audience was familiar with *The Taming of the Shrew*, point to an early date which has been variously placed between 1604 and 1607. Petruchio, now living in London instead of Italy, has after his first wife's death just married the elder daughter of Petronius, hitherto apparently the 'gentle, tame Maria'. But she is now resolved to avenge :

> all the several wrongs
> Done by imperious husbands to their wives
> These thousand years.

In a succession of uproariously farcical scenes, including a rebellious stand in which Maria and her kinswomen are supported by an amazonian array of city and country wives (Act II. v), she carries through her purpose till Petruchio feigns death and her tears restore him to life, whereupon she declares, 'I have tam'd ye, And now am vowed your servant'. The play shows at an early stage Fletcher's facility in invention and his linguistic dexterity, but the variations on the elementary theme of sex antagonism become too protracted for modern taste, even with the relief of the successful struggle of Maria's younger sister to secure the youthful

Rowland as her husband instead of her father's choice, the 'old, rich, doting' Moroso.

If, in a sense, Shakespeare was the sponsor of *The Woman's Prize*, it was Guarini, author of *Il Pastor Fido*, who gave Fletcher the cue for *The Faithful Shepherdess*, acted, as Jonson told Drummond, in 1608–9.

The earliest quarto is undated, but probably appeared about 1609–10. It was followed by four others between 1629 and 1665, showing that the play found more favour with readers than with the audience in the theatre which, as Fletcher complained, expected to find 'hired shepherds in gray cloaks, with curtailed dogs in strings, sometimes laughing together, and sometimes killing one another'. He claimed to represent them with their actions and passions, their natural arts of singing and poetry, and their knowledge of herbs and fountains, of the sun and the stars. But the Jacobean playgoers may be excused if in Fletcher's representation of the dream-world of Italian pastoral they failed to find the likeness to anything known to them in the English countryside. The shepherds, of both sexes, have no other concern than love, in its various aspects. Hence the play on its revival on Twelfth Night 1633/4, before the King and Queen found much more favour with the sophisticated Court audience.

The faithful shepherdess is Amoret, who is impersonated for a time through the magic arts of the sullen shepherd by the light-of-love Amaryllis, and who is wounded by Perigot, who thinks that she has betrayed his love. After she has been healed in an enchanted well by the river-god, a second time he wounds her, believing that her protestations of constancy are from the lips of Amaryllis in her shape, and again a kindly satyr has to render aid before she is finally cured and united to Perigot. The cure is effected by another faithful shepherdess Clorin, versed in the healing virtues of herbs, who has consecrated herself to the memory of her dead lover, and who is adored in Platonic fashion by Thenot because of this unique example of chastity. Another singular type is the too modest shepherd Daphnis, whose innocence is a complete shield against the allurements of the outrageously lustful Cloe. But these characters, one and all, have little more life than the figures woven in an exquisite piece of tapestry. The enduring charm of *The Faithful Shepherdess* lies in the loveliness of its imagery and in the lyrical enchantment of its verse, where Fletcher for his special purpose shows himself a master of the rhymed metres which, as a rule, he did not use.

In his prefatory epistle Fletcher called *The Faithful Shepherdess* a pastoral tragi-comedy, and went on to say that 'A tragi-comedy is not so called in respect of mirth and killing, but in respect it wants deaths, which is enough to make it no tragedy, yet brings some near it, which is enough to make it no comedy'. This definition has been criticized as not indicating precisely enough the type of tragi-comedy which was to be the joint achievement of Fletcher and his fellow-dramatist. As has been recently said, the distinctive element is the mood of the play which lies 'somewhere between the light-heartedness of unshadowed comedy and the apprehension of shock and mystery, which attend a tragic catastrophe. If this indeed be the fundamental distinction between tragicomedy and the other two kinds . . . then it is the creation of this middle mood which is the contribution of Beaumont and Fletcher to the subsequent drama.'[1]

According to Dryden in his *Essay of Dramatic Poetry* it was *Philaster* that first brought Beaumont and Fletcher into esteem, 'for before that they had written two or three very unsuccessfully'. Though he speaks of these 'two or three' as if they were joint efforts, he may be referring in part to the ill-fortune on the stage of *The Faithful Shepherdess* and perhaps *The Woman-Hater* or *The Woman's Prize*. The only play by the two dramatists which, owing to the names of the cast, there are grounds for dating before *Philaster*, be-

[1] Una Ellis-Fermor in *The Jacobean Drama* (1936), 204–5.

tween 1608 and 1610, is *The Coxcomb*. It was performed at
Court by the Queen's Revels Company on 2 and 3 November
1612, and revived on 5 March 1622 and 17 November 1636.
It must therefore have found favour in high circles, but the
prologue, written for one of the revivals, and printed when
the play was included in the 1647 folio, stated that this piece
'long forgot' was condemned by some of the ignorant multi-
tude for its length. Their censure had, however, other justification. *The Coxcomb* exhibits in one of its most repellent
forms the decadent attitude of Beaumont and Fletcher
towards sexual relations which is the stain upon their brilliant theatrical achievement. Antonio, the coxcomb, will not
rest till he procures his wife's dishonour through his friend,
Mercury, and by his plots and subterfuges involuntarily causes
the pair to be charged with his supposed murder. There is
relief in the sub-plot where the gentle Viola by her constancy
and sweetness of temper under every trial brings to repentance the lover who in a drunken fit fails to keep tryst with her
and leaves her to be a helpless fugitive from her father's
house.

The date of *Philaster* must be previous to 1611, when
it is alluded to under its second title, *Love Lies A-Bleeding* by
John Davies of Hereford, in an epigram. 1609–10 is approximately right. No edition appeared till 1620, when T. Walkley
published an imperfect text. Two years later he issued a
second impression cured 'of some dangerous and gaping
wounds'. The rapid succession of later editions in 1628, 1634,
1639, 1652, and 1660 testified to the remarkable popularity
of the play, and even after its inclusion in the folio of 1679
two further quartos were called for in 1687 and 1717.

No source of the play has been traced, but Shakespearean
influence is visible in various ways and especially in the
parallel between the situation of Philaster in the earlier
scenes and that of Hamlet. Philaster is the rightful heir to
the throne of Sicily, of which he has been wrongfully deprived by its union through force with Calabria under one

king. The usurping monarch has even sought to imprison him, but has been restrained by a popular rising in his support. To secure the succession the king has chosen the Spanish prince, Pharamond, to be the husband of Arethusa, his daughter and sole heir. But when Pharamond arrives to claim her hand with characteristic self-praise, Philaster defies him in front of the Court:

> This earth you tread upon
> (A dowry, as you hope, with this fair princess)
> By my dead father (oh, I had a father
> Whose memory I bow to!) was not left
> To your inheritance, and I up and living . . .

Phar. He's mad, beyond cure, mad.

*   *   *

King.   Sure he's possessed.
Phil. Yes, with my father's spirit. It's here, O King,
A dangerous spirit! Now he tells me, King,
I was a king's heir, bids me be a king,
And whispers to me, these are all my subjects.

The prince of Sicily, who is directed by his dead father's spirit and who is suspected of madness, must owe descent to the prince of Denmark. But his fortunes from this point are far different. Arethusa confesses to him that it is he whom she loves:

> Philaster, know,
> I must enjoy these kingdoms. . . . I must have them
> and thee.

Phil. And me?
Are.   Thy love, without which all the land
Discovered yet will serve me for no use
But to be buried in.

To carry news between them Philaster puts at her service a boy, Bellario, whom he has found sitting orphaned, at a fountain's side, and who does not hide his grief at the transfer:

Are. You are sad to change your service, is't not so?
Bel. Madam, I have not changed; I wait on you,
To do him service.

But unforeseen and dire consequences follow. A wanton Court lady, Megra, discovered in guilty intercourse with the dissolute Spanish prince, takes revenge by accusing Arethusa to her father of having the boy as her lover. An old lord, Dion, repeats this charge to Philaster that it may stir him to revolt against the usurping royal house, and even meets the prince's indignant denial with a declaration that he himself took them in the act. Here, as yet unknown to the audience is a masterly piece of dramatic irony, for Bellario is no other than Dion's own daughter, Euphrasia, who for love of Philaster, and to be near him, has adopted the disguise of an orphaned boy. This, too, lends an ironic undercurrent to the jealous reproaches of Philaster which force Bellario and Arethusa to take flight from the Court to the neighbouring woods, where the prince himself also in desperate mood seeks shelter. Here Philaster bids Arethusa kill him or suffer death. 'We are two earth cannot bear at once.'

Are.   Yet tell me this, will there be no slanders,
        No jealousies in the other world, no ill there?
Phil.   No.
Are.   Show me then the way.

But as he strikes her a countryman comes between them and wounds him, and as he takes flight he finds Bellario sleeping, whom he wounds before he falls fainting on the ground. When they are discovered by a hunting party Bellario seeks to shield Philaster by declaring that it was he who attacked the princess, and at her request they are both committed to her charge that she may 'appoint their tortures and their death'. It is a ruse by which she may claim Philaster in prison as her husband, and appear before the amazed king in nuptial array. While he threatens that they shall keep their wedding in the citadel news comes of a rising in the city to rescue Philaster. The king bows before the storm, restores the prince to his inheritance and blesses his union with Arethusa. But to clear his daughter's name

he demands that Bellario should be put to torture. To escape
this ordeal the supposed boy is at last constrained to confess
her true sex and parentage.

The plot, thus summarily analysed, is ingenious and never
loses interest, though it transports us into the 'escapist'
atmosphere removed from realities, which pervades the tragi-
comedy of Beaumont and Fletcher. Philaster himself, though
sound at heart, is too impulsive and credulous to be a very
sympathetic figure. But in Arethusa and Bellario-Euphrasia
the dramatists created two figures that justify Swinburne's
eulogy on *Philaster* as 'the loveliest though not the loftiest
of tragic plays which we owe to the comrades or successors
of Shakespeare'. If I may repeat with full conviction words
that I used many years ago of Bellario, she is 'one of the
most exquisite children of the lyric muse that has ever
strayed from her native haunts into the dramatic sphere.
She lives and moves in an atmosphere of ideal beauty, and
her lips are musical with the very quintessence of silvery
eloquence'. Hers is in its perfection the limpid diction which
sheds its charm over the play as a whole.

Philaster had a rival for enduring popularity in *The Maid's
Tragedy*, which probably succeeded it in 1610–11. The first
quarto of the play, as acted at the Blackfriars by the King's
men, appeared in 1615. A second revised and enlarged
edition was issued in 1622, and others followed in 1630, 1638,
1641, 1650, and 1661, before its inclusion in the 1679 folio.
As the title indicates, here Beaumont and Fletcher crossed
the line which in *Philaster* had by an inch stopped short of
'killing', and with a minimum of relieving 'mirth' presented
a tragedy bound to have an overwhelming effect on an
audience which was being grounded in the doctrine of the
divine right of kings.

The soldier, Melantius, returning from the wars to Rhodes
on the day that his friend Amintor has married, as he thinks,
the long-loved maid, Aspatia, is astounded to hear that his
own sister, Evadne, has, by the king's command, become

Amintor's bride. Evadne reveals the reason when in their
bedchamber she tells Amintor that she will be his wife
merely in name:

> I do enjoy the best, and in that height
> Have sworn to stand or die: you guess the man.

Amint. No, let me know the man that wrongs me so.
> That I may cut his body into motes.

Evad. Why 't is the King.

Amint.   The King!

               *   *   *

Evad.   What will you do now?

               *   *   *

Amint. O, thou hast named a word that wipes away
> All thoughts revengeful; in that sacred name
> There lies a terror; what frail man
> Dare lift his hand against it?

Amintor next morning plays the part of the joyful bridegroom so deceptively that the king forces the truth from
Evadne's lips. Then Amintor cannot withhold the withering
reproaches:

> Y' are a tyrant; and not so much to wrong
> An honest man thus, as to take a pride
> In talking with him of it.

Yet even so he feels himself powerless:

>   As you are mere man,
> I dare as easily kill you for this deed,
> As you dare think to do it; but there is
> Divinity about you that strikes dead
> My rising passions; as you are my King,
> I fall before you.

But he cannot conceal his inward misery from the eyes of
Melantius. It is something of a paradox that Beaumont and
Fletcher, so often the offenders where sex is involved, are
unrivalled in their presentation of friendship between men.
Melantius now invokes that sacred word:

> You may shape, Amintor,
> Causes to cozen the whole world withal
> And yourself too; but 'tis not like a friend
> To hide your soul from me.

And when Amintor affirms that 'there is nothing', he bids him farewell with the reproach, 'From this time have acquaintance but no friend'. Thereupon Amintor reveals the terrible secret to the incredulous Melantius, who at first draws his sword to defend his sister's honour. But Amintor's bearing convinces him of the truth, and with the cry,

> The name of friend is more than family
> Or all the world beside,

he resolves on vengeance on the king. This dialogue and that in which he swears Evadne to this dread task and drives her to a repentant appeal for pardon from her husband are masterly in their sustained power. Thus the tragedy mounts step by step to the culminating scene where Evadne in her bedchamber executes justice on her seducer:

> This for my lord, Amintor;
> This for my noble brother; and this stroke
> For the most wronged of women!

With the knife in her blood-stained hands she rushes to her husband, crying, 'Joy to Amintor, for the king is dead!' But even in death the royal divinity still casts its spell over the outraged subject:

> Joy to Amintor! thou hast touched a life
> The very name of which had power to chain
> Up all my rage and calm my wildest wrongs.

He thrusts Evadne away and as he flies from her she stabs herself, crying, 'Evadne whom thou hat'st will die for thee'. The spectacle of such volcanic passion is so overpowering that the reappearance of the wronged Aspatia after a long absence from the stage falls in part short of its intended effect. In the guise of her brother she provokes Amintor to a duel in which she offers her breast to his sword. As she is dying on the ground she hears him proclaim his penitence for his faithlessness to her, and she reveals herself to him. He can clasp her hand for a moment before he stabs himself to keep her company in another world. But she has been too fragile a figure for her fate to move us deeply. Even her brother, Melantius, mourns not for her but for Amintor:

> Here was my sister, father, brother, son;
> All that I had.

It is friendship, not love, that sounds the dominant note at the close.

A King and No King was licensed for performance by Sir George Buck in 1611 and on December 26 of that year it was acted at Court by the King's men; and again in 1612–13, and at Hampton Court in 1636. An edition of the play, as written by Beaumont and Fletcher, and acted at the Globe appeared in 1619. A second quarto as acted at the Blackfriars followed in 1625. The popularity of the play was proved by a succession of later editions in 1631, 1639, 1653, 1661, and 1676.

As in *The Maid's Tragedy* an amorous monarch gives rise to the action of the play, though here this does not end in catastrophe. Arbaces, King of Iberia, has victoriously completed a long campaign against Tigranes, King of Armenia, and displays his lack of self-control by boasting of his conquest while affecting modesty:

> Far then from me
> Be ostentation! I could tell the world
> How I have laid his kingdom desolate
> By this sole arm propt by divinity. . .
> Did I but take delight
> To stretch my deeds, as others do, on words
> I could amaze my hearers.

'So you do', interjects the captain, Mardonius, another of the blunt-spoken, loyal-hearted soldiers dear to Beaumont and Fletcher. He does not hesitate to rebuke his sovereign:

> You told Tigranes you had won his land
> With that sole arm propt by divinity.
> Was not that bragging, and a wrong to us
> That daily ventured lives?

Arbaces' self-flattery takes the singular form of ordering

that Tigranes for his ransom shall marry his sister, Panthea, whom, as a campaigner, he had not seen since her childhood, but whom report declares to be a 'miracle'. Tigranes is, however, already pledged to his countrywoman, Spaconia, who journeys to Iberia and enters Panthea's service to dissuade her from the imposed union.

But she finds the most unexpected of allies. As Arbaces returns to his Court, where the old noble, Gobrias, has been in his absence Lord-Protector, and is greeted by Panthea, who kneels before him, he is struck so dumb that the amazed bystanders, one after another, beseech him to speak to her. Mardonius puts it in his forcible fashion:

> A tree would find a tongue to answer her,
> Did she but give it such a lov'd respect.

The first sight of Panthea has influenced Arbaces with an irresistible unlawful passion which, when he at last breaks silence, finds vent in disordered, laconic queries:

Arb. Where's my sister? I bade she should be brought.
Mar. What, is he mad?
Arb.   Gobrias, where is she? . . .
Gob. Do you not see her there?
Arb.   Where?
Gob. There.
Arb.   There ! where?
Mar. · 'Slight, there, are you blind?

He disbelieves them all:

> She is no kin to me, nor shall she be;
> If she were ever, I create her none:
> And which of you can question this? My power
> Is like the sea that is to be obeyed
> And not disputed with.

It is a masterly presentation of the effect of delirious passion on a nature already intoxicated with the sense of absolute power. Nor does it refrain from inconsistencies. When Tigranes, overcome by Panthea's charms even in Spaconia's presence, salutes her as his queen, Arbaces orders

him to prison for changing words with her whom he now
proclaims

> My hope, the only jewel of my life,
> The best of sisters, dearer than my breath.

He seals these words with kisses which so inflame his senses
that in self-protection he commits the bewildered girl to
prison in her chamber. His passion takes yet another turn
when he finds Spaconia with Tigranes. He is convinced, in
spite of all denials, that she carries love-letters from Panthea
to the Armenian king and condemns them to the closest
confinement. In fear of a rival he confesses to Panthea the
reason of her imprisonment and learns that she returns
his love:

Arb.   Is there no stop
    To our full happiness but these mere sounds,
    Brother and sister?
Pan.   There is nothing else,
    But these, alas, will separate us more
    Than twenty worlds betwixt us.
Arb.   I have lived
    To conquer men, and men are overthrown
    Only by words, brother and sister; where
    Have those words dwelling? I will find them out,
    And utterly destroy them. . .
Pan.   But 'tis not in the power of any force
    Or policy to conquer them.

Baffled in his desires Arbaces turns upon Gobrias and
threatens him with death for implanting in him love for
Panthea with praise of her beauty before he saw it. Whereupon Gobrias stays him with the cry, 'If you kill me, you
kill your father'. Arbaces, it is revealed, is a supposititious
child of the late King of Iberia and his queen, Arane, and
is not of kin to Panthea, who is their daughter and the lawful
heir to the throne. He is therefore proved 'no king', but by
his union with Panthea, to which there is now no impediment,
he will share reflected royalty.

Beaumont and Fletcher have many offences to answer for
at the bar of an outraged moral sense, but I at least cannot

S

count among these their treatment of the love between
Arbaces and Panthea, or take the view that it could only
have been justified by a tragic outcome. The struggle of
Arbaces between his nobler impulses and the passion that
whirls him towards what he believes to be the fulfilment of
incestuous desire is treated throughout with unfaltering
dignity. And there are subtle suggestions even before the
secret is disclosed that the *horror naturalis* is not in truth
being violated in the love of Arbaces and Panthea.

From the violent tension of the main plot relief is afforded
by the poltroonery of Bessus, colleague and foil to Mardonius. One of the most contemptible variants of the *miles
gloriosus* he helps to win a battle by taking flight with his
company so precipitately that he charges into the enemy.
Though he thus gains a false reputation for valour he lets
himself be beaten by the king and kicked by a lord. Two
swordsmen to whom he puts the question of his honour
decide that injuries from a royal hand must be regarded as
favours, and that the kicking may be overlooked because he
laughed during it. Thus by the crazy dialectic of the duelling-
code the honour of Bessus is saved.

The publishers of the 1679 folio showed discrimination
when they placed *The Maid's Tragedy*, *Philaster*, and *A King
and No King* in the forefront of the volume. This trio of
plays, in which Beaumont's hand has been recognized as
predominant represents the peak of the achievement of the
two partners. They were followed in the folio by another
piece, *The Scornful Lady*, which shared their seventeenth-
century popularity, and which in a quarto of 1616 was the
first to bear the authors' joint-names, but which was very
different in type and quality. The play had been acted by
the Children of the Queen's Revels at Blackfriars. The date,
therefore, cannot be later than 1609, but various internal
references, especially to the Cleve wars and to the Spanish
ambassador, Sarmiento (afterwards Count Gondomar), suggest
a revision, between 1613 and 1615. In any case, Fletcher's

was the chief hand and the success of the play, after it had passed to the King's men, is proved by the series of editions in 1625, 1630, 1635, 1639, 1651, and 1677 before its inclusion in the 1679 folio.

But in spite of the racy vigour of much of its dialogue, which is mainly in prose, *The Scornful Lady* has to-day lost most of its attraction. The chief characters represent conventional and outmoded types. The central figure is a woman, not even distinguished by a name, who out of caprice and self-will keeps her lover at a distance and imposes on him for a trifling indiscretion the penance of a year's travel abroad. Feigning obedience, he leaves his house in the charge of his scapegrace younger brother, under the supervision of his hitherto trusty steward. He returns disguised, with a tale of his death by drowning, to find his house filled with his brother's riotous boon-companions, the steward corrupted into a drunkard, and the estate about to be sold to a usurer. He tells the same story to the lady, who sees through his disguise, mocks him by declaring her love for another suitor, Welford, and then again bids him go into banishment. But in the end he turns the tables on her by making love before her face to Welford, dressed as a woman, and thus drawing from her the confession that she is ready to marry him. There was a spice of novelty in a male character donning feminine attire on the Elizabethan stage instead of the customary *vice-versa*. And another unusual feature is the usurer's conversion to benevolence which may be set against the steward's fall from grace.

Another play acted by the Children of the Queen's Revels, *Cupid's Revenge*, was ascribed in the first quarto of 1615 to Fletcher, but more correctly in a 1630 edition to Beaumont also. As only one further edition in 1635 was called for before its inclusion in the 1679 folio, it seems to have made less appeal than *The Scornful Lady* to contemporary taste, but it is of greater permanent interest as more distinctive of the work of the two collaborators. They borrowed their plot from Sidney's *Arcadia*, but they modified it in characteristic ways. Leontius, King of Lycia, grants the birthday prayer of his daughter, Hidaspes, that the 'loose naked statues through the land' of Cupid be broken down and destroyed. The god announces that he will take a mighty revenge upon the rebels. Thus, strictly speaking, the freedom of will out of which dramatic conflict arises is paralysed under the domination of supernatural power. But the characters act so much after the same fashion as their fellows in the abnormal world of the twin dramatists' tragi-comedy that we scarcely think of them as Cupid's puppets. His first victim is Hidaspes herself, who becomes enamoured (not as in the *Arcadia*, of a low-born youth) of a hideous dwarf whom the king has executed and grief for whose loss kills her. Then the god's wrath falls on her kinsfolk. Her brother, Leucippus, has been carrying on an intrigue with a young widow, Bacha, whom the king denounces for corrupting him. In a perverted spirit of chivalry Leucippus declares:

> She is, by Heaven,
> Of the most strict and blameless chastity
> That ever woman was . . . by this light she is
> A most obstinate modest creature.

This false defence has an amazing sequel. The king, overcome by Bacha's beauty and supposed chastity, determines to make her his wife. Once more Leucippus displays a distorted moral sense. When she appears as queen he assures her,

> I will bear myself
> To you with all the due obedience
> A son owes to his mother.

When she vainly tempts him to renew their former intercourse and declares that she will make away with the king if he will marry her, or else she will undo him, he gently begs her

> To lay what trains you will for my wish'd death
> But suffer him to find his quiet grave
> In peace.

The 'trains' are soon laid and Leucippus, accused of conspiracy against his father and of a plot to murder him, is sentenced to public execution, from which he is saved by a popular rising on his behalf. He flies to the solitude of a forest, whither he is followed by Urania, Bacha's daughter, in the disguise of a page. She is an addition by the dramatists to the story in the *Arcadia* and has a place in their favourite gallery of devoted maidens eager for every self-sacrifice on love's behalf. She is individualized by adopting the dialectical accents of a country lad, but as she is introduced abruptly in Act IV she fails, like Aspatia in *The Maid's Tragedy*, to win the full sympathy designed for her, when she saves Leucippus from the sword of a villainous agent of Bacha, and herself receives a death-wound.

Even in this extremity, when the queen, again widowed, is led in by friends of Leucippus to meet judgement at his hands, he is restrained by the tie that binds him to her:

> Live, wicked mother! that reverend title be
> Your pardon! for I will use no extremity
> Against you, but leave you to heaven.

With the cry, 'let heaven fall', Bacha stabs Leucippus and then turns her weapon against her own breast. With his dying breath he orders the broken images of Cupid to be re-edified. But it is a tribute to this striking, if unequal, play that its catastrophe does not seem due to the *deus ex machina* but to the welter of human passions and to the singular 'correctitude' of Leucippus, who is only indirectly the sport of the god of love.

Recent criticism has thrown doubt on the inclusion in the strict Beaumont and Fletcher canon of *Four Plays in One*, first published in the 1647 folio. Both the date of this series of 'moral representations', and the performing company are uncertain, though the music and dancing suggest that boys were the actors.

In honour of the wedding of King Emmanuel of Portugal and Isabella of Castile in 1497 four *Triumphs* are supposed

to be set forth of *Honour, Love, Death,* and *Time.* The versification and style of the two latter pieces indicate Fletcher's
hand. The first two have been traditionally ascribed to
Beaumont, but have now on internal evidence been assigned
by several well-qualified critics chiefly to Nathan Field.
They are both founded on stories in *The Decameron,* and the
Triumph of Love, whether fashioned by Beaumont or not,
contains in Violante another of the devoted sisterhood eager
to sacrifice all for love. She has given herself to a wooer
supposedly unmatched with her in birth, and by the laws
of Milan both are to suffer death. But she looks forward to
the perfecting of their union in heaven:

> We shall meet
> Where our condemners shall not, and enjoy
> A more refined affection than here;
> No law nor father hinders marriage there
> 'Twixt souls divinely affied as, sure, ours were.

Her lover, however, proves to be a long-lost son of the duke,
and their joys begin on earth.

It thus appears that prior to Beaumont's death only about
a dozen 'Beaumont and Fletcher' plays were written, and
scarcely more than a half of these seem to be of joint-author-
ship. But these include the masterpieces of the group, and
Beaumont's influence on his colleague's technique, especially
in the constructive side, must have remained even after their
collaboration had ceased. For a time, however, Fletcher found
an even greater partner than Beaumont. *King Henry VIII,*
dating from 1612–13, was included by the editors of the 1623
folio as a Shakespearean play, but there is the strongest internal evidence that many of the most familiar scenes are from
Fletcher's hand. *The Two Noble Kinsmen,* about 1613, is
ascribed to 'the memorable worthies of their time', Fletcher
and Shakespeare, in the quarto of 1634, and the internal
metrical evidence supports this attribution.[1] A third play,

[1] For a detailed discussion of the authorship of *King Henry VIII* and
The Two Noble Kinsmen see E. K. Chambers, *William Shakespeare,* II.
495–8 and 528–32, and my *Shakspere and his Predecessors,* 545–50.

Cardenio, may also have been their joint work. It was acted by the King's men at Court in 1612–13 and on 8 June 1613, and was based on a story in *Don Quixote*. H. Moseley registered on 9 September 1653 amongst other plays, '*The History of Cardenio*, by Mr. Fletcher and Shakespeare', which has been lost, though it may possibly have been used by Theobald as a basis of his *Double Falsehood* in 1728.

XI

JOHN FLETCHER

COMEDIES AND ROMANTIC PLAYS

WHEN Shakespeare retired from the theatre Fletcher turned to Philip Massinger as his chief collaborator, but he also produced a large number of plays single-handed, of which some may be here taken as representative of different aspects of his dramatic art. *Wit Without Money* is ascribed, apparently without warrant, to Beaumont also in a quarto of 1639. It had been presented at the Cockpit in Drury Lane and was written soon after 1614, as it has an allusion to a dragon in Sussex discovered in that year. It is a lively comedy on lines broadly similar to *The Scornful Lady*. Here it is a widow, Lady Heartwell, who takes up an attitude of defiance towards the other sex and scorns the idea of a second wedlock. She has a counterpart in Valentine, who thinks ill of all women, especially widows. He also has the more unusual quality on the Stuart stage of holding property, including his own, in contempt, and of putting his trust for advancement in wit or intelligence without money. In the extremity, however, of the widow's attitude he finds a challenge, and in the end he overcomes by wit her aversion to a renewal of matrimony, and has also to surrender, in making a wealthy match with her, his prejudice against money.

In *Monsieur Thomas*, first printed in 1639, with Fletcher's name on the title-page, a comedy of humours is combined with a romantic plot. As the latter is based on a story in the second part of D'Urfé's *Astrée*, published in 1610, the play must be after that date, and there are indications in it of a later revision. In the relations of Thomas, who gives the piece its name, and his father, Sebastian, there is a variation from the conventional attitude of the elderly parent towards a scapegrace son. Thomas has acquired the style of 'Monsieur' on his travels, from which he has just returned, but to his father's chagrin he is no longer ' mad' Thomas, but has become apparently a reformed character. As Sebastian laments:

> Did not I take him singing yesternight
> A godly ballad, to a godly tune too,
> And had a catechism in 's pocket? . . .
>   When was my house
> At such a shame before, to creep to bed
> At ten o'clock and twelve for want of company?
> No singing, nor no dancing, nor no drinking?

On the other hand to his lady-love, Mary, who has been alienated by reports of his *amours* abroad, he writes a letter that is 'the rarest inventory of rank oaths' and that 'roars like thunder'. Eventually with the help of his resourceful twin-sister, Dorothea, and through a series of stratagems and disguises, he succeeds in the double reconciliation with his father and his mistress. It is spirited fooling though, after Fletcher's manner, somewhat too long-drawn-out for modern taste. His higher quality is shown in his treatment of the romantic borrowed plot. Valentine has brought up in his house as his ward the girl Cellidè, and in spite of their difference of age looks forward to making her his second wife. On his travels he has formed a strong affection for a young stranger, Francisco, and has brought him back to live with him. Soon Francisco falls ill, and three doctors differ in their diagnosis of remedies. But Valentine divines the real nature of the malady—undisclosed love for Cellidè. In a dialogue of exquisite delicacy the guardian reveals this to his ward (II. i), and in a spirit of true chivalry bids her give preference to her younger lover. But when, in obedience to this command she offers her love to Francisco, he shows himself as self-sacrificing as Valentine (III. i):

> Hold, for heaven's sake!
> Must my friend's misery make me a triumph?
> Bear I that noble name, to be a traitor!

> O virtuous goodness, keep thyself untainted!
> You have no power to yield, nor he to render:
> Nor I to take: I am resolv'd to die first.

To escape temptation he makes an unavailing attempt at flight, and Cellidè an equally unavailing attempt to become a nun. But all ends happily when Francisco is discovered to be Valentine's son supposed to have been lost at sea in infancy.

D'Urfé's *Astrée*, Part II, ch. xii, furnished Fletcher with the main source of another play of a very different type in *Valentinian*, though he probably also owed something to the *De Bello Vandalico* of Procopius. The play was included in the folios of 1647 and 1679. The latter gives the names of the principal actors, all members of the King's company, including Burbage, Condell, Lowin, Ostler, and Underwood. As Ostler died on 16 December 1614 the play must have been produced between that date and the publication of Part II of *Astrée* in 1610. Internal evidence suggests that it is entirely from Fletcher's hand, and it may probably be placed about 1613–4.

Though the play takes its title from the emperor Valentinian III, the interest does not centre in him. He is the conventional figure of the tyrant who stops at nothing to satisfy his desires. He has cast lustful eyes on Lucina, wife of the renowned soldier Maximus, of whom it is said,

> She has in her
> All the contempt of glory and vain seeming
> Of all the Stoics, all the truth of Christians
> And all their constancy.

When every allurement and bribe fail to tempt her to sin the emperor brings her to the palace by a trick and ravishes her. The dialogue that follows between him and his victim rises to a majestic level as Valentinian meets her curses and call for vengeance with a reiteration of his omnipotence (III. i):

> *Luc.*   As long as there is motion in my body
> And life to give me words, I'll cry for justice.

Val.   Justice shall never hear you; I am justice. . .
       Your husband cannot help you, nor the soldier;
       Your husband is my creature, they my weapons,
       And only where I bid 'em, strike; I feed 'em;
       Nor can the gods be angry at this action,
       For as they make me most, they mean me happiest,
       Which I had never been without this pleasure.

The divine right of kings to do wrong here finds its consummate expression and nothing is left for Lucina but to die.

Then follows the situation which gives the play its distinctive quality. Maximus is eager to avenge his wife's dishonour, but finds an obstacle in his friend, the general Aëcius, who though outspoken in his criticism of Valentinian's vices, puts loyalty to him before everything. He has already dismissed the brave Captain Pontius, who has been spreading sedition among his troops because they have no warlike employment. Friendship between men is, as has been seen, a sacred obligation in the Beaumont and Fletcher canon, and it is only after a heart-rending struggle that Maximus can bring himself to violate it (III. iii. 1 ff):

       There's no way else to do it; he must die;
       This friend must die, this soul of Maximus. . .
                Why should I kill him?
       Why should I kill myself? for 'tis my killing;
       Aëcius is my root, and, wither him,
       Like a decaying branch I fall to nothing.
       Is he not more to me than wife? than Caesar?

For a moment he is tempted to let friendship outweigh honour, but he fortifies himself with the thought of Lucina's perfect virtue. His distraught bearing provokes Aëcius to cry: 'You look strangely'.

Max.   I look but as I am: I am a stranger.
Aëcius. To me?
Max.   To every one; I am no Roman.

And he is indeed 'no Roman' in the stratagem that he uses to procure the death of Aëcius. He sends to the emperor a forged letter implying that the general is about to take advantage of his popularity with the army to make a bid for the supreme power. Valentinian bribes the discharged Pontius to make away with him by promising him the succession to his office. In a superbly handled scene (Act IV. iv) Fletcher shows his insight into the spirit, at its finest, of the Roman legionaries. Pontius bluntly tells Aëcius that he has come to kill him, and that he is to have his place in the army. The old general has no thought of self:

> Now I fear thee,
> And not alone thee, Pontius, but the empire.
> *Pont.*   Why I can govern, sir.
> *Aëcius.*   I would thou could'st,
> And first thyself! Thou can'st fight well and bravely...
>   were thy mind
> But half so sweet in peace as rough in dangers,
> I died to leave a happy heir behind me.
> Come, strike and be a general!

Pontius bids him defend himself, but the soldierly instinct of discipline is too strong and Aëcius refuses to treat as an enemy any one 'sent from Caesar'. Thereupon Pontius crying, 'Then, have at you!' stabs himself, and with his dying breath protests to Aëcius:

> You mistook me:
> If I were foe to anything, 'twas ease; ... ,
> Not to the state or any point of duty.

Aëcius gasps forth admiringly:

> Thou hast fashion'd death
> In such an excellent and beauteous manner
> I wonder men can live,

and falls upon his own sword.

Up to this point the play has been sustained at a level of tragic grandeur from which there is a descent in the last act. Vengeance for Aëcius is taken by two eunuchs who had been in his service, and the death agonies of Valentinian from poison are unduly protracted on the stage. A contrast is provided by the festivities of Maximus, whom the soldiers elect as Valentinian's successor. But his inauguration is also the end of his reign, for Valentinian's widow, Eudoxia, crowns him with a poisoned wreath. His treachery to Aëcius deserves retribution, but it does not come with dramatic fitness from the hand of Eudoxia, who makes no appearance in the play till after the general's death.

In *Bonduca* Fletcher again chooses a theme from Roman imperial history, but transports us from the fifth to the first century and from Italy to Britain. His source, direct or indirect, is Book IV of the *Annals* of Tacitus. The play was included in the folios of 1647 and 1679, and the latter gives the list of the principal actors Besides the five mentioned for *Valentinian* there were Egglestone, Tooley, and Robinson. As Egglestone and Ostler seem to have acted together only in 1609–11 and 1613–14, the play belongs to one of these two periods, more probably the latter.

As with *Valentinian*, the titular part in *Bonduca* does not provide the main interest. Indeed, it is difficult to recognize at first the heroic queen of the Iceni, more familiarly known as Boadicea, in the virago who is rebuked by her commander-in-chief, Caratach, for taunting her foes as 'fearful, fleeing Romans and Roman girls'. Later, when the fortune of war has turned, he again has to reproach her (III. v) for 'playing the fool, the fool extremely, the mad fool' by giving an order that causes the Britons to lose the battle. Her daughters also provoke his wrath. In a piece of dubiously 'romantic' embroidery Junius, one of the Roman captains, figures as the lover of the queen's younger daughter, who treacherously lures him and other officers into the British camp, where only Caratach's intervention saves them from death. It is only at their last appearance (Act IV. iv), when besieged, in their fort, that Bonduca and her daughters arouse sympathy. All offers of mercy if she yields the British queen repels with scorn, which is echoed by the elder girl. But the younger shrinks from the suicide which Bonduca ordains:

> Oh, gentle mother!
> Oh, Romans! Oh, my heart, I dare not . . .
> Oh, persuade her, Romans!
> Alas, I am young and would live! Noble mother,
> Can you kill that you gave life? Are my years
> Fit for destruction?

But at last when told that she will meet her father among the blessed she stabs herself and is followed by her sister, while the queen drains a poisoned cup and dies with a touch of her former braggadocio:

> If you will keep your laws and empire whole,
> Place in your Roman flesh a Briton soul.

The true champion of Britain, however, is Caratach, though he is too idealized a type of the *chevalier sans peur et sans reproche* to fit in fully with his surroundings. When the British cause is lost through Bonduca's rashness he seeks to save their nephew Hengo. In the whole range of Elizabethan drama there is no more appealing figure of a child than this high-spirited, finely-tempered boy, with his questions to his uncle about the other world where he hopes to meet no Romans (IV. ii):

> *Car.*   No ill men
> That live by violence and strong oppression
> Come thither; 'tis for those the gods love, good men.
> *Hengo.* Why then I care not when I go, for surely
> I am persuaded they love me: I never
> Blasphem'd 'em, uncle, nor transgressed my parents;
> I always said my prayers.
> *Car.*   Thou shalt go then.
> Indeed thou shalt.

And all too soon a Roman arrow speeds him to 'that great blessedness'. But he has lived long enough to prove that Fletcher could draw the picture of a real boy to match those of such exquisite maidens in masculine guise as Bellario and Aspatia.

With the last hope of the royal house of Britain gone Caratach yields to the offer of the Roman general Suetonius that converts him from a brave foe into a noble friend.

Suetonius in his chivalrous bearing is a worthy counterpart
to Caratach, and in the individualized portraits of his large
group of subordinate officers Fletcher shows on a wider scale
than in *Valentinian* his interest in Roman military types.
Contrasted with those of a more orthodox pattern is Poenius,
a captain, of whom Tacitus had given a brief description
which Fletcher elaborates. Believing that it is madness to
attack an overwhelmingly superior British force he disobeys
the general's command to bring up his regiment. But when
the Romans are victorious he is overcome with shame and,
though Suetonius magnanimously forgives him, he falls upon
his own sword. It is another case like that of Pontius in
Valentinian of a true-hearted soldier proving a rebel against
discipline and having to pay the price.

The later plays which there is reason to assign to Fletcher
alone add to the range and volume of his work, but they do
not materially increase its dramatic significance and may be
considered more briefly. With one or two exceptions they
are found only in the 1647 and 1679 folios, and their approximate dates depend on internal evidence. *The Loyal Subject*
(*c.* 1618) is in its title and general theme allied to a play of
Heywood,[1] though in its treatment and setting it diverges
widely. Once again a highly placed soldier carries the
doctrine of passive obedience to fantastic limits. The young
Duke of Muscovy discharges and banishes to his country
house the aged general Archas. But at the news of a Tartar
invasion the duke has to recall the general, whom the soldiers
demand as their leader. When he has won the day he is
treacherously summoned to the Court and subjected to
torture by the evil-hearted favourite who has supplanted
him. Enraged by his ill-treatment the soldiers mutiny and
threaten to desert to the Tartars. With a magnanimity that
is wellnigh incredible Archas appeases them and brings about
a reconciliation with the sovereign who has so despitefully
used him.

[1] See above, p. 187.

Another abnormal military figure is the titular character of *The Humorous Lieutenant*, of which there is a manuscript text, 1625, prior to its inclusion in the folios, and which can be dated 1618, as it was 'allowed' by Sir George Buck on 16 November of that year. 'Humorous' is here used by Fletcher in its Jonsonian sense of temperamental. It is the peculiarity of the lieutenant in his career as a soldier that when he is in his usual ill-health, owing to his dissipated habits, he fights bravely. But when he has been paradoxically cured by a wound received in battle his longing for the fray quite leaves him. It is only when he has been tricked into the belief that he is suffering from a mortal illness that he is again roused to a display of excessive martial valour. It is a whimsical conception, but it is carried through with unflagging zest.

The Wild-Goose Chase could not be included in the 1647 folio because the manuscript had been lent to a person of quality and, as the publisher feared, irrevocably lost. But it was found later and published in quarto in 1652. It was acted at Court in 1621, and this may have been its first production ; it was revived in 1631. In a dedication prefixed to the quarto two of the principal actors, Lowin and Taylor, testified that the play was 'of so general a receiv'd acceptance' that they have known Fletcher himself when a spectator, 'in despite of his innate modesty, applauding this rare issue of his brain'. Its contemporary popularity is not difficult to understand. It belonged to the same type of comedy as *The Scornful Lady* and *Monsieur Thomas* in which a member of one sex affects to wage war *á l'outrance* against the other, in respect of marriage, but capitulates at the close. Here the militant attitude is assumed by 'the wild-goose', Mirabel, just back from his travels and from a series of amours, of which he keeps a record in an 'inventory' of his mistresses. His father is anxious that he should marry, and he has before leaving home contracted himself to Oriana, who loves him. But on his return he disavows the pledge and tells her that he must not lose his liberty. Then begins her chase of the wild-goose in which she is helped by her brother and by the ingenious tutor of two of her friends, Rosalura and Lillia Bianca. The chase involves a variety of stratagems, including Oriana's pretence of madness and her disguise as an Italian heiress to a fortune, by which Mirabel is finally tricked into marriage with her. In an effective complement to the main action, the underplot shows how Rosalura and Lillia Bianca adopting poses enjoined by their tutor first scare away their suitors, Mirabel's fellow-travellers, but finally secure them as husbands. The play owed its success to the fertility of Fletcher's invention, the briskness of its dialogue and (it must be added) the grossness of much of its wit. It has lost a good deal of its savour for an age not so preoccupied with every phase of the matrimonial 'chase'.

Another play presented at Court in 1621 was *The Pilgrim*, based upon a story by Lope de Vega. Pedro, a Spanish gentleman of Segovia, adopts the disguise of a pilgrim to carry on his wooing of Alinda, whose father wishes her to marry Roderigo, a wealthy suitor, who for political reasons has been banished from the city and has become captain of an outlaw band. Flights, pursuits, and disguises, strange happenings in the outlaws' camp and the surrounding woods and in the city mad-house (so attractive to Stuart theatre-goers) end in Pedro's union with Alinda and their all-round reconciliation. Though *The Pilgrim* is not one of Fletcher's more noteworthy works, it was adapted in 1700 by Vanbrugh with a prologue, epilogue, and masque written by Dryden.

Three other plays have association with the *Novelas Exemplares* of Cervantes. A story appended to a French translation of this work is the source of *The Island Princess* acted at Court on 26 December 1621. The play carries us into a region unfamiliar to London theatre-goers of the period, the Molucca islands. The King of Tidore has been seized and imprisoned by the Governor of Ternate, and his place as ruler has been taken for the time by his sister, Quisara. She

T

has many wooers, including the Governor, two neighbouring potentates, and Ruy Diaz, a leader among the Portuguese, who have a fort in Tidore. Quisara promises her hand to the rescuer of her brother, who bears his captivity and tortures with exaggerated Stoic constancy. He is delivered by a newly arrived Portuguese, Armusia, who then claims the princess 'by her own word and honour'. She hesitates to give herself to a stranger, and when he has shown proof of his noble nature and his devotion, she puts him suddenly to 'the utmost trial' by bidding him 'worship our gods, renounce the faith you are bred in'. Religion plays but a small part in the Beaumont and Fletcher dramatic canon, but here something of sacred fire touches Fletcher's pen in Armusia's indignant refusal to forsake his faith :

> *Quis.* The sun and moon we worship (these are heavenly)
> And their bright influence we believe.
> *Arm.*   Away, fool!
> I adore the Maker of that sun and moon,
> That gives those bodies light and influence,
> That pointed out their paths, and taught their motions;
> They are not so great as we; they are our servants. . .
> Shall I fall from this faith to please a woman,
> For her embraces bring my soul to ruin?
> I look'd you should have said, 'Make me a Christian:
> Work that great cure'; for 't is a great one, woman.

For once we are reminded that Fletcher was the son of a Bishop of London and that he was the cousin of Giles, the author of *Christ's Victory and Triumph*. In less lofty vein Armusia declares to Quisara that he will kick her 'mammet-gods' into puddles. He thus plays into the hands of the Governor of Ternate who, disguised as a Moorish priest, urges the reluctant King of Tidore to seize and threaten with torture and death his erstwhile deliverer for dishonouring their gods. The unflinching composure of Armusia effects what his eloquence could not do—Quisara announces that she will embrace his faith and share his fate. But in animated closing scenes the Portuguese rescue them by turning the guns of their fort upon the city, and the villainous Governor of Ternate is unmasked.

The Chances, published only in the two folios, and of uncertain date, is more directly indebted to Cervantes as it is based on one of the *Novelas Exemplares*. We turn back from the 'spicy breezes' of the Moluccas and the high argument of rival faiths to the more familiar Fletcherian background of an Italian city and the strange adventures in which two young Spanish gallants become involved there. The one has an unknown infant thrust into his arms, and the other becomes the protector of a beauty in distress. A breathless series of happenings, including street-brawls and highly embarrassing mistakes of identity, results in the revelation that the lady is the contracted bride of the Duke of Ferrara, and that the child is theirs. Two well-drawn secondary characters are a suspicious and loose-tongued landlady and a teacher of grammar and music who affects to be a conjurer. Adaptations of *The Chances* by the Duke of Buckingham and by Garrick, and a musical version in 1821 prove its enduring popularity.

Another of the *Novelas Exemplares* furnished the underplot of *Rule a Wife and Have a Wife*, published in quarto in 1640 and in the 1679 folio. Sir H. Herbert records that it was acted at Court on 2 November and 26 December 1624. In the underplot Estefania, a lady's maid to the rich Seville heiress, Margarita, entraps into a marriage with her Captain Percy by a pretence that she is the owner of her mistress's house and fortune. Margarita's unexpected return from the country forces her into a further series of lies and shifts till the truth has at last to be revealed. Meanwhile the heiress herself has contracted a marriage which provides the main plot and which is another variant of the matrimonial theme which had so strong a fascination for Fletcher. Margarita wants a 'shadow' husband who will fetch and carry for her and let her have her own will in everything. Her other attendant, Altea, recommends the 'alferez' or ensign Leon,

gentle and soft spoken, who is really her brother. As soon
as the match is made Leon assumes in the fullest manner the
status and rights of a husband and master of the house and
the wealthy termagant is tamed as effectually as Kate in
Shakespeare's play.

To May of the same year, 1624, belongs, as Herbert records,
A Wife for a Month, included in the 1679 folio. Here at the
very close of his career Fletcher turned back from his lighter
comic vein to a theme reminiscent in some respects of his
and Beaumont's masterpiece, *The Maid's Tragedy*. Frederick,
King of Naples, sits on the throne which should have been
Alphonso's, his elder brother, who is a victim of melancholia
and lives retired in a monastery. Frederick, though he has
a devoted wife, Maria, has cast a lustful eye on Evanthe,
and he is abetted by her villainous brother, Sorano, the
anthithesis to Melantius in *The Maid's Tragedy*. Evanthe
turns a deaf ear to the king ; she loves and is beloved by
the young lord Valerio, who in a 'sonnet' to her has avowed:

> To be your own but one poor month, I'll give
> My youth, my fortune, and then leave to live.

In a cynical spirit of revenge Frederick ordains that Valerio
is at once to be married for a month to Evanthe, and then
to die, and that she is also to die unless she can find another
husband on the same condition. Valerio is ready to prove
the truth of his sonnet's declaration.

> Think but man's life a month and we are happy.
> I would not have my joys grow old for anything:
> A Paradise, as thou art, my Evanthe,
> Is only made to wonder at a little.

But Sorano announces to Valerio on his wedding night that
it is the king's will that if he does more than merely kiss
Evanthe she is at once to die. He therefore has to offer her
instead of bridal joys to 'feed on the sweets of one another's
souls', and finally to pretend impotence. Thereupon Frederick renews his suit to Evanthe, and in scenes of striking
psychological subtlety her faith in Valerio is for a brief time

shaken, but they are reunited in love and look for one final night of bliss when Valerio is summoned to meet his fate.

But Sorano has over-reached himself. To secure his patron Frederick's position, he has administered to Alphonso a drug which instead of acting as a poison has proved a cure for his melancholia. The followers of the rightful king revolt against Frederick and seize him; they set Valerio free, and Alphonso blesses his union with Evanthe. His miraculous recovery and the instant success of the revolt are unconvincing, and Sorano's devilry throughout is dramatically incredible, but the lovers are drawn with insight and feeling and Fletcher's handling of their abnormal situation proves that to the end he had a grasp of tragi-comedy in which Beaumont and he had shown their highest powers. Meanwhile in Massinger he had found another notable collaborator and their joint achievement has now to be considered.

XII

JOHN FLETCHER AND PHILIP MASSINGER

TRAGI-COMEDIES—COMEDIES OF SPANISH SOURCE

PHILIP MASSINGER was the son of Arthur Massinger, horse-steward to Henry Herbert and afterwards to William Herbert, Earls of Pembroke. Philip was baptized in St. Thomas's Church, Salisbury, on 24 November 1583. In 1602 he entered St. Alban's Hall, Oxford, but left without a degree in 1606. He then appears to have gone up to London to try his fortunes as a playwright, but nothing is known of his earlier years in the capital. He began as a collaborator and from about 1613 was associated chiefly for a decade with Fletcher, writing for the King's men. In the 1647 and 1679 folios, however, his share is ignored, and, as has been seen, it is to Sir Aston Cokayne that we are indebted for contemporary testimony to his close partnership. For a time he worked for other companies. *The Virgin Martyr* by him and Dekker licensed on 6 October 1620, and first published in 1622, was acted by the Revels company at the Red Bull. Three of his plays in 1623–4 were written for the Lady Elizabeth's Cockpit company. Thereafter he again worked for the King's men till his death in 1639, when he was buried on 18 March in St. Saviour's, Southwark. In the lines which Cokayne addressed to the printer of the 1647 folio he declared:

> Beaumont in those many writ in few,
> And Massinger in other few; the main
> Being the issues of sweet Fletcher's brain.

Cokayne did not specify the plays in which Massinger joined hands with Fletcher, and we have to fall back upon internal evidence, which is not entirely conclusive. Critics, therefore, differ considerably in their estimates and attributions, but, broadly speaking, Massinger may be traced by his constructive power, his style more eloquent and impressive than lyrical or imaginative, and his preference for run-on ten-syllable lines in contrast with Fletcher's end-stopped feminine endings. On these grounds his hand has been detected or conjectured more frequently in acts I and V of the composite plays than in the central scenes.

Certainly in *The Knight of Malta* the first and last acts have the impress, especially metrically, of Massinger and not of Fletcher. The play appeared only in the two folios, but must have been performed before the death of Burbage, who is mentioned among the principal actors, in March 1618/9. No source has been found for this tragi-comedy which has as its background the conflict between the Knights of St. John and the Turks. But the interest lies in the rivalry of three suitors of different nationality for the love of Oriana, sister of the Grand-Master of the Order. The valiant but evil-hearted Frenchman, Mountferrat, one of the Knights, seeks to win her, though by the vows of his Order he is bound never to marry. For her sake, though they allege unworthiness of the honour, the Italian, Miranda, and the Spaniard, Gomera, decline to be admitted into the Order of the knights. In jealous fury, Mountferrat, with the aid of Oriana's Moorish waiting-woman, brings against her a forged charge of treason to which (it is a weakness in the plot) her brother lends at once a credulous ear. Gomera appears as her champion and is opposed in disguise by Miranda, who lets himself be defeated to save Oriana's honour. The Grand Master as 'umpire' between these two claimants gives her in marriage to Gomera, while consoling Miranda with the assurance,

> I have provided
> A better match for you, more full of beauty;
> I'll wed you to our Order.

But it is to him that Oriana has given her love, and by her artless praise of him she wakes her husband's jealousy.

Stung by his reproaches (another unconvincing episode) she
falls in a swoon, which by the machinations of the Moor is
turned into a death-like stupor. In impressive scenes reminiscent of *Romeo and Juliet* she is buried in the family
monument in the Temple of St. John and rescued by
Miranda. In the finest scene of the play (V. i), which on
metrical grounds must be assigned to Massinger, Miranda
pleads for her love, but she forbids him to offer her even a
kiss, which is now 'due to my lord, to none else'. Miranda
confesses himself overpowered:

> Husband! wife!
> There is some holy mystery in those names
> That sure the unmarried cannot understand.

Oriana responds with a rapturous declaration of a supersensual communion of souls:

> Now thou art straight, and dost enamour me
> So far beyond a carnal earthly love,
> My very soul dotes on thee, and my spirits
> Do embrace thine; my mind doth thy mind kiss;
> And in this pure conjunction we enjoy
> A heavenlier pleasure than if bodies met:
> This, this is perfect love.

With this bond between them Miranda hastens to restore
Oriana to her repentant husband, who is mourning her as
dead. The play has a spectacular close in the expulsion
before an altar of Mountferrat from the Order of St. John
and the admission into it of Miranda, welcomed in song as
'fair child of virtue, honour's bloom'.

The Queen of Corinth, acted by Burbage and his fellows,
is also laid in the Mediterranean neighbourhood, but is of
slighter interest. It is notable less for its main plot concerning a despotic queen's relations with her heir and a favourite
than for its ridicule in a trio of minor characters of pre-
tentious travellers, especially Tom Coryate, against whom
there are several palpable hits, probably soon before or
after his death in 1617.

Beggars' Bush, besides its inclusion in both folios, appeared in quarto in two issues in 1661, and is also extant in a MS. version. It was acted at Court at Christmas 1622, but may date somewhat earlier. Here again it is not the main plot that gives the play its interest. It is a complicated story of the restoration to his rights of the true heir, through his mother, to the earldom of Flanders which has been seized by a usurper. The heir's father, Gerrard, and a group of loyal subjects have adopted the disguise of beggars and have joined a band of real 'knavish beggars', appropriately named Higgen, Prig, and Snap. It is the jovial atmosphere in the camp of this fraternity, among whom Gerrard is elected king, that lends the play an exhilarating open-air feeling. Their rousing, spicy songs and their prodigal use of the 'canting' lingo of the thieves' highway give glimpses of the Stuart underworld that are unusual in 'Beaumont and Fletcher' plays.

It was not the legendary chronicles of Flanders but a contemporary event in its blood-stained history that inspired *Sir John Van Olden Barnavelt*. The execution of this famous Advocate of Holland for conspiracy against the State took place in May 1619 and the play, as contemporary letters prove, was being acted by the King's men in the following August. Its omission from the folios is strange, for it deserved a place on its merits, and the objections raised to its performance by the Bishop of London would not have had any weight in 1647, still less in 1679. It has survived in a manuscript (now British Museum Add. MS. 18,653) and was printed by Bullen in *Old English Plays* (1883), vol. II. The MS. is anonymous, but if internal evidence can prove anything, Bullen's identification of Fletcher as part author is certain and scarcely less so is that of Massinger as his collaborator. The names of some of the actors of minor parts written in the margin of the MS. prove that it was a King's company's play.

The tragedy was evidently hurriedly written to exploit for stage purposes the popular interest in a striking contem-

porary event. In such circumstances it could scarcely have
been a masterpiece, and Bullen's claim that it is a 'magnificent tragedy' is exaggerated. Even at the time the position
of Barnavelt as the champion, religiously, of the Arminians
against the Calvinists, and, politically, of the province of
Holland against the States General cannot have meant very
much to the average London playgoer. And there was the
further difficulty that King James had strongly sided with
Barnavelt's enemies though history has proved that his
execution was a judicial murder.

Thus from the first Barnavelt appears not in a patriotic
light, but as jealous of Prince Maurice of Nassau, whom the
dramatists call Prince of Orange.

> Shall I then,
> Now in the sunset of my day of honour,
> When I should pass with glory to my rest,
> And raise my monument from my country's praises,
> Sit down and with a boorish patience suffer
> The harvest that I labour'd for to be
> Another's spoil?
> No! this ungrateful country, this base people,
> Most base to my deserts, shall first with horror
> Know he that could defeat the Spanish counsels,
> And countermine their dark works, he that made
> The State what 'tis, will change it once again
> Ere fall with such dishonour.

On the other hand the Prince of Orange is favourably
.represented. As one of his followers declares:

> Like a true noble gentleman he has borne himself,
> And a fair fortunate soldier. I hold the State, sir,
> Most happy in his care, and this torn country,
> Whose wounds smart yet, most bound to his deliverance.

He shows himself merciful to the conspirators and it is only
by the advice of his council that he proceeds to extremities
against them. Barnavelt's defence of himself, a narrative of
his past services, falls flat in the light of his present plots.
When he receives his sentence, he cries, 'I shall not play my

last act worst', but even on the scaffold, when bidden to confess his faults, he maintains his self-righteous attitude:

> I came not hither
> To make myself guilty; yet one fault I must utter,
> And 'tis a great one . . .
> I die for saving this unthankful country.

It is only with his last breath, before the axe falls, that he changes his tune:

> Honour and world I fling ye thus behind me,
> And thus a naked poor man, kneel to heaven.

Whatever the dramatists' intention may have been, the fate of Barnavelt, as he is thus equivocally portrayed, does not move the true tragic pity and fear. The attraction of the play lies rather in some of the incidental scenes, especially those in which Barnavelt's fellow-plotter, Leidenberck, figures. He has been arrested and made confession and is thereafter visited in prison by Barnavelt, who, in Fletcher's exquisite verse, bids him with his own hand seek death (III. iv):

> *Leid.* 'Tis no great pain.
> *Bar.*   'Tis nothing:
> Imagination only makes it monstrous.
> When we are sick we endure a hundred fits—
> This is but one—a hundred ways of torture. . .
> One blow, one short piece of an hour does this,
> And this cures all.

But the sight of his boy sleeping near him almost stays Leidenberck's hand:

> To die were nothing—simply to leave the light;
> No more than going to our beds and sleeping;
> But to leave all these dearnesses behind us,
> These figures of ourselves that we call blessings
> Is that which troubles. Can man beget a thing
> That shall be dearer than himself unto him?

Such lines alone would give cause for gratification in the rediscovery of the play. Equally notable, in a very different

vein, is the scene (V. ii) in which the three executioners of
Harlem, Leyden, and Utrecht contend as to their respective professional merits and throw dice for the honour of
cutting off Barnavelt's head, in which Utrecht is winner. In
its grim humour this scene may take rank with that of the
grave-diggers in *Hamlet*.

Among the 'Beaumont and Fletcher' problems of date and
authorship those relating to *Thierry and Theodoret* may claim
pre-eminence. An anonymous quarto of this tragedy, as
acted at the Blackfriars by the King's men, was published
by T. Walkley in 1621. Another quarto, published by
H. Moseley in 1648, assigned it to Fletcher, but a further
issue of this quarto in 1649 with a new title-page gave
Beaumont's name also. It was omitted in the 1647 folio, but
included, with part of Act V left out, in the 1679 collection.
The stylistic evidence shows that Fletcher had a collaborator
whom, since Swinburne suggested him, critics have mostly
identified as Massinger. On internal grounds there might be
found traces of Beaumont's hand, but as the prologue to the
1649 quarto speaks of the play as having been in fashion
twenty years ago, it appears to date after his death.

Thierry and Theodoret is loosely based on historical events
in the later sixth century, and the fiendish queen-mother,
Brunhalt, had an actual prototype. But the weakest element
in the tragedy is the lack of sufficient motive for her appal-
ling crimes, and we echo the words of one of the characters,
'Why art thou such a monster?' Because her elder son,
Theodoret, prince of Austrasia, reproaches her for her sinful
life, she flies with her paramour Protaldy, and her servile
physician Lecure to the Court of his brother, Thierry, King
of France, whither he follows her only to be treacherously
stabbed to death by Protaldy at her command. Subtler
means have to be used to get rid of a yet more dangerous
obstacle. Thierry announces the arrival of his contracted
bride, Ordella, daughter of the King of Arragon. Brunhalt
angrily forsees that with this

> all my power
> Must suffer shipwreck. For me now,
> That hitherto have kept the first, to know
> A second place, or yield the least precedence
> To any other, 's death.

She administers to Thierry a potion compounded by Lecure which will prevent him from consummating the marriage and will, as she believes, estrange him from Ordella. But with her entrance the play mounts from the region of melodrama into a loftier sphere. To Thierry's lament that he can make her a wife but not a mother she gives the nobly reassuring answer (III. i):

> 'Tis true
> That to bring forth a second to yourself
> Was only worthy of my virgin-loss;
> And should I prize you less unpattern'd, sir,
> Than being exemplified? Is't not more honour
> To be possessor of unequall'd virtue
> Than what is parallel'd?

Again Brunhalt employs Lecure, disguised as an astrologer, to tell Thierry that he will beget children if he kills the first woman that he sees coming from Diana's temple—that woman being Ordella veiled and unrecognized by him. As he imparts to her that she must bring a general blessing on the king and kingdom by her own self-sacrifice, Fletcher (for the verse can be none but his) achieves an unsurpassed union of his lyrical and dramatic powers (IV. i):

Thi.   Suppose it death.
Ord.   I do.
Thi.   And endless parting
> With all we can call ours, with all our sweetness,
> With youth, strength, pleasure, people, time, nay, reason:
> For in the silent grave no conversation,
> No joyful tread of friends, no voice of lovers,
> No careful father's counsel; nothing's heard,
> Nor nothing is, but all oblivion,
> Dust and an endless darkness: and dare you, woman,
> Desire this place?

Ord.   'Tis of all sleeps the sweetest.
        Children begin it to us, strong men seek it,
        And kings from height of all their painted glories
        Fall like spent exhalations to this centre;
        And those are fools that fear it. . .
Thi.   Then you can suffer?
Ord.   As willingly as say it.

Here with the sacrificial ardour of a Bellario or an Aspatia for love's sake Ordella blends 'a spirit masculine and noble' that makes her glad to surrender life for the kingdom's sake. But as she raises her veil Thierry lets fall his uplifted sword. His confidant, Martel, however spreads a report of her death, and Brunhalt, to prevent Thierry from marrying again, traps him into a torture of sleeplessness that must prove fatal. Martel turns the tables on her in similar fashion and the play reverts to melodrama in her own and Lecure's suicide and the breaking of her paramour on the wheel. But the close is irradiated by the reappearance of Ordella, whom her husband takes to be a spirit, a 'happy, happy soul' in everlasting life, till he realizes that she is 'the same Ordella still', and they have an ecstatic moment of reunion before their joy proves too much for them to bear. There are few Stuart plays which glow at the end with so spiritual a light.

In *The False One*, where Massinger's is the predominant hand, the chief figures, Caesar and Cleopatra, had already been presented on the stage by Shakespeare. But as the prologue pleads, the play shows Caesar not dying in the Capitol but in his 'amorous heats', and Cleopatra not in her fatal love for Antony, but in her youthful days. *The False One* appeared only in the two folios. As Burbage is not in the list of principal actors it was later than his death.

The play opens after Pompey's defeat by Caesar at Pharsalus, and closely following and adapting Lucan's *De Bello Civili*, it deals in spirited fashion with Pompey's flight to Egypt, his murder by his former centurion Septimius, and the arrival of Caesar at Ptolemy's court to mourn the fate of his defeated rival and to reproach those who have instigated the crime. But his mood is soon changed by Cleopatra whose portraiture is the most striking feature of the play. Young as she is she has the imperious temper of one born to royal station:

> There is no place in Egypt where I stand,
> But that the tributary earth is proud
> To kiss the foot of her that is her queen.

She bitterly resents the gilded captivity to which she has been confined by the jealousy of Ptolemy's chief minister, the eunuch Photinus, and it is to escape from this that by a characteristic ruse she gets herself conveyed into the presence of Caesar and bewitches him by her charms. The reproaches of his blunt-spoken captain Scaeva cannot move him, but the display before him at Ptolemy's command, of the matchless treasures of Egypt, with a masque of their parent, 'the reverend Nile', diverts his eyes from his enchantress. It is at this point that the two dramatists give an original turn to their characterization of Cleopatra by making her jealous of the wealth that has outvied for Caesar her attractions. As she laments to her sister (IV. ii):

> To prefer
> The lustre of a little earth, Arsinöe,
> And the poor glow-worm light of some faint jewels,
> Before the life of love and soul of beauty.
> O, how it vexes me! He is no soldier;
> All honourable soldiers are Love's servants:
> He is a merchant, a mere wandering merchant,
> Servile to gain; he trades for poor commodities,
> And makes his conquests thefts.

In similar vein, when he again approaches her, she upbraids him, and bids him 'farewell, unthankful':

Caesar Stay!
Cleop.　　　　I will not.
Caesar　　　　　　　　I command.
Cleop. Command, and go without, sir.
　　　I do command thee be my slave for ever
　　　And vex while I laugh at thee. . . . Farewell, conqueror !

Her defiance spurs him to win again this 'miracle' among women. And this he does in unforeseen fashion. By his courage he quells a rising of the Egyptian mob incited by Photinus, in which King Ptolemy loses his life. Cleopatra sees him again as truly a conqueror, and renews her allegiance:

> He is all honour,
> Nor do I now repent me of my favours,
> Nor can I think Nature e'er made a woman,
> That in her prime deserv'd him.

The Egyptian queen in *The False One* is not the Cleopatra of Shakespeare or Dryden or Bernard Shaw (though with him too she is Caesar's, not Antony's, charmer), but she is worthy to take her place with the other figures in this resplendent gallery.

From the above series of more or less historical tragedies let us pass to some among a group of lighter plays in which the two dramatists were associated in the final phase of Fletcher's career. Though *The Spanish Curate* appeared only in the two folios, it can be dated in 1622, when it was licensed by Herbert on 24 October, and acted at Court on 26 December. Its source is an English translation published in 1622 of a Spanish novel by Gonzalo de Cespedes, *Gerardo, the Unfortunate Spaniard*. One tale in this novel provides the basis of the more serious plot. Don Henrique, a grandee, has an unacknowledged son, Ascanio, by Jacinta, a woman of humble birth, to whom he was contracted, but whom he has repudiated and who is supposed to be the wife of a disbanded captain, Octavio. Don Henrique is now living with the high-born Violante, supposed to be his wife, but who is childless. To prevent his estate from passing to his younger brother, Don Jamie, he determines to have Ascanio legally recognized as his heir, though this involves the revelation of his own and Jacinta's shame. He effects this by means of the venal lawyer, Bartolus, and a corrupt 'assistant' or judge. But Violante, enraged by the entrance of the 'bastard' into her childless home, proves a very Brunhalt in a more domestic sphere. She plans with Don Jamie to kill Ascanio and Don Henrique, and when he suggests Octavio and Jacinta as further victims, she cries 'that's glorious'. But his compliance is merely a ruse to defeat her criminal purpose. She is arrested and sentenced to life-long confinement in a nunnery, to be built out of her dowry, while Don Henrique is reunited to Jacinta and reconciled with the brother who has saved his wife. The redeeming figure in this somewhat sordid story is Ascanio, who in the homes both of his foster-parent and of his father is the very model of a dutiful and loving son. He is drawn with a wistful and tender charm that allies him to the sacrificial sisterhood of the 'Beaumont and Fletcher' creation.

It is however in the lighter plot, based upon another tale in *Gerardo*, that the chief attraction of the play lies. The main link between the two actions is the lawyer, Bartolus, who keeps jealous guard over his beautiful young wife Amaranta. The young gallant Leandro, hearing of her charms, resolves to woo her and gets admitted to her husband's house under the pretence that he is a law-student ready to pay handsomely for tuition. He is introduced to Bartolus by the curate Lopez, who deservedly gives the play its title, for though his is a minor part in the action he provides the richest entertainment. This is increased by the addition of a figure not found in *Gerardo*, his sexton Diego. The pair lament in chorus that nothing happens in the parish to bring them in fees (II. i):

Lop. When was there a christening, Diego?
Dieg.   Not this ten weeks;
   Alas, they have forgot to get children, master. . .
   They are so hard-hearted here too,
   They will not die; there's nothing got by burials. . .
Lop. We must remove into a muddy air,
   A most contagious climate.
Dieg.   We must, certain.

When Leandro enters with a bogus letter from an imaginary

father in Nova Hispania to his old fellow-student, Lopez,
the curate naturally cannot remember him. But when
Leandro produces five hundred ducats which he was to
deliver to him, the curate's memory, prompted by Diego,
starts to life in such amazing clearness that Leandro may
well whisper:

> The money rubs 'em into strange remembrances:
> For as many ducats more they would remember Adam.

The episode is a masterpiece of humour, not so wildly
farcical as a later scene (IV. v) where Diego pretends to be
dying, makes Lopez write his will in which he leaves immense
fictitious legacies, and appoints Bartolus his full executor
with two thousand ducats for his pains. Meanwhile, the
lawyer is being fooled in a different fashion in his own house.
The sly, bookish student who, as Bartolus thinks,

> knows not how to look upon a woman
> More than by reading what sex she is,

finds opportunity of declaring his passion for Amaranta by
lute and song, and through the *double-entendre* of the moves
on a chess-board.[1] This is followed by an assignation at a
'private fine house' which, in another highly entertaining
scene, Amaranta declares to her husband was a visit to
church, where Leandro fell asleep and snored. Thus it is
surprising that Leandro can afterwards assure Bartolus
that he   made trial of this lady's constancy,
> And found it strong as fate,

and that Don Jamie supports him and declares her 'fair and
virtuous'. Even a less jealous husband than Bartolus might
have found cause for suspicion, but the dramatists are bent
on putting the rascal always in the wrong. Yet he fares
better than in the novel, where he finds Leandro in his wife's
bedchamber, and in a struggle is stabbed by him to death.

[1] This episode is taken from the novel, but Fletcher (the scene bears his
mark) works the technical terms of the game into the dialogue as Heywood
and Middleton have also done.

The venal advocate like Bartolus is a stock character in Stuart drama: it is a more unusual figure that gives the title to *The Little French Lawyer* included in the two folios and, as is suggested by the list of principal actors, performed by the King's men about 1620.

This singular representative of the Paris Bar is a creation of the dramatists, but he is ingeniously grafted into a plot borrowed, in modified form, from an episode in Guzman d'Alfarache's *The Spanish Rogue*. Dinant, a young gallant, has loved Lamira, daughter of the judge, Vertaigne. But when the play opens she has just been married to Champernel, an elderly 'naval warrior', who has lost an arm and leg in the service, but has the advantage over his rival in wealth. Dinant, meeting the wedding party on their way back from the church, uses such insulting language to the bride, her father, and her husband, that he is challenged to a duel by Champernel's nephew, Verdone, with Vertaigne's son, Beaupré, as his second, while Dinant's friend, Cleremont, acts similarly for him. But on the morning of the encounter Lamira sends a message to Dinant—this is the most artless part of the action—which prevents him from keeping his tryst. Cleremont thus left alone to face two adversaries spies the little lawyer, La-Writ, hurrying across the field with his bag full of cases, and forces him, in spite of his protests, to take his stand beside him in the duel. He has beginner's luck and disarms in turn Beaupré and Verdone. His success so inflames him that he becomes 'metamorphosed, nothing of lawyer left'. Fighting's his occupation, and because he fails to appear in court his clients are non-suited by Vertaigne. Thereupon he sends a challenge to this elderly judge, whose nephew Sampson takes it up on his behalf. Their encounter (Act IV. iv) is an exquisitely comic satire on the punctilios of the duelling-code and may take rank on its own lines with the meeting between Sir Andrew and Viola in *Twelfth Night*. Cleremont, acting as second to La-Writ, asks his foe:

> You come with no spells nor witchcraft?
>
> *Samp.*   I come fairly,
> To kill him honestly.
>
> *La-Writ.*   Hang spells and witchcraft!
> I come to kill my lord's nephew like a gentleman,
> And so I kiss a hand.

Then, a gentleman who is Sampson's second, objects that La-Writ's doublet is too stiff, and both duellists 'uncase'. Thereupon Sampson raises another objection—that La-Writ has no lace in his shirt, and asks,

>   May I fight
> With a foul shirt?
>
> *Gent.*   Most certain, so it be
> A fighting shirt, let it be ne'er so foul or lousy;
> Caesar wore such a one.
>
> *Samp.*   Saint Denis, then!
> I accept your shirt.

While they are parleying the seconds run off with their doublets and swords and they are left shivering and with chattering teeth, in the cold morning air. At last to keep up their circulation they have to go off kicking and beating each other. That is the end of La-Writ's 'occupation' as a fighting-man.

It is unnecessary to follow the development of the somewhat unedifying and not entirely lucid main plot, but in addition to the little lawyer the play presents us with a Nurse who is of kin to her namesake in *Romeo and Juliet*, and it has a number of verbal Shakespearean echoes.

This survey of the Fletcher and Massinger group of plays may end with *The Elder Brother*, a comedy whose unusual popularity is attested by the number of editions in which it appeared. Two quarto issues in 1637 spoke of it as written by Fletcher and acted by the King's men at Blackfriars. It was not included in the 1649 folio, but another quarto in 1651 'corrected and amended', ascribed it to Beaumont and Fletcher. A 1661 quarto mentioned Fletcher only, but in 1678 yet another reverted to Beaumont and Fletcher. It was included in the 1679 folio, where unaccountably the verse was throughout printed as prose, and where the prologue speaks of the play as an 'orphan' left by Fletcher. There is now general agreement that Massinger had a hand in the play, though whether as a collaborator or reviser after Fletcher's death is uncertain.

The plot, of which no source has been traced, is simpler than is usual in Stuart plays of joint authorship, and is based on the contrast between two brothers, a scholar and a courtier, sons of a wealthy justice, Brisac. This philistine and (as it proves) immoral dignitary looks scornfully upon his elder son Charles, who is absorbed in 'bookish contemplation' and who replies to the paternal precepts about the management of an estate:

> I may do this
> From what I've read, sir; for what concerns tillage
> Who better can deliver it than Virgil
> In his *Georgics*? and to cure your herds
> His *Bucolics* is a masterpiece.

Charles, too, has no interest in the other sex except as he finds them in his reading. Brisac therefore resolves to marry his younger son Eustace, just returned from Court, to Angelina, daughter of a neighbouring lord, Lewis, and to make him his heir. As he assures Lewis,

> Charles has given o'er the world; I'll undertake,
> And with much ease, to buy his birthright of him
> For a dry-fat of new books.

But unexpected obstacles arise. Brisac's own elder brother, Miramont, though himself no student, gives support to Charles. Angelina does not find in Eustace 'that grac'd excellence' promised by her father. Charles at first sight of her calls her 'a curious piece of learning, handsomely bound, and of a dainty letter'. When he hears that the surrender of his inheritance to Eustace means the parting with this 'inimitable piece of beauty', he refuses to sign, and cries in new-found rapture:

> We'll live together like two wanton vines,
> Circling our souls and loves in one another,
> We'll spring together and bear one fruit;
> One joy shall make us smile and one grief mourn. . .

Ang.   And one hand seal the match, I'm yours for ever.

She follows Charles to Miramont's house, while Brisac
enraged with Eustace for his defeat by a 'bookish boy' turns
him out of doors until he can recover the lost Angelina. With
two lily-livered courtier companions he makes an attempt
to carry her off, but when he is baffled by Charles, he shakes
off the contemptible pair and, to reclaim 'the reputation of
a man' challenges Charles to a duel. Miramont roused by
the clashing of swords near his house parts the two brothers,
but rejoices to find a new Eustace, 'a brave spark, a true
tough-metall'd blade', who is 'turn'd an Oliver and a Rowland'. The brothers unite with their uncle in bringing to
reason Angelina's father, who has taken out a writ for the
'rape' of his daughter against Brisac, who fears the revelation
in court of an intrigue with a tenant's wife. All ends in a
general reconciliation.

The Elder Brother is an entertaining piece and it ends on
an exceptionally edifying note. But the conversions through
which its chief characters go are too abrupt and it does not
rival in rich humour the best scenes in *The Spanish Curate*
and *The Little French Lawyer*. For us to-day its main attraction lies in the humanist atmosphere which towards the close
of the Jacobean period recalls the ardours of the early
Renaissance. Marlowe himself might have put into the
mouth of Charles the lines:

> That place that does contain
> My books (the best companions) is to me
> A glorious Court, where hourly I converse
> With the old sages and philosophers.

Even more striking as the tribute not of the scholar but of
the man of the world is Miramont's declaration to Brisac:

Though I can speak no Greek, I love the sound on't.
It goes so thundering as it conjur'd devils.
Charles speaks it loftily, and if thou wert a man,
Or had'st but ever heard of Homer's *Iliads*,
Hesiod and the Greek poets, thou would'st run mad,
And hang thyself for joy th' hadst such a gentleman
To be thy son.

Even at so late a date the very mention of the old sages and philosophers, of Homer and Hesiod, lends a glow and splendour to the rhythm of the verse.

XIII

PHILIP MASSINGER—NATHAN FIELD

RELIGIOUS, POLITICAL, AND SOCIAL DRAMAS

BEFORE passing to the consideration of plays written by Massinger alone, or jointly with the actor-dramatist, Nathan Field, note may here be taken of the highly popular religious tragedy in which he collaborated with Dekker, *The Virgin-Martyr*. The play must date before 6 October 1620, when Sir George Buck entered 40s. in his office-book 'for new reforming *The Virgin-Martyr*'. A quarto edition of the play, as acted by the Revels company, and written by Massinger and Dekker, appeared in 1622, and was followed by other quartos in 1631, 1651, and 1661. Massinger's name comes first on the title-pages and his appears to have been the predominant hand. The classical setting and the pre-occupation with the theme of religious conversion are characteristic of him and not of Dekker, to whom, however, with his gift for fine feminine portraiture, may be ascribed at least in part the creation of the heroine, Dorothea, and (in his least happy comic vein) the prose scenes in the play.

The persecution of the Christians under Diocletian offers a lofty tragic theme, and the fundamental conception underlying the play is a noble one. Yet in spite of some striking poetic and rhetorical flights, and of the contemporary popularity of *The Virgin-Martyr*, the two dramatists just failed to reach the full height of their great argument. The scene is laid in Caesarea where Theophilus is a fierce persecutor of the 'new-found religion' and is incited by his secretary, Harpax, who is really an evil spirit. The audience of the period was avid of supernatural effects and was as ready to swallow them in the crude form of a Harpax as in the imaginative grandeur of Marlowe's Mephistopheles. He has already served his master by teaching him to reclaim his two daughters who had joined the 'new-sprung sect', but who have now forsaken it and become vestals in the temple of Jupiter. Theophilus can thus present them with pride to the Emperor, when he visits the city, as proof of his zeal for the Roman gods. Diocletian, too, has a dutiful daughter, Artemia, to whom in recompense he offers any husband of her choice. When she singles out Antoninus, son of the Governor, he astounds her by declining her proffered hand on the plea that he dare not look so high, but in reality because he loves the daughter of a senator, the Christian Dorothea. She in turn spurns his suit and the dramatists fail in making it plausible that devotion to Christ implies such an icy rejection of human love (II. iii):

> Sir, for your fortunes, were they mines of gold,
> He that I love is richer; and for worth,
> You are to him lower than any slave
> Is to a monarch.

Dorothea's two villainous servants, Hircus and Spungius, have brought Artemia, with the Governor and Theophilus, to overhear from the gallery 'above', the declaration of Antoninus that he offers Dorothea a heart for which great Caesar's daughter sues in vain. Artemia in fury decrees that they both shall die, but yields to the plea of Theophilus that 'this Christian thing' shall, by his daughter's arguments, be brought back creeping 'to kiss the pavements of our paynim gods'. But in what is the central scene of the play (III. i) the tables are turned and it is Dorothea who reconverts her childhood's friends to her own faith. Here again she would be a more sympathetic figure if she prevailed by an exhibition of Christian graces instead of by an intemperate denunciation of the most disreputable features of classical mythology. But an extremely effective *coup de théâtre* follows. Theophilus greets joyfully his daughters leading in Dorothea, preceded by a priest with an image of Jupiter, and bids them pay their vows to the god. To the father's horror they spit

at the image and throw it down, while Dorothea cries in
mockery :

> Alack, poor Jove!
> He is no swaggerer! how smug he stands!
> He'll take a kick or anything.

Incited by Harpax, Theophilus not only kills his daughters,
but in melodramatic fury bids Hell's dreadful porter receive
their damned souls.

Dorothea is reserved for more lingering torment, but the
blows of the traitors Spungius and Hircus fall harmlessly
on her, for she too has a supernatural minister in her page
with the revealing name of Angelo, and who, when at last
she falls beneath the headsman's axe, appears in his heavenly
shape to carry her soul to joys eternal, and with it the soul
of her ever faithful Antoninus.

Here with the fourth act the tragedy of the virgin-martyr
really ends. But a fifth act exhibits the greatest wonder of
all—the conversion of the arch-persecutor, Theophilus. In
mockery he had asked the dying maid to send him some of
the 'curious fruit' which she looked forward to enjoying in
'the blessed garden'. It is brought to him by Angelo, and in
spite of the threats of Harpax appearing 'in a fearful shape,
fire flashing out of the study', he eats it and feels his soul
illumined, and puts Harpax to flight by holding up a cross
of heavenly flowers. This again must have been a theatrically
effective scene, though the spectators in the Red Bull may
even so have scarcely been prepared for the complete
recantation of Theophilus that follows, and his death by
torture in the presence of Diocletian, with a vision before him
of Dorothea and her companion martyrs.

Massinger's preoccupation with religious problems, almost
unique among Stuart playwrights, takes an even more
unusual form in *The Renegado*, licensed according to Herbert's office-book, on 17 April 1624 for performance at the
Cockpit, then occupied by the Lady Elizabeth's company,

and afterwards acted at the same theatre, as the 1630 quarto states, by Queen Henrietta's men.

The renegade Venetian Grimaldi who gives the play its title is not its central character. After profaning the service in St. Mark's, where the Jesuit Francisco is celebrating the Mass, he has turned Mahomedan, and as a pirate has entered the service of Asamberg, the Viceroy of Tunis, where the scene is laid. He has kidnapped and sold to the Viceroy Paulina, sister of a Venetian gentleman Vitelli, who in the disguise of a shopkeeper has come to Tunis to find his sister and to save her from dishonour in the Viceroy's seraglio. But she is preserved by wearing a holy relic given to her by the Jesuit and it is Vitelli himself who in amazing fashion comes within an ace of a tragic fate. Dorusa, niece of the Sultan Amurath, is in Tunis to meet Mustapha, bashaw of Aleppo, to whom she has been betrothed, but on visiting Vitelli's shop she falls violently in love with him and bids him bring his bill to the palace, where she loads him with treasure and offers herself to him. It is a more extravagant and incredible version of the situation in *The Virgin-Martyr* where Artemia chooses a mate in Antoninus—but here the princess meets with no refusal for the time.

In *The Renegado*, however, Francisco controls the issues after the fashion of the central figure in several of Chapman's plays. By his direction as his father confessor Vitelli returns her gifts to Dorusa and rejects a second proffer of her embraces. But the scorned Mustapha, in another situation reminiscent of *The Virgin-Martyr*, has brought the Viceroy to witness this shameful scene from 'above', and he arrests the pair, to wait the Sultan's pleasure.

The edict comes that Dorusa must die unless she can atone for her guilt with a Christian by prevailing upon him to change his faith and marry her. But as in *The Virgin-Martyr* it is the Christian who triumphs and makes the convert, though again the argument would be more effective if less one-sided (IV iii):

> Dare you bring
> Your juggling prophet in comparison with
> That most inscrutable and infinite Essence
> That made this all and comprehends His work? . . .
> I will not foul my mouth to speak the sorceries
> Of your seducer.

To complete Dorusa's regeneration, in a scene alien to the predominantly secular temper of the Stuart theatre, she is baptized by Vitelli at the place where they are to suffer death together, and makes the joyful profession (V. iii):

> I am another woman; till this minute
> I never lived, nor durst think how to die.

But in *The Renegado* there are to be martyrs only in will, not in deed. A *dea ex machina* appears in Paulina, who has witnessed the scene and pretends that 'such ridiculous follies' have made her 'turn Turk' and ready to fall into the Viceroy's arms, if he will grant a brief reprieve to the 'base couple', that she may gloat over Dorusa's sufferings. It is merely a feint by which she may carry out a plan devised by Francisco through which all the Christians are delivered and carried to safety in a ship captained by the 'renegado' Grimaldi, who had been dismissed from the Viceroy's service, had repented of his crimes, and been reconciled by Francisco to the Church. Of the many surprising features in the play the most astonishing is that within twenty years after the Gunpowder Plot, and almost on the eve of Phineas Fletcher's fierce poetical denunciation of the Jesuits in his *Appolyonists*, a member of the Order should be represented as the good genius of the characters in Massinger's drama.

Another play with a religious stamp, though in less predominant and controversial form, is *The Maid of Honour*, published in quarto in 1632, and acted between 1625 and that date 'with good allowance' by the Queen's men at the Phoenix. The beautiful and wealthy Camiola, who gives the title to the play, is besieged by suitors, the fantastic fop Sylli, King Roberto of Sicily's 'minion', Fulgentio (in whom a likeness has been detected to the Duke of Buckingham), the faithful family retainer, Adorni (whose love is unspoken), and Bertoldo, the king's bastard brother, who is a Knight of Malta. Her heart is given to Bertoldo, who in her soul's judgement is 'a man absolute and circular'. But she refuses to marry him on the plea that she is not his equal, and that as a Knight of Malta he is bound to a single life. In her rejection of his passionate vows there is the austere touch which just takes the bloom from the virtue of Massinger's heroines.

Bertoldo turns from love to arms. Duke Ferdinand of Urbin, besieged by the Siennese in their capital, which he had attacked, has sent to his ally, King Roberto, for help. The cautious King of Sicily refuses to imperil the lives of his subjects, but on Bertoldo's appeal,

> May you live long, sir,
> The King of peace, so you deny not us
> The glory of the war,

he allows those who wish 'as adventurers and volunteers' to go to Ferdinand's aid. The censorship of the Stuart stage was so increasingly strict that it is risky to find political references, but it is tempting to see here an allusion to the hesitating foreign policy of James I, especially as Bertoldo holds up to Sicily the inspiring example of the northern island under Elizabeth (I. i):

> Look on England,
> The empress of the European isles;
> And unto whom alone ours yields precedence:
> When did she flourish so, as when she was
> The mistress of the ocean, her navies
> Putting a girdle round about the world;
> When the Iberian quaked, her worthies named?

On the battlefield Bertoldo meets another Knight of Malta, Gonzaga, general to the Duchess of Sienna, by whom he is wounded and taken prisoner, and who on recognizing him as one of their Order denounces him as false to his vows by drawing his sword against a lady, the Duchess of Sienna. Gonzaga tears the cross from his breast, condemns him to

rigorous imprisonment and puts the enormous ransom of
fifty thousand crowns upon his head.

Meanwhile Camiola has again forfeited something of sympathy by harshly rebuking Adorni, who has been wounded
in a duel with Fulgentio in defence of her honour. Yet when
she hears of Bertoldo's captivity and the amount of his
ransom, which the king, his brother, refuses to pay, she
chooses Adorni as her messenger to the Knight to tell him
that she will redeem him—and marry him. Then follows
another of those abrupt reversals of situation which are the
least convincing feature in Massinger's powerful constructive
technique. When Bertoldo learns that he owes his freedom
to Camiola, and to discharge his debt must marry her, he
cries in protest (IV. i):

> A payment! an increase of obligation,
> To marry her!—'twas my *nil ultra* ever;
> The end of my ambition:

and he swears by heaven and hell that he will never be false
to her. Yet when the Duchess of Sienna, in an uncontrollable
amorous ecstasy, characteristic of so many of Massinger's
royal ladies, offers him her love at first sight, after short
hesitation, he declares, 'I am wholly yours'.

While her lover is proving false Camiola's nobler nature
has been more and more clearly shining forth. When the king
visits her on Fulgentio's behalf she dares to confront him
in terms which it is surprising were ever allowed to pass by
the censor (IV. v):

> When you are unjust, the deity
> Which you may challenge as a king parts from you ...
>   Tyrants, not kings,
> By violence from humble vassals force
> The liberty of their souls.

The king's answer is in truly royal strain:

> While I wear a crown, justice shall use her sword
> To cut offenders off, though nearest to us.

He has soon to make good his words. While he is accompany-

ing Bertoldo and the Duchess to the church for their wedding
Camiola throws herself at his feet crying (V. ii):

> He's the man,
> The guilty man, whom I accuse; and you
> Stand bound in duty, as you are supreme,
> To be impartial. Since you are a judge,
> As a delinquent look on him, and not
> As on a brother.

The recital of her wrongs follows, and on Bertoldo's confession of guilt and remorse, she forgives him and invites him
to her 'marriage', which, to the general amazement, is her
reception as a 'maid of honour' by her father confessor into
the religious life as a nun. Her last entreaty to Bertoldo is
to resume his order as a Knight of Malta, whereupon Gonzaga
restores to him his white cross and greets him as once more
a brother-in-arms. The climax to the play again shows
Massinger as a master of the *coup de théâtre*, and though the
austere strain in Camiola fits her better to be a heavenly
than an earthly bride, it required unusual courage to present
such a solution before a Stuart audience.

Similar courage, as has been seen, was shown by Massinger
in his political allusions and in some instances he went so
far as to defeat his own ends. Thus Sir H. Herbert records
that Charles I, after reading his lost play *The King and the
Subject*, wrote: 'This is too insolent and to be changed',
against a passage in which a King of Spain declares:

> Monies! we'll raise supplies which way we please,
> And force you to subscribe to blanks, in which
> We'll mulct you, as we think fit. The Caesars
> In Rome were wise, acknowledging no laws
> But what their swords did ratify..

In the light of the slightly veiled allusions in *The Bondman*
to contemporary events, it is surprising that Herbert licensed
it on 3 December 1623 for performance by the Lady Elizabeth's men without exacting reformation of some passages,
and that Charles (then Prince of Wales) was present at
apparently its first production at Whitehall on the following

St. John's night. A quarto edition was entered on 12 March 1623/4 and was at once issued; it was followed by another in 1638, and by an adapted version in 1719.

The background of the play, a rising of slaves quelled by their masters not by the use of weapons but by a display of whips, could have been borrowed from various sources, Justin, Herodotus, Giles Fletcher's *Russ Commonwealth*, or Diodorus, who alone, like Massinger, makes Sicily the scene of the event. With it the dramatist interweaves another episode of Sicilian history, the defeat of the Carthaginians with the aid of the Corinthian general Timoleon, who was the subject of one of Plutarch's *Lives*. Further upon the historical features he grafts a romantic love plot of his own invention.

Massinger evidently chose Sicily as the *locale* of the play because the island-state suggested parallels with the England of his own day. Corinth comes to her help against Carthage as Holland was eager for an alliance with Britain against Spain. Timoleon in *The Bondman* may have embodied some of the characteristics of Prince Maurice of Orange. In any case, on his arrival in Syracuse in Act I. iii, he indicts the very evils deplored by the opponents of James I's and his Court's timid foreign policy and financial abuses:

> You have not, as good patriots should do, studied
> The public good, but your particular ends. . .
> The treasure of the city is ingross'd
> By a few private men: the public coffers
> Hollow with want . . . Yet in this plenty,
> And fat of peace, your young men ne'er were trained
> In martial discipline and your ships unrigged
> Rot in the harbour, no defence prepared,
> But thought unuseful, as if that the gods
> Indulgent to your sloth, had granted you
> A perpetuity of pride and pleasure.

He stirs up the islanders to march forth to victory under his leadership, but during their absence another Greek leader, the Theban Pisander, who has taken the disguise of a bondman to be near the praetor's daughter, Cleora, incites the slaves to mutiny. He bases his argument on the Stoic principle that all men were originally on the same level (II. iii. 31 ff.):

> Equal nature fashioned us
> All in one mould: the bear serves not the bear,
> Nor the wolf, the wolf; 'twas odds of strength in tyrants
> That pluck'd the first link from the golden chain
> With which that thing of things bound in the world.

He assures them they are as fit as their masters to be senators or burghers, and he urges them

> by strong hand to revenge
> Your stripes, your unregarded toil, the pride,
> The insolencie of such as tread upon
> Your patient sufferings.

The scene (III. iii) in which the victorious rebels turn the tables upon their domestic tyrants must have been highly entertaining on the stage. When Timoleon returns in triumph he is amazed to find himself defied by the slaves mounted on the city walls. Pisander acts as their apologist (IV. ii. 52 ff.):

> Your tyranny
> Drew us from our obedience. Happy those times
> When lords were styl'd fathers of families,
> And not imperious masters; when they numbered
> Their servants almost equal with their sons,
> Or one degree beneath them.

All this is changed, and man, more cruel to his fellow-man than to his beasts, 'appoints no end to the sufferings of his slave'. To the cry of death or victory the bondmen charge their foes, but at the sight of the whips they throw away their weapons and run off. When however Pisander, after a brief imprisonment, casts off his disguise, and confesses that he was their ringleader, partly as a warning to their masters against their cruel usage, and partly as a means of forcing 'a grant of fair Cleora', Timoleon pardons the offenders on promise of future good behaviour.

It is in its political and social aspects that the main attraction of the play lies. The love-story of Pisander, the

pseudo-'bondman', who has the titular part, is ingenious
and moving, but too involved. To become her father's slave,
and to raise a revolt among his fellows, seems a singularly
indirect way of winning Cleora, and the revelation that his
rival, Leosthenes, has been contracted to and seduced his
sister, Statilia, is too long deferred to be fully effective.
Leosthenes in the earlier acts has appeared as a valiant
soldier not unworthy of Cleora's love, though his mistrust
of her during his absence leads her to the fantastic resolve
of staying blind and dumb in her chamber till his return.
The chivalrous conduct of Pisander when during the rising
he has her in his power is an inadequate motive for the
sudden transfer of her love to one whom she believes to be a
slave. It is the most extreme instance of Massinger's fond-
ness for linking high-born ladies with men far below them
in station, and even Pisander's noble nature and the revelation of his true rank do not make the *dénouement* dramatically
convincing.

In another, later, play, *Believe as You List*, Carthage again
appears, in relation not to Sicily but Rome. Here with
Massinger it was not a matter of choice but of constraint.
The original setting of the action had by Herbert's order on
11 January, 1630/1 to be remodelled because 'it did contain
dangerous matter, as the deposing of Sebastian, King of
Portugal, by Philip II, and there being a peace sworn 'twixt
the Kings of England and Spain'. Massinger used as his
sources an English tract, *The Strangest Adventure* (1601), and
P. Cayet's *Chronologie Septenaire*, relating the career of a
claimant to the throne of Portugal who professed to be the
Don Sebastian, believed to have been killed in the battle of
Alcazar in 1578. To meet the censor's objections Massinger
had to throw back the action into the classical era and to
substitute Antiochus, King of Lower Asia, for Sebastian,
with Rome and Carthage taking the place of the modern
countries. As thus revised it was licensed by Herbert on
7 May 1631 for performance by the King's company.

Believe as You List, preserved only in MS. Egerton 2828 in the British Museum, was supposed to have been one of the plays destroyed by Warburton's cook, but it was rediscovered in 1844. The MS. as recast still gives some indications of the original form of the drama. The most striking is in I. ii. 186, where it is said of Antiochus, 'his nose, his German lip', corresponding with 'the lip of Austriche' in *The Strangest Adventure*. Afterwards 'German' was cancelled and 'very' written above it. In other cases the earlier names are discernible under those that have been written over them.

The transformation of the play cannot have been an easy task, for Antiochus, the exiled monarch cast in Stoic mould, is a very different figure from a refugee claimant to the crown of Portugal, and Spain even at the height of her power did not aspire to such world 'dominion as does Rome represented by Flaminius, her ambassador to Carthage. He is the dominant figure of the action, secure in the conviction that

> In the brass-leaved book of fate it was set down
> The earth should know no sovereign but Rome,

and that his mission on her behalf justifies his every act:

> By my birth
> I am bound to serve thee, Rome, and what I do
> Necessity of state compels me to.

Though he learns from three former servants of Antiochus that he is no impostor, he affirms him to be one and orders them to be poisoned so that their lips may henceforth be sealed. In an elaborately worked-up scene (II. ii) Flaminius so intimidates the Carthaginian senate that though Antiochus brings forward incontrovertible proofs of his identity, they refuse him any longer sanctuary, though they decline to deliver him up to Rome. When he takes refuge with the friendly King of Bithynia, Flaminius pursues him and overawes Prusias into compliance on the same totalitarian plea that he himself has used (III. iii):

Pru.   The gods can witness
How much I would do for you; and but that
Necessity of state——

Ant   Make not the gods
Guilty of your breach of faith! From them you find not
Treachery commended; and the state that seeks
Strength from disloyalty in the quicksands which
She trusteth in is swallowed.

In the lofty spirit of this utterance Antiochus, as the prisoner
of Flaminius, endures every indignity and alternatively every
temptation with the aim of making him confess that he is
an impostor. Even a Roman captain is moved to cry, 'I
never saw such magnanimity'. He does not quail even before
the crowning humiliation of becoming a galley-slave.

Up to this point, the close of Act IV, the sustained conflict
between the inflexible tyranny of Flaminius and the equally
inflexible long-suffering of Antiochus has been extraordinarily
impressive. But Act V is something of an anti-climax. The
scene shifts to Sicily, where Cornelia, wife of the proconsul
Marcellus, gets leave to have a view of Antiochus, who when
on his throne had shown favours to her and her husband.
Again the 'impostor' gives such convincing proofs of his
identity that Cornelia cries:

                    This is
The King Antiochus, as sure as I am
The daughter of my mother.

Flaminius angrily retorts, 'This is little less than treason',
and is taking leave abruptly when Marcellus orders him to
stay 'as a prisoner, not a guest'. He has been found guilty
of corruption and is to pay the penalty. This is another of
the sudden reversals of fortune characteristic of Massinger's
technique, and is so unlooked for that it fails to carry conviction. Nor does it satisfy justice, dramatic or otherwise,
that Antiochus, though released from the galleys, should be
confined in a penal settlement, where he knows that he shall
not have long to live.

As Flaminius till his fall impersonates the massive power

of republican Rome, so Domitian in *The Roman Actor* embodies in the similitude of divinity the still mightier sway of the imperial world-state. The play was licensed by Herbert on 11 October 1626 and was published in quarto in 1629, as acted by the King's company 'with good allowance' at the Blackfriars theatre. In it Massinger skilfully combined material taken from Suetonius and Dio Cassius with episodes of his own invention. It has been seen that the sudden passion of a woman of royal status for a man much inferior to her in position is something of a *cliché* in Massinger's dramatic technique. It was natural therefore for him to exploit on the stage the notorious infatuation of the empress Domitia for the actor, Paris. Formerly the wife of the senator, Ælius Lamia, she had by her beauty fascinated Domitian, who in the exercise of his arbirary power had forced her husband to divorce her and had made her his consort, to whom his own kinswomen had to render servile obeisance.

The subject had the further attraction for Massinger that it enabled him through the lips of Paris before his fatal entanglement with Domitia to give voice to an eloquent 'apology for actors'. Aretinus, a spy, had indicted him and the profession of which he was the head before the Senate as 'libellers against the State and Caesar'. In his spirited defence Paris claims that the stage furnishes a more powerful incentive to noble living than all the sects of the philosophers (I. iii):

> They with cold precepts (perhaps seldom read)
> Deliver what an honourable thing
> The active virtue is; but does that fire
> The blood, or swell the veins with emulation
> To be both good and great, equal to that
> Which is presented on our theatres?

From this he proceeds to the far more disputable argument,

> When do we bring a vice upon the stage,
> That does go off unpunished?

so that the spectators inclined thereto 'go home changed

men'. And if some of the audience are conscience-stricken by the presentation of various types of iniquity, 'we cannot help it'. It is unfortunate (though this does not seem to have struck Massinger) that the attempt of Paris soon afterwards to use the stage for a remedial purpose should fail completely. His performance of an interlude 'A Cure of Avarice', instead of working a reformation in an elderly miser, only confirms him in the resolve to die as he has lived and causes the infuriated emperor to order his instant execution.

In another, more unaccountable, fashion the performance falsifies the tribute of Paris to the moral influence of the actor's art, for during it Domitia conceives her infatuation for him. She is not content till she sees him in another 'play within the play', of her own fashioning, 'Iphis and Anaxarete', in which he acts the part of a despairing lover. Nothing is more masterly in *The Roman Actor* than Domitia's uncontrollable display during the progress of 'Iphis and Anaxarete' of sympathetic emotions of which the emperor fails to realize the significance, even when she starts from her seat crying, 'not for the world', when the rejected lover declares that he will hang himself. But Domitian hears the truth from his wife's jealous enemies and is convinced of it sorely against his will when he sees her and Paris locked in close embrace.

At this point in the play Massinger shows fine psychological instinct. The emperor has hitherto been a monster of cruelty, and as such he orders the spy, Aretinus, who has been foremost in denouncing Domitia, to be immediately strangled, as his 'reward'. But even after the revelation of their guilt he cannot bring himself to take summary vengeance on his adored wife and his favourite actor. For the latter he devises a unique and honorific way of death, though in historic fact he had him murdered in the street. He orders a third 'play within the play', the tragedy of 'The False Servant', who during his generous master's pretended absence becomes his wife's paramour. While Paris acts the

servant the emperor himself takes the part of the injured
lord and using his own sword instead of a property foil stabs
Paris, crying,

> as thou didst live
> Rome's bravest actor, 'twas my plot that thou
> Shouldst die in action, and, to crown it, die
> With an applause enduring to all times
> By our imperial hand.

Paris removed, he surrenders himself again to his passion
for Domitia, but she treats his forgiveness with contempt
(V. i):

> Thou being my beauty's captive,
> And not to be redeemed, my empire's larger
> Than thine, Domitian, which I'll exercise
> With rigour on thee for my Paris' death.

At last she overplays her hand. Domitian realizes, 'I am lost;
nor am I Caesar', and forces himself to write her name among
the proscribed who are to die to-morrow. While he sleeps
she steals the fatal table-book, and gathering a band of
those inscribed in the 'bloody scroll', with them she sends
the tyrant to his doom.

In one of the exceptional cases where a dramatist indicates
a preference for one of his own works, Massinger in his
dedication of the 1629 quarto of *The Roman Actor* declares,
'I ever held it the most perfect birth of my Minerva'. He
was justified in his partiality for a play which revealed with
striking fidelity the decadent Court atmosphere of imperial
Rome, which was a masterpiece of construction, and which
included among its protagonists the most attractive man of
the theatre presented on the Stuart stage.

The Duke of Milan, acted by the King's men at Blackfriars, and published in quarto in 1623, serves as a convenient
transition from Massinger's remarkable series of plays with
a classical setting. For the titular character in his relation to
those nearest to him presents a striking parallel to Domitian.
Duke Sforza, like the emperor, is enslaved in dotage upon
his beautiful wife, Marcella, and has aroused the anger of

his mother and his sister, Mariana, by making them sub-
servient to her. In the war between Francis I and the
Emperor Charles he has become the former's ally, and when
he hears of his defeat at Pavia, and the impending vengeance
of Charles upon Milan, his only thought is of Marcella's
safety. But his love takes a strangely paradoxical form.
Before setting out for a personal interview with Charles, he
binds by an oath his favourite Francisco, who has married
his sister, to murder Marcella in case he does not return. He
cannot live apart from her in this world or the next:

> There is no heaven without her, nor a hell
> Where she resides.

Swiftly on this surprise follows another. Francisco, the
duke's trusted deputy, makes a passionate avowal of love
to Marcella and seeks to convince her of her husband's
hatred by showing her the warrant for her execution as if
it were an unconditional order. It is never fulfilled, for
Charles is so affected by Sforza's declaration of his unflinching allegiance to his 'good angel' Francis, whether in good or
evil fortune, that he chivalrously buries all former passages
of hate, accepts the duke's friendship, and sets his crown
again upon his head. But before his return to Milan Francisco
has confessed to Marcella the real purport of Sforza's warrant
and she determines

> to make him know a constant wife
> Is not so slaved to her husband's doting humours,
> But that she may deserve to live a widow,
> Her fate appointing it.

Chilled by her 'discreet' reception of him the duke moans,

> By all the joys of love, she does salute me
> As if I were her grandfather,

and with another of the incredibly violent revulsions of
feeling typical of Massinger's characters, orders her from his
sight without reply, and proclaims that he will 'never think
of cursed Marcella more'. But, as with Domitian, his dotage
overpowers him and he seeks to appease her. And again

as with the Roman emperor the jealousy of his women kinsfolk plays a disastrous part. His mother and sister accuse
Marcella of infidelity with Francisco, who himself declares
that she is mad for him and pursues him hourly. In another
access of fury the duke stabs her, only to hear her dying
cry, 'Francisco was not tempted, but the tempter'. In
repentant anguish he is about to kill himself when the
doctors persuade him that his wife's wound is not mortal,
and there is a grimly effective stage-spectacle when, with his
mother and sister forced to kneel beside him, he invokes
what is really lifeless clay. Another doctor of wonderful
powers is announced. He is the disguised Francisco, with a
sister in male attire who, as in the parallel case in *The Bondman*, we learn too late had been seduced by the duke, and
for whose sake Francisco has sought revenge upon him.
This he now consummates by giving with a 'ceruse' Marcella's
body a delusive semblance of life, and by offering Sforza a
poisoned cup. With his dying breath the duke pronounces
his own apt epitaph, 'My whole life was a frenzy', and it is
because the plot is largely a series of phases of this 'frenzy'
that in spite of its ingenious working it fails to get across.

The *Great Duke of Florence*, licensed by Herbert on 5 July
1627, 'often presented' by the Queen's men at the Phoenix,
and published in 1636, is akin in its title and its Italian Court
background to *The Duke of Milan*, but is very different in
its plot and spirit. Here young love meets with cross-
currents but comes safely into port at last. Cozimo, the
widowed and childless Duke of Florence, has designed his
nephew Giovanni to be his heir and has appointed as his
tutor and trusted confidant, Charomonte. It is a refreshing
change from sophisticated Court surroundings to the wholesome atmosphere of the tutor's country-house, with its
training in liberal arts and accomplishments, and where an
idyllic affection springs up between the youthful prince and
Charomonte's lovely and innocent daughter, Lydia, most
charming of Massinger's heroines. The duke has also under

his care as guardian the young Duchess of Urbin, Florinda,
who, after the fashion of Massinger's royal ladies, has become
enamoured of Cozimo's favourite, Count Sanazzaro. He is
far from being, like others of his type, a mere minion, for he
has given proof of his skill and devotion in the wars. But
when entrusted by the duke with a secret errand to report
on Lydia's charms, he falls a victim to them, and fearing
that Cozimo intends himself to marry her, he damns her with
faint praise and persuades Giovanni, whose prospects of
inheritance are threatened by a second marriage, to do
likewise.

The duke, however, resolves to see Lydia in her home,
and the conspirators are forced to appeal to her for help.
In an improbable but entertainingly farcical scene she allows
herself to be impersonated by her rustic maid Petronella,
who however overdoes her part by dancing with the duke
when she is drunk, and rousing him to solve the riddle of
these 'strange chimaeras'. This is done when the real Lydia
is led in by her father, and the duke, enraged at the deception
practised on him, orders the arrest as traitors of his nephew
and Sanazzaro. But in accents of touching humility Lydia
pleads for her royal lover (IV. ii):

> For me, poor maid,
> I know the prince to be so far above me
> That my wishes cannot reach him. Yet I am
> So much his creature that, to fix him in
> Your wonted grace and favour, I'll abjure
> His sight for ever and betake myself
> To the religious life (where in my prayers
> I may remember him) and ne'er see man more
> But my ghostly father.

But Lydia is not to share the fate of Camiola in *The Maid
of Honour*. The duke makes the belated revelation that he
had sworn on his wife's monument never to marry again.
Sanazzaro's fears were therefore unfounded, and while
Giovanni, in spite of his lapse, deserves the hand of Lydia,
the favourite is rewarded beyond his desserts by winning

Florinda, whose love for him has even withstood the shock of his desertion of her for one of lower birth and fortune.

Though *The Guardian* is some years later in date than *The Great Duke of Florence* and has more of the features of a tragi-comedy, it recalls it in various ways. The Italian background shifts from the city, Naples, to the neighbouring countryside; an uncle, 'the guardian', is concerned with the fortunes of a nephew; the tangles of young love are finally smoothed out in unexpected fashion. *The Guardian* was licensed by Herbert on 31 October 1633, and was acted at Court on 12 January 1633/4 by the King's men, who also performed it 'with great applause' at the Phoenix. It was not published till 1655, when Moseley issued it with *The Bashful Lover* and *A Very Woman* in an octavo volume entitled *Three New Plays*.

Durazzo, the guardian, is one of Massinger's most vigorously drawn but provoking characters. He is good-hearted and witty, but completely lacking in moral sense. When he is reproached for feeding his nephew's loose riots he retorts:

> Riots? what riots?
> He wears rich clothes, I do so; keeps horses, games, and
> wenches;
> 'Tis not amiss, so it be done with decorum:
> In an heir 'tis ten times more excusable
> Than to be over-thrifty.

But nothing that we see of Caldoro, the nephew, corresponds with this description. He is wooing in honourable wise, Calista, who cares nothing for him and offers herself in marriage to Adorio, a young libertine, who scornfully refuses to wear such a heavy yoke on his neck. In his distress Caldoro threatens suicide, and as a cure for his 'lovesick ague' Durazzo, in a speech wherein Massinger shows himself an adept in the technicalities of hawking and falconry, prescribes a visit to his country villa, with rising before the sun and field-sports from morning to night.

Calista's father, Severino, has been banished because he

is supposed to have killed his brother-in-law, Monteclaro, in a quarrel, and has become the chief of a gang of banditti. His wife, Iōlante, acts as a rigorous duenna to her daughter, forbidding her to stir abroad or look upon a man, though from a window. Yet she herself falls in love at first sight with Laval, who has come in the train of a Milanese general, and sends her repulsive confidante, Calipso (as vicious as Durazzo, without his redeeming qualities), to invite him to her house. Meanwhile Calista through her maid, Mirtilla, has arranged to elope with Adorio, who is so affected by her letter to him that in a moment, quite unconvincingly, he is converted from his 'sensual, loose and base desires'.

Scarcely less incredible are the complications that follow. In the darkness Calista mistakes Caldoro for Adorio and flies with him while Adorio is tricked into going off with Mirtilla. At the same hour and place Laval, on his way to Iōlante, is intercepted by Severino, whom he mistakes for the watch, but who is taking his life in his hands to visit his 'chaste wife' He finds her not in mourning but in gala dress, with a rich banquet before her, evidently prepared for a guest. The punishment that in his fury he intends for her— wounds on her face and arms—falls by another confusion in the darkness on Calipso. And then, as the crowning impro- bability, Iōlante persuades Severino that she has been miraculously cured of her disfigurement and thus proved innocent, and together they fly to join his bandit crew.

When Calista discovers that it is Caldoro whom she has embraced, he pleads with her that they have been united by a decree of fate (IV. i):

> O, dear madam,
> We are all the balls of Time, tossed to and fro,
> From the plough unto the throne, and back again:
> Under the swing of destiny mankind suffers,
> And it appears by an unchanged decree
> You were appointed mine.

But such reasoning has far less effect on Calista than the sight of Adorio sleeping with his head on Mirtilla's lap. In a final scene it is revealed that this very sprightly maid is of gentle birth, daughter of a drowned noble captain and thus fit to pair off with Adorio as Calista with Caldoro. There is a still more astonishing disclosure when Laval confesses that he is no other than the Monteclaro left as dead on the field, but recovered by the Milanese general's care. Thus the king can revoke his edict against Severino, though the audience is left to digest as best it can the unpalatable consequence that Iölante had made an assignation with her own brother. *The Guardian*, in spite of its improbabilities, shows much ingenuity of technique, but it is remarkable that in so late a play Massinger should show a kinship to Fletcher in his most questionable aspects.

Further features of Massinger's dramatic art, in its treatment of romantic themes, are illustrated in *The Unnatural Combat*, *The Parliament of Love*, *The Picture*, *The Emperor of the East*, and *The Bashful Lover*. But speaking generally they are inferior in interest and execution to the plays of which an account has been given above. Nor do these exhaust his prolific output. Bishop Warburton, in the list of plays in his collection (Lansdowne MSS. 807), includes eleven (or ten, if two titles are alternatives) by Massinger, of which nothing further is known. It may be that not all these plays were possessed by Warburton and destroyed by his cook[1] and that there may be mistakes in his list, as when he attributed *The Parliament of Love* to William Rowley. But evidently the complete Massinger canon would contain additional pieces to those that have survived.

With this wide range and variety of Massinger's work for the stage it is a paradox that his reputation as a vital force in the theatre should have long been maintained by the relatively small section of his dramatic canon which dealt with the evil consequences in his own day of the unbridled pursuit of wealth and of advance in the social scale. His plays of that type have special associations with the actors

[1] See W. W. Greg, 'The Bakings of Betsy' in *The Library*, July 1911.

of them. *The City Madam* was licensed by Herbert on 25 May
1632 for performance by the King's company, but it was not
printed till 1658, when it was 'redeemed from the teeth of
Time' by Andrew Pennycuick, who had appeared in it and
who asserted that it 'may justly be ranked' among its
author's best. The claim is excessive, but the play, according
to Pennycuick, was when performed 'the object of love and
commendations', and as late as 1810 a version of it was
successfully produced at the Lyceum.

The title, *The City Madam*, is somewhat misleading, for
the central figure is not Lady Frugal, wife of the rich city
merchant, Sir John Frugal, but Sir John's brother, Luke.
Through his excesses he had incurred imprisonment from
which he was delivered by Sir John, in whose house he is
treated as 'an under-prentice or a footman', not as a relative.
His chief tormentors are Lady Frugal and her two daughters,
who employ him in menial services and treat him as a male
Cinderella. Their ambition is to rise out of their class and
they affect the luxuries and the airs and graces of Court
ladies. The girls by their extravagant demands repel their
respective suitors, Sir Maurice Lacy and the wealthy countryman, Mr. Plenty.

Sir John has his part in the ill-treatment of his brother,
yet is moved by his entreaties to deal leniently with three
of his debtors, though he enjoins secrecy:

> Do you hear, no talk of 't;
> Should this arrive at twelve on the Exchange,
> I shall be laughed at for my foolish pity,
> Which money-men hate deadly.

Lord Lacy, father of Sir Maurice, bids him extend this pity
to his brother, whom he keeps as a parasite scorned by his
proud wife. But the plot devised by the worthy lord to right
these wrongs is one of Massinger's major improbabilities.
He announces that Sir John has retired to an overseas
monastery and has by his will appointed Luke the sole heir
to his estate and bestowed on him the key of his counting-

house. By his last request Luke is to receive into his house three Indians sent from Virginia who are to be converted to Christianity. Massinger does not hesitate to assume that such astounding news will be instantly credited by all concerned. But he then proceeds to make a yet more unexpected demand—not now on his stage-characters, but on his audience. Hitherto he has worked up their sympathies with Luke as the ill-treated younger brother. In his sudden reversal of fortune he might be justified in turning the tables upon Lady Frugal and her daughters, in stripping them of their finery and lecturing them with a profusion of detail upon their aping of the fashions of Court ladies. But it was to be expected from his previous words and actions that he would show himself generous and merciful in the hour of his miraculous transformation. Instead he proves even more hard-hearted than Sir John to the debtors, exercising against them the extreme severity of the law. And to crown all when the 'Indians', who are Sir John and the two suitors in disguise, ask for two Christian virgins and a matron as an offering to their god, the devil, he tempts Lady Frugal and his nieces to go to Virginia by the assurance that they will there have the rank of queens. This is a *reductio ad absurdum* of Luke's hypocritical villainy and makes it difficult to take seriously the final scene, ingenious and theatrically effective as it is, in which the plot by which he has been tricked is revealed and he is turned out of doors to beggary. For the penitent ladies there is pardon and the promise of a happy future, though to-day there would not be the same obligation on them as in the Stuart period to confess,

> In their habits, manners, and their highest port,
> A distance 'twixt the City and the Court.

The high rank among Massinger's plays claimed by Pennycuick for *The City Madam* has been recognized by posterity as the due of another tragi-comedy dealing with kindred themes in more powerful fashion. The date of production of *A New Way to Pay Old Debts* is uncertain, but it was published in quarto in 1633 as often acted by the Queen's men at the Phoenix. Here Massinger does not, as with Luke Frugal, for a time lead his audience astray. The central figure, Sir Giles Overreach, is drawn from the first with bold and masterful strokes. Of citizen birth he has risen to fortune by his ruthless and unscrupulous arts.

> He frights men out of their estates,
> And breaks through all law-nets, made to curb ill men,
> As if they were cobwebs. No man dares reprove him;
> Such a spirit to dare and power to do were never
> Lodged so unluckily.

Among those whom he has thus jockeyed out of their lands and revenues and reduced to penury is his good-hearted but prodigal nephew, Wellborn. As his agents in his nefarious courses he employs the gluttonous Justice Greedy, 'arch-president of the boiled, the roast, the baked', whose excitement about culinary items makes him a farcical rather than a melodramatic figure, and a sycophantic limb of the law, Marrall. Overreach is no mere miserly usurer. He is the Stuart protagonist of a type of which there have been many later examples, the 'racketeer' on a grand scale.

> This Sir Giles feeds high, keeps many servants,
> Who must at his command do any outrage;
> Rich in his habit, vast in his expenses.

He is the masculine counterpart to Lady Frugal, with an overweening ambition to rise in the social scale. He has sought in vain to become a suitor to the widowed Lady Allworth, but his aspirations are above all for his only child, Margaret, who, he is resolved, shall

> write honourable,
> Right honourable, my right honourable daughter,
> If all I have, or e'er shall get, will do it.

He flatters himself that he has secured her marriage with an elderly colonel and man of rank, Lord Lovell, who, however, plays the part of a good genius by hoodwinking

Overreach and contriving that the girl shall be married to her young lover, Lady Allworth's stepson and his own page. Lady Allworth acts in a similarly delusive and beneficent fashion by showering such attentions on Wellborn that Overreach is convinced that she intends to marry him and therefore begins to pay court to the nephew, whom he had treated as an outcast. Lady Allworth's behaviour is the weakest feature in this realistic and closely compacted play. At one moment she is crying out to Wellborn, 'Thou son of infamy, forbear my house', and then, when he reminds her of how he had delivered her husband from want, she feasts him and loads him with favours.

As soon as Overreach thinks that his nephew is married he shows his hand by pressing for the immediate pledging of some of his new possessions as security for the loan he has made him of a thousand pounds. Wellborn makes the defiant answer (V. i):

> Either restore my land, or I'll recover
> A debt, that's truly due to me from you,
> In value ten times more than what you challenge.

To make Wellborn give himself 'the lie, the loud lie', Sir Giles produces from a box as evidence of the sale the bond with his hand and seal—only to find that the parchment has on it neither wax nor words. It is the most effective of Massinger's *coups-de-théâtre*. Only later does Marrall, who had drawn the deed, reveal that in revenge for Overreach's ill-treatment of him, he had so doctored the ink and wax that they had disappeared.

Sir Giles calms his mounting fury by the prospect of welcoming from her wedding 'my honourable, my right honourable daughter', but her entrance with Allworth as her husband so inflames his rage that he tries to kill her, and then rushes out to get friends and servants to second him. But he returns alone, delirious, flourishing his sword sheathed, and battling with visionary hangmen and furies, till he falls foaming at the mouth and biting the ground.

Y

Lovell points an appropriate moral, declares himself umpire between Wellborn and Overreach's heir, Margaret, concerning the disputed land, and proclaims that Lady Allworth, with whom he has exchanged vows, will henceforth be his anchor. Wellborn promises that, if Lovell will confer a company in his command upon him, he will redeem his reputation by doing service to his king and country. It was not, however, this edifying conclusion that kept *A New Way to Pay Old Debts* in the living theatrical repertory when so many contemporary plays equally popular in their own day had become museum pieces. It was the full-blooded character of Sir Giles Overreach and above all his final maniacal frenzy that made it a favourite role of star tragedians on both sides of the Atlantic till the close of the nineteenth century.[1]

NATHAN FIELD

It was probably either before or at an early period of his association with Fletcher that Massinger collaborated with Nathan Field in *The Fatal Dowry*. Field had already an established reputation as an actor and playwright, especially the former. He was the son, born in 1587, of a noted puritan preacher, and it is therefore surprising that he should have been impressed as one of the Children of the Chapel. He is mentioned first among the 'principal comedians' in Jonson's *Cynthia's Revels* (1600) and *Poetaster* (1601). He appeared later in *Bussy d'Ambois*, *The Silent Woman* and in his own *A Woman is a Weathercock* (1610), and *Amends for Ladies* (*c.* 1611). In 1611 he became the leader of the Lady Elizabeth's men, and Jonson testifies to his high professional reputation in *Bartholomew Fair* (1614), where he speaks of 'Your best actor, your Field'. He afterwards, probably about 1616, joined the King's men. His name appears in the livery list of the company in May 1619 and in the Shakespeare first

[1] See *The Amazing Career of Sir Giles Overreach*, by R. H. Ball (1939).

folio (1623). But he had died before 2 August 1620, when letters of administration were granted to his sister.

According to Field's preface 'to the reader' in *A Woman is a Weathercock*, he was driven to play-writing in self-defence. 'I have been vexed with vile plays myself a great while, hearing many; now I thought to be even with some and they should hear mine too.' His two unaided dramatic ventures are certainly not 'vile plays', but they cannot make much claim to originality. Their merits lie chiefly in sprightly dialogue and in a 'slickness' of plot management natural to Field from his experience as an actor. Thus in the opening scene of *A Woman is a Weathercock*, when Scudmore is in ecstasies over a letter from Bellafront, 'Yours through the world and to the end of time', there is a highly effective surprise when his friend Nevill tells him that he is on his way to attend the lady's wedding to Count Frederick. It is this eldest daughter of Sir John Worldly (typified by his name) who is the leading weathercock in the comedy. Yet even she, in answer to Scudmore's reproaches, declares that she was enforced by her severe father's threats, and when her wedding to the Count proves to have been performed by Nevill in clerical disguise, she is at once ready to go through a real ceremony with her lover. Frederick instantly consoles himself with Worldly's second daughter, Lucida, who has worn the willow for his sake. Here it is the man rather than the woman who is the weathercock. She has been courted by Sir Abraham Ninny, the most amusing figure in the play, a knight of the new creation, a simpleton, with a coarser strain, of the Sir Andrew Aguecheek class, who is paired off with his bibulous mother's waiting-woman, Mistress Wagtail. Kate, Worldly's third daughter, is so far a weathercock in that she gives up Captain Pouts for the wealthy young merchant, Strange. But the surly captain, a braggart and a slanderer, is so inferior to his rival, even as a swordsman in a duel, that Kate is well justified in her second choice. In fact, it might be urged that the play's real significance is to be found not so much in its proverbial title as in the claim made in the final couplet :

> Ne'er was so much (what cannot heavenly powers?)
> Done and undone and done in twelve short hours.

When, however, the comedy was published in 1612 Field thought it well to announce that it would be found when his next play was printed that he had made amends to the female sex. Thus, *Amends for Ladies* must have been written and probably acted before 1612 by the Lady Elizabeth's company, though the quarto did not appear till 1618. As in the earlier play there are three women weathercocks, so in the later there are three who are examples of constancy. They are Lady Honour, a maid, Lady Perfect, wife of Sir John Loveall, and Lady Bright, a widow. It is Lady Perfect who endures the severest test. Field may have been influenced by the tale of the 'Curioso Impertinente' in *Don Quixote* when he turned to account the highly unpleasant plot of a husband using his best friend as the tempter of his wife's virtue. The friend plays the husband false by revealing the trick, seeks in earnest to seduce the wife, and is foiled by her unwavering loyalty to her spouse, who is driven to seek her forgiveness.

Nor does the taste of to-day find much more agreeable the plot of which the widow, Lady Bright, is won by her young wooer, Bold, who to be near her adopts the disguise of a waiting-woman, and is thus admitted to an intimacy which, though just not criminal, leads to marriage as the only solution. A much more attractive instance of disguise is that of Lady Honour, who after repulsing her lover, Ingen, with a declaration that she will never marry, comes to him as an Irish footman, and, with a feigned message from a 'distressed, forsaken virgin', gives voice to her own love. Her brother, Lord Proudly, believing that Ingen has carried her off, demands her in a fury, and a duel follows in which Lady Honour, who seeks to prevent it, is stabbed by her brother and then forced to reveal herself. To calm Proudly's rage she pretends to accept as her husband a rich, old Count, with a racking cough, but by a further stratagem she becomes Ingen's bride. In Lady Honour Field reproduces with a less delicate touch an exquisite Beaumont and Fletcher model, while in Lord Feesimple, who shrinks from the sight of cold steel, the set of tavern 'roarers' and Moll Cutpurse, there are echoes of Jonsonian humours and London types.

Our first knowledge of Field's association with Massinger is about 1613, when together with Robert Daborne they were engaged upon a play for Henslowe and applied to him for a loan. Two similar letters from Daborne and Field and one from Field alone followed. Nothing more is known about these joint activities, but it was probably about 1619 that Massinger and Field collaborated in *The Fatal Dowry*, acted at the Blackfriars by the King's men, and published in 1632. Whatever were exactly their respective shares in this remarkable play, Massinger, with his more sombre and moralizing gifts, was the predominant partner.

The play starts with an unusual variation on what is one of his constant themes, the corrupting influence of financial greed. Grasping creditors have thrown an old and brave Burgundian Marshal into prison and on his death there they claim by the State law a right over his body and refuse him Christian burial. In vain an advocate and a gallant officer, Romont, plead before the 'parliament' or judicial court of Dijon for a relaxation of the law. Only when the marshal's son, Charalois, offers to take his place in the prison do the creditors consent to the release of the dead hero's body, which is carried to the grave in a solemn funeral procession, with a military escort, which must have been an impressive stage spectacle. Over the coffin Charalois cries to those near (II. i):

> What! weep ye, soldiers? blanch not.—Romont weeps!
> The gaolers and the creditors do weep;
> Even they that make us weep, do weep themselves.
> Be this thy body's balm!

The son's sacrifice for his father has another more unexpected consequence than mourners' tears. The retiring chief justice of the parliament Rochfort is so moved by it that he frees him by paying the marshal's debts and offers him in marriage his only child, Beaumelle, with all his fortunes as her dowry. Their wooing is the shortest on the Stuart, or probably any, stage:

Char. Fair Beaumelle, can you love me?
Beau.   Yes, my lord.

And at Rochfort's bidding the wedding follows at once. In such impulsive action lies the seed of catastrophe. Even on her way to the ceremony Beaumelle is hailed as 'mistress' by young Novall, son of the new chief justice, who has courted her, and to whom she now whispers:

> O, servant! Virtue strengthen me:
> Thy presence blows round my affection's vane:—
> You will undo me, if you speak again.

And it is not long till Romont finds the pair kissing and embracing. In the unduly protracted Act III he urges Rochfort and afterwards Charalois to be on their guard, but his warnings are shattered upon their trust in Beaumelle's virtue, and it is not till her husband catches her *flagrante delicto* that his faith is overthrown, and he kills her seducer.

Thereupon follows one of the most original and moving trial-scenes in Elizabethan drama. Before Rochfort in the judgment-seat, blindfolded to ensure impartiality, and with Novall's body borne into the room, Charalois charges Beaumelle with adultery, and she confesses that she is 'most miserably guilty'. Her father declares that she must die, and when Charalois asks whether her one fault may not be forgotten in her fair life hereafter, he replies (IV. iv):

> Never, sir
> The wrong that's done to the chaste married bed
> Repentant tears can never expiate;
> And be assured—to pardon such a sin
> Is an offence as great as to commit it.

Char. I may not then forgive her?

Roch.   Nor she hope it.
Nor can she wish to live. . .
Char.   Let her die, then! [*He stabs her*
Better prepared, I am sure, I could not take her,
Nor she accuse her father as a judge
Partial against her.
Beau.   I approve his sentence
And kiss the executioner.

But the moment that she has suffered by Rochfort's
'doom' he is startlingly transformed. These sudden conversions are frequent with Massinger, but here there is
psychological justification for Rochfort's plea:

> I pronounced it
> As a judge only and a friend to justice;
> And zealous in defence of your wronged honour
> Broke all the ties of nature, and cast off
> The love and soft affection of a father. . .
> I looked on you as a wronged husband but
> You closed your eyes against me as a father.

But while Rochfort laments for his daughter, Novall's father
bursts in with officers, shrieking, 'Lay hold on him! My son,
my son!'

After such a powerfully moving scene the trial of Charalois,
with its detailed pleadings, is something of an anti-climax.
And when the court acquits him, though he has gone beyond
the letter of the law in avenging his injuries, we have not
been adequately prepared for his death at the hand of so
secondary a figure as Pontalier, young Novall's friend. He
in turn is killed by Romont in his last act of loyalty to
Charalois, who with his final breath confesses:

> What's fallen upon me
> Is by Heaven's will, because I made myself
> A judge in my own cause without their warrant.

This is emphasized by one of the judges:

> We are taught
> By this sad precedent how just soever
> Our reasons are to remedy our wrongs,
> We are yet to leave them to their will and power
> That, to that purpose, have authority.

Thus the final 'moral' of the play stresses the tragic consequences of private vengeance which has precipitated the catastrophe far more than 'the fatal dowry', brought by Beaumelle which, though it gives the title, has had little influence on the action. The play after exhausting its own contemporary popularity had a further vicarious lease of life as the origin of Rowe's *The Fair Penitent* (1703), which achieved great success, and which in the gay Lothario contributed the permanent personification of the stage *roué*.

XIV

JOHN FORD

TRAGEDIES OF MELANCHOLY

I T was approximately during the last decade of Massinger's career that John Ford produced the some half-dozen plays that bear his name alone. There could scarcely be a greater contrast between two contemporary dramatists. Massinger was highly prolific with a remarkably varied range of theatrical achievement; he was a rhetorician and a robust moralist. Ford, if we may judge by his surviving pieces, did not aim at an extensive output, and worked for the most part a particular dramatic vein; he had a finely sensitive poetic gift and his chosen themes took little heed of conventional ethical standards.

John Ford was baptized on 17 April 1586 at Ilsington in Devon. He was a member of a well-to-do landed family, and may have been the John Ford who matriculated at Exeter College, Oxford, in 1601. If so, his academic career seems to have been short, for he was entered at the Middle Temple on 16 November 1602. It has recently been shown that his career at the Inn was chequered, for he was expelled for debt but readmitted on 10 June 1608 on payment of a forty shillings fine. As late as May 1617 he seems to have been involved in a protest against the wearing of caps in the Inn Hall.

He began as an author in 1606, with *Fame's Memorial*, an elegiac poem on Charles Blount, Earl of Devonshire. In the same year, in celebration of the visit of King Christian of Denmark, he produced a pamphlet, in verse and prose, *Honour Triumphant, or the Peers' Challenge*, with an appended poem, *The Monarchs' Meeting*. In May 1609, on the death of his father, he received the small bequest of ten pounds. He fared better in September 1616, on the death of his

brother Henry, who left him on certain conditions an
annuity of twenty pounds for the term of his life. Another
poetic elegy on *Sir Thomas Overbury's Life and Untimely
Death* is known only from an entry in the Stationers' Register
25 November 1615. His last non-dramatic work was a
moralizing tract, *A Line of Life*, published in 1620.

Henceforward till his death, of which no record has yet
been found, he was occupied with writing for the stage. His
earlier plays were in collaboration with older dramatists.
With Dekker and Rowley he was associated in *The Witch of
Edmonton* (1621)[1]; with Dekker in *The Sun's Darling*, and
two lost plays, *The Fairy Knight* and *The Bristow Merchant*
(known from Herbert's note-book), all licensed in 1624. In
the same year he was allied with Dekker, Rowley, and
Webster in the production of *Keep the Widow Waking* and
the scandal that resulted from its performance.[2] Another
lost play, *Beauty in a Trance*, is known from a recently discovered bill to have been performed at Court by the King's
men on 28 November 1630.[3]

Ford had too individual a temperament to remain merely
a collaborator, and after a time he found his distinctive field
in the stage-presentation of melancholy. It was a theme that
in different ways had been made familiar to theatre-goers in
Shakespeare's Jacques, Marston's Malevole, and Jonson's
Malicente and Crites. But the publication in 1621 of
Richard Burton's *Anatomy of Melancholy* had given a semi-
scientific basis to the study of this type of temperament. To
Ford it made a peculiar appeal, and in his earliest surviving
play, *The Lover's Melancholy*, he acknowledges his debt. The
piece was licensed by Herbert in 1628, acted by the King's
men at the Blackfriars and the Globe, and published in 1629.
In its plot there is little that is not common form in the
romantic drama of the period. Palador, prince of Cyprus,
had been betrothed to Eroclea, elder daughter of the old

---

[1] See above, p. 162. [2] See above, p. 164.
[3] Sec G. E. Bentley, *Jacobean and Caroline Stage*, I. 28.

statesman, Meleander, but had to fly from an attempted rape by agents of the prince's father, who had since died. She had lived in Greece in the disguise of a youth named Parthenophil. There she had been found by Menaphon, nephew of Meleander, lover of Thamasta, the prince's cousin, who brought her back with him to Cyprus, where Thamasta, taking her for a handsome young man, declares her sudden passion. Admetus, brother of Thamasta and bosom friend of Menaphon, pines for the love of Cleophila, younger daughter of Meleander, who is solely devoted to the cure of her father, crazed by the loss of Eroclea and confinement in his castle.

In the end after the traditional fashion all these love-tangles are resolved. But there are two elements in the play distinctive of its author. The first is the frequent lyrical beauty of the verse. Though the theme is borrowed from Strada's *Prolusiones Academicae*, how exquisitely does Ford retell the tale of 'music's first martyr', the nightingale, that failing to rival the sweetness of Parthenophil's melody upon the lute, dropped upon the instrument and broke her heart, while the conqueror wept upon her hearse 'a funeral elegy of tears'. How haunting is the cadence of Eroclea's lament in Act IV. iii:

> Minutes are numbered by the fall of sands,
> As by an hourglass; the span of time
> Doth waste us to our graves, and we look on it:
> An age of pleasures, revelled out, comes home
> At last, and ends in sorrow; but the life,
> Weary of riot, numbers every sand,
> Wailing in sighs, until the last drop down,
> So to conclude calamity in rest.

The second distinctive feature is not merely the dramatic presentation of melancholy in Prince Palador but its analysis by his physician, Corax (III. i):

> Melancholy
> Is not, as you conceive, indisposition
> Of body, but the mind's disease. So ecstasy,

> Fantastic dotage, madness, frenzy, rapture
> Of mere imagination, differ partly
> From melancholy; which is briefly this,
> A mere commotion of the mind o'ercharged
> With fear and sorrow; first begot i' the brain,
> The seat of reason, and from thence derived
> As suddenly into the heart, the seat
> Of our affection.

To illustrate the sundry kinds of this mental commotion Corax produces before the prince a masque in which six varieties of melancholy as described by Burton are impersonated; but one—of which Palador is the victim—

> Is only left untouched: 'twas not in art
> To personate the shadow of that fancy;
> 'Tis named love-melancholy. . .
> Love is the tyrant of the heart; it darkens
> Reason, confounds discretion; deaf to counsel,
> It runs a headlong course to desperate madness.

Though Palador's own melancholy finds its cure, it is with love in its sombre, tumultuous manifestations that Ford's art is predominantly concerned. But in the later scenes of this play—and it is a fault in construction—the interest is largely shifted from the prince's love-melancholy to the distraction of Meleander, caused by his wrongs. In the picture of the frenzied old statesman, tended by his daughter Cleophila, and waking through his physician's art to sanity anew, it is difficult not to think that Ford was following in the steps of Shakespeare, though Meleander's restoration and reunion are lasting and not merely for the moment, as with Lear.

Of the three plays by Ford published in 1633, *Love's Sacrifice*, acted at the Phoenix by Queen Henrietta's men and 'received generally well', is the most closely related to *The Lover's Melancholy*, and has part of its inspiration from Burton's psychological analysis. Caraffa, Duke of Pavia, is swayed by two overmastering affections, for his young bride, Bianca, of modest birth and fortune, whose beauty has enchanted him; and his favourite, Fernando, 'thou half myself', as he calls him. He confidently proclaims:

> I am a monarch of felicity,
> Proud in a pair of jewels, rich and beautiful,
> A perfect friend, a wife beyond compare: . .
> > Look, Bianca,
> On this good man; in all respects to him
> Be as to me; only the name of husband,
> And reverent observance of our bed,
> Shall differ us in person, else in soul,
> We are all one.

It sounds like to a challenge to fortune, and there are two close to him, his cynical widowed sister, Fiormonda, and his treacherous secretary, D'Avolos, evidently modelled on Iago, who see to it that the challenge shall be taken up.

Fernando and Bianca play into their hands by a violent yet strangely equivocal form of passion. The Duchess, after repeated rejection of the favourite's avowals of love, visits him in his chamber at night, and declares that in her heart he is the only king, but that if she gives up her body to his embraces, she will kill herself before dawn. It is for him to choose. Ford is apparently influenced by the prevalent cult of Platonic love in the Court of Queen Henrietta Maria when he makes Fernando answer (II. iv):

> > Heaven forbid that I
> Should by a wanton appetite profane
> This sacred temple . . . I'll master passion, and triumph
> In being conquered.

The revelation of their secret passion, on which he puts the worst construction, by D'Avolos to the duke stirs him to a jealous distraction and melancholy which have a Burtonian stamp. And it is an even thinner line that keeps the pair from actual guilt when Bianca cries (V. i):

> Why should'st thou not be mine? Why should the laws,
> The iron laws of ceremony, bar
> Mutual embraces? What's a vow? a vow?
> Can there be sin in unity?

When the duke enters with his sword drawn and threatens
her with death her one aim is to shield Fernando:

> I must confess I missed no means, no time,
> To win him to my bosom; but so much,
> So holily, with such religion,
> He kept the laws of friendship, that my suit
> Was held but, in comparison, a jest.

Fiormonda's taunts steel his wavering arm to strike the
duchess dead and to challenge her lover to mortal combat.
But Fernando offers his bosom to the sword (V. ii):

> If the chaste Bianca
> Be murdered, murder me. . .
> Unfortunate Caraffa, thou hast butchered
> An innocent, a wife as free from lust
> As any terms of art can deify.

In his zeal to 'whitewash' his paramour he rises to the
highest poetic level in the play:

> O, Duke!
> Could'st thou rear up another world like this,
> Another like to that, and more, and more,
> Herein thou art most wretched; all the wealth
> Of all those worlds could not redeem the loss
> Of such a spotless wife.

The crowning paradox is that the duke believes him, does
penance at his wife's tomb, and even when Fernando rises
from out the tomb in his winding-sheet and takes poison,
he cries to Fiormonda:

> Sister, when I have finished my last days,
> Lodge me, my wife and this unequalled friend
> All in the monument.

Whereupon he stabs himself, with an appeal to heaven to
wipe out the writing of his sin, and with Bianca's name upon
his lips. One wonders how far the sympathies of the Phoenix
audience responded to this remarkable instance of confusing
moral values.

In any case, Ford did not hesitate to handle with 'general
commendation' an even more perilous problem in another

play, acted like *Love's Sacrifice* at the Phoenix and also published in 1633. The incestuous love between a brother and sister, which had been the apparent theme of Beaumont and Fletcher's *A King and No King*, is in fact that of Ford's *'Tis Pity She's a Whore*. In the opening scene Giovanni gives voice to his defiance of the convention that stands between him and Annabella:

> Shall a peevish sound,
> A customary form, from man to man,
> Of brother and of sister, be a bar
> 'Twixt my perpetual happiness and me?

Though at the bidding of his confessor, a friar, he struggles against his infatuation by prayer and fasting, it is in vain, and he justifies himself by the plea that it is not his lust but his fate that leads him on. So when he discloses his passion to his sister, he proclaims:

> 'Tis my destiny
> That you must either love or I must die.

And he urges that their consanguinity is an argument for, not against, their union:

> Wise Nature first in your creation meant
> To make you mine; else't had been sin and foul
> To share one beauty to a double soul.
> Nearness in birth and blood doth but persuade
> A nearer nearness in affection.

It is subtly suggested that the pair are driven into each other's arms not by sensual desire but by an irresistible dynamic force. It is an elemental background to the conventional wooing of Annabella by a trio of suitors, Soranzo, a noble, Grimaldi, a soldier, and Bergetto, a booby. Her father favours Soranzo, and urged by the friar, for her honour's safety she marries him. The wedding-feast is darkened by an ominous fatality. Soranzo had seduced Hippolita, wife of Richardetto, and in revenge she seeks in a masque to offer him a poisoned cup, but through treachery drinks it herself. Thus Soranzo is spared to discover that his bride is already with child by her brother, and he plans revenge at a feast in celebration of his birthday. Annabella warns her brother of what is afoot, and in the moving dialogue between them Giovanni's sceptical temper strikes its deepest note (V. v):

Ann.	This banquet is an harbinger of death
	To you and me; resolve yourself it is,
	And be prepared to welcome it.
Gio.	Well, then;
	The schoolmen teach that all this globe of earth
	Shall be consumed to ashes in a minute.
Ann.	So I have read too.
Gio.	But 'twere somewhat strange
	To see the waters burn: could I believe
	This might be true, I could believe as well
	There might be hell or heaven.
Ann.	That's most certain.
Gio.	A dream, a dream! else in this other world
	We should know one another
Ann.	So we shall.
Gio.	Have you heard so?
Ann.	For certain.
	But d'ye think
	That I shall see you there, you look on me?
	May we kiss one another, prate or laugh,
	Or do as we do here?

However this may be, Annabella is to him white in her soul, and to save her fame, and to forestall her husband's cruelty, he kills her upon a kiss with his own hand. From the lovely pathos of their parting it is somewhat disconcerting to turn to the last scene, where Giovanni rushes in among the guests with Annabella's heart upon his dagger, fights with and kills Soranzo, and himself is slain by the husband's retainer. There are not wanting clerical and other voices to point the moral of these fatal consequences of sin. But Giovanni, unrepentant to the last, cries with his dying breath:

> Where'er I go, let me enjoy the grace
> Freely to view my Annabella's face.

And we feel that his love for her, though outside 'the laws of conscience and of civil use', is a worthier thing in the dramatist's eyes than that of the profligate Soranzo.

The Broken Heart, another of the plays published in 1633, was acted by the King's men at the Blackfriars. The date of performance is unknown, but the versification which is less lyrical in quality, and the diction which is compressed and occasionally less lucid than that of the plays noticed above, suggest that it was of later composition. It is one of the few Stuart dramas of which the scene is laid in ancient Greece, and though no source has been traced, it is difficult to accept the assertion in the prologue that 'what may here be thought fiction was known as a truth'.

It may also be a sign of Ford's maturer art that he here almost discarded the comic episodes wherein he was at his weakest and concentrated his powers on the elaboration of tragic issues. He ran some risk, however, of defeating his own purpose, for in the earlier acts he engages so deeply our sympathies for the disappointed lover, Orgilus, that we think that his is 'the broken heart'—only to find later that the title is intended for the princess Calantha. Orgilus has been contracted to Penthea, but her brother, the victorious Spartan general and royal favourite, Ithocles, has forced her into marriage with the rich nobleman, Bassanes, who is insanely jealous of his young bride and keeps her mewed up in his house. Orgilus, feigning a journey from Sparta to Athens, makes his way in disguise into her presence and claims her for his own. Once more the doctrine of Plantonic love asserts its influence (II. iii):

> *Org.* I would possess my wife; the equity
> Of very reason bids me.
> *Pen.* Is that all?
> *Org.* Why 't is the all of me, myself.

Mastering her own feeling she bids him be happy in a next choice and declares that they must part.

z

Org.   Part! yet advise thee better:
      Penthea is the wife to Orgilus,
      And ever shall be.

Pen.   Never shall nor will.

Meanwhile, Ithocles, with a sudden conversion more characteristic of Massinger's dramatic figures than Ford's, has repented of his action. He now knows what true love means, for he has become enamoured of the princess Calantha, who is about to be contracted to Nearchus, prince of Argos. He tells his secret to Penthea ; she reveals it to Calantha, who shows her feeling by casting before Ithocles a ring for which Nearchus has begged.

But Penthea still holds the centre of the stage. Under the stress of her wrongs, though Bassanes also is suddenly repentant, her wits become crazed, and in a scene (IV. ii) reminiscent in some points of Ophelia's madness, she wakes the pity of the bystanders who are soon to hear that she has starved herself to death. Yet even this tragic fate does not prepare us for the sequel. Orgilus, in revenge, to prevent the union of Ithocles and Calantha, traps the general in a chair fitted with an engine that pins him down, and then stabs him to the heart. Such treachery alienates at a blow the sympathy which by his sufferings Orgilus has hitherto earned.

In contrast with these grim fatalities the course of love has been running smooth between Prophilus, the dearest friend of Ithocles, and Euphranea, sister of Orgilus. During the revels that celebrate their nuptials word is brought successively to Calantha that the king, her father, is dead, Penthea starved, and Ithocles murdered. At last the princess, hitherto a somewhat shadowy figure, captures the imagination when with supreme self-control, as one tragic report follows the other, she bids the dance in which she partners the bridegroom proceed, and after the third and direst tidings, she cries indignantly (V. ii):

    How dull this music sounds! Strike up more sprightly!
    Our footings are not active like our heart
    Which treads the nimbler measure.

So, when the dance is done, with lofty composure she announces, 'we are queen', and on the confession of Orgilus that it was he who killed Ithocles, sentences him to whatever form of death he may choose. And thus in stark contrast to the nuptial revels there follows the spectacle of a condemned man letting out his own life by bleeding on the stage. Then in the solemnly impressive last scene the enigma of the play's title is resolved. Before an altar the body of Ithocles crowned is borne on a hearse and is met by Calantha, also crowned, with her attendant Court. After announcing future arrangements of state, she places a wedding ring on the finger of Ithocles:

> Thus I new-marry him whose wife I am;
> Death shall not separate us. O, my lords,
> I but deceived your eyes with antic gesture,
> When one news straight came huddling on another
> Of death! and death! and death! still I danced forward,
> But it struck home, and here, and in an instant.

With a kiss on the lifeless lips she dies to the strains of a dirge that she has fitted for her end:

> Love only reigns in death, though art
> Can find no comfort for a broken heart.

It is the heart of Calantha that is broken, and Ford's portrayal of her in the last act of the play ranks among his finest achievements. But her fate would touch us more had more been made of her living love for Ithocles and had not the sorrows of Orgilus and Penthea so long been in the foreground of the stage.

In 1634, the year after the publication of the above trio of plays, appeared *Perkin Warbeck*, acted at the Phoenix. Its date is uncertain, but in its versification and diction it is allied to *The Broken Heart*. This is the more striking because Ford has here turned from romantic love-stories to

> A history of noble mention, known,
> Famous and true; most noble, 'cause our own;
> Nor forged from Italy, from France, from Spain,
> But chronicled at home.

It is curious that the dramatist should have thus brought on the stage an example of 'studies', which, according to the prologue, 'have been of late so out of fashion', but he may have been partly attracted by the account in his source, Bacon's *Life of Henry VII*, of Lady Katherine Gordon's devotion to her husband, Perkin, 'whom in all fortunes she entirely loved'. In any case, Ford showed his mastery over the chronicle-history, and his *Perkin Warbeck*, together with Marlowe's *Edward II* and the anonymous *Edward III*, worthily fits in with Shakespeare's English history plays to form an almost unbroken sequence of the finest dramatic interpretation of this country's annals during more than two centuries.

Ford shows his skill in keeping the events with which he deals, ranging from Westminster to Edinburgh and thence to Cornwall, in clear perspective, and making them subordinate to his portraiture of the chief characters. The two kings, Henry VII of England and James IV of Scotland, are vividly contrasted. Henry is the shrewd, diplomatic, parsimonious statesman. James is the chivalrous but shortsighted ruler, deluded by Warbeck's personal charm, and ready to undertake single combat on his behalf till he is undeceived by the complete failure of the northern English to rally to his cause. Among the Scottish nobles two stand out conspicuously, Katherine Gordon's blunt-spoken, warmhearted father, Huntley, and her lover, Dalyell, faithful to her even when she has become Warbeck's wife and is in exile from their country.

The least convincing feature in the play is that Katherine, after listening to such a wooer as Dalyell, should, on the king's persuasion, so swiftly give her heart to Warbeck. But if this be overlooked, there is no nobler and more appealing figure in Stuart drama than this 'great miracle of constancy', who at the lowest ebb of Perkin's fortunes can declare:

> Thou art my husband, no divorce in heaven
> Has been sued out between us; 'tis injustice
> For any earthly power to divide us:

and draw from him the response:

> Even when I fell, I stood enthroned a monarch
> Of one chaste wife's troth pure and uncorrupted.

In the closing scenes Katherine's devotion invests Warbeck with a reflected halo which cannot be dimmed, however fictitious his claims may otherwise be. And without violating historic truth by representing these claims as genuine, Ford tactfully succeeds in keeping his imposture in the background and in bringing to the front the qualities which made him a formidable pretender to the English crown. Thus when Warbeck has for the first time appealed to James for recognition of him as Edward's heir, the Scottish sovereign replies:

> He must be more than subject who can utter
> The language of a king, and such is thine.

At all times his speech and bearing have a princely dignity, as when he declares to his 'royal cousin' that when he sits on his own throne,

> Then James and Richard, being in effect
> One person, shall unite and rule one people,
> Divisible in titles only.

Even when James announces that he must seek a harbour elsewhere than with him, Warbeck's gratitude does not fail (IV. iii):

> Two empires firmly
> You're lord of—Scotland and Duke Richard's heart:
> My claim to mine inheritance shall sooner
> Fail than my life to serve you, best of kings.

So when all is lost he disdains to listen to his predecessor in counterfeit, Lambert Simnel, who urges him to confess and hope for pardon. He is resolved to suffer a ' martyrdom of majesty', and as he goes to execution at the head of his followers, the idea of sovereignty is with him to the last:

> Illustrious mention
> Shall blaze our names and style us kings o'er Death.

It is curious, if the dates of publication are a guide, that after this fine 'study' in English history Ford should have turned to unrewarding themes with an imaginary Italian background. *The Fancies, Chaste and Noble* and *The Lady's Trial*, both acted at the Phoenix, appeared in quarto respectively in 1638 and 1639. Both are written in Ford's later compressed style, which does not make for easy reading and which must have strained the attention of audiences who had come to listen to a comedy. 'The Fancies' are the nieces of the Marquis of Sienna who, for no obvious reason, kept them secretly as his close companions, and thus gave rise to unjustified scandal which is exposed only at the very close of the play. The scandal also involves another 'chaste and noble' lady, Castanda, who becomes an associate of the Fancies, and is reviled by her brother and her former wooer till by another last minute revelation she turns out to be the bride of the nephew of the marquis. Loosely connected with the main plot are the fortunes of the unhappy Flavia, whose first marriage to a merchant has been dissolved by a Papal dispensation that she may become the wife of a nobleman and who is torn between two loyalties. In the comic episodes provided chiefly by attendants on the marquis Ford touches the nadir of his attempts at dramatic humour.

In *The Lady's Trial* feminine virtue is again under unfounded suspicion, though here in the more traditional form of aspersions cast on a wife during her husband's absence. While Auria, a Genoese noble, is fighting on behalf of the State, his too officious friend Aurelio finds her in what he takes to be a compromising situation with the young Lord Adurni. The clearing up of the lady's reputation is tediously drawn out and is not sufficiently relieved by the humours of the under-plot in which the chief figures are the lisping Amoretta, the whistling coxcomb Fulgoso and the braggart Spaniard Guzman, of the same kin as Shakespeare's Don Armado. In the prologue to the play which he spoke and may have written the actor, Theophilus Bird, declares on behalf of the 'fearless author':

If he so have not hit all right,
For wit, words, mirth and matter as he might,
He wishes yet he had for your delight.

It was not in *A Lady's Trial*, but in the plays where he had plumbed the tragic depths of broken hearts that Ford had 'hit all right' and given the delight which springs from seeing human sufferings transmuted into high artistic form.

XV

JAMES SHIRLEY—RICHARD BROME

COMEDIES OF MANNERS—ROMANTIC DRAMAS—
PLAYS OF TOWN AND COUNTRY

I N the comic sphere where Ford's genius was at its weakest two contemporaries of less lofty, but in one case of more versatile, dramatic gifts were to win the last laurels before the dark shadows of the Civil War fell over the theatre. James Shirley was born on 18 September 1596 in the parish of St. Mary Woolchurch, London. He was educated at Merchant Taylors' School, at St. John's College, Oxford, where he spent a short time when Laud was President, and at Catherine Hall, Cambridge, where he graduated and began to publish verse in 1618. Soon afterwards he took orders in the Church of England and was appointed to a living in St. Albans, which he resigned on joining the Church of Rome. He remained at St. Albans as master of the Grammar School from 1623 to 1625. In the latter year his first comedy, *Love Tricks*, was acted, and thenceforth Shirley gave up teaching and 'set up for a playmaker'. He settled in London at Gray's Inn, and won popularity both with his fellow-dramatists and the Court circles. King Charles himself, according to the Master of the Revels, supplied him with the plot of *The Gamester*, acted in 1634, and in the same year Shirley was chosen to compose the masque, *The Triumph of Peace*, offered to the King and Queen by the four Inns of Court.[1]

The more unusual honour fell to him, on a visit to Dublin in 1636, to have one of his plays performed before the Lord Deputy, then Lord Wentworth. During further visits to the Irish capital several other of his plays were produced there. On his return to London in 1639–40 he continued to write

[1] See below, pp. 393–4.

for the theatres till they were closed in September 1642. His only further association with the drama was the printing of a number of his previously written plays in 1653, 1655, and 1659, and the contribution of the 'address to the reader' prefixed to the 1647 Beaumont and Fletcher folio. He returned to the teaching profession, and also assisted John Ogilby, formerly manager of the Dublin theatre, in his work of translation from the classics. Overcome by the loss of their home during the Great Fire in September 1666 he and his wife died shortly afterwards and were buried together in the churchyard of St. Giles-in-the-Fields.

Of the more than thirty surviving plays by Shirley his comedies form the largest and most distinctive group, and amongst them the most notable are those of which the scene is laid in London and which deal with the life and manners of its fashionable society. Probably the first in date of this London series is *The Witty Fair One*, licensed by Herbert in October 1626, acted by the Queen's men at the Phoenix and published in 1633. The verse passages are in the easy, lucid, though not distinguished, style characteristic of Shirley, but there is a larger proportion than usual of prose. Sir George Richley, as described by his brother Worthy, a Londoner, is the good old-fashioned country squire. He

> takes no lordly pride
> To travel with a footman and a page
> To London; humbly rides in the old fashion
> With half a dozen wholesome liveries
> To whom he gives Christian wages, and not countenance
> Alone, to live on; can spend by the year
> Eight hundred pounds and put up five.

He is leaving in Worthy's care during a short absence his only daughter and heiress, Violetta, whom he intends to marry to a rich but brainless young knight, Sir Nicholas Treedle, still attended by a tutor who frankly dubs him an ass. But the girl herself favours a less wealthy suitor, Aimwell, who wins her in the end while Treedle is tricked into marrying a chambermaid, impersonating her mistress in a masque. The witty fair one of the title is however not Violetta, but her cousin, Penelope, Worthy's daughter, who also changes places with her chambermaid to befool him. The richest vein of comedy is in the last act, when Fowler, Penelope's scapegrace lover, who had shammed illness, hears talk that he is dead and is to be buried from Worthy's house:

I am so thin and airy, I have slipped out o' the world, it seems, and did not know on't. If I be dead, what place am I in? Where am I? This is not hell, sure. I feel no torment, and there is too little company; no, 'tis not hell—and I have not lived after the rate of going to heaven, yet . . . Where am I, then? Umph! I'll go to Worthy's before they bury me, and inform myself better what's become of me.

There he finds Penepole with her father and friends sitting in mourning round a hearse, and addressing him as dead. When he asks, 'Where am I dead?' she answers:

> Here, everywhere
> You're dead to virtue, to all noble thoughts,
> And till the proof of your conversion
> To piety win my faith, you are to me
> Without all life; and charity to myself
> Bids me endeavour with this ceremony
> To give you burial.

Fowler thereupon bids all witness his 'death to vanity', and promises, if she will revive him in her thoughts, to love her, as she taught him, nobly. It is an ingenious and original stage method of reforming a rake.

Hyde Park, licensed in 1632, acted at the Phoenix by the Queen's men, and published in 1637, shows less skill in plot and characterization, but won much popularity and is still specially interesting as a picture of a particular aspect of London social life. The play was performed on the occasion of the opening of the Park, which was presented by the first Lord Holland, to whom the quarto is dedicated. Of the three threads in the plot the best worked out concerns Julietta, whose suitor, Trier, employs his friend Lord Bonvile to test her virtue by advances which she repels with fine scorn:

> I must
> Be bold to tell you, sir, unless you prove
> A friend to virtue, were your honour centupled,
> Could you pile titles till you reach the clouds . . .
> Yet I, I, in such infinite distance, am
> As much above you in my innocence.

Julietta's brother, Fairfield, is one of three 'amorous servants' to the petulant Mistress Carol, and finally wins her hand by the paradoxical method of making her swear that she will never love him nor desire his company. He is more fortunate than Lacy, who after seven years' wooing of the supposed widow, Mistress Bonavent, gains her consent just when her husband, who had been lost at sea, reappears to claim her again. Such entanglements are common form in Stuart comedy, but the distinctive feature of the play is found in the scenes, in Acts III and IV, in Hyde Park, where the chief characters gather to see the foot- and horse-races and to bet upon them, the men in pieces of silver, and the ladies in gloves or silk stockings. We are made to share the excitement as the backers of the Irish 'footman' who is competing with an Englishman, cry 'a Teague! a Teague!' and the two runners cross the stage. Then follows the even more breathless sport of the horse-race, in which the gentleman, Venture, rides his mare against the mount of a professional jockey, and bids fair to win till he is thrown by the mare into the mud and his rival returns in triumph, played in by a bagpiper and greeted with cries of 'a jockey, a jockey!' A further touch of realism was added to this vivid picture after the Restoration, when Pepys saw horses led over the stage in a presentation of the play.

A different aspect of the London social life of the period is dealt with in the *The Ball*, licensed to Shirley in November 1632, and printed in 1639, as presented by the Queen's men at the Phoenix, with the names of Chapman and Shirley on the title-page. It is difficult to find traces of Chapman's hand in the play, which is in essentials a comedy of manners wherein originally 'there were divers personated so naturally both of lords and others of the Court' that omissions had to be made before performance was allowed by the Master of the Revels. In the amended text there are only two figures who appear to be topical rather than conventional comedy types, Bostock, inordinately boastful of his blue-blooded descent, and Monsieur Le Frisk, the dancing-master, with his mixed jargon of French and broken English. More traditional is Freshwater, the pretended traveller, but in his grotesque account of his imaginary continental tour there is an interesting allusion to the Parisian stage (V. i): 'There be no such comedians as we have here; yet the women are the best actors, they play their own parts, a thing much desired in England by some ladies, inns o' court gentlemen, and others.'

There is nothing very distinctive in Lord Rainbow for whom two Court ladies feign to be rivals in love or in the two knightly suitors of the rich young widow, Lady Lucina. But to her relations with her favoured suitor, Colonel Winfield, Shirley gives a characteristically ingenious turn which leads up to what is the main topical feature of the play, the defence of the institution of 'the Ball'. Lucina promises that she will marry Winfield on condition that he swears that he has always been 'honest', strictly moral. He turns the tables on her by casting doubts on her sex's honesty (IV. iii):

> I do allow you Hyde Park and Spring Gardens—
> You have a recreation called THE BALL,
> A device transported hither by some ladies
> That affect tennis; what do you play a set?
> There's a foul racket kept under the line,
> Strange words are bandied, and strange revels, madam.

To convince him that some malice has corrupted his opinion of the Ball, she invites him to be present at it, where the purity of the entertainment is symbolized in a masque where

Diana puts to flight Venus, and allows Cupid to remain, if
he throws away his licentious shafts: 'Love is welcome while
he's chaste'. Thereafter the golden ball from which the revel
took its name (now of derived wider application) was 'tossed'
to the lady who became president of the ceremony.

In *A Lady of Pleasure*, licensed in October 1635 and
printed in 1637, as acted by the Queen's men at the Phoenix,
Shirley gives his most comprehensive picture of fashionable
London life. The titular role is filled by Lady Bornwell, who
has forced her husband, Sir Thomas, to bring her up to the
capital because she can no longer endure the country where
the men are so primitive that 'they retain a sense of nothing
but the earth'. Here she has launched forth on extravagant
courses with which her husband upbraids her (I. i):

> Your change of gaudy furniture, and pictures
> Of this Italian master, and that Dutchman;
> Your mighty looking-glasses, like artillery,
> Brought home on engines; the superfluous plate,
> Antique and novel; varieties of tires;
> Fourscore-pound suppers for my lord, your kinsman.

Amongst her other dissipations Sir Thomas includes the
Ball, and it is curious that Shirley puts unto his mouth an
indictment of the entertainment which he had vidicated in
his earlier play:

> Another game you have, which consumes more
> Your fame than purse; your revels in the night,
> Your meetings called THE BALL, to which repair,
> As to the court of pleasure, all your gallants
> And ladies thither bound by a subpoena
> Of Venus, and small Cupid's high displeasure.

Her husband's 'lecture', as she calls it, has no effect on Lady
Bornwell, who immediately afterwards is getting the latest
gossip of the town from two frivolous gallants, Kickshaw
and Littleworth, and who has called her nephew, Frederick,
from the University to teach him the manners of the capital.
The scene in which the conversion of the young scholar

begins is in Shirley's happiest vein. Frederick on his entrance
is the model studious undergraduate (II. i):

> I never knew
> More sweet and happy hours than I employed
> Upon my books.

His aunt makes mock of his black suit, the fashion of his
hair, and the way in which he holds his hat, in terms that
bewilder him:

> I understand not this; Latin or Greek
> Are more familiar to my apprehension:
> Logic was not so hard in my first lectures
> As your strange language.

She commends him to the tuition of the two gallants and he
soon proves himself an apt pupil. Sir Thomas also, as the
only way of curing his wife, determines to play the prodigal
rake, and proceeds to pay court to a young widow, Celestina,
whose ways are even more sumptuously lavish than his wife's,
though she is careful in the pursuit of her pleasures to keep
the security of her honour. By becoming, however, the guest
of Sir Thomas in his house she excites the jealousy of Lady
Bornwell, who puts on Kickshaw and Littleworth to jeer at
her, to which she retorts in kind.

Just when Bornwell begins to find himself becoming
seriously enamoured of Celestina, a rival for her favours
appears in a lord whom (perhaps in fear of the Censor who
had ruled out personal allusions in *The Ball*) Shirley desig-
nates merely by the initial A. He had been constant in his
mourning for a dead mistress, but is persuaded to visit the
beautiful young widow. In a scene of admirably polished
high comedy (IV. iii) she tells him of the world's flattering
opinion of his qualities and its regret that 'against the
imperial laws of love' he has buried with a mistress all that is

> Hoped for in love's succession, as all beauty
> Had died with her and left the world benighted:
> In this you more dishonour all our sex
> Than you did grace a part.

He showers compliments on her in return, and kisses her hand and lips—and then declares that he is proof against all temptation to profane the memory of his mistress; 'This magic has no power upon my blood'. Whereupon Celestina turns the tables upon him by declaring that she can 'now glory that you have been worth my trial', and that she has found that his constancy springs not 'from melancholy for some female loss', but from his truth and love of innocence. This so works upon Lord A that he suggests to her

> To become mistress to a noble servant
> In the now Court Platonic way.

Her reply is that she can help him to sell his ancient family's glorious coat of arms, and when he indignantly refuses, she upbraids him with trying to buy her honour from her:

> Honour that is not worn upon a flag
> Or pennon, that without the owner's dangers
> An enemy may ravish and bear from me;
> But that which grows and withers with my soul
> Beside the body's stain; think, think, my lord,
> To what you would unworthily betray me,
> If you would not, for price of gold or pleasure
> (If that be more your idol) lose the glory
> And painted honour of your house.

Here, both in the thought and the rhythm of the verse, Shirley rises to a peak point, and nothing is left to Lord A but to offer Celestina, and her to accept, his chaste love. They have so occupied the forefront of the stage in the later acts of the play that they have somewhat unduly diverted the attention of the audience from Sir Thomas and his wife, who has been frightened by his threatening prospects of their imminent bankruptcy into abandoning her spendthrift ways, and who, after a touching reconciliation with her husband, promises her after life to virtue.

While these comedies of manners are Shirley's most individual contribution to the Stuart stage, there is a considerably larger group of his plays which may be classed as romantic comedies or tragi-comedies, and of which some of the more representative may be here considered. *The Wedding*, acted by the Queen's men at the Phoenix, was printed in 1629 and again in 1633 and 1660. Though the scene is again laid in London the main interest is not topical but lies in the relations, which come near to being tragic, between Beauford and Gratiana, daughter of Sir John Belfare. On the day before their wedding, when the guests have been bidden to the festivities, Beauford's friend and kinsman, Marwood, intervenes to save him from 'a lasting shipwreck' by marriage with an unchaste woman who has been his own paramour. In defence of her honour Beauford fights a duel with Marwood in Hyde Park, here seen in a different aspect from that of a race-course, and gives him a seemingly mortal wound. Even then he retracts nothing:

> Take my last breath; I sinfully enjoyed her,
> Gratiana is a blotted piece of alabaster.

Convinced that his friend would not die with a lie upon his lips, Beauford tells the horror-stricken girl that they are eternally divorced, and will not listen to her protests (II. iii):

> *Gra.*　　　　　　　Have you done?
> Then hear me a few syllables:—you have
> Suspicion that I am dishonoured.
> *Beau.*　　　　　　　　　　　　No,
> By heaven I have not; I have too much knowledge
> To *suspect* thee sinful; but in the assurance
> Of it I must disclaim thy heart for ever.

One friend, however, believes in her innocence, Captain Landby, who brings Beauford a letter from her which ends, 'Farewell! I am carrying my prayers for thee to another world. Her own martyr, drown'd Gratiana'. Stricken with remorse he vows to make his own chamber, strewn with funeral herbs, into a coffin. Seldom does Shirley reach so high a level of poetic imagination as here (IV. iv):

> Gratiana had ne'er a coffin; I have one
> Spacious enough for both of us; but the waves
> Will never yield to't, for it may be they,

Soon as the northern wind blows cold upon them,
Will freeze themselves to marble over her,
Lest she should want a tomb.

But when all seems set for a tragic close there is an over-whelming dramatic reversal. It is revealed that Marwood had unconsciously lied. He had planned to seduce Gratiana, and believed he had done so, but her attendant for mercenary reasons had substituted her own daughter, Lucibel. Gratiana makes a startling reappearance from a chest which was supposed to contain the body of Marwood, who also comes to life again, having been cured by a park-keeper, and offers marriage to the injured Lucibel. All this is slick 'theatre', which was doubtless effective on the stage, and this main plot of *The Wedding* displayed favourably Shirley's gifts for dealing with serious emotional situations. His powers as a comic dramatist make on the whole a poorer showing in the sub-plot in the rivalry for the hand of Captain Landby's cousin, Jane, between Rawbone, a thin and miserly citizen, and the abnormally fat Lodam. The most amusing feature is a duel at Finsbury—a burlesque counterpart of that between Beauford and Marwood in Hyde Park—in which Lodam surrenders his sword, as he thinks, to Rawbone, who is impersonated by Haver, a gallant masquerading as the citizen's servant, who wins and weds Jane.

The plot of *The Gamester*, acted by the Queen's men at the Phoenix and at Court on 6 February 1633/4, and printed in 1637, was (according to Herbert) provided by King Charles. But in some of its leading incidents it is akin to *The Wedding*, though Shirley with his versatile skill placed them in a new setting. Will Hazard fills the titular role, but his gambling propensities do not furnish the main interest, though they enable the dramatist to depict some dicing scenes in an 'ordinary' which give the play in part the character of a comedy of manners. When ill luck with the dice-box has brought Hazard into low water his fortunes are suddenly bettered by a paradoxical offer which sets on foot

Aa

some episodes of excellent fooling. Old Barnacle, a rich
citizen, is anxious that his nephew, his namesake and heir,
who, like Frederick in *The Wedding* has been 'almost spoiled'
by the university, should be transformed into a fine gentleman.
As he explains to Hazard (I. i):

> We that had
> Our breeding from a trade, cits as you call us,
> Though we hate gentlemen ourselves, yet are
> Ambitious to make all our children gentlemen.

He therefore is prepared to give Hazard a hundred pieces
if he will allow his nephew to gain credit for valour by letting
him beat him in public. The plan succeeds only too well.
Young Barnacle, after giving Hazard a box on the ears, turns
into a 'blade' or 'roarer', who dices in the tavern, spreads
the latest news, in an admirable burlesque, from the 'Coranto',
and paints the town red. His uncle, terrified that he will
come to a criminal's end, bribes Hazard with another
hundred pieces to 'unblade' him. He thereupon gives him
two blows, 'there's first your principal; take that for the use',
and then has him kicked by all the company, last of all by
old Barnacle, who on promise of his reformation takes him
again into his love.

From another quarter there comes to Hazard a no less
unexpected and more heinous proposal. The merchant,
Wilding, has become enamoured of Penelope, his wife's rich
kinswoman and his own ward. She is as quick-witted as she
is beautiful, and she makes it a condition of granting his
desires that his wife will give her consent. With revolting
brutality he forces her to become the girl's temptress, though
she does so only to test her, and finds her the soul of purity.

> I have no life
> Without my innocence, and you cannot make
> Yourself more miserable than to wish if from me.

But she consents to play a part in a plot by which Penelope
is to make a midnight assignation with Wilding in the dark
and in silence, and his wife is to take her place and receive

his embraces. It promises to be another case of substitution, akin to that of Lucibel for Gratiana in *The Wedding*. But the sequel is doubly surprising. Wilding, after an unlucky evening with the dice, borrows from Hazard in the hope of winning the gold of a merchant who has just come into the tavern, and in return bids Will impersonate him in the midnight meeting with Penelope. No sooner has Hazard reported his enjoyment of this in luscious phrases than mistress Wilding tells her husband of the trick that she has played, as she thinks, on him, so that by his own act he finds himself fitted with the horns of which Stuart husbands, at any rate on the stage, went in constant terror. To blind the world to his shame he bribes Hazard to marry the supposed victim of the midnight encounter, Penelope, by the offer of her whole portion, two thousand pounds. After a lively verbal duel the pair agree to go through the ceremony. Then follows the disclosure of what is perhaps the best-kept secret in the whole range of Stuart drama. Hazard reveals that his report to Wilding was entirely faked (V. ii):

> Your wife expected you, but when I came
> She had prepared light, and her cousin here,
> To have made you blush and chide you into honesty.
> Seeing their chaste simplicity, I was won
> To silence, which brought on my better fortune.

Mistress Wilding assures her husband that her plot was only to betray him to love and repentance, and he confesses his follies and begs her forgiveness.

In singular contrast to this highly ingenious but far from edifying main action is the romantic and finely tempered sub-plot. It opens very effectively when Delamore is carried over the stage wounded and is afterwards followed by Beaumont, who has been arrested for the assault. They have had a quarrel in their cups about their mistresses, Leonora and her friend, Violante. The former is the daughter of Sir Richard Hurry, who has forbidden her marriage with the impecunious Delamore and rejoices when news is brought

that he has died of his wounds. He orders the grief-stricken
girl to give her love to Beaumont, whom by his authority he
will get freed from prison. She turns upon him indignantly
(II. iii):

> I shall commit a sin, foul as his murder,
> Upon poor Violante, and rob her:
> Their hearts' love hath seal'd up i' the eye of heaven,
> 'Twere sacrilege to part 'em; she's my friend, too,
> One that will rather die than injure me:
> And he will rather suffer, if he be
> Noble, as you profess him, than consent to
> So foul a guilt.

When, nevertheless, Hurry offers the girl's hand to Beaumont he too rejects scornfully the prospect of relief from
prison and execution: 'These things may bribe an atheist,
not a lover'. But then comes an unforeseen sorer temptation.
Violante has visited the prison and overheard what has passed
between Hurry and her lover, and she now adjures him:

> O do not lose yourself in a vain passion
> For thought of me! I cancel all your vows
> And give you back your heart . . . be Leonora's,
> For being mine, thou art lost to all the world.
> Better a thousand times then be made hers
> Than we both lose; I'll pawn my faith she'll love thee.

But Beaumont's constancy is unshaken, 'I will not leave thee
for the world's kingdom'. It is a noble rivalry in self-
sacrifice and it soon has its reward, for, as spectators of *The
Wedding* will probably have guessed from the first, Delamore's death, like Marwood's, has been a false report, and
Beaumont is set free to take Violante to his arms It was not
only his suggestion of the plot that entitled King Charles to
say that *The Gamester* was the best play he had seen for
seven years. It has its drawbacks in the pruriency of much of
the dialogue and in the exaggerated brutality of Wilding and
Hurry, as husband and father. But it weaves together with
even more than Shirley's wonted technical skill remarkably
varied threads of interest and it goes with uninterrupted
swing to its astonishing close.

It may be fairly claimed for the king that he showed himself a more discerning critic than his Master of the Revels, who entered in his office-book an extravagant eulogy of another of Shirley's romantic comedies, *The Young Admiral*, which was licensed 3 July 1633, acted by the Queen's men at the Phoenix, and at Court on 19 November 1633, and printed in 1637. This comedy, wrote Herbert, 'being free from oaths, profaneness, or obsceneness, hath given me much delight and satisfaction in the reading, and may serve for a pattern to other poets. . . . When Mr. Shirley hath read this approbation, I know it will encourage him to pursue this beneficial and cleanly way of poetry', and others to imitate him for their own credit. Herbert not only here makes what may be called its negative qualities the criterion of a 'pattern' play, but takes, by modern standards, a somewhat lax view by allowing the earlier part of Act. IV. iii to pass as a 'cleanly way of poetry'.

Later critics than Herbert on other grounds than his have rated *The Young Admiral*, as I think, above its merits. Neither in its graver dialogue nor in its humorous episodes is Shirley seen at his best, and his technical ingenuity in the creation of well-nigh tragic dilemmas is pushed to nearly fantastic limits. The scene is laid in Naples and its neighbourhood. Vittori, the young Neapolitan admiral, is returning from a victory over the fleet of the Sicilian king who has been provoked to warfare by the slighting behaviour to his daughter of Cesario, prince of Naples, who had come to woo her. His heart was not in his courtship, though he had found grace with Rosinda, the Sicilian princess, because he had become violantly enamoured of Cassandra, the beloved of Vittori. He had hoped for Vittori's death in the sea-battle, and now to dishonour him in his hour of triumph he orders no man to go forth from the city to meet him and his troops, and without cause arrests his father, Alphonso, as a traitor. The astonished victors are met only by Cassandra, who tells Vittori of the prince's overtures to her and of Alphonso's

fate, and when the king appears his reward to the admiral
is to banish him with his father and Cassandra from Naples.

The king hopes thus to prevent further trouble with
Cesario, and Shirley shows dramatic power in the contrast
between the weak soveriegn and his self-willed heir, who
defies him by seeking to prevent the flight of the banished
trio, though he succeeds only with Alphonso, who scornfully
bids the monarch, 'turn friar and make the young man king'.
But a storm at sea drives Vittori and Cassandra back to the
coast of Naples, where they fall into the hands of the
Sicilians seeking to retrieve their naval defeat by a siege of
the city. The King of Naples confronts Vittori with one of
those tragic alternatives which figure so largely in Shirley's
dramatic technique. 'Be our soldier, fight against your
country—we have pledge for this trust in Cassandra, whose
head shall be the price of your disobedience.'

The young admiral bursts out indignantly (III. i):

> To fight against my country!
> 'Tis a less sin to kill my father there,
> Or stab my own heart; these are private mischiefs
> And may in time be wept for; but the least
> Wound I can fasten on my country makes
> A nation bleed, and myself too.

But he remembers that (unlike Beaumont in *The Gamester*)
it is not his own life but that of Cassandra that is at stake,
and though she bids him not value it above his honour, he
takes arms, to save her, against his country. He even in
disguise revisits the Court of Naples to announce that he is
now the Sicilian general, and hears from Cesario that the
price of his attack will be Alphonso's head. Here is a further
tragic dilemma:

> If I refuse their war
> I lose my wife, Cassandra; if I fight,
> My father bleeds.

But this is not enough for Shirley. Alphonso is offered his
liberty by Cesario if he will dare his traitor son to single
combat. The old father moans that he (IV. ii):

> Could wish Vittori dead; but 'twill not satisfy,
> Unless we murder one another too,
> And I must challenge him; he is my son,
> Although he be a rebel.

But it is Cesario himself who by a strange complication is to prevent Vittori from leading Sicily's army. A letter from Cassandra to the prince, which sounds as a declaration of her love, but is written on behalf of the enamoured princess Rosinda, beguiles him into the Sicilian camp, where he is seized as a hostage by the King, who thereupon dismisses Vittori from his service. Rosinda, fearful of the fate that Cesario may meet at her father's hands, flies with Vittori to the palace at Naples, where she offers herself to make the balance even as a pledge for the prince's safety. Instead she brings him into immediate danger, for the King of Sicily, enraged at his daughter's disappearance, declares to him, 'I will have her, or your head shall off'; and still more closely anticipating the Queen of Hearts in *Alice*, he shrieks:

> Where is Cassandra?
> Off with her head and his!

With her return and confession of her motive all is made plain, and the general reconciliation is completed by Cesario's acknowledgment to Rosinda that she has made him fit to know her and be worthy of her love.

The ingenuity of the plot cannot be denied, but it makes the impression of an over-artificial arrangement of checks and balances. Nor does Shirley's humour shine in the sub-plot, where the cowardly Pazzarello is tricked by two of his fellow servants into the belief that by a witch's enchantment he can be made 'slick and shot-free'—till he finds that he can be beaten and bruised.

Another play acted by the Queen's men at the Phoenix, in 1634, and printed in 1637, is *The Example*. Here Shirley reverts to London as the scene; but with the romantic main plot he here combines features not of a comedy of manners, but of humours. Sir Solitary Plot, in whose house most of

the action takes place, has two humours indicated by his
name. He goes to bed at daylight and thus never meets his
wife. And when the rest of the world is asleep he sits up
brooding upon 'this world of plots and close conspiracy'
which he sees everywhere. For once he has some reason in
suspecting a plot in the daily visits of the rich young lord
Fitzavarice to his niece, Lady Peregrine, whose soldier
husband, Sir Walter, is absent fighting in the Low Countries.
Fitzavarice has a hold over the spendthrift knight, whose
estate is mortgaged to him, and he is now intent upon the
conquest of his wife by costly gifts and the tinsel rhetoric
of his parasite, Confident Rapture. To the fustian praise of
Fitzavarice by this 'pretended wit'—a most diverting piece
of burlesque—Lady Peregrine retorts:

> Cry mercy, sir,
> I know him, and you might, with half the expense
> Of so much wit in blank verse, have express'd
> His purpose and himself.

That purpose is soon made clear by Fitzavarice himself,
but Lady Peregrine is adamant to his pleading. Thereupon,
the gamesome Lady Plot, true to her name, gives him the
key of her niece's room, where he renews his solicitations in
vain, and at last threatens her with his poniard. When she
falls down in a faint, he cries our despairingly, 'Ha! madam!
dead! help! I did but try thee.' At this tense moment, by
an extremely deft stroke, the 'humours' element is reintroduced. Plot's servant, Dormant, rushes in 'above', calling
(III. i):

> Peace! you'll wake my master.
>
> *Lord F.* Help here! the lady Peregine is dead.
>
> *Dor.* If she be dead, she will not make a noise,
> Would all i' the house were dead! we should be at quiet.

There is less psychological than theatrical justification for
the developments that follow. Lady Peregrine's swoon converts Fitzavarice from his vicious aims, and in proof of his
repentance he sends her the mortgage bond and a magnificent carcanet. When Lady Peregrine innocently reports

this to her husband, unexpectedly on furlough from the wars, he at once concludes that these gifts from 'the wanton lord' must be the price of her guilt during his absence. He rushes with his sword drawn to find him, and instead wakes Plot, who flies from him in his nightshirt, shrieking, 'a plot! a plot to murder me!' and 'resolving 'to sleep hereafter in a shirt of mail'.

Peregrine thereupon sends a challenge to Fitzavarice by a captain of his company, who agrees to be his fighting second, while Fitzavarice chooses for the same role Confident Rapture, who assents in flowery phrases, but to save his own skin has Sir Walter arrested on a pretended action for debt by Fitzavarice. The lord at once sets him free by discharging the debt, and Peregrine, now convinced that his suspicions were groundless, welcomes his wife to his heart and begs Fitzavarice for pardon. But the young lord (by one of Shirley's characteristically ingenious turns of action) maintains that he is bound in honour to accept the challenge, and in a duel they wound each other and then are reconciled.

Fitzararice's chivalry has its reward. Lady Peregrine's wealthy and vivacious sister, Jacinta, is the central figure of an underplot, in which two foolish wooers, Varnnion and Pumicestone, are rivals for her hand. She leads them a merry dance in farcical scenes (IV. ii and V. i), where they try to comply with preposterous conditions as a test of their vows. But her heart has been given to Fitzavarice, with whom she has had verbal passages-at-arms, in which she has declared that she will never marry while she has any wit, and he has retorted:

> Pray, lady, do not fear I come a-wooing. . .
> Yet if I could love, I would marry thee
> Of all women alive.

Fitzavarice overhears her confession of a feeling that she can no longer conceal, and turning to Lady Peregrine he cries:

> Let me salute THE EXAMPLE of chaste honour:
> Sister I now must call thee, and shall glory
> To own that title by Jacinta's love.

And here the play with its remarkably skilful interlacing of the various actions, its mixture of farcical humours with poignant emotions, may serve as 'the example', of Shirley's matured comic art before we turn finally to other features of his work.

Most of the plays acted first in Dublin while Shirley was in Ireland are in the same general tradition as his previous romantic comedies. They include *The Royal Master* (printed 1638), performed in Ogilby's theatre in 1635 and in the Castle, on New Year's Day 1636, before the Lord Deputy, to whom an epilogue is addressed; *The Doubtful Heir* (licensed 1640) and *The Constant Maid* (printed 1640). Also printed in 1640 and previously performed in Dublin was a play of more distinctively local flavour and difficult to classify, *St. Patrick for Ireland*. It holds as exceptional a place in Shirley's canon as *Perkin Warbeck* in Ford's, for supernatural agencies play in it a predominant part. Archimagus, chief priest of the pagan gods of Ireland, finds their and his own power challenged by the landing of 'a tame, a naked churchman', Patrick, apostle of Christianity. The evil spirits whom he summons by his magic arts to blast the newcomer fly away as Patrick appears, escorted by his angelic guardian, Victor, bearing a banner with a cross. When Leogarius, the king, bids him quit this kingdom speedily, Patrick answers that he has commission for his stay, as a legate from the supreme King,

> Who sent me hither to bring you to him,
> And this still wand'ring nation to those springs
> Where souls are everlastingly refreshed.

When Dichu, a nobleman, seeks to strike him, the saint by a miraculous act effects his conversion, and Archimagus counsels the king to change his tactics and get Patrick into his power by a hypocritical display of friendliness.

So far the play has kept close to its religious theme, but

with characteristic ingenuity Shirley proceeds in Act II to complicate this with love entanglements. The king has vowed that Dichu's two sons shall be thrown into the sea unless he recants. They are the lovers of the princesses Ethne and Fidella, and Archimagus, to save them, disguises them as idols in the temple where the King and Court come to worship. It is odd that the scholarly Shirley should here represent them as Jupiter and Mars, though he calls the chief of the Irish pantheon Ceanerarchius. This deity in turn is impersonated by the king's elder son, Corybreus, who under cover of his disguise ravishes Emeria, daughter of the 'great officer', Milcho, whose love is given to his brother, Conallus. In revenge she stabs the lustful impostor to death, and becoming a convert is hailed by Patrick as 'spouse to an eternal bridegroom'.

Even more exalted converts are gained by the saint's miraculous powers. The queen begs to be received as his 'weak disciple' and is imprisoned by the king in the house of Milcho who, while Patrick is visiting it, sets it on fire. But the saint is preserved from harm by his angelic guardian while Milcho leaps into the flames rather than hear Patrick preach his 'cursed faith'. In the last act all the characters are brought to the mouth of a cave, where the first convert, Dichu, has made his cell, and here Patrick accomplishes his crowning miracle of banishing for ever from Ireland the poisonous serpents which Archimagus had summoned for a last assault upon the saint's life. The baffled pagan high-priest sinks into the earth, and the king kneels to Patrick, who has proclaimed to Conallus the glorious future of the kingdom to which he now is heir (V. iii):

> This nation
> Shall in a fair succession thrive, and grow
> Up the world's academy, and disperse,
> As the rich spring of human and divine
> Knowledge, clear streams to water foreign kingdoms,
> Which shall be proud to owe what they possess
> In learning to this great all-nursing island.

Such a prophecy must have sounded strangely ill-suited to the distracted Ireland of 1640, and Shirley was evidently not encouraged to write the second part of the play to which he had looked forward in the prologue and epilogue. The work as it stands, including also a farcical element of a servant in love with the queen, and a Bard whose songs form a semi-operatic feature, is a curious *pastiche*, but has the special interest of the last excursion of the English theatre into the supernatural before the Civil War.

From *St. Patrick for Ireland*, which includes tragic episodes, we turn finally to the series of some half-dozen tragedies with which Shirley varied his prolific output as a comic playwright. *The Maid's Revenge* in 1626, at the beginning of his dramatic career, was followed by *The Traitor* and *Love's Cruelty* in 1631, *The Duke's Mistress*, 1636, *The Politician*, before 1639, and *The Cardinal*, 1641. Of these *The Traitor* and *The Cardinal* are the outstanding examples.

The titular part of *The Traitor*, printed in 1635, is the Florentine Lorenzo de Medici. But Shirley recks little of the historical facts of his career, and in characteristic fashion complicates them with amorous entanglements which push the political action of the plot into the background. Pisano is betrothed to Amidea, and his friend Cosmo is the lover of Oriana. Duke Alexander has cast a lustful eye on Amidea, and his kinsman and favourite Lorenzo has persuaded Pisano to throw her over and transfer his affections to Oriana, thus proving false both to his mistress and his friend. Lorenzo, pursuing his tortuous path, while serving as agent of the Duke's vices, stirs up Sciarrha, Amidea's high-souled, fiery brother, to join him in a plot against Alexander:

> *Lor.*   Let me advance
>   Our liberty, restore the ancient laws
>   Of the republic, rescue from the jaws
>   Of lust your mothers, wives, your daughters, sisters.
> *Sci.*   Sisters!
> *Lor.*   From horrid rape—'las, Amidea!
> *Sci.*   I am resolved; by all that's blest, he dies.

The Duke seems to put himself into his power by visting Sciarrha's house when, something after Hamlet's fashion with the 'mousetrap', he presents a symbolic masque in which a Young Man crowned follows Lust with her circle of Pleasures, with whom he dances till Death enters with a train of Furies, who join in the dance and then carry the Young Man away. Whether or not, as some hold, Claudius was too much occupied with Polonius to note the dumb-show, the Duke in Shirley's play is too much engaged with Amidea to mark the meaning of this masque. But she herself averts for the time her brother's threatened vengeance by wounding herself in the arm, that it may teach the Duke to 'correct' his blood. Her action (not too convincingly) forces from him a prayer for pardon, and a declaration that he is reconciled to virtue.

This is the prelude to an ingeniously contrived episode of double-crossing. Sciarrha (again somewhat too lightly) gives full credit to the Duke's 'conversion', confesses that he had intended to kill him that night, and warns him that Lorenzo expects every minute to hear that he is dead. To convince Alexander of his favourite's treachery, Sciarrha announces this to Lorenzo in the Duke's hearing, and is so astounded when Lorenzo denounces the deed that he is about to stab him when the Duke comes forward, crying:

> Hold! . . .
> You are too passionate, Sciarrha, and
> Mistook Lorenzo . . .
> You shall be friends; you shall, I say.

It is only a feigned reconciliation, for Lorenzo craftily stirs Sciarrha to renewed murderous rage by the news that Pisano having jilted Amidea is to be married to Oriana on the morrow. As Sciarrha rushes out to intercept the bridal procession Lorenzo cries jubilantly:

> Farewell, dull, passionate fool! How this doth feed me!
> Kill and be lost thyself; or, if his sword
> Conclude thy life, both ways I am revenged.

Deaf to a warning from Amidea, still faithful to her love for
him, Pisano is stabbed to death by Sciarrha, who thus places
himself in the favourite's power. For the Duke's guilty
passion for Amidea has revived, and as the price of his pardon
for murder, Lorenzo bids him speed his sister to Alexander's
arms. In the finest scene of the play (V. i), where the situation is akin to that between Claudio and Isabella in *Measure
for Measure*, Sciarrha pleads with Amidea to save his life by
surrendering to the Duke's desires. Whe she answers 'Never,
never', he stabs her, and she dies, *splendide mendax*, with the
cry, 'I drew the weapon' that gave the wound. In a scene
of the fantastic horror that appealed so strongly to Stuart
playgoers her dead body is laid on a bed as if to welcome
the Duke, who starts back with an agonized cry from kissing
her frozen lips. But soon, falling beneath the daggers of
Lorenzo and an accomplice, he does share her bed—in death.
For a moment we are brought back to the almost forgotten
political aspect of the play when Lorenzo announces that
he will now wear the title of Duke, but divide the power
with Sciarrha (V. iii):

> *Sci.*   I like this well:
> You told a tale once of a commonwealth
> And liberty.
> *Lor.*   It was to gain a fiction
> With discontented persons, a fine trick
> To make a buzz of reformation,
> My ends are compassed; hang the ribble-rabble!

But in the very hour of his apparent triumph the hypocrite
traitor meets his doom from the 'dull, passionate fool' who
too is slain in their duel. As the doors are flung open Cosmo
voices the general horror at the bloody spectacle: 'Here is a
heap of tragedies'. But the test of tragic art does not lie in
the number of victims at the close, and *The Traitor*, as I
think, in spite of its skilful technique and its effective
dialogue, hovering often on the borderland between rhetoric
and poetry, does not reach as high a level as some have
claimed for it. Of the principal characters, Amidea alone

excites sympathetic interest; the Duke's relapse after his conversion is a forbidding feature; the tortuous windings of Lorenzo's mentality, and in a minor degree of Sciarrha's, are more suitable material for the analysis of a psychologist than for the traffic of the stage.

Ten years after *The Traitor* Shirley produced *The Cardinal*, acted by the King's men at Blackfriars. It appears to have been its author's favourite work, for not only does the prologue declare that he thought 'this play might rival with his best', but in the dedication to the 1652 octavo Shirley calls it 'the best of my flock'. With this overestimate of his last tragedy the dramatist seems almost to be applying to himself a line in the play, 'Dost think, he has no more wit than to write a comedy?' *The Cardinal* in respect of its style is among Shirley's plays what *Perkin Warbeck* is among Ford's. It is in the main exceptionally austere, and the meaning is at times more obscure than is usual with Shirley. Though the plot is unhistorical and laid in the kingdom of Navarre, the audience, as indeed the prologue indicates, must have seen a prototype of the titular figure in the Cardinal who was holding the reins of government at Paris. Even more than in *The Traitor* amorous rather than political complications fill the forground of the plot. The young widowed Duchess Rosaura has given her heart to Count D'Alvarez, but the Cardinal has forced upon her a contract of marriage with his nephew, the quick-tempered, rough-hewn soldier, Columbo. She catches eagerly at a chance of deliverance when the king appoints Columbo general in a war against Arragon, from which he may not return alive. But this does not explain what is a weakness in the plot— that she should write to him when he is in camp bidding him send her back 'a free resign' of all his interest in her 'person, promise or love'; nor that to test her he should return an affirmative answer. The Duchess immediately claims from the King the right to marry D'Alvarez, and to the reproaches of the Cardinal for her desertion of his nephew she retorts in

words applicable to Richelieu or, from the Puritan stand-
point, to Laud (II. iii):

> How vast are your corruptions and abuse
> Of the king's ear! at which you hang a pendant,
> Not to adorn, but ulcerate, while the honest
> Nobility, like pictures in the rooms,
> Serve only for court ornament. If they speak,
> 'Tis when you see their tongues, which you wind up
> Like clocks, to strike at the first hour you please.

Even the return of Columbo from a victorious campaign
cannot console the Churchman for his nephew's defeat at
home.

The festivity that celebrates the wedding of D'Alvarez and
the Duchess gives Columbo the opportunity of his revenge.
There is nothing more effective in the whole play than the
scene (III. ii) in which the Duchess's servants get ready to
act a comedy before her and the King on the wedding night,
and make a fuss about the beards, heads, and doublets in
which they are to play their parts. It calls back a similar
making-up scene before the catastrophe in Kyd's *The Spanish
Tragedy*, and, like it, is a prelude to fatal doom. But the
comedy is not acted, for Columbo and five accomplices enter
as masquers, dance, beckon D. Alvarez to go out with them
and return with his dead body. Columbo confesses the
murder and makes a sophistical defence of it as an act of
justice which does not prevail with the King who, however,
afterwards at the Cardinal's instigation pardons him.

An avenger appears in a figure who has hitherto played
a minor part, Colonel Hernando. During the Arragon campaign he had been dismissed by Columbo on a charge of
cowardice for urging delaying tactics. Nursing already a
sense of injury against his general, he is horrified by the
murder and challenges him on the plea that

> the inborn right
> Of every gentleman to Alvarez' loss
> Is reason to engage their swords and lives
> Against the common enemy of virtue.

In the duel he kills Columbo, whose dying words, 'I forgive thee—when shall we meet again?', he answers icily, 'Never, I hope'. The victim deserves his doom, but Shirley does not win our sympathy for the executioner.

But it is in the last act that the dramatist more signally fails in his aims. The Duchess, though she has strengthened Hernando's sword with 'the prayers of a wronged widow', now as a safeguard pretends to have gone mad, and is given the Cardinal as a guardian. Hitherto he has been presented as an ambitious and ruthless master of intrigue. But he is now transformed into a lustful and inhuman monster—a Borgia, not a Richelieu. To kill the distracted Duchess will not be enough, it will be merely to 'wound her with a two-edged feather'. He tries to ravish her and is prevented by Hernando, who stabs him, and then takes his own life. The Cardinal makes a feigned confession to the Duchess that he has poisoned her and offers her an antidote—in reality a poison. Mistakenly believing that his wounds are mortal he drinks first of it himself, and thus becomes a suicide, and is followed swiftly in death by the Duchess, murmuring, 'I come, I come, Alvarez'.

Though *The Cardinal* has its merits of dialogue and situation, posterity has not endorsed Shirley's preference of it among the plays of his canon. But on other grounds it is of special interest. It is the last tragedy written and acted before the outbreak of the Civil War, and thus closes the great series beginning with *The Spanish Tragedy* and *Tamburlaine* which for over half a century were the crowning glory of the Tudor and Stuart stage. By 1641 the shadow of the coming Civil War and the Puritan domination was falling across the scene, and when the Duchess warns the Cardinal,

> By timely care
> Prevent a shame, before the short-haired men
> Do crowd and call for justice.

Shirley must have had in view the close-cropped Roundheads whose call for 'justice' was to involve as far as in them lay the destruction of the theatre and all its works.

RICHARD BROME

The dramatic career of Richard Brome ran chronologically closely parallel with that of Shirley, and his best work lay in the kindred sphere of stage-presentations of contemporary social life. But his talent was more derivative and limited and of a coarser texture. Of his birth and earlier years nothing is known. The first allusion to him is in the Introduction to *Bartholomew Fair* (1614), as Ben Jonson's 'man'. Eighteen years later, in an affectionate sonnet prefixed to *The Northern Lass*, Jonson wrote, 'I had you for a servant once, Dick Brome'. Whatever the exact nature of his service may have been, Brome was of good education and won the regard of Dekker, who styled him 'my son', and of Ford, who signed himself his 'very friend'. He may have been the Richard Brome who was married on 8 July 1616 to Frances Lott, a widow, and who was subsequently twice married. On 2 October 1623 *A Fault in Friendship*, not extant, by Brome and 'young Jonson' (probably a son of Ben) was licensed for performance by Prince Charles's men. On 30 June 1628 he was mentioned fourth among the Queen of Bohemia's players granted a warrant as Groom of the King's Chamber.

In 1629 he was writing for the King's company, as on 29 July of that year Herbert licensed *The Northern Lass* for performance by them. They also acted his and Heywood's *The Late Lancashire Witches* in 1634.[1] But on 20 July 1635 he signed a contract with the Salisbury Court theatre to write three plays a year for three years. *The Sparagus Garden* was produced there by the King's Revels company in that year, and *The Antipodes* by the Queen's men in 1638. Both plays were published in 1640. In August 1638 the contract was renewed for seven more years, but Brome wrote

[1] See above, pp. 188–90.

only two more plays for Salisbury Court, and then left this theatre for the Cockpit, under the management of his 'most deserving friend, William Beeston'. It was there in 1641 that *A Jovial Crew* was presented, on the eve of the outbreak of the Civil War. It was not published till 1652, with the last of the dedications that he penned. Eleven further comedies acted before 1642 at uncertain dates appeared in print between 1653 and 1657, after his death.

The four comedies mentioned by name above may be taken as representative of Brome's best work for the theatre at the beginning, middle, and close of his active career. *The Northern Lass* was first published in 1632 and two further editions appeared in 1663 and 1684. Its popularity was doubtless in part due to the novelty in a play laid in London of making the heroine a country girl speaking throughout in her local dialect. Constance, coming up to the capital with her shrewd governess, Mistress Trainwell, has fallen passionately in love with a new-made knight, Sir Philip Luckless, who had paid her some attention. But Sir Philip has contracted himself to a wealthy widow, Fitchow, and, in spite of the protests of his kinsman Triedwell, they go through a wedding ceremony. But, not very plausibly, before the marriage is consummated, they turn against each other and find that by canon law they can be divorced. Mistress Fitchow urges her nincompoop brother, Widgeon, to become a suitor to Constance, while her uncle, Sir Paul Squelch, favours an equally doltish Cornish squire, Master Nonsense. Constance is deaf to their pleas, for she has run melancholy-mad for love of Sir Philip. In the end she secures him without a divorce, for it is revealed that the ceremony between Sir Philip and the widow was performed by a mock-parson at the instigation of Triedwell, who himself wins Mistress Fitchow, while Sir Paul pairs off with Mistress Trainwell.

The plot is somewhat unpleasant and is over-complicated by disguisings and impersonations. It seems scarcely adapted to fulfil Brome's wish expressed in the prologue of making his audience merry. But he holds the strings of the action well in hand, and in Anvil, the braggart governor of Widgeon, and Howder, the widow's gentleman-usher, he supplies two 'humorous' types. A masque and a number of songs, in which Constance forgets her dialect peculiarities of speech, helped to brighten *The Northern Lass* as a stage entertainment.

The Sparagus Garden, like Shirley's *Hyde Park* and *The Ball*, takes its title from a fashionable London resort and festivity. The garden where a novel delicacy could be enjoyed attracted many visitors, and became noted as a centre of scandalous assignations. It is as such that it figures in the play, but so far as the development of the plot is concerned the scene might almost equally well be laid elsewhere. It is predominantly a comedy of Jonsonian humours in their most extravagant form. Two elderly irascible justices of the peace, Touchwood and Striker, cannot meet without boiling over into mutual vituperation. Their wrath is intensified by the news that Touchwood's son, Samuel, and Annabel, Striker's grand-child, whom he treats as his daughter, have become lovers. After running a tortuous course the affair ends happily. But they are a colourless pair. The interest centres mainly in technically subordinate characters in whom Brome again exploits the contrast between town and country manners and speech. Timothy Hoyden has come from Somerset in search of an uncle whom he has never seen and to learn to be a gentleman. He is a gull of the Jonsonian pattern, who is fleeced and fooled to the top of his bent. As Mathew in *Everyman in his Humour* takes as his model Bobadill, so Hoyden copies in deportment and language Striker's impecunious son-in-law, Sir Hugh Moneylacks, who lives by shifts. He even lets himself be bled to get rid of the vulgar fluid in his veins. But he proves after all to be of gentle though illegitimate birth, for it is revealed that he is the son of Touchwood and

Striker's sister whom he had seduced, and who had disappeared and afterwards married a yeoman, Hoyden. Their child, Thomas, had taken after his rustic father. He is a shrewd countryman, who talks in broad Somerset dialect, and who hurries up to London to save his step-brother from his cheating guides to fashionable life. 'Icha made a sweet jaunt after you, and have I vound a vine vool o' thee; where's thy vour hundred pound? is that made a vool on too, tro?' The 'humours' are completed by Sir Arnold Cautious, a bachelor who 'is an admirer and hunter after the sight of beauty', but never ventures to go further, though he is manoeuvred into being for a time a half-hearted suitor for Annabel. London is presented in the play as a centre of intrigue, folly, and fraud, but if Brome's strokes are coarse they are driven home with vigour and gusto.

In *The Antipodes* he displays a more imaginative vein. Again country visitors, Joyless with his young second wife, Diana, and his son, Peregrine, with his wife, Martha, come up to London to stay with Blaze, a herald-painter. But not much is made here of the contrast between London and Derbyshire manners, and everyone speaks standard English. The provincials have come up not to enjoy the pleasures of the capital, but in quest of a cure for Peregrine, who is afflicted with a strange form of melancholy-madness. From boyhood he had been a reader of Mandeville and other travellers' tales, and when he grew up,

> His mind was all on fire to be abroad;
> Nothing but travel still was all his aim.

His parents, hoping it would prove a remedy, had argued him into an early marriage, but after three years it was still unconsummated, and his talk was only of monsters:

> Pygmies and giants, apes and elephants,
> Griffins and crocodiles.

His wife, owing to his treatment of her, is almost as distracted as he, and Joyless himself is madly jealous of his young Diana.

The trio are fit patients for Dr. Hughball, a Caroline psycho-analyst, who effects cures not by physic but by 'medicine of the mind'. He has a patron in an eccentric lord, Letoy, who dresses like a pedlar in broadcloth out of doors, but who at home lives sumptuously, feasting and keeping his own companies of musicians and actors. The doctor assures Peregrine that he can transport him to the furthest part of the Antipodes, which is foot to foot against England. There the people appear like English

> To the exterior show, but in their manners,
> Their carriage and condition of life
> Extremely contrary.

Giving him a potion which sends him asleep for twelve hours, he persuades him that he has arrived in the Antipodes. Peregrine is such a country cousin that he has never seen a play, and when Hughball gets Letoy's actors to perform a number of scenes in which everyone's behaviour is exactly opposite to that of his English counterpart, Peregrine takes it all as real.

There is much acute observation in these scenes of the seamier sides of London life, presented in inverted form, but this paradoxical 'play within the play' is unduly dragged out, and in a postscript to the printed text Brome informed his readers that when *The Antipodes* was performed at Salisbury Court the actors had omitted part of it 'for superfluous length'. At last Peregrine, arraying himself in the property crown and royal robes from the tiring-house, believes himself King of the Antipodes and accepts as his queenly bride his own wife, with whom he enters into marital relations, thus effecting both his and her cure.

The progress of the play within the play has been enlivened by the vivacious comments of Diana and the surly retorts of her husband, Joyless, jealous of the attention to her of Letoy. But this scarcely prepares us for the scene in Act V in which Letoy seeks by every means to draw Diana astray, and she parries his attacks with the sanctity of the word 'husband'. It is then disclosed that Letoy has arranged for Joyless to overhear this encounter to cure him of his jealousy. But a greater surprise is in store. The revelation of a long hidden relationship is a favourite feature of Brome's technique. Diana is supposed to be the daughter of Letoy's friend, Truelock, who now discloses that her father is Letoy himself, who had, in unjust suspicion of his wife's fidelity, substituted her for an infant of Truelock who had died at birth. Thus Letoy had himself been a victim of Joyless's disease of jealousy. But the revelation comes unpleasantly after the temptation scene and is another example of Brome's liking for over-complication of plot.

In *A Jovial Crew, or The Merry Beggars* Brome's imaginative vein finds lighter expression. In a prologue he explains why in 'these sad and tragic days' he has chosen a mirthful theme. He is emulating the popular 'comic writers' of romantic plots who bring together lovers, 'afflicted wanderers', after they have been separated, apparently for ever, 'through much travail and distress'. Brome is therefore writing to some extent with his tongue in his cheek, but nevertheless with gaiety and zest.

Oldrents, a wealthy and benevolent county squire, has been plunged into melancholy, despite the protests of his merry friend Hearty, because a fortune-teller has told him that his daughters will live to be beggars. He is also distressed because his trusty steward, Springlove, after a year's interval, now that May has come, is possessed again with a 'gadding humour' that takes him off for a summer vagary far afield. In vain Oldrents pleads:

> Does not the sun as comfortably shine
> Upon my gardens as the opener fields?
> Or on my fields as others far remote?
> Are not my walks and greens as delectable
> As the highways and commons?

This cannot avail against Springlove's 'inborn strong desire of liberty', and he goes off to be welcomed as their king with song and dance by the crew of merry beggars. He is followed by the two daughters of Oldrents, Meriel and Rachel, who also have been tempted by the prospect of 'absolute freedom, such as the very beggars have', and who bring their lovers, Vincent and Hilliard, in their company. Brome's delight in dialectical speech reaches its peak in his rendering of the 'canting' lingo of the vagabonds. But the girls and their swains have difficulty in learning the lingo, and when they start begging their speech betrays them. The action after Brome's method is unduly prolonged and complicated with the underplot of the flight from her home of the niece of the garrulous Justice Clack. He seeks to force on her an elderly, detested suitor from whom she takes refuge, with the aid of the justice's clerk, with the beggars. Here she and Springlove at once fall in love. Then follows the most surprising of the disclosures with which Brome delights to wind up a fifth act. Springlove's roaming instinct in summertime is explained when it is revealed that his mother was a beautiful beggar, of gentle descent, but it is a thunderclap that his father is none other than Oldrents, who had sent 'his blood a-begging with her' in his youthful days.

In contrast with Shirley, whose 1641 tragedy, *The Cardinal*, was touched by the chill of the fast approaching catastrophe, Brome on the even of the crisis produced this merry, if somewhat over-weighted, comedy. It 'had the luck', as he stated in the dedication, 'to tumble last of all in the epidemical ruin of the scene'. This alone would give it a secure place in the history of Stuart drama.

XVI

MASQUES AND UNIVERSITY PLAYS

I N the Tudor period, in addition to the professional stage, notable contributions to drama had been made by the Inns of the lawyers, the universities, the schools, and festivities at Court and great houses. They all continued their activities under the Stuarts, but the Inns (except for masques) and the schools ceased to produce new theatrical pieces of importance. On the other hand, the universities and the Court took an increasingly prominent part. The cardinal contribution made by the Court entertainments, the great series of Ben Jonson's masques, has been discussed in an earlier chapter. Some account must be added here of masques provided by other accomplished hands. The sequence begins with Samuel Daniel's *The Vision of the Twelve Goddesses*, presented at Hampton Court on 8 January 1604 by the 'most magnificent Queen' Anne and eleven of her ladies. Iris, the messenger of Juno, decked like the rainbow, descends to a temple of peace and announces to its priestess, a Sybil, that the goddesses leaving 'their ancient delighting places of Greece and Asia, made now the seats of barbarism and spoil, vouchsafe to recreate themselves upon the western mount of mighty Britanny, the land of civil music and of rest'. As they appear the Sybil describes each of the twelve in graceful four-lined stanzas, beginning with Juno, goddess of empire, and ending with Tethys representing power by sea. Preceded by the three Graces, hymning in a song

> Desert, reward, and gratitude,
> The graces of society,

and attended by torch-bearers, the goddesses present symbolic gifts which the Sybil places on the altar. They then dance their own measures and, after a pause for rest during another

song by the Graces, they take out the lords from among
the audience and dance lively corantos and galliards with
them. Thereafter Iris notifies that the goddesses are about
to depart, having vouchsafed to appear in the forms of the
best of ladies and her choicest attendants, being otherwise
no objects for mortal eyes. With this hyperbolical compliment to the Queen and her train Daniel closed this masque
of slender texture, in which his own lyric gifts counted for
less than the spectacular and musical effects. He himself
makes this plain in his dedication to the Countess of Bedford
prefixed to the quarto of 1610. An 'indiscreet printer' had
soon after the performance 'very disorderly set forth' a
corrupt and unauthorized version. Daniel therefore felt
compelled to 'describe the whole form' of the masque as it
was performed. This detailed analysis makes clear much
that not only the 'captious censurers' whom he attacks, but
more friendly spectators and readers might easily miss. And
it shows that Daniel's purpose was not only to present the
queen in flattering guise, but to pay tribute to the blessings,
symbolized by the twelve deities, that 'this mighty kingdom'
enjoyed through the accession of the Stuart sovereign.

King James was also present on Twelfth Night 1607, when
a masque by Thomas Campion was presented at Whitehall
in honour of the wedding of his favourite, Lord Hay (afterwards Earl of Carlisle) and Honora, daughter of Lord Denny.
A detailed 'Description' of this masque, with the full text
of the dialogue and songs, was published in 1607. A full
account is given of the spectacular and musical effects, with
the names of the nine courtiers who 'presented in their
feigned persons the Knights of Apollo, who is the father of
heat and youth, and consequently of amorous affections'.
Campion terms their number nine 'the best and amplest of
numbers framed by the Muses and Worthies and . . . of all the
most apt for change and diversity of proportion'.

The scene opens with a view of a bower, with Flora and
Zephyrus, the mild west wind, plucking flowers and throwing

them into baskets, after which there is a song in which, as throughout this masque, Campion shows a far higher lyric quality than Daniel in *The Vision of the Twelve Goddesses*.

> Now hath Flora robb'd her bowers
> To befriend this place with flowers:
>   Strow about, strow about.
> The sky rain'd never kindlier showers.
> Flowers with bridals well agree,
> Fresh as brides and bridegrooms be:
>   Strow about, strow about:
> And mix them with fit melody.

A veil is withdrawn discovering a grove with nine golden trees, and on the left hand Night in her house with her nine hours, each bearing a black torch painted with stars and lighted. Night, on behalf of Diana, the moon and queen of virginity, upbraids Flora for gracing the thief Hymen, who has stolen a nymph out of her train,

> And matched her here, plighted henceforth to be
> Love's friend, and stranger to virginity.

Hesperus descends to appease the 'needless jars', and to pay a rhapsodical compliment to King James:

> Cynthia is now by Phoebus pacified,
> And well content her nymph is made a bride,
> Since the fair match was by that Phoebus grac'd
> Which in this happy western isle is plac'd
> As he in heaven, one lamp enlightening all
> That under his benign aspect doth fall.
> Deep oracles he speaks, and he alone
> For arts and wisdom's meet for Phoebus' throne.

Cynthia (Diana) also sends word that the Knights of Apollo, whom she has transformed to trees for seducing her nymphs with love, may now be restored to their rightful shapes. The trees were then cleft asunder by an engine under the stage and from them came forth the nine masquers in robes of green cut into leaves, and began to dance. This done, Night led them, one by one, to her house, each preceded by one of her hours as a torch-bearer, where each received from his attendant hour his helmet, and was stripped of his

green robe and appeared 'in his glorious habit', in which
they again danced. Then they took forth the ladies from
the audience and trod measures with them. Hesperus thereupon announces that he must away and give 'place and
honour to the nuptial night', and after further songs and
'lighter dances' one of the most artistically designed of
Stuart masques of the simpler pattern comes to its close.

The nation's grief for the untimely death of Prince Henry
in November 1612 was deep, but not prolonged, for it soon
found relief in the joy over the marriage between princess
Elizabeth and the Elector Palatine on 14 February 1613.
The event was celebrated by an elaborate series of festivities,
including masques on the evening of the wedding and (as
was intended) the two succeeding nights. The first of these
entertainments was provided by Campion and Inigo Jones,
to whose workmanship showing 'extraordinary industry and
skill' the poet paid generous tribute when the text, with a
full description, was printed later in the year, with the title,
The Lords' Masque. Campion's lyric gifts were now combined
with a more complex design, including anti-masques, than
in his 1607 composition. Orpheus bids Mania, goddess of
madness, set free from her cave Entheus or Poetic fury,
though this means the temporary release also of twelve
frantics of both sexes, who 'fell into a mad measure fitted
to a loud fantastic tune'. Entheus has been given liberty
by order of Jove, who commands him

> to create
> Inventions rare, this night to celebrate,
> Such as becomes a nuptial by his will
> Begun and ended.

A curtain then falls down and reveals eight enormous stars
in clouds of various colours, with Prometheus in front of the
scene. To the accompaniment of a song they 'moved in an
exceeding strange and delightful manner' and then vanished
to reappear in their own human form as masquers sumptuously
attired. A change of scene discovers four women-statues of

silver, to whom Prometheus had given life by his fire and whom Jove had thus transformed. But that they may celebrate this nuptial night he gives them life again, and they are courted by the eight lords, while the chorus sings:

> Woo her, and win her, he that can:
> Each woman hath two lovers,
> So she must take and leave a man,
> Till time more grace discovers.
> This doth Jove to show that want
> Makes beauty most respected;
> If fair women were more scant,
> They would be more affected.

But they are not 'scant' for long. Four more statues appear and are transformed into women, so that each masquer can entertain his lady in a 'first new entering dance', before they take out others from the audience to dance with. 'And first of all the princely bridegroom and bride were drawn into those solemn revels which continued a long space'. Then another change of scene presented an obelisk, all of silver, with statues of the bridegroom and bride beside it, 'all of gold in gracious postures'. The obelisk was drawn forth with a thread of gold by Sybilla, who

> in her native tongue,
> Wherein old prophecies she sung,

foretells in Latin verse happiness for the royal pair and their progeny.

The second evening's entertainment, *The Masque of the Middle Temple and Lincoln's Inn*, was (according to the title-page of the 1613 quarto) 'invented and fashioned . . . by our kingdom's most artfull and ingenious architect Inigo Jones: supplied, applied, digested and written by George Chapman'. The quarto begins by an elaborate description of the procession of the performers from the house of the Master of the Rolls to the Court at Whitehall—'a show at all parts so novel, conceitful and glorious as hath not in this land . . . been ever before beheld'. In the hall a rock reaching nearly to the ceiling and veined with gold had on one side a hill crowned by the temple of Honour and on the other a grove ending in a withered and hollow tree. Plutus, the god of riches, appears and is followed by Capriccio, 'a man of wit', strangely attired and having a pair of bellows on his head with which he 'can puff up with glory all those that affect him'. They have a long prose dialogue, after the fashion of Jonson in some of his masques, but without his trenchant quality, and evidently from Chapman's angry retort found tedious by some of the audience. Capriccio explains his presence at the nuptials by having the charge of 'a company of accomplished travellers that are excellent in antimasques'. They are a set of baboons who come forth from the hollow tree and perform an 'antic and delightful dance'. Plutus gives in reward a wedge of gold, and after this 'low induction' the main masque begins with Honour descending from her temple and announcing the arrival of the princes of Virginia, to do homage to the nuptials of love and beauty, and of the Phoebades, the priests of the Virginian deity, the Sun. The rock opens and discloses a mine of gold, beneath which are seated the twelve princes, attended by their torch-bearers, while above them appears a setting sun, to which the priests sing their hymn. Chapman's powerful genius did not include the lyric faculty, but this 'evening service' is made notable by the way in which Honour contrives that each stanza of the superstitious invocation shall be countered by a parallel observance to the true Phoebus, King James! And when the song ends Eunomia, or Law, Honour's priestess, drives the contrast home:

> Viriginian princes, you must now renounce
> Your superstitious worship of these suns,
> Subject to cloudy darkenings and descents,
> And of your fit devotions turn the events
> To this our Briton Phoebus, whose bright sky,
> (Enlightened with a Christian piety)
> Is never subject to black Error's night,
> And hath already offer'd heaven's true light
> To your dark region.

After this missionary note, incongruous in the festive setting, the torch-bearers danced a second antimasque, as a prelude to the dances of the main masquers, first by themselves and then with ladies among the spectators. So closes a masque with original features, but by its somewhat exotic and laboured design scarcely appropriate to nuptial festivities.

The third entertainment, *The Masque of the Inner Temple and Gray's Inn*, by Francis Beaumont, was to have followed on the next evening, Shrove Tuesday, and the procession by river from Winchester House to Whitehall, led by two admirals, took place on that day. But the King was tired out and the performance was postponed till the Saturday, when it was held in the banqueting room. Beaumont's scheme is on traditional classical lines. Iris, the messenger of Juno, appears to do honour to this union of the rivers Thames and Rhine. She is followed by Mercury, the enemy of Jove, who as king of gods claims the first part in 'these high joys'. Mercury summons Naiads from the fountains, Hyades from the clouds, Cupids from a grove, and, lastly, statues 'attired in cases of gold and silver', who all take part in various dances as the first antimasque. Iris retorts with a second antimasque of a dozen rural figures dancing in may-games to music of 'a spirit of country jollity'. Thereupon Mercury announces that Jove in honour of these nuptials has revived the Olympian games. A change of scene reveals Jove's altar, with the priests about it and on either side pavilions in which lie the Olympian knights, who form the main masque. They dance their measures, while the priests sing in the intervals. After they have taken out the ladies for the lively dances of galliards, durets, and corantos, loud music summons them away to the Olympian games, while a charming lyric petitions that for once Time's 'wild wings' may be stayed.

> But though these games must needs be played,
> I would this pair, when they are layed,
>   And not a creature nigh them,

> Could catch his scythe, as he doth pass,
> And cut his wings and break his glass,
>   And keep him ever by them.

The royal union so auspiciously inaugurated was to end in political disaster. A still more ill-starred wedding, that of the divorced Countess of Essex and the Earl of Somerset, was celebrated in the same Whitehall banqueting room by Campion in a masque presented on 26 December 1613. It contains some songs worthy of Campion's lyric vein, but owing (as he states) to the failure of his collaborator, the Italian architect Constantine, to carry out the main invention, it is short and, according to a contemporary, had 'little or no consideration, either of device or dancing, only it was rich and costly'.[1]

A more notable entertainment, though it remained in manuscript till 1772, was William Browne's *The Inner Temple Masque*, presented by the members of the Inn on 13 January 1614/5. Here the author went for his inspiration in part direct to Homer, as shown in marginal notes, and takes as his theme the tale of Ulysses and the enchantress Circe:

> She that can cold December set on fire
> And from the grave bodies with life inspire;
> She that can cleave the centre and with ease
> A prospect make to our Antipodes;
> Whose mystic spells have fearful thunders made,
> And forc'd brave rivers to run retrograde.

By her charms and the songs of the sirens she draws Ulysses from his ship into her domain and exhibits to him an antimasque of her human victims, whom she has transformed into brute shape. When Ulysses protests that the sight has made him 'most wretched', she retorts that she is blameless for their degradation, and is too easily believed. In striking contrast the second antimasque consists of the nymphs who attend on Circe, bearing wicker baskets in which they gather the simples for her enchantments. In the main masque

---

[1] For Jonson's *The Irish Masque* presented on 29 December, in honour of the same wedding, see above, pp. 93–4.

Ulysses wakes with Circe's wand his sleeping shipmates, inappropriately called knights, who tread their various measures, including the usual sprightly dances with ladies from the audience. The sweetness of Browne's verse both in the dialogue and the songs is not unworthy of the fascinating Odyssean theme, and the last song, almost echoing the close of Beaumont's masque, is a reproach to Time for not staying his flight.

> Who but Time so hasty were
> To fly away and leave you here?
>   Here where delight
>   Might well allure
> A very Stoic from this night
>   To turn an Epicure.

In the years that followed till 1631 Jonson was the undisputed masque-maker, and it was not till 1634 that successors appeared for a brief period in James Shirley and Thomas Carew.

On 3 February of that year the gentlemen of the four Inns of Court presented before the King and Queen in the Whitehall banqueting house a masque, *The Triumph of Peace*, 'invented and written' by Shirley, himself a member of Gray's Inn, with the collaboration of Inigo Jones and of the musicians, Simon Ives and William Lawes. As in the case of the two 1613 masques provided by the lawyers in honour of the royal wedding, *The Triumph of Peace* was preluded by a gorgeous procession of those taking part in it from Ely and Hatton houses to Whitehall. The expenses of the masque amounted to over £20,000, and the quarto published soon after the performance described it, 'for the variety of the shows and richness of the habits', as 'the most magnificent that hath been brought to Court in our time'. Yet as a literary and semi-dramatic achievement it is somewhat disconnected. The stage is first occupied by a group of allegorical characters, including Opinion, Confidence, and Fancy, who asks,

cc

How many antimasques have they? of what nature?
For there are fancies that take most; your dull
And phlegmatic inventions are exploded.
Give me a nimble antimasque. . .
No antimasque!
Bid 'em down with the scene and sell the timber.

Fancy may well voice here the majority view for, as has
been seen, the antimasques had progressively multiplied and
taken a more predominant part in the entertainment. And
so it is here, for Fancy is persuaded to act (in modern par-
lance) as *compère* and to preside and comment on a series
of antimasques. The first is danced by himself and the other
allegorical figures. The scene changes to a tavern, and the
second antimasque is danced by the host, his wife and
servants, and some wantons of both sexes. The third anti-
masque is of six 'projectors' or hare-brained inventors whom
Fancy satirically describes. There is another change of scene
to a wood, with an owl on an ivy-bush, surrounded by a
crow, a kite, a jay, and a magpie, represented by little boys,
who 'dance and wonder at the owl'. Further antimasque
episodes follow. Then the tone of the entertainment alters,
and there appears charioted in heaven Irene or Peace, who,
to the accompaniment of songs, is joined by her sisters,
Eunomia, or Law, and Dike, or Justice. They salute as their
parents, Jove and Themis, the King and Queen, and the
earth on which they move as 'the paradise of love'.

Once more the scene changes and the sixteen masquers
are seen sitting on the ascent of a hill, representing the sons
of Peace, Law, and Justice. After they have descended and
danced their main dance there is another irrelevant episode
when a number of working men and women burst their way
in through the guard to see the show and have 'a lively
frisk themselves'. When they have gone the masquers revel
with the ladies and as day dawns they depart. The King
and Queen were so delighted with this entertainment that
when they soon afterwards visited the City they commanded
its repetition.

Carew's *Coelum Britannicum*, his only venture outside the lyrical sphere, was presented in the Whitehall banqueting-room on Shrove Tuesday. After the later Jonsonian fashion the masque proper has a lengthy semi-dramatic prelude. Mercury, in a speech addressed to the King and Queen, unfolds the ingenious conception that accounts for the entertainment's title. The chaste example set by Charles and his consort has influenced the Olympian deities:

> Jove rivals your great virtues, royal sir,
> And Juno, madam, your attractive graces.

The king of the gods had transformed his earthly paramours to stars, but he is now determined to chase these 'infamous lights from their usurped sphere', and to replace them by the British royal pair and their train:

> So to the British stars this lower globe
> Shall owe its light, and they alone dispense
> To the world a pure refined influence.

Thereupon Momus, the god of envious mockery, enters 'in a long, darkish robe, all wrought over with poniards, serpents' tongues, eyes, and ears'. His speeches prove that Carew, when he chose, was a master of nervous and sharp-pointed prose. 'My natural qualities are to make Jove frown, Juno pout, Mars chafe, Venus blush, Vulcan glow, Saturn quake, Cynthia pale, Phoebus hide his face, and Mercury here take his heels'. In his own cynical fashion Momus, too, describes the Olympian transformation, with sly references to contemporary abuses in England itself.

Heaven is no more the place it was: a cloister of Carthusians, a monastery of converted gods . . . Monopolies are called in, sophistication of wares punished and rates imposed on commodities . . . Edicts are made for the restoring of decayed house-keeping, prohibiting the repair of families to the Metropolis. Bacchus hath commanded all taverns to be shut, and no liquors drawn after ten at night.

He announces that the guilty stars, Hydra and the rest, at the waving of Mercury's wand will fall down and appear in their natural deformities, in which they dance the first antimasque. Next the Crab, and the nine topazes that adorn his shell, are deposed and restored to human shapes, in which they dance the second antimasque 'in retrograde paces, expressing obliquity in motion'. Six other antimasques of the most varied types follow.

The scene changes, and midway up a mountain appear three seated figures in regal habits and crowned, representing the kingdoms of England, Scotland, and Ireland, and above them a winged young man impersonating the Genius of these kingdoms, who summons from forth a cave a troop of British worthies. These are the main masquers richly attired like ancient heroes and preceded by young men of noble birth bearing lighted torches, with which they dance. Then the masquers, who included the King himself, tread their first measure and Genius announces:

> These must in the unpeopled sky
> Succeed and govern destiny.

When the kingdoms protest that they cannot lend heaven so much treasure Genius calms their fears:

> Jove shall not, to enrich the sky,
> Beggar the earth; their fame shall fly
> From hence above, and in the sphere
> Kindle new stars, whilst they rest here.

The masquers thereupon dance their main dance, and afterwards 'the revels with the ladies, which continued a great part of the night'. Then the emblematic figures of Religion, Truth, and Wisdom, and of Concord, Government, and Reputation appear from the clouds and salute the sovereigns, while in the midst sits Eternity on a globe. 'In the firmament about him was a lamp of fifteen stars, expressing the stellifying of our British heroes; but one more great and eminent than the rest, which was over his head, figured his Majesty'. The King and Queen were naturally highly gratified by an entertainment in which the customary flattery was given so original a turn, and which enlisted the united gifts of Carew, Inigo Jones, and the musician, Henry Lawes.

The Master of the Revels declared enthusiastically that it was 'the noblest masque of any time to this day; the best poetry, the best scenes and best habits' [costumes.] It certainly ranks high, but in its excessive elaboration, especially of the antimasques, it overweights the delicate framework of the masque of which the best of Jonson's remain the outstanding models.

In this same year 1634 an even greater name than Jonson's was to claim association with the masque. The figure of Comus, as has been seen, had made a brief and silent appearance in Ben's *Pleasure Reconciled to Virtue*.[1] When Milton with the collaboration of Henry Lawes presented an entertainment at Ludlow Castle in September in honour of the Lord President of Wales he transformed the coarse belly-god into the enchanter who by his dazzling rhetoric and spells takes captive and strives to subdue to his will the lady who embodies chastity. In its union of exquisite verse and exalted tone *Comus* stands in the forefront of all 'occasional' pieces in the Stuart age. But though when published it was entitled a masque, it does not strictly come under that heading. It has some of the features, dances, songs, and a kind of antimasque in the victims of the enchanter's magic. But it lacks the fundamental masque structure. The three youthful Egertons representing the lady and her two brothers do not assume any disguise. Nor do they go through the customary succession of dances culminating in the revels where the masquers choose partners of the other sex from among the spectators.

Another notable entertainment, bearing the title of a masque, but approximating more closely to a play, was Heywood's *Love's Mistress, or The Queen's Masque*, which was thrice presented in November 1634. It was designed by Henrietta Maria to celebrate the king's birthday on 19 November by a performance at Denmark House. But there was a preliminary performance before the royal pair by the

[1] See above, pp. 97-8.

Queen's company at the Phoenix theatre. For the Denmark House presentation 'that admirable artist', Inigo Jones, devised scenic effects, to which Heywood paid enthusiastic tribute when *Love's Mistress* was published in 1636. So great was the success of the birthday performance that a third repetition was commanded within a week.

Not only was the 'first night' of *Love's Mistress* in a theatre but the performers were all professionals. There were no gallants or Court beauties on the stage, to take part in the dances, though just before the close Cupid appears to invite members of the audience to join in treading a measure. The entertainment thus lacked the amateur element which was one of the most distinctive features of the masque, and in its division into five acts it had the full proportions of a play. On the other hand, in its wealth of dances and songs, its spectacular effects, and in what are virtually antimasques provided by a clown and four rustics, and various grotesque figures, *Love's Mistress* has distinctive masque elements. It is presented by Apuleius, from whose *Golden Ass* Heywood borrowed the story of the well-nigh tragic love of Cupid and Psyche. Apuleius, representing Art, discourses between the acts with the Philistine Midas representing Ignorance and interprets the allegorical meaning of the story.

> Psyche is Anima, Psyche is the soul,
> The soul, a virgin, longs to be a bride.
> The soul's immortal; whom then can she woo,
> But Heaven? Whom wed, but Immortality?

The main attraction of the piece however lies not in its ethical significance but in the portrayal of Psyche in her suffering womanhood. Under Heywood's sympathetic touch she becomes a vital, pathetic figure, scorned by her two elder sisters; wedded to an invisible spouse, who is suspected to be a serpent till he is revealed a deity; subjected by his jealous mother, Venus, to seemingly impossible tasks, ending in a descent into hell; and at last proclaimed by Jove himself an immortal and Cupid's bride. Into this central theme

are skilfully interwoven various other mythological episodes
—Venus mourning for Adonis, Vulcan at his smithy with his
attendant Cyclopes, Apollo and Pan in musical rivalry,
Proserpine returning to earth for a day when her mother,
Ceres, holds her annual sowing feast. Though *Love's Mistress*
is something of a dramatic hybrid, it provided first-rate
entertainment and merited the signal royal favour which
it received.

After 1634, except for William Davenant's *Temple of Love*,
on Shrove Tuesday 1634/5, there was an interval of several
years before masques were again presented at Court. The
ceiling of the banqueting-house in Whitehall had been
adorned by paintings 'figuring the acts of King James of
happy memory', which would have suffered from the smoke
of many lights. King Charles therefore ordered the erection
of a temporary timber hall. Here on Twelfth Night 1637/8
Britannia Triumphans, by Davenant in collaboration with
Inigo Jones, was performed. There is a long series of preliminary episodes introducing Action and Imposture, Merlin,
Bellerophon, six antimasques of varied type, and a 'mock
romanza' of giant, damsel and knight. The masque proper
begins with a view of Fame in her glorious palace singing an
invocation to Britanocles, impersonated by the King:

> How hath thy wisdom rais'd this isle!
> Or thee by what new title shall we call?
> Since it were less'ning of thy style,
> If we should name thee Nature's Admiral.

Britanocles appears accompanied by the other masquers in
costumes 'beautiful, rich, and light for dancing'. He is again
saluted by Fame and a chorus of poets. Finally the scene
changes to a view of the sea, over which Britanocles rules,
where 'a great fleet was discovered which . . . with a pros-
perous gale entered into the haven, this continuing to
entertain the sight whilst the dancing lasted'.

Two years later, on 21 January 1639/40 both Charles and
Henrietta Maria appeared in another masque by Davenant

and Inigo Jones, *Salmacida Spolia*.[1] Though written in the
same vein of courtly flattery as its predecessor, there may
be heard in it some undertones of the wrath that was soon
to come. It opens with 'a horrid scene of storm and tempest', in which Furies threaten this 'too much happy isle',
and though there is then a change to a calm and to a serene
sky from which descends in a chariot the good Genius of
Britain and Concord, their dialogue betrays the sense that
all is not well between the people and their sovereign.

> O who but he could thus endure
> To live and govern in a sullen age,
> When it is harder far to cure
> The people's folly than resist their rage?

After a medley of antimasques the good Genius and
Concord lead forth 'the chorus of the beloved people', but
even in their song of invitation to the King to mount the
throne of Honour there is an uneasy note:

> Or are you slow 'cause th' way to Honour's throne
> In which you travel now is so uneven,
> Hilly and craggy, or so much unknown
> As that uncertain path which leads to Heaven?

Then the King and the other masquers were discovered
sitting in Honour's throne, 'his Majesty highest in a seat of
gold, and the rest of the lords about him'. To them descended
a cloud of various colours within which the Queen sat,
'representing the chief heroine, environed with her martial
ladies'. Thereupon the King took out the Queen and the
lords the ladies, and came down into the room and danced
their entry and then a second dance. The scene then changed
again, and from the highest part of the heavens came forth
a cloud in which were eight persons richly attired, representing the spheres, and above 'a heaven opened full of deities,
which celestial prospect with the chorus below filled all the
whole scene with apparitions and harmony'. The masque
ended with the spheres passing through the air and the

[1] An allegorical title from the mollifying effect of drinking from the
fountain Salmacis.

deities ascending. It must have been a brilliant climax and it was acclaimed by those present as 'the noblest and most ingenious that hath been done here in this kind'. But it was to be one of Time's ironies that the last Court masque before the outbreak of the Civil War should conclude with a song celebrating the harmonious union of the royal pair and proclaiming them to be exemplars to their subjects:

> So musical as to all ears
> Doth seem the music of the Spheres,
> Are you unto each other still,
> Tuning your thoughts to either's will. . .
> Live still the pleasure of our sight,
> Both our example and delight,
> So long until you find the good success
> Of all your virtues in one happiness.

UNIVERSITY PLAYS

Another source of entertainment for the Stuart royalties was provided by the plays performed at the Oxford and Cambridge colleges. Elizabeth had been similarly fêted on her visits to Cambridge in 1564 and to Oxford in 1566 and 1592. But with James and Charles and their consorts such visits were more frequent, and it was during them that nearly all the outstanding Stuart academic performances took place. But there is a unique memorial of University drama in the early Jacobean period which may be first noticed. A manuscript preserved in St. John's College, Oxford, contains the record of the presentation of a series of anonymous plays in Latin and English by members of the College in honour of Thomas Tucker, Bachelor of Arts, who according to a traditional custom was elected to be a mock sovereign or 'Christmas Prince'. The festivities under his rule lasted from All Saints' Eve (31 October) 1607 till the first Sunday in the following Lent. He was formally installed on St. Andrew's Day, when in a Latin device, *Asa*

Fortunae, he visited the temple of Fortune and was assured of the favour of the goddess. On Christmas Day a boar's head was served to him at the college high table, and afterwards a short show in Latin, appropriate to the season, was presented. The first of the full-dress performances, a Latin tragedy in Senecan style, on the subject of Philomela, was to have been held on Innocents' Day, but owing to various mishaps it had to be postponed till the following day, when it was favourably received, with Tucker acting the part of Tereus.

On New Year's Day the first of the English pieces *Time's Complaint* was staged. It too suffered through mishaps and its mixture of allegorical and farcical features left the audience cold, though it is of interest to-day for its sketches of various contemporary social types, including the cashiered soldier and the professional beggar. Ten days afterwards another English show, *The Seven Days of the Week*, was staged at the President of St. John's Lodging. Each of the days appears in turn and describes itself in amusing rhymes. The show was so much liked that it was repeated a week later by request before the Vice-Chancellor. Afterwards Latin again took the place of English in a much applauded comedy, *Philomathes*, partly after the manner of Plautus.

On Shrove Tuesday the Prince in another Latin device, *Ira Fortunae*, again visited the temple of Fortune. The capricious goddess had grown angry with him, and unable to appease her, he discards the emblems of his sovereignty and his reign thus comes to an end. But as the stage was still standing, and as an English tragedy on Periander, the tyrant of Corinth, had been prepared, it was arranged to perform it on the following Sunday. Such crowds flocked to hear it that they could not get into the college hall, and the result was a riot in which stones were thrown and windows broken, and the St. John's officials had to come out with drawn swords and arrest the ringleaders. It was an inappropriate ending to several months of merry-making

under a Christmas Prince, which did not produce any play
of first-rate quality, but the record of which is of the highest
value for the intimate insight that it gives into the methods
of the academic stage.

Some two years before its Christmas Prince festivities
John's had been the first college to greet in dramatic fashion
the reigning sovereign. On 27 August 1605 King James with
his Queen and Prince Henry began a visit to Oxford. Outside St. John's he was met by three young scholars dressed
as nymphs who announced in Latin verse written by one of
the Fellows, Matthew Gwinne, that they were the sybils who
foretold to Banquo that his descendants would bear rule, and
that they had come again to prophesy that his stock would
be perpetual on the British throne. They then saluted the
king, queen, and prince in turn with a triple *salve*. Even if
it is nothing more, it is a striking coincidence that this
academic 'conceit' 'should have been followed in about a year
by the vision of Banquo's descendants with which the three
witches horrify *Macbeth*.

Lavish preparations had been made for the entertainment
of the royal visitors, but the results at first were disappoint-
ing. The Latin plays performed on the first three nights
were all unsuccessful. On the first night James was with
difficulty persuaded from leaving in the middle of the performance. On the second he openly expressed his dislike of
the production. On the third he fell asleep while the play
was being acted. But fortunately the balance was redressed
on the fourth and last night by the resounding triumph of
Samuel Daniel's English pastoral, *The Queen's Arcadia*. It
owed a debt to Italian pastoral drama in general and especially to Tasso's *Aminta*, but the plot is developed on original
lines. Two ancient Arcadians, Meliboeus and Ergastus, are
sorely disturbed by a change that they perceive in their
country, which has lost its plain honesty and simple innocence and has become like unto ruder lands. They determine
to find out the source of the contagion and remain in the

background throughout the action, commenting as a chorus at the end of each act. The first two troublers of Arcadian peace appear in the persons of Colax, 'a corrupted traveller', and Techne, a subtle wench of Corinth. Their design is to spread dissension and jealousy among the amorous Arcadian swains and maids. As they listen to the debate between Amyntas and Corinus, rivals for the love of Cloris, Colax declares that he will forestall them both, though this will mean his forsaking Dorinda. In a passage characteristic of Daniel's sweet and limpid verse he makes his defence:

> I have heard abroad, where best experience
> And wit is learned, that all the fairest choice
> Of women in the world serve but to make
> One perfect Beauty, whereof each brings part.
> One hath a pleasing smile, and nothing else:
> Another but some silly mole to grace
> Th' air of a disproportioned face;
> Another pleases not but when she speaks,
> And some in silence only graceful are. . .
> So that we see how Beauty doth consist
> Of divers powers, and yet all attract;
> And therefore unto all my love aspires:
> As beauty varies, so doth my desires.

Through Techne's machinations Cloris is decoyed into a cave where Colax attempts in vain to win her forcibly, and Amyntas seeing her rush from the cave followed by Colax is persuaded that she has given herself to him and in despair flies to a desert spot and takes poison. But Techne herself has become enamoured of Amyntas, and to save his life entreats Cloris to come to his aid. As he regains his senses under her touch he fixes his gaze upon her.

> That look did read t' her new conceiving heart
> All the whole tragic lecture of his love,
> And his sad sufferings, all his griefs and fear,
> And now in th' end what he had done for her,
> And with that powerful force of moving too
> As all the world of words could never do.
> Ah! what a silly messenger is speech

> To be employ'd in that great embassy
> Of our affection, in respect of th' eye:
> Ah! 't is the silent rhetoric of a look
> That works the league betwixt the states of heaven.

Here as often in this pastoral the movement of the verse is lyrical rather than dramatic, but it proves how truly the epithet 'well-languaged' fits Daniel.

Other pairs of Arcadian lovers are deceived and separated for a time by the wiles of Colax, though they do not come so near to tragedy as Amyntas. There are also mischief-makers of another type in Arcadia. Lincus is a pettifogger who poses as a great man of law and is nonplussed by a social order where things are held in common. He aims at dissolving the frame of this strange-built State

> by drawing them
> To apprehend of these proprieties
> Of *mine* and *thine*.

Alcon, a quack doctor, is in happier case, for he finds that the Arcadian maidens will be sick for company.

> I have now seventy patients at this time,
> That know not what they ail, no more do I.

He gives them a drug which

> Doth neither good nor hurt, but that's all one;
> For if they but conceive it doth, it doth,
> And it is that physicians hold the chief
> In all their cures, *conceit and strong belief*.

He has also another specific, a herb from the island of Nicosia brought by a seaman:

> And this in powder made, and fired, he sucks
> Out of a little hollow instrument
> Of calcinated clay, the smoke thereof:
> Which either he conveys out of his nose
> Or down into his stomach with a whiff.
> And this, he said, a wondrous virtue had
> To purge the head and cure the great catarrh.

This testimony by a charlatan to the medicinal powers of

tobacco was of course intended to tickle the ears of James, who had published a 'counterblast' against the weed. The two impostors flourish for a time, but in the end, together with Colax and Techne, they are banished from Arcadia by Meliboeus and Ergastus, who have overheard all their machinations, and who now proclaim a restoration of the former state of innocence:

> Let us all
> Exile with them their ill example too. . .
> And be again Arcadians as before
> In manners and in habits as we were.

Ten years later, on 7 March 1615, James, accompanied by Prince Charles, visited Cambridge, where he was entertained at Trinity College. On the first night a Latin comedy, written by a member of St. John's, was not much to his taste. But on the following evening another Latin comedy, *Ignoramus*, proved to be one of the high lights of academic drama. It was from the pen of George Ruggle, a Fellow of Clare Hall, who had been a scholar of Trinity. It was based upon an Italian comedy *Trappolaria*, by G. della Porta, but the central figure who gives his name to the play was transformed from a soldier into a lawyer. It was a period of sharp hostility in Cambridge between town and gown, and the attack on the privileges of the scholars had been led by the deputy-recorder, Francis Brackyn. He had already been satirised in the St. John's play, *Part II of the Return from Parnassus* (1602), and now Ruggle pilloried him still more derisively under the figure of Ignoramus. As a common lawyer he was anathema to the academic jurists who were upholders of the civil law which favoured the royal prerogative. They therefore scoffed when Ignoramus on the Trinity stage spouted common-law technicalities while the scholars made mock of his barbarous Latinity. In the course of the action he suffers a series of humiliations. He is outwitted by a rival for the hand of a girl with whom he falls in love and is tricked instead into the arms of an elderly virago. His unintelligible outcries when she attacks him give the impression that he is bewitched and he is subjected to exorcism as a cure for his possession.

The King was so fascinated by this brilliant burlesque that he revisited Cambridge in the following May to see it a second time. Nor did it have merely a short-lived triumph. Two editions were published in 1630, and by 1737 they had increased to nine. In 1787 these were supplemented by an edition with notes and glossary by Sir John Hawkins. In 1763 an abbreviated version was acted at Merchant Taylors' School, and in 1794 it was performed at Westminster School with an English prologue and epilogue. In 1662 an English translation by R. Codrington had been published, and in 1678 a version by E. Ravenscroft, *The English Lawyer*, was acted at the Theatre Royal, Drury Lane.

The first-night of *Ignoramus* on the Trinity stage was succeeded on the next evening, 9 March, by an adaptation of another of della Porta's plays, *L'Astrologo*. This English comedy, *Albumazar*, was from the pen of Thomas Tomkins of Trinity, who had already written the successful allegorical play, *Lingua*, of uncertain date, first published in 1607. Albumazar is an astrologer who by his mischievous and fraudulent arts brings about a tangle of amusing complications. The play, though it did not win the same royal favour as *Ignoramus*, had a share of its later popularity. Four editions appeared between 1615 and 1634, and a fifth in 1668, with a prologue by Dryden for its production at the Duke of York's theatre. In the next century it was revived by Garrick on 3 October 1747.

Albumazar was followed on 10 March by a Latin pastoral. It was hoped that James would remain to see on the next evening a specimen of a more unusual dramatic type, the piscatory or fisher-play, *Sicelides*, by John Fletcher's cousin, Phineas. The impatient King, however, had hurried off, and *Sicelides* was not performed till some days later. It has a measure of poetic charm, but its unduly intricate plot and its weak characterization showed that Phineas did not share his cousin's dramatic power.

James visited Cambridge for a third time in March 1622 /3, but on this occasion no new plays were produced, though the performance of John Hacket's *Loida* on the Trinity stage on 28 February 1622 /3 may have been intended as a rehearsal of its presentation before the King on 12 March. This clever Latin comedy was a two-handed engine striking impartially at the Jesuits in the person of the title-part, and at the Calvinists through Martinus, a canting elder of Amsterdam. Such a salty piece was better calculated to appeal to James than the popular but more conventionally romantic Latin comedy, *Labyrinthus*, adapted by William Hawkesworth from della Porta's *Cintia*, and originally acted at Trinity in 1602, which was now revived in his honour.

Ten years later, in March 1631 /2, Cambridge welcomed King Charles and Henrietta Maria. They were without the pedantic learning of James and it is significant that the plays provided for their entertainment were not in Latin but in English. And they were influenced by the fantastic 'Platonic' idealism which Henrietta Maria had fostered in Court circles. In *The Rival Friends*, written by Peter Hausted, a Fellow of Queen's, and acted on 19 March at Trinity, two friends in love with the same girl prove themselves ready to surrender their claims in favour of each other. The result of their self-abnegation is that the lady finally gives herself to a third wooer. Incongruously combined with this romantic complication is a realistic sub-plot attacking the abuses of simony and introducing some figures from rustic life. These appear to have been considered too low for so august an occasion by many of the spectators. When Hausted soon afterwards appealed to a wider circle by publishing the play, he spoke of it as 'cried down by boys, faction, envy and confident ignorance, approved by the judicious, and now exposed to the public censure [judgement] by the author'.

No such appeal was needed on behalf of the second English

play presented at Trinity during this royal visit. Thomas
Randolph had already won his spurs as an academic dramatist with two short productions, *Aristippus, or The Jovial
Philosopher* and *The Conceited Pedlar*, published together in
1630. He now achieved a resounding success with his final
full-length play, *The Jealous Lovers*, where 'jealous' has its
earlier meaning of 'suspicious'. As in *The Rival Friends*,
though after a different fashion, the plot is spun out of
emotional extravagance. Without cause Tyndarus doubts the
constancy of his beloved Evadne, and similarly the maiden,
Techmessa, mistrusts her adoring Pamphilus. The jealous
lovers have recourse to the fantastic expedient of a mock
funeral to see whether death will shake the loyalty of the
suspected pair. They pass this acid test. But jealousy has
now to pay a surprising penalty. Hymen appears to forbid
the banns of what would be incestuous unions, for Tyndarus
is found to be the brother of Evadne and Techmessa the
sister of Pamphilus. It is the antithetical and more un-
wholesome solution of the matrimonial problem of Beaumont
and Fletcher's *A King and No King*.

Since the visit of James to Oxford in 1605 Cambridge had
had the monopoly of the royal presence at its entertainments.
But in August 1636, for the last time before the Civil War,
Charles with his queen and his two nephews went on a
progress to Oxford and made his headquarters at Christ
Church. On 29 August *The Floating Island*, by William
Strode, the public orator, was performed. If Phineas Fletcher
had failed to make much dramatic mark with his *Sicelides*
at Cambridge in 1615, he can almost certainly claim to have
helped to inspire Strode's successful Oxford play with his
allegorical poem, *The Purple Island, or The Isle of Man*,
published in 1633. For the island as conceived by Strode is
the mind of man afloat on the sea of the passions. These
form a conspiracy against their king, Prudentius, who
resigns the throne, which is occupied by Fancy as queen.
She gives a free vein to all to act according to their humours

and such confusion results that Prudentius is entreated to resume his crown. This portrayal of an unsuccessful rebellion, even if only in the psychological realm, was quite to the taste of the Stuart king. On the following afternoon one of the chief pillars of his government, Archbishop Laud, as Chancellor of the University, entertained him at his own college, St. John's, where an amusing comedy, *Love's Hospital*, by George Wilde, one of the Fellows, was performed. It was never published, but has been preserved, with an earlier St. John's play by Wilde, and a pastoral, perhaps his, in manuscript form.

On the same evening at Christ Church the entertainment of the royalties closed with the notable performance of *The Royal Slave*, by William Cartwright, one of the University proctors, who enjoyed an exceptional degree of academic reputation and influence. Both the subject and the treatment were worthy of the occasion, which was to mark the end of Oxford college performances on the grand scale. The scene is laid in Sardis. Cratander, a slave of Ephesus, captured by the Persian king, Arsamnes, is, according to a traditional custom, invested with the prerogatives of majesty for three days before being doomed to execution. He confronts his victor after the high Stoic fashion, reading

> A discourse o' th' nature of the soul,
> That shows the vicious slaves, but th' well-inclined
> Free and their own though conquer'd.
Ars.   Thou dost speak
> As if thou wert victorious, not Arsamnes.
Crat. I not deny your conquest, for you may
> Have virtues to intitle 't yours; but otherwise,
> If one of strange and ill-contriv'd desires,
> One of a narrow or intermperate mind,
> Prove master of the field, I cannot say
> That he hath conquer'd.

In this lofty spirit he bears himself throughout his period of sovereignty. He spurns the sensuous pleasures with which he is tempted. He rejects a proposal from two of his dis-

guised countrymen to betray the Persians into their hands
and to come home as king where he had been a slave. The
queen, Atossa, is so impressed by his nobility that she throws
down to him a chain of gold, but he realizes that her feeling
for him is supersensual, belonging to

> The pure, clearer flames that shoot up always
> In one continued pyramid of lustre,
> Know no commerce with earth, but unmixt still,
> And still aspiring upwards (if that may
> Be called aspiring which is nature) have
> This property of immortality,
> Still to suffice themselves, neither devouring,
> And yet devour'd; and such I knowledge yours,
> On which I look as on refin'd ideas
> That know no mixture or corruption.
> Being one eternal simpleness.

Henrietta Maria must have been pleased to hear from the
Christ Church stage this echo of the Platonic love doctrine
that she had been spreading in Court circles. Atossa pleads
to Arsamnes for Cratander's life, and he grants her prayer.
But the Persian priest demands the promised sacrifice and
Arsamnes yields with the cry,

> I know
> Thy virtue's such that thou had'st rather suffer
> Thyself than heaven should be violated.

But as the king prepares to give the fatal stroke, the sun
is eclipsed and rain dashes out the altar fire. It is a sign that
heaven would have Cratander spared, and Arsamnes declares
that

> in a just reward I must
> Myself conduct thee into Greece and there
> Continue thee a king; that what was meant
> For sport and mirth may prove a serious honour,
> And thy three days pass o'er into a long
> And happy government.

These were ironical last words to fall on the ears of a king
who was to return next to Oxford as a city of refuge in the
heat of a civil war. But at the time *The Royal Slave* ended

with loud acclaim, and after the departure of the royalties was performed again before members of the University.

The success of the play was due not only to the author and actors, but to Inigo Jones, who devised the scenery and settings, and to Henry Lawes, who composed the music. It so captivated the queen that she borrowed from Christ Church the costumes which had been used there for a repetition of the play at Hampton Court, where it was acted by the King's company on 12 January 1636/7. No less than £224 was spent on this elaborate performance, including £40 to Cartwright who was present and £30 to the company. Yet, if Anthony Wood is to be believed, 'by all men's confession the players came short of the University actors'. It is remarkable that just near its close the academic stage should have received so flattering a tribute.

XVII

THE DROLLS—SIR WILLIAM DAVENANT

O N 2 September 1642 the following ordinance was passed by Parliament:

Whereas public sports do not well agree with public calamities, nor public stage-plays with the seasons of humiliation. . . . It is therefore thought fit and ordained by the Lords and Commons in this Parliament assembled that while these sad causes and set times of humiliation continue, public stage-plays shall cease, and be forborne.

The chief theatres were in turn pulled down, and many of the actors enlisted in the army, the majority on the king's side, but a few, strangely enough, in the Parliamentary forces. Nevertheless, as recent research has shown, the suppression of stage performances was less complete than has often been assumed, though the names of the plays acted are not usually recorded. We learn from a contemporary account that as the players at the Fortune persevered 'in their forbidden art', on 2 October 1643 'there was set a strong guard of pikes and muskets on both gates of the play-house, and in the middle of their play they unexpectedly did press into the stage upon them'. Thus 'the actors' comedy was turned into a tragedy, their richest clothes were taken from them and they were left nothing but their necessities now to act and learn a better life'.

As in happier days the sovereigns during their progresses had entertainments for their pleasure, so now the royalties in their exile from the capital continued them as a consolation. In January 1646 a play was acted at Oxford before King Charles, 'to keep up his spirit instead of good successes from his soldiery'. In Paris Prince Charles maintained for some time a company of actors for whose plays the Marquis of

Newcastle wrote prologues and epilogues. But in November
1646 the company had to be dissolved for want of pay, and
owing to the audience being so poor and few.

Throughout the struggle the actors looked forward to a
return to their old life. Of the King's men it was reported
in August 1645, 'when the stage at Westminster where the
two Houses now act is once more restored back again to
Blackfriars, they have hope they shall return to their old
harmless profession of killing men in tragedies without man-
slaughter'. After the Royalist defeat at Naseby they threw
themselves upon the mercy of Parliament.

In 1647, in defiance of the 1642 ordinance, performances
were resumed at Salisbury Court, the Cockpit, and the
Fortune. At the first named house a revival of *A King and
No King* was announced for 5 October, but the City of
London sheriffs prevented the performance, and the large
audience, including some young lords and other eminent
persons, were left crying out for the return of their money.
The King's men began to repair the Blackfriars for a reopen-
ing. As a check to these renewed theatrical activities,
Parliament enacted on 22 October that all common players
found acting should be imprisoned and proceeded against at
the next Sessions of the Peace as 'Rogues'. A still more severe
ordinance on 9 February 1648, in addition to the above,
empowered the Lord Mayor and Sheriffs to pull down all
stage-galleries, seats, and boxes, and not only to confiscate
the money paid by spectators but to fine them as well. Yet
in spite of these legal terrors acting continued. A contemporary account proves that on New Year's Day 1649 performances were taking place at three theatres, in addition
to rope-dancing at the Fortune, and were suppressed by
force. At the Cockpit the actors resisted the raiding soldiers,
and were accordingly imprisoned for two days and then
released on bail to appear before the Lord Mayor. At
Salisbury Court the soldiers arrived when the play was almost
ended, and carried the actors to Whitehall, where, as they

had submitted quietly, they were allowed to retain their costumes. The players at the Red Bull got wind of the raid and escaped in time with 'all their acting clothes'. They had even better luck later in the year, when Salisbury Court, the Cockpit, and the Fortune were dismantled by order of Parliament, but their own house was spared. For a time it attracted a more select audience than in the days of its popular vogue. But on it too the blow fell on 22 January 1649, when 'the State Janizaries' invaded the theatre, imprisoned the players and 'listed all the Lords, Ladies and Gentlewomen' present for penalties.

Nevertheless, even during the Commonwealth performances continued at this theatre. On 30 December 1654, when they were about to act Fletcher's *Wit Without Money*, the soldiers swooped down upon them and despoiled them of their costumes, though on this occasion they 'carried themselves very civilly towards the audience'. In a later raid on 14 September 1655 the spectators fared worse for each of them had to pay five shillings or leave some article of clothing behind as a gage.

The mention of *Wit Without Money* shows that full-length plays were at times revived. But it was easier to stage selected scenes from them under altered titles. According to Francis Kirkman, who published twenty-seven of them in a collection called *The Wits*, the chief contriver of these 'drolls' was Robert Cox, who also played the principal parts in them. Their popularity was immense.

These being all that was permitted us, great was the compliance of the auditors; and these small things were as profitable and as great get-pennies to the actors as any of our late famed plays. I have seen the Red-Bull playhouse, which was a large one, so full that as many went back for want of room as had entered.

Yet even the drolls were not always permitted. It had been announced that on 9 June 1653 there would be an entertainment at the Red Bull, where after rope-dancing and

a new country dance 'there will also appear a merry conceited fellow which hath formerly given content'. This was
Robert Cox, who was to act a droll of his own devising, *John
Swabber*. But though the audience had been assured, 'you
may come and return with safety', two jealous actors gave
information to the soldiers who broke up the performance,
and made each of the spectators pay five shillings 'for their
coming out as well as for their going in'. Another droll of
Cox's own invention was *Humours of Simpleton the Smith*.
But for the most part these pieces were brief comic adapta-
tions from favourite plays. The earliest was *The Merry Conceits of Bottom the Weaver*, and other borrowings from
Shakespeare included *The Grave Diggers' Colloquy* from
Hamlet and *The Buckbasket Mishap* from *The Merry Wives*.
An even more popular source was provided by Beaumont
and Fletcher, who supplied fourteen of the twenty-seven
adaptations in *The Wits*, including *The Encounter* from *The
Knight of the Burning Pestle*, *The Testy Lord* from *The Maid's
Tragedy*, and *The Club-man* from *Philaster*.

SIR WILLIAM DAVENANT

It was not, however, through the drolls but by a bolder
and more original venture that the way was to be opened
for the full revival of drama after 1660. The man who has
to be given the credit of this achievement, Sir William
Davenant, is a remarkable link between the Elizabethan and
the Restoration stage. He was the fourth son of John
Davenant, vintner, of Oxford, and was christened on
3 March 1605/6 at St. Martin's Church, with William Shakespeare, a frequent guest of the tavern household when
travelling between London and Stratford, standing (if tradition can be trusted) as godfather to the boy who was given
his Christian name. John Davenant, after rising to be mayor
of Oxford, died in April 1622, when William was sixteen
years old, and the enterprising youth, instead of remaining

at home to enter the University, set out at once for London, where he became a page in the household of the Duchess of Richmond. Thence he passed into the service of a survivor of the great Elizabethan age, Fulke Greville, Lord Brooke, the friend of Sir Philip Sidney, whose poems and neo-classical dramas must have been of lively interest to his young retainer. They probably helped to stimulate his own first dramatic efforts, but Brooke's death on 30 September 1628 threw Davenant again upon his own resources, complicated by an improvident first marriage in or before 1624, and the birth of a son. Yet he found himself able to enter the Middle Temple, where he shared quarters for a time with Edward Hyde, the future Lord Chancellor Clarendon. A slightly later and closer aristocratic connexion was with the influential courtier, Endymion Porter, who stood his good friend through the serious troubles of which the story has recently been reconstructed from legal documents.[1]

In February 1633, in a quarrel at Braintree in Essex, Davenant killed a tavern servant, Thomas Warren, and fled for refuge overseas, probably to Holland. A warrant of transportation to America and confiscation of goods was issued against him, but a petition by his wife to the King procured a suspension of the sentence. Though a pardon was not granted till 1638 Davenant was able to return to London and resume his dramatic activities, and in 1634 he received a signal mark of royal favour by being chosen to provide the libretto for the masque, *Temple of Love*, dealing with the subject of Platonic love, which the Queen herself had chosen and in which she personally appeared at Shrovetide 1634/5. Even more decisive recognition by King Charles followed in 1638, when at last Davenant was granted a formal pardon for his 1633 homicide and was appointed Poet Laureate in succession to Ben Jonson.

In the years that followed, however, neither the muse nor the theatre could claim him chiefly. During the two 'Bishops'

[1] See Arthur H. Nethercot, *Sir William D'Avenant* (1938), pp. 101–7.

Wars' against the Scots in 1640 he held a post as paymaster
in the ordnance department. In May 1641 he was arrested
for complicity in a royalist plot to attempt the rescue of
Strafford from the Tower and to bring over French forces
for the King's support. Parliament treated him leniently,
but he found it advisable in 1642 to depart for the Continent.
There Henrietta Maria found him a helpful agent, and he
was employed as an intermediary between her and the
royalist commander, the Earl of Newcastle, under whom he
was advanced to the rank of lieutenant-general. For his
services during the siege of Gloucester he was knighted in
1643, and thereafter was busily employed in the Royalist
cause in Holland and France and as a privateer on the seas.
In October 1646 he was an emissary from the Queen in Paris
to her husband at Newcastle in an unsuccessful attempt to
induce him to end the Civil War by taking the Covenant.
After the King had paid the final penalty for his loyalty to
the Anglican Church on 30 January 1649, Prince Charles in
Jersey had himself proclaimed as successor to the throne and
began to bestow offices upon his adherents. Amongst them
Davenant was appointed Lieutenant-Governor of the 'planta-
tion' of Maryland, and set sail for the New World, but was
intercepted by a privateer, Captain Green, who delivered
him into the hands of the Parliament. He was confined first
in Cowes Castle and afterwards in the Tower as 'an active
enemy of the Commonwealth'. But again he got off comparatively lightly. On 7 October 1651 he was granted 'the
liberty of the Tower' which enabled him to move about
London, on bail. As he was now a widower he took advantage
of his conditional freedom to marry the twice-widowed Lady
Cademan, who brought to her impoverished third husband
some fortune and four stepsons, but who died in March
1654/5, seven months after Davenant had obtained a full
pardon from Cromwell, as previously from King Charles, and
had his discharge from the Tower. He soon afterwards
crossed again to France and took as his third bride a wealthy

widow whom he had met there in earlier days. She was to survive him for many years and was to help him in carrying out projects that he had long entertained.

For the many vicissitudes of Davenant's career throw into stronger relief what was its dominating purpose—to achieve success in the theatrical field. To this were subordinated not only his varied practical activities, but his literary ambitions, of which the chief fruit was his Lombard epic, *Gondibert*, published in two editions, quarto and octavo, in 1651. His dramatic output falls into two periods separated by an interval of about sixteen years. The earlier period, though the longer and more fertile, is the less important historically, for the plays belonging to it, though they have notable merits, especially the comedies, are for the most part derivative and traditional in type. *The Tragedy of Albovine, King of the Lombards*, apparently not acted but printed in 1629; *The Cruel Brother*, acted at the Blackfriars, and printed in 1630, belong to the blood and lust school. *The Just Italian*, acted at Blackfriars in 1629, and printed in 1630, is a tragi-comedy showing the influence of Fletcher and Jonson.

In the comedies that followed Davenant struck a more original note. The earliest of them, *The Wits*, made a troubled entry in January 1633/4. The Master of the Revels dealt with it severely, and King Charles had to intervene. As Herbert relates, the King 'went over all that I had crossed in Davenant's play-book, and allowing of *faith* and *slight* to be asseverations only, and no oaths, marked them to stand, and some few other things, but in the greater part allowed of my reformations'. When the 'reformed' play appeared on the Blackfriars stage it had a hostile reception from a 'cruel faction'; but at a Court performance before the King and Queen on 28 January it was 'well liked', and after the Restoration it was remarkably popular.

The Wits of the title are the two country gentlemen, the elder Pallatine and Sir Morglay Thwack, who, though they are rich and beyond middle age, set out to conquer the town and the favours of its ladies merely by the exercise of their wits. But they find themselves outmatched by Pallatine's younger, impecunious brother and his lady-love, Lucy, allied with Lady Ample, the rich ward of the miserly Sir Tyrant Thrift. They go through humiliating and unsavoury experiences, especially the elder Pallatine, who is trapped into a house of ill-fame, bundled into a chest which is lowered into a crypt, and arrested for sacrilege by the constable and the watch. In the end he makes open confession of his follies and is rewarded, somewhat too easily, by the hand of Lady Ample, who tricks him into a settlement on his brother which, with her own bounty to Lucy, enables them to marry. The plot is somewhat too long spun out, and there are echoes of *The Merry Wives* and *Much Ado*. But the dialogue is brisk and entertaining and enriched, even overloaded, with detail from Davenant's close observation of both town and country life.

Later in 1634 Davenant returned to tragi-comedy in *Love and Honour*, acted in November at Blackfriars. Alvaro, Prince of Savoy, takes prisoner during a war Evandra, daughter of the Duke of Milan, and conceals her from his father, the Duke of Savoy, who because of a blood-feud is determined to execute her. Alvaro has fallen in love with his captive but finds rivals in his friend Prospero and in Leonell, who is later revealed as the Prince of Parma. Each of the three lovers seeks to become a sacrifice for Evandra, who is resolved to suffer herself while Melora, sister of Leonell, tries to avert this by impersonating her and becoming the victim. But a tragic close is averted by the discovery that the blood-feud arose from an error. Evandra is united to Leonell and Alvaro pairs off with Melora. The success of the play, which was more immediate than that of *The Wits*, was due to its ingenious handling of the two themes of its title in the exaggerated vein which anticipated Restoration heroic tragedy. Yet in his next play Davenant, returning to satirical comedy, dealt effective blows at a kindred affectation of Stuart society.

The Platonic Lovers, licensed in November 1635, acted at Blackfriars and printed in 1636, turns to ridicule the fantastic theory of sexual relations which, as has been seen, had been made fashionable in Court circles, and of which there are many echoes in Caroline drama. A Sicilian duke, Theander, and his 'mistress' Eurithea are

> lovers of a pure
> Celestial kind, such as some style Platonical;
> A new Court epithet scarce understood;
> But all they woo, sir, is the spirit, face,
> And heart.

Contrasted with them are Duke Phylomont, Eurithea's brother and his 'mistress' Ariola, who are eager for the 'natural ends' of matrimony, but who are thwarted by the refusal of Theander, Ariola's brother, to give his consent to a union of bodies as well as of souls. A change is wrought in Theander by the philtres of Buonateste, a physician and sceptical philosopher, who is the most attractive figure in the play. He protests against the calumny on his 'good old friend Plato':

> They father on him a fantastic love
> He never knew, poor gentleman.

When asked, 'But did not Plato write of love?' he answers with deeper truth than probably Davenant realized:

> Divinely, sir, but not such kind of love
> As ladies would have now: they mistake him.

Another cure effected by Buonateste is on the young soldier, Gridonell, whose father has directed

> That he should never learn to write nor read,
> Nor never see a woman.

The plot is complicated by various intrigues and frustrations, even Ariola becoming temporarily converted by her brother's 'holy lectures', and asking her bewildered wooer,

> What need we marry? . . . Is it not better to live thus,
> In a perfection that we know than to attempt
> New joys, which our unskilfulness should make
> Us doubt? This is the angels' life.

In the end natural matrimonial love in all cases triumphs over perverted Platonism and, in spite of some almost inevitable pruriency in the treatment of such a theme, Davenant's comedy brings fresh air into a dangerously overheated atmosphere.

Fresh air, in a more literal sense, blows through another comedy licensed at almost the same time as *The Platonic Lovers*, but acted at the Globe, *News from Plymouth*. It is one of the few plays of the period set in a seaside town and with sailors among the chief characters. The three naval captains with the descriptive names, Seawit, Topsail, and Cable, are on a similar quest to the country gentlemen in *The Wits*. But unlike them they are financially on the rocks and they find cold comfort in Plymouth. As Cable moans,

> They would make us pay
> For day-light, if they knew how to measure
> The sunbeams by the yard . . .
> If you walk but three turns
> In the High-street, they will ask you money
> For wearing out the pebbles.

They see an opportunity of mending their fortunes by paying court to the wealthy widow Carrack—another significant name—and her two guests, Lady Loveright, possessor of £4,000 a year, and the lady's cousin, Mistress Jointure, also well endowed. Lady Loveright is the ward of her uncle, Sir Solemn Trifle, a Jonsonian figure whose 'humour' is for endless, interrupting talk, so that his niece cries, 'The perpetual motion is in his tongue, I think'. He has a counterpart in Seawit's 'charge', Sir Furious Inland,

> a gentleman
> Of fair descent and ample means, but subject
> To their disease of quarrelling,

especially as a 'ready champion' of ladies. When Cable and

Topsail quarrel about the favours of Lady Loveright he offers himself as second to both the duellists. But the Lady has in the background another suitor, Sir Studious Warwell, learned, brave, rich, whom in a spirit of whimsical idealism she is subjecting to cruel tests. At her command, his money has vanished, and he has sold his books:

> To serve you shall be
> My only study. If you search my pockets
> And find the *Tale of Troy*, or an Almanack there,
> Or William Wisdom's metres, yet renounce me.

He now promises to sell or pledge his lands to pious uses, but she declares that the 'rest is nothing', unless he can prove himself a perfect soldier, after a type 'writ with my father's hand'. It is the last straw, however, when he overhears her take Mistress Jointure to task for beguiling Seawit to an assignation, 'although belov'd of me, and first my choice'. He challenges the captain to a duel, which is averted by the arrival on the field of the other characters and by Lady Loveright's confession that she had come to Plymouth to meet Warwell, and her promise to cast by her imperious humours and embrace him as a husband. This abrupt change of attitude, preceded by her ambiguous claim upon Seawit's affections, is the least satisfactory feature in this otherwise well-contrived and lively comedy which is rounded off by the prospect of lawful unions between Seawit and Jointure and Cable and Carrack, and by the penalties on Sir Solemn for spreading news of his own invention, while Sir Furious is promised that he shall kill the king's enemies by dozens.

After an interval of two years, during which the theatres were usually closed owing to the plague, Davenant in April 1638 produced *The Unfortunate Lovers* at the Blackfriars. Though it gained the royal favour and was frequently revived after the Restoration, the play of which the scene is laid in Verona, was mainly a variation on the blood and lust theme with some features of the 'love and honour' type. He was

more happily inspired in the tragi-comedy, *The Fair Favourite*
licensed later in the same year, in November, when he
returned, in a romantic not a satirical vein, to the theme of
The Platonic Lovers. The title-part is that of Eumena,
Platonic favourite of a king, whose equivocal position
arouses suspicions and conflicts which come within an ace
of tragedy for her brother and his dearest frined. The king
himself tempts Eumena to become his paramour, but she is
steadfast to her idealistic creed, and sends him back at last
into the arms of his faithful queen. A year later, in November 1639, Davenant closed the decade of his pre-Civil War
dramatic activity with *The Distresses*, a romantic and over-
complicated comedy of which the scene is laid in Cordova,
and which shows, not happily, the influence of the Spanish
theatre.

It was not till the spring of 1656, or somewhat earlier, that
Davenant was able, 'wearing his rue with a difference', to
resume work for the stage. Protected by his friendship with
the two highly placed Puritans, John Thurloe and Bulstrode
Whitelocke, he set himself to give a systematic revival, under
an ingenious camouflage, of those theatrical activities which
since September 1642 had been, though never entirely dis-
continued, sporadic and furtive. The evidence of a ballad
printed in April 1656, *How Daphne Pays His Debts*, whose
importance has been recently recognized,[1] shows that he had
before that date four 'houses' in which he was giving entertainments with players, and 'clothes to make them trim'.
They were Apothecaries' Hall, Gibbons's Tennis-Court in
Lincoln's Inn Fields, the Phoenix in Drury Lane, and 'St.
John's', probably Rutland House, near the dissolved priory
of St. John in Clerkenwell, which he had recently taken as
his private residence. An ambitious scheme to found a new
theatre in Clerkenwell, in which he got several rich venturers
to invest considerable sums, came to nothing, and led later
to proceedings at law.

[1] See Leslie Hotson, *The Commonwealth and Restoration Stage* (1928),
pp. 141–8.

But Davenant was not to be baffled. On 23 May 1656 in his own mansion he produced *The First Day's Entertainment at Rutland House*, which was described in preliminary bills as 'The Entertainment by Music and Declamations after the manner of the Ancients'. Though a charge of five shillings a head was made, Davenant adroitly avoided any reference to a 'theatre' or a 'play'. The prologue speaks of 'our cupboard scene', and of the auditorium as

> the narrow way
> To our Elysian field, the opera.

A contemporary reporter of the performance also calls it Davenant's 'opera', and under this disguise for the first time since the closing of the theatres a stage-show was presented without fear of its being forcibly broken up. It is significant that, according to the reporter, the piece ended with songs in honour of 'the Victor' (the Protector Cromwell), though they were omitted from the printed version. The composers of the music which preceded each of the 'declamations' were Henry Lawes and Charles Coleman.

The piece is entirely devoid of action, and is written, except for the songs, in prose. Its first part is a debate between the cynic Diogenes and the poet Aristophanes 'against, and for, public entertainment by moral representations'. It is a spirited argument in which the cynic voices the Puritan view while the Athenian poet-playwright speaks the convictions of Davenant himself. The second part shifts to an entirely different theme, a discussion between a Parisian and a Londoner on the claims to superiority of their two capitals. To the Frenchman Paris is 'the school of Europe', and though he calls London a 'noble city', he dilates upon all the weaker features in its buildings and streets and in the demeanour of its inhabitants. The Londoner retorts in kind, and both speeches show that Davenant retained his power of close observation of detail which had enriched his comedies. It is to be hoped that, in spite of the high price of admission, it ran for the ten days which, according to the reporter,

Davenant anticipated. In any case, it found sufficient favour to be published by Herringham in the following year, 1657.

The First Entertaiment was the prelude to a greater undertaking, *The Siege of Rhodes*, of which, as is known from a letter of Davenant to Whitelocke, dated September 3, he had the text printed before its production in the autumn of 1656. In an address 'to the reader of this first edition' Davenant made an elaborate apology for the limitations forced upon him by the confined space available in Rutland House:

It has been often wished that our Scenes . . . had not been confined to eleven foot in height, and about fifteen in depth, including the places of passage reserved for the Music. This is so narrow an allowance for the fleet of Solyman the Magnificent, his army, the island of Rhodes, and the varieties attending the siege of the city, that I fear you will think we invite you to such a contracted trifle as that of the Caesars carved upon a nut.

As these limits have hindered the splendour of the scene, so we are like to give no great satisfaction in the quantity of our argument, which is in story very copious, but shrinks to a small narrative here, because we could not convey it by more than seven persons; being constrained to prevent the length of *recitative* music, as well as to conserve, without encumbrance, the narrowness of the place.

On the other hand he claimed that the scenes had the advantage of the art and industry of John Webb, son-in-law and pupil of Inigo Jones, six of whose designs for *The Siege of Rhodes* have been discovered at Chatsworth; and that the music had been composed by 'the most transcendent of England' in that art, including Henry Lawes. Another attraction, though he does not specify this, was the novelty of a woman, Mrs. Coleman, taking the part of the heroine.

With these features the success of the opera was assured. But it is largely due to Dryden that it has till recently unduly displaced Davenant's earlier work for the stage in an estimate of his dramatic powers. In his *Essay of Heroic Plays* (1670) Dryden declared that the 'first light we had of them was from Davenant in *The Siege of Rhodes*, and in his dedication to *The Rival Ladies* (1664) claimed that the 'noblest use' of rhymed verse was made by Davenant, 'who at once brought it upon the stage, and made it perfect in *The Siege of Rhodes*'. Such panegyrics made more impression than the qualifying criticism that 'these wanted the fulness of a plot, and the variety of characters', that 'there might have been something added to the beauty of the style', that the dramatist 'complied not enough with the greatness and majesty of a heroic poem'.

Dryden was speaking of the opera in its completed form in two Parts, and with additional characters in Part I. This enlarged text of the piece as it was 'lately represented in the Duke of York's Theatre in Lincoln's Inn Fields', was not published till 1663, and there is no record of a performance of Part II earlier than in June 1661 at Lisle's Tennis Court, though the recent critical view is that there probably was a production of it at the Cockpit in 1658–9.[1] In any case, it was the original representation of Part I at Rutland House in 1656 that was historically of most significance. In the previous *First Entertainment* the musical element had been limited to an introductory instrumental 'concert' and to the songs. In *The Siege of Rhodes* the whole dialogue was delivered to a recitative accompaniment after the Italian operatic fashion. This had the important consequence that Davenant not only used rhyme throughout but introduced 'frequent alterations of measures which . . . are necessary to recitative music for variation of airs'.

Here, as in the use of 'Entries' instead of 'Acts', he was bent on circumventing his Puritan censors, and he must be given full credit for his bold innovation. But among Davenant's varied gifts the lyrical faculty was not included, and the 'libretto' (as it would now be called) of *The Siege of*

[1] The only late seventeenth century testimony to this is by John Aubrey who is not an entirely trustworthy authority. But on various grounds, W. J. Lawrence, A. Nicoll, A. Harbage, and A. H. Nethercot are iuclined to accept his statement. In any case the Second Part was written before the Restoration, for it was entered on the *Stationers' Register* on 30 May, 1659.

Rhodes will disappoint those in whom Dryden's eulogy of its 'perfect' rhymed verse has raised high expectations.

To Davenant's contemporaries, however, this mattered as little as the slightness of the plot or the representation of a battle by seven singing characters, ridiculed later by Buckingham in *The Rehearsal*. What appealed to them was that on the story of the early sixteenth-century siege of Rhodes by the Turks under Solyman the Magnificent the dramatist had engrafted a conjugal romance based on the themes of love and honour. Alphonso, a recently wedded Sicilian duke, and a Knight of Rhodes, has come to attend the sacred annual feast held by Vallerius, the grand master of the Knights, when the approach of the Turkish fleet is announced. Vallerius bids him hasten back to his bride, but Alphonso proudly disobeys:

> Honour is colder virtue set on fire;
> My honour lost, my love would soon decay.

It is the bride, Ianthe, who comes to seek her lord and braves the perils of the sea-voyage. When she is taken captive and led veiled into the presence of Solyman by his 'bassa', Mustapha, the Sultan asks: 'What is it thou wouldst show, and yet dost shroud?' Mustapha's answer, 'I bring the morning pictur'd in a cloud', was guyed in *The Rehearsal*, 'Ah, gadzookers, what a conceit is there!' Solyman shows himself quixotically magnanimous. He not only offers Ianthe a safe conduct to Rhodes, but orders the assault to be delayed till she and her husband have made their escape. Alphonso rejects so extravagant a bounty:

> Are we besieg'd then by a friend?
>   Could honour such a present make,
>   Then when his honour is at stake?
> Against itself does honour booty play?
>   We have the liberty to go away!

He even doubts whether Ianthe's virtue has not paid the price.

When Solyman hears that the pair have refused his pass-

port and are resolved rather to die 'for company', he speaks
the finest lines in the piece:

> O Mustapha, our strength we measure ill,
>> We want the half of what we think we have;
> For we enjoy the beast-like power to kill,
>> But not the God-like power to save.
> Who laughs at death, laughs at our highest pow'r,
> The valiant man is his own emperor.

When Ianthe, with a change of mood, urges Alphonso to
accept Solyman's 'obliging offer',

> For why should honour scorn to take
> What honour's self does to it offer?

he is strengthened in his suspicion of her and becomes
distraught with jealousy. Yet he takes the lead in the
defence of the beleaguered town, while Ianthe, in disguise,
hazards her life fighting at the side of the valiant English
auxiliaries to whom Davenant pays a deft partiotic tribute.
She is wounded, and at the same time the grand master,
Vallerius, with the French allies is in danger of being overpowered. Alphonso is faced with the dilemma of deciding
which of the two he is to aid:

> The riddle is too sad and intricate,
> The hardest that was e'er proposed by fate.
>> Honour and pity have
> Of both too short a time to choose;
>> Honour the one would save,
> Pity would not the other lose.

Pity conquers, and he flies to Ianthe, who forgives him
for his sin of suspicion, which he declares that he will mourn
away.

The success of the opera led to the addition of a longer
second Part. Whether or not this was of pre-Restoration
date, it does little more than develop the themes of Part I.
with greater emphasis on that of jealousy. The siege continues and the Rhodian authorities are forced by the clamour
of the starving population to send Ianthe to seek to make
terms with Solyman. Trusting to his magnanimity she enters

his camp without even asking for a passport, but is dismayed
to hear from him, 'Your business will all night require your
stay.' The Sultan sees in the visit of the Sicilian beauty the
chance of a countermove against his ambitions and 'tempestuous' wife, Roxolana. He sends Ianthe to the tent of
the Sultana, who fired by jealousy writes secretly to Alphonso
that Solyman

> to Ianthe lays
> A closer siege than e'er he did to Rhodes.

The Rhodian leaders headed by the grand master vow to
rescue her. But Roxolana shows herself generous to one
whom she takes to be a rival, and it is the Sultan whom she
denounces for fickleness and for his preference of the 'meaner
conquests' of war over those of love. When the Rhodian
sally has failed and Alphonso, wounded and captured, is
handed over by Solyman to Roxolana to be punished at her
hands, she gives him over freely to Ianthe. The Sultan, to
crown all, cries:

> Go back, Ianthe! Make your own
> Conditions boldly for the town.
> I am content it should recorded be,
> That when I conquered Rhodes, you conquer'd me.

The somewhat more complicated action in the second Part
is a doubtful advantage for the moods of the characters are
at times difficult to follow. But in the printed text Davenant
discarded 'Entries' for 'Acts'; he showed a greater command
of terse, epigrammatic, rhymed verse, while in the tempestuous but generous Roxolana he created a character which,
as impersonated by Mrs. Davenport, overshadowed the
original self-sacrificing heroine, Ianthe.

Whether or not the second Part of *The Siege of Rhodes* was
of pre-Restoration date, it was not in Davenant's nature to
rest satisfied with the cramping conditions imposed on his
'operas' by Rutland House. It was probably (though the
exact date is uncertain) as a prelude to another phase of his
guerrilla warfare against the Puritan enemies of the stage

that he addressed a remarkable paper to Thurloe as Secretary of State urging the necessity of public entertainments.[1]

The people of England are observed by writers of other nations and by our own to require continual divertisements, being otherwise naturally inclined to that melancholy that breeds sedition; which made our ancestors entertain them with public meetings for prizes in archery, horse-races, matches at football, wakes, may-poles, and sports of Christmas, theatres, and other public spectacles.

Which examples and the former reasons may (especially at this time) put the public authority in mind that the city hath occasion of divertisements. . . . If moral representations may be allowed (being without obsceneness, profaneness, and scandal) the first arguments may consist of the Spaniards' barbarous conquests in the West Indies and their several cruelties there exercised upon the subjects of this nation.

The last sentence shows that Davenant had already planned to write the strange, dramatic hotch-potch, *The Cruelty of the Spaniards in Peru*, published on or before July 1658, with the statement that it was 'represented daily at the Cockpit in Drury Lane'. Thus by the favour of Thurloe, and perhaps of the Protector himself, Davenant had realized the aim, which he had pursued by a circuitous route, of again presenting a piece in dramatic form on a recognized public stage, where the performance could be on a much ampler scale than in Rutland House, and he could indulge in 'the great expense necessary to scenes, and other ornaments in this entertainment.' The incidents were mainly drawn from a recent translation, dedicated to Cromwell, of a Spanish work, *The Tears of the Indians*. But these incidents were of minor importance, for the piece has been described as 'a succession of speeches, songs, and dances presented against a background of painted scenes', varied by the acrobatic feats of the attendant on an Inca priest, who gave among other displays of agility 'the double somerset', the 'porpoise' and the 'sea-horse'.

[1] Printed in full by Sir Charles Firth in *The English Historical Review* (1903), XVIII. 320. It is undated but bound up with other papers belonging to January 1657.

Later in the same year there followed another 'opera', *The History of Sir Francis Drake*, dealing with earlier episodes relating to Peru and the West Indies. Performed at the Cockpit and published in 1659, the piece had more action than its predecessor, and was more elaborately staged. The chief figures are Drake senior (Sir Francis), Drake junior, his younger brother, Captain Rouse, and an enfranchised slave, Pedro, who acts as their guide. Among the episodes in the six 'entries' are the welcome of Drake by the Moorish Symerons who had revolted against their Spanish oppressors; his arrival at Venta-Cruz and the rescue there of a beautiful Spanish bride from their avenging fury; and the capture of a mule-train richly laden with treasure. The bride and the mules, as well as Drake's ships only appeared in perspective on the back-cloths, but the choruses and dances by sailors soldiers, and natives provide lively entertainment, and (as Harbage has noted) dialogues in song here appear in Davenant's operas for the first time, though duets are still absent.

With the death of Oliver on 3 September 1658 and the succession of his son Richard, Davenant's position grew more precarious. On 14 September a correspondent writes: 'It is thought the opera will speedily go down; the godly party are so much discontented with it.' On 23 December an order was passed by the Council of State 'for taking into consideration the opera showed at the Cockpit in Drury Lane', and on 5 February 1659 the House of Lords appointed a committee to deal with 'stage-plays, interludes, and things of the like nature called Opera, acted to the scandal of religion and the Government'. Yet Davenant's show must have gone on, for on 6 May John Evelyn went 'to see a new opera, after the Italian way in recitative music and scenes much inferior to the Italian composure and magnificence. . . . I being engaged could not decently resist the going to see it, though my heart smote me for it.'

But the day was at hand when lovers of the drama could

again visit the theatre without inward searchings or fears of violence from without. On 3 February 1660 General Monck entered London with his troops and summond a Parliament which in the following May voted for the recall to the throne of Charles II. Davenant with characteristic promptness welcomed Monck with a poetical *Panegyric*. With his further activities as theatrical manager and playwright in the Restoration period we are not here concerned. It may well have seemed to Davenant an act of *pietus* to revive on the Lincoln's Inn Fields stage a number of the plays in adapted form of his reputed godfather. But his true service to the 'very spirit' of William Shakespeare was that in the theatre's darkest days he did not despair of the commonwealth, and that during them more than any other single man by mingled courage and craft he kept unbroken the chain which stretches over a century and half and links the early Tudor drama of Medwall, Rastell, and John Heywood with the heroic plays of Dryden and Lee and the comedies of the Restoration age.

INDEX

PRINTED IN GREAT BRITAIN
AT THE UNIVERSITY PRESS, OXFORD
BY VIVIAN RIDLER
PRINTER TO THE UNIVERSITY